LITERATURA CHICANA

LITERATURA

antonia castañeda shular

tomás ybarra-frausto

joseph sommers

text and context

CHICANO

PRENTICE-HALL, INC.

CHICANA

texto y contexto

LITERATURE

ENGLEWOOD CLIFFS, NEW JERSEY

Library of Congress Cataloging in Publication Data

CASTAÑEDA SHULAR, ANTONIA, 1942–   COMP.
  Literatura chicana: texto y contexto.

  Spanish or English.
  1. American literature—Mexican-American authors
—History and criticism. 2. Spanish-American
literature—History and criticism. I. Ybarra-Frausto,
Tomás, 1938-   joint comp. II. Sommers, Joseph,
1924-   joint comp. III. Title.
PS153.M4C3   810.98'6872073   79-175809
ISBN 0-13-537563-O
ISBN 0-13-537555-X (pbk.)

LITERATURA CHICANA
Antonia Castañeda Shular, Tomás Ybarra-Frausto, Joseph Sommers

10 9 8 7 6 5 4 3 2 1

Printed in the United States of America

Prentice-Hall International, Inc., *London*
Prentice-Hall of Australia, Pty. Ltd., *Sydney*
Prentice-Hall of Canada, Ltd., *Toronto*
Prentice-Hall of India Private Limited, *New Delhi*
Prentice-Hall of Japan, Inc., *Tokyo*

ACKNOWLEDGMENTS

We gratefully acknowledge permission to quote from the following:

Fernando Alegría, "¿A qué lado de la cortina?," from *El poeta que se volvió gusano,* Mexico, 1956; by permission of the author.

Alurista, "Must be the season of the witch," "Nuestro barrio," and "We've played cowboys," from *Floricanto,* Los Angeles, 1971; by permission of the author.

Fernando Alvarado Tezozómoc, "Así lo vinieron a decir," and "Principio de la crónica," from *Crónica mexicayotl,* Mexico, 1949; by permission of the Universidad Nacional Autónoma de México.

Fernando Alvarado Tezozómoc, "Thus they have come to tell it," from Miguel León-Portilla, *Pre-Columbian Literatures of Mexico,* Norman, Okla., 1949; by permission of the University of Oklahoma Press.

Anonymous, "American Me," presented by Beatrice Griffith in *American Me,* Boston, 1948; by permission of Houghton Mifflin Company.

Anonymous, "Carta a la raza," from *The Daily Collegian,* Fresno, 1969.

Anonymous, "Corrido de José Apodaca," from J.D. Robb, "The Matachines Dances," in *Western Folklore,* 1961; by permission of The California Folklore Society.

Anonymous, "Corrido de Kiansis," from Brownie McNeil, "Corridos of the Mexican Border," in *Mexican Border Ballads and Other Lore,* ed. Moady C. Boatright, Publications of The Texas Folklore Society, XXII; by permission of The Texas Folklore Society.

iv

Anonymous, "Décima anónima," from Pablo González Casanova, *La literatura perseguida en la crisis de la colonia,* Mexico, 1958; by permission of El Colegio de México.

Anonymous, "Deja de arar, campesino," from Rubén M. Campos, *El folklore literario de México,* Mexico, 1929.

Anonymous, "Defensa de los norteños," and "Los deportados," from Paul S. Taylor, "Songs of the Mexican Migration," in *Puro Mexicano,* ed. J. Frank Dobie, Publications of The Texas Folklore Society, XII; by permission of The Texas Folklore Society. Trans. by Paul S. Taylor.

Anonymous, "El hijo desobediente—A Pachuco Version," collected by George C. Baker, in "Pachuco: An American Spanish Argot and its Social Functions in Tucson, Arizona," *University of Arizona Social Science Bulletin,* Vol. XXI, 1950; by permission of The University of Arizona Press.

Anonymous, "Doble bola de la huelga de Cananea," from Armando de María y Campos, *La Revolución Mexicana a través de los corridos populares,* Mexico, 1962; by permission of the Instituto Nacional de Estudios Históricos de la Revolución Mexicana.

Anonymous, "En este oscurecer," from José María Arguedas, *Canto Kechwa,* Lima, 1938.

Anonymous, "The Impartiality of Death," from Aurora Lucero White-Lea, *Literary Folklore of the Hispanic Southwest,* San Antonio, 1953; by permission of The Naylor Company.

Anonymous, "La llorona en California," from Elaine K. Miller, *Mexican Folk Narrative from the Los Angeles Area,* University of California, Los Angeles (Doctoral dissertation); by permission of Elaine K. Miller.

Anonymous, "La llorona en Texas," from Soledad Pérez, "Mexican Folklore from Austin, Texas," in *The Healer of Los Olmos and Other Mexican* Lore, ed. Wilson M. Hudson, Publications of The Texas Folklore Society, XXIV; by permission of The Texas Folklore Society.

Anonymous, "La persecución de Villa," from Merle E. Simmons, *The Mexican Corrido,* Bloomington, 1957; by permission of Indiana University Press.

Anonymous, "Life Story of a Vato," from *La Raza Yearbook,* Los Angeles, 1968; by permission of El Barrio Communications Project.

Anonymous, "Lo que digo lo sostengo," from *La Raza,* Los Angeles, Vol. I, 1968; by permission of El Barrio Communications Project.

Anonymous, "Los americanos," recited by Juan Chaves y García to Aurelio M. Espinosa, author of "Romancero nuevomexicano," in *Revue Hispanique,* XXXIII, Paris, 1915.

Anonymous, "Los animales," from *Journal of the Folklore Institute,* Bloomington, 1966; by permission of Indiana University Press and Américo Paredes, collector.

Anonymous, "Los reenganchados a Kansas," from Brownie McNeil, "Corridos of the Mexican Border," in *Mexican Border Ballads and Other Lore,* ed. Moady C. Boatright, Publications of The Texas Folklore Society, XXII; by permission of The Texas Folklore Society. Trans. by Brownie McNeil.

Anonymous, "Poema azteca," in Miguel León-Portilla, *Los antiguos mexicanos a través de sus crónicas y cantares,* Mexico, 1961; by permission of the Fondo de Cultura Económica.

Anonymous, "Poema popular," from María Cadilla de Martínez, *La poesía popular en Puerto Rico,* Madrid, 1933.

Anonymous, "Remedies of Don Pedrito Jaramillo," in Ruth Dodson, "Don Pedrito Jaramillo: The Curandero of Los Olmos," *The Healer of Los Olmos and Other Mexican Lore,* ed. Wilson M. Hudson, Publications of The Texas Folklore Society, XXIV; by permission of The Texas Folklore Society.

Anonymous, "Sin nadie, sin nadie," from José María Arguedas, *Canto Kechwa,* Lima, 1938.

Anonymous, "to brothers dead crossing the rapido river," from *La Raza,* Los Angeles, Vol. I, 1968; by permission of El Barrio Communications Project.

Anonymous, "Vida, proceso y muerte de Aurelio Pompa," from Manuel Gamio, *Mexican Immigration to the United States,* Chicago, 1930; by permission of the University of Chicago Press. "Life, Trial and Death of Aurelio Pompa," trans. by Margaret Redfield.

Anonymous, "Viva huelga en general," from *Canción de la Raza,* Coachella, Calif., 1968; by permission of *El Ideal.*

Juan José Arreola, "Baby H.P.," *Confabulario,* Mexico, 1952.

Juan José Arreola, "Baby H.P.," *Confabulario and Other Inventions,* trans. by George Schade, Austin, 1964; by permission of the University of Texas Press.

Mariano Azuela, *Los de abajo,* Mexico, 1958; by permission of the Fondo de Cultura Económica.

Leonor Barrientes de Maldonado, "La mano negra,"; by permission of the author.

Julia de Burgos, "Letanía del mar," from Yvette Jiménez de Báez, *Julia de Burgos, Vida y poesía,* Puerto Rico, 1966; by permission of the author.

Eliu Carranza, "The Mexican American and the Chicano," from *Pensamientos on Los Chicanos, A Cultural Revolution,* Berkeley, 1969; by permission of the California Book Company and the author.

Celso de Casas, "And Another Piece of Litter is Thrown on the Junk Heap,"; by permission of the author.

Irene Castañeda, "Crónica personal de Cristal," from *El Grito,* Berkeley, IV, 1971; by permission of the author.

Rosario Castellanos, "Silence Concerning an Ancient Stone," trans. by George Schade, from *The Muse in Mexico,* ed. Thomas M. Cranfill, Austin, 1959; by permission of The University of Texas Press.

Carlo Antonio Castro, *Los hombres verdaderos,* Jalapa, Veracruz, 1959; by permission of the author.

Carlo Antonio Castro, *The True Men,* trans. by Mauda Sandvig; by permission of Mauda Sandvig.

Chicano Coordinating Council on Higher Education, "Manifesto," from *El Plan de Santa Bárbara,* Santa Barbara, 1969; by permission of La Causa Publications.

Jesús Colón, "Little Things Are Big," from *A Puerto Rican in New York,* New York, 1961; by permission of New Outlook Publishers.

Sor Juana Inés de la Cruz, "Against the Inconsequence of Man's Desires. . . ," trans. by Robert Graves, from *Encounter,* London, I, 1953; by permission of A.P. Watt & Son.

Rubén Darío, "Fatality," trans. by Lysander Kemp, from *Selected Poems of Rubén Darío,* Austin, 1965; by permission of the University of Texas Press.

Abelardo Delgado, "El imigrante," and "El río grande," from *Abelardo—Twenty Five Pieces of a Chicano Mind,* Denver, no date; by permission of the author.

María del Refugio, "La llorona," from *Mesoamerican Notes,* Mexico City College, 1950.

Jorge Enciso, design motifs, from *Design Motifs of Ancient Mexico,* New York, 1947; by permission of Dover Publications, Inc.

Tony "Chato" Estrada, "Letter to Society," *La Palabra,* McNeil Island Federal Penitentiary, 1969; by permission of the author.

Carlos Fuentes, "La herencia de la Malinche," from *Todos los gatos son pardos,* Mexico, 1970; by permission of Siglo Veintiuno Editores, and Brandt & Brandt.

Carlos Fuentes, *La muerte de Artemio Cruz,* Mexico, 1962; by permission of the Fondo de Cultura Económica.

acknowledgments vii

Carlos Fuentes, *The Death of Artemio Cruz,* trans. by Sam Hileman, New York, 1964; by permission of Farrar, Straus, & Giroux, Inc.

Carlos Fuentes, *La región más transparente,* Mexico, 1959; by permission of the Fondo de Cultura Económica.

Carlos Fuentes, *Where the Air is Clear,* trans. by Sam Hileman, New York, 1960; by permission of Farrar, Straus, & Giroux, Inc.

Gabriel García Márquez, "El escritor y el sistema," from *Mundo Nuevo,* Paris, June, 1970; by permission of *Mundo Nuevo.*

Elías Garza, "Narración de Elías Garza," from Manuel Gamio, *El inmigrante mexicano: la historia de su vida,* Mexico, 2nd. ed., 1969; by permission of the Universidad Nacional Autónoma de México.

Elías Garza, "Narración de Elías Garza," in Manuel Gamio, *The Mexican Immigrant: His Life Story,* trans. by Robert C. Jones, Chicago, 1930; by permission of the University of Chicago Press.

Jovita González, "Mi caballo bayo," and "Mi querida Nicolasa," in "Folklore of the Texas-Mexican Vaquero," from *Texas and Southwestern Lore,* Publications of the Texas Folklore Society, VI; by permission of The Texas Folklore Society.

José Luis González, "La carta," from *El hombre en la calle,* San Juan, Puerto Rico, 1948; by permission of the author.

Rodolfo Gonzales, "I am Joaquin," Denver, 1967; by permission of the author.

Steve Gonzales, "The Advertisement," from *El Grito,* Berkeley, I, 1967; by permission of the author.

Nicolás Guillén, "Balada de los dos abuelos," from *Antología mayor,* La Habana, 1964.

Nicolás Guillén, "Ballad of the Two Grandfathers," trans. by Langston Hughes and Ben F. Carruthers, in *Cuba Libre,* Los Angeles, 1948. Copyright © 1948 by Langston Hughes and Benjamin Carruthers, reprinted by permission of Harold Ober Associates, Inc. and the publisher, Ward Ritchie Press.

José Angel Gutiérrez, "22 Miles," in *El Grito,* Berkeley, I, 1968; by permission of the author.

José Hernández, "El gaucho Martín Fierro," trans. by C.E. Ward, Albany, N.Y., 1967; by permission of the State University of New York Press.

Armando Liszt Arzubide, "Corrido de la muerte de Emiliano Zapata," from Armando de María y Campos, *La Revolución Mexicana a través de los corridos populares,* Mexico, 1962; by permission of the Instituto Nacional de Estudios Históricos de la Revolución Mexicana.

Ronald W. López, "The El Monte Berry Strike," in *Aztlan,* Los Angeles, I, 1970; by permission of the author.

Jesús Maldonado, "Loa al frijol," "No nomás tú eres," and "Trio Mexicano," from *El Grito,* Berkeley, IV, 1971; by permission of the author. "El molcajete," and "Under a Never Changing Sun," also by permission of author.

Gabriela Mistral, "Madre mexicana," in *Lecturas para mujeres,* Mexico, 1967; by permission of Editorial Porrúa.

Gabriela Mistral, "Yo no tengo soledad," in *Ternura,* Montevideo ,1925.

Gabriela Mistral, "I am not Lonely," from *Selected Poems of Gabriela Mistral,* ed. and trans. by Langston Hughes; by permission of Indiana University Press.

José de Molina, "Del Bravo a la Patagonia," in Méri Franco-Lao, *¡Basta!: Canciones de testimonio y rebeldía de América Latina,* Mexico, 1970; by permission of Editorial Era.

Augusto Monterroso, "El eclipse," in *Obras completas y otros cuentos,* Mexico, 1959; by permission of Universidad Nacional Autónoma de México, 1959.

José Montoyoa, "El Louie," from *Rascatripas,* Oakland, Calif., II, 1970; by permission of the author.

Pablo Neruda, "Canción," from *Fulgor y muerte de Joaquín Murieta,* Santiago, 1967, and "Poema XX," from *Veinte poemas de amor y una canción desesperada,* Santiago, 1924; by permission of the author. "Tonight I Can Write," from *Twenty Love Poems and a Song of Despair,* trans. by W.S. Merwin, London, 1969; by permission of Jonathan Cape Ltd.

Nezahualcóyotl, "Xopan cuicatl," (Nahuatl version) and "Canto de primavera" (Spanish version of same poem) in Miguel León-Portilla, *Trece poetas del mundo azteca,* Mexico, 1967; by permission of Universidad Nacional Autónoma de México.

Salvador Novo, "El chile," in *Cocina mexicana: historia gastronómica de la ciudad de México,* Mexico, 1967; by permission of Editorial Porrúa.

Alberto Ordóñez Argüello, "Canto de Nezahualcóyotl," from *New Voices of Hispanic America,* Boston, 1962; by permission of Beacon Press. "Song of Nezahualcóyotl," trans. by Darwin Flakoll and Claribel Alegría.

José Ortega, "Trasquilador," collected by Antonia Castañeda Shular, 1971; by permission of José Ortega.

Pedro Padilla, "La sepultura del diablo atrevido," in *El Grito del Norte,* Feb., 1969; by permission of the author.

Luis Palés Matos, "Danza negra," from *Poesía: 1915–1956,* Río Piedras, Puerto Rico, 1971; by permission of Universidad de Puerto Rico.

Américo Paredes, "The Anglo-American in Mexican Folklore," from *New Voices in American Studies,* ed. Ray B. Browne, Donald M. Winkel and Allen Hayman, Lafayette, Indiana, 1966; by permission of Purdue Research Foundation.

Octavio Paz, "The Return," trans. by Tim Reynolds, in *TriQuarterly Anthology of Contemporary Latin American Literature,* Evanston, Illinois, 1969; by permission of Northwestern University Press.

Elena Poniatowska, "La tortilla," from *Artes de México,* Vol. V, 1959; by permission of *Artes de México.* "The Tortilla," trans. by *Artes de México.*

John Rechy, "El Paso del Norte," from *Evergreen Review,* New York, II, 1958, by permission of the author.

Arnold Rojas, Selections from *The Vaquero,* Santa Barbara, 1964; by permission of McNally & Loftin.

Bernardino de Sahagún, "De la comida de Moctezuma," and "De la comida que usaban los señores," from *Historia general de las cosas de Nueva España,* Mexico, 1938.

Hugo Salazar Tamariz, "Las raíces," from *New Voices of Hispanic America,* Boston, 1962; by permission of Beacon Press. "The Roots," trans, by Darwin Flakoll and Claribel Alegría.

Luis Omar Salinas, "Aztec Angel," and "Death in Vietnam," in *Crazy Gypsy,* Fresno, 1970; by permission of the author.

raúlsalinas, "A Trip Through the Mind Jail," and "Los Caudillos," from *Aztlan,* Leavenworth Federal Penitentiary, I, 1970; by permission of the author.

Luis Rafael Sánchez, "Tiene la noche una raíz," from *En cuerpo de camisa,* Puerto Rico, 1966; by permission of the author.

Pedro Juan Soto, "Bayaminiña," from *Spiks,* Mexico, 1956.

Luis Spota, *Murieron a mitad del río,* Mexico, 3rd. ed., 1969; by permission of the author.

Mario Suárez, "El Hoyo," from *Arizona Quarterly,* III, 1947, and "Maestría," from *Arizona Quarterly,* IV, 1948; by permission of the author.

Piri Thomas, "If you ain't got heart, you ain't got nada," and "Puerto Rican Paradise," from *Down These Mean Streets,* New York, 1968; by permission of Alfred A. Knopf, Inc.

Carmen Toscano, *La llorona,* Mexico, 1959; by permission of El Fondo de Cultura Económica.

United Farmworkers Organizing Committee, "El plan de Delano," Delano, 1966. "The Delano Manifesto," trans. by U.F.W.O.C.; by permission of U.F.W.O.C.

Luis Valdez, "Las dos caras del patrón," from *Actos,* Fresno, 1971; by permission of the author.

César Vallejo, "Masa," trans. by H.R. Hays in *Twelve Spanish American Poets,* New Haven, 1943; by permission of the translator.

Roberto Vargas, "Homenaje a la tercera marcha de Delano," from *El Pocho Che,* Berkeley, I, 1969; by permission of the author.

Mario Vargas Llosa, "La literatura es fuego," from *Mundo Nuevo,* Paris, Nov. 1967; by permission of *Mundo Nuevo.*

José Vasconcelos, *La raza cósmica,* Paris, 1925.

Enriqueta Vásquez, "La santa tierra," from *El Grito del Norte,* Dec., 1970; by permission of the author.

José Antonio Villarreal, *Pocho,* New York, 1959; by permission of Doubleday & Company, Inc.

Tomás Ybarra-Frausto, "Chicano Theatre: Punto de Partida," in *Latin American Theatre Review,* IV, 1971; by permission of the *Latin American Theatre Review.*

Leopoldo Zea, "El Indio," from *La filosofía como compromiso,* Mexico, 1952; by permission of Colegio de México.

Así lo vinieron a decir,
así lo asentaron en su relato,
y para nosotros lo vinieron a dibujar en sus papeles
los ancianos, las ancianas.
Eran nuestros abuelos, nuestras abuelas,
nuestros bisabuelos, nuestras bisabuelas,
nuestros tatarabuelos, nuestros antepasados.
Se repitió como un discurso su relato,
nos lo dejaron,
y vinieron a legarlo
a quienes ahora vivimos,
a quienes salimos de ellos.
Nunca se perderá, nunca se olvidará
lo que vinieron a hacer,
lo que vinieron a asentar en las pinturas:
su renombre, su historia, su recuerdo.
Así en el porvenir
siempre lo guardaremos
nosotros, hijos de ellos, los nietos,
hermanos, bisnietos, tataranietos, descendientes,
quienes tenemos su sangre y color,
lo vamos a decir, lo vamos a comunicar
a quienes todavía vivirán, habrán de nacer,
los hijos de los mexicas, los hijos de los tenochcas...

Crónica mexicayotl. Texto náhuatl de F. Alvarado
Tezozómoc.

Source: *Cuadernos del México Prehispánico,
Los Mexicas,* Museo Nacional de Antro-
pología, No. 4.

Thus they have come to tell it,
thus they have come to record it in their narration,
and for us they have painted it in their codices,
the ancient men, the ancient women.
They were our grandfathers, our grandmothers,
our great-grandfathers, great-grandmothers,
our great-great-grandfathers, our ancestors.
Their account was repeated,
they left it to us;
they bequeathed it forever
to us who live now,
to us who come down from them.
Never will it be lost, never will it be forgotten,
that which they came to do,
that which they came to record in their paintings:
their renown, their history, their memory.
Thus in the future
never will it perish, never will it be forgotten,
always we will treasure it,
we, their children, their grandchildren,
brothers, great-grandchildren,
great-great-grandchildren, descendants,
we who carry their blood and their color,
we will tell it, we will pass it on
to those who do not yet live, who are to be born,
the children of the Mexicans, the children of the Tenochcans . . .

Crónica mexicayotl. Nahuatl text by F. Alvarado Tezozómoc.

contents

LO MERO PRINCIPAL

III. el humor   123

IV. los barrios de aztlán   151

DEJANDO HUELLAS...
CAMINOS DE LA MIGRACION

LITERATURA DE LA RAZA—
THE CONTEXT OF CHICANO LITERATURE

preface

The present volume was composed with the Chicano reader in mind. This orientation does not exclude other readers. On the contrary, it presents them with the challenge to approach material which contains a cultural reference different from their own. Most of the texts, if not originally written completely or partly in English, are accompanied by translations into English. On the other hand, there are texts which stand alone in their Spanish or largely Spanish versions. We are confident that the excellence of these texts will function as magnet and stimulus—in the first place to Chicano readers, but also to others—as literary motivation to master the language in all its own original subtleties, shadings, and tones. In this sense, the volume embodies the statement that the Spanish language is ultimately indispensable in understanding the developmental process of Chicano literature and culture.

The heart of this book lies in the three units based on Chicano literary expression. Each is organized around a major characteristic or pattern in the Chicano experience: social protest, the essence of culture, the migratory experience. While the units are not uniformly organized along historic lines, each one does present antecedent Mexican texts, including pre-Hispanic literary selections. The effort is to show continuity where it exists, and creativity when the writer breaks with the past to find a new form or a new theme. The units, each in its own way, attempt to show continuity and change as Chicano literary expression sets itself off from Mexico. In each of these three units, however, the majority of the texts are by Chicano authors.

The unit on social protest, presented in historical progression, shows the Chicano facing his reality at each stage in his history, and engaging actively in protest aimed at transforming it.

The second unit embodies our conception of culture as a creation which has evolved along with changes in the people's material and spiritual conditions. The essence of Chicano culture is dynamic, rather than static. In this sense, the four cultural patterns presented in this unit show the process by which Chicano culture, built on a Mexican base, has forged its own characteristics, and continues to manifest the dialectic of continuity and change.

The third unit deals with migration, a root experience of socioeconomic nature which has been a fact of life imposed on the Chicano and his ancestors across the centuries. To this pattern which continued in seemingly repetitive cycles, the Chicano has forged a many-faceted response, the literary reflection of which is the basis of this unit. One dimension of the response has been resistance through struggle, another has been the retention and assertion of cultural strength, with the result of constantly renewed social and human bonds.

Stated simply, the Chicano has not only endured the changes brought about by the migratory process, he has in turn affected the process itself, placing upon it the imprint of his own response. He has not only reacted to history—he has acted upon it.

The fourth and final unit seeks to place Chicano literature in a number of larger contexts. Firstly, we felt the Mexican context to be important, beyond the mere inclusion of Mexican texts as antecedents, as we did in other units. Secondly, Puerto Rican literature, from both the island and the American mainland, seemed vital because of the parallels and contrasts which it reflects in historical and cultural experience. Awareness of similarity in heritage and of a shared encounter with imperialism has awakened new interest in Puerto Rican language and literature among Chicano students. And finally we have presented a limited but significant sample of Latin American writing because this is yet another context for Chicano literature. In their language, their themes, and their forms, Latin American poets and *cuentistas* often share the same preoccupations as Chicanos, often see reality in similar ways, often express themselves through images and symbols which strike echoes when we read Chicano poems or stories. For the language and many literary and historical antecedents, if not identical, are certainly close.

Our effort has been to include the richest diversity of literary forms and themes, in order to encompass experiences that were characteristic of different areas, periods, social strata, and cultural types—for all of these, in their plurality of modes, are part of the Chicano literary heritage.

Antonia Castañeda Shular
Tomás Ybarra-Frausto
Joseph Sommers

introduction

Every book represents an effort to grapple with some sort of problem. The central question which faced us when we began to formulate plans and ideas for this book was, "Is it valid to speak of Chicano literature?" As we worked out our answer, two other questions then presented themselves: If there is such a body of literary expression, what are its most important characteristics? Further, why has there been such a scarcity of publication, over the years, of Chicano novels, plays, and poetry, and of historical and critical studies about Chicano literary achievements?

We pose these questions at the start to the readers of this volume for several reasons. One is the hope that it will stimulate interest in the literature itself. More important is our confidence that some will be motivated to seek answers which may be different from ours, or more complete, or based on other arguments and literary evidence. We see this work as more tentative than definitive, as one approach among several that have been made and many that will be made—as one step on the road to definition.

To begin with, we formulated an understanding of what constitutes literary expression. Acknowledging our debt to a wide range of writers who have helped to clarify this basic issue, we came to a statement of norms: that literature comes out of the imaginative use of language to interpret human experience. The focus may be individual or collective, and the kind of experience may be emotional, spiritual, sensual, or social in the broadest of terms. But literary value is present in the many and diverse verbal creations—oral and written, printed, and scrawled—by which man has seen fit to respond to the range of experiences with which life has confronted him.

Literature, then, plays a number of possible roles. It interprets existence —and in so doing it not only provides understanding but also touches emotional chords. In this way it links our enjoyment of the art of verbal expression with our response to ideas. In effect, it changes our experience. At times literature communicates protest against life and society, at times it serves as a release for anguished feelings, at moments it harks back to the past, at moments it strengthens the will to act, or it may express a reaction to pain, to beauty, to fear, or to what seems contradictory or absurd. But at all times, it is the artist's reflection of what life is all about.

With this conception of what constitutes literature, we were able to answer our early question. Chicano literature, for us, is indeed a valid concept, for it covers a rich and varied body of creative material. This conception also provided us with guidlines in selecting texts. We have looked for depth of experience, for imaginative use of language, and for treatment of the important themes of Chicano life, past and present. These three categories, which make up our index of literary quality, may vary from traditional standards of literary criticism, which place much emphasis on formal traditions. We feel, however, that they flow logically from our view of the nature and the function of literature.

Further, our literary values free us from traditional limitations in identifying literary texts of quality. The reader will notice a range of authors in this anthology, which is as broad as the range of Chicano experience. As antecedents, for example, not only an Aztec king or a seventeenth century Mexican nun are represented, but also the anonymous authors of popular corridos and folk legends. The Chicano authors include published poets and novelists as well as students, migrant workers, and prisoners in federal penitentiaries.

These then are the ideas behind our approach to Chicano literature. What can we say about its major characteristics? Two fundamental propositions suggest themselves concerning the nature of Chicano literature: 1) that it is rooted in human experience within two cultures, that of Mexico and that of the United States. 2) that the Mexican War of 1846–1848 is a historical point of departure for the development of a Chicano literature. From these general assumptions, a number of more specific observations can be made about this literature.

Chicano literature in one sense creates new themes, new language, new expressive forms, and in another sense continues ancient Mexican themes and forms.

Cultural continuity with Mexico is certainly evident in Chicano poetry. From the time of the Nahuas, our poets have sung of the human struggle against oppressive social forces, they have sung of the brevity of life, of death, of love and nature. These ancient and universal themes have been passed on to the Chicano poets in the campos and barrios of Aztlan.

If Chicano writers have elaborated on Mexican themes, they have also borrowed and maintained Mexican forms. This is especially evident in the rich and abundant folkloric tradition of corridos, décimas, and coplas.

From 1848 on, the literature *de acá de este lado* begins to treat old themes in new ways and to reflect others not found in the Mexican heritage. Dislocation and migration, social exploitation by the gavacho, barrio life, struggle for self definition in a colonized situation, and myriad other Chicano experiences form the basis for new expression.

The literary forms in which these themes are expressed are varied. In poetry there is a preference for traditional forms like the décima and the corrido; in prose, the short narrative had been more cultivated than the novel. Political essays and social manifestos are abundant, as is the continuation of folk forms like inditas and coplas.

Moving to contemporary Chicano literature, an outstanding characteristic is the experimentation with language. In a fluid, complex, and expressive manner, Chicano authors write in Spanish, in English, in combinations of Spanish-English, in Pachucano, and in combinations of Pachucano-Spanish-English. This process involves the forging of new vocabulary and new images of reality. Often a single piece of writing will contain several variations of these linguistic modes, creating multiple levels of meaning and emotional response. Thus linguistic innovation influences both form and substance.

The present period, dating from the mid-1960s, represents a new level of development, "la regeneración." While incorporating established cultural values, Chicano writers are at the same time breaking new ground in all forms: theater, cuento, essay, novel, poetry. More notable than in the past is the response to diverse literary influences, including Anglo-American and international writing.

These being the general characteristics of Chicano literature, why is there such a dearth of published literary representation of this experience? Why are Chicano authors not included in anthologies of North American literature used in junior and senior high schools and colleges throughout the country? Why, when the above antecedents go back ten centuries in two cultures, is Chicano literature so unavailable?

As we have seen, our literary traditions are multiple and complex, and the Chicano has been neither inarticulate nor nonliterary. The lamentable lack of published Chicano literature is due to a variety of reasons that must be examined from a historical and sociological as well as a literary perspective. We do not pretend to have arrived at the definitive explanation for the unavailability of material, but we offer the following series of working hypotheses.

It is impossible to separate the fulfillment of a people's artistic and esthetic sensibility from the question of their access to power in economic and political terms, as well as to education and social justice. The scarcity of Chicano literature is primarily the result of an exclusionist and intolerant American society that has maintained a purist and static view of literature. The basis for what is literarily valid and thereby publishable has been the degree of conformity to pre-established literary, ideological and linguistic norms—norms which reflected the interests of the groups in power.

It has been the nature of these oppressive socio-political and educational structures, impeding publication of non-English works, that in effect discouraged literary expression which may have portrayed a negative image of the United States. The movement of Anglo-Saxons into the Southwest and the subsequent establishment of Anglo institutions that sought to exclude Chicanos from participation in the new order, in effect suppressed much of the publication and the dissemination, although not the growth of Chicano literature.

As Anglos displaced the people from the land, burned or destroyed valuable historic documents, began to patrol the border with armed men, and integrated the wealthy Mexican Americans into Anglo society, many nascent literary efforts that may have been occurring at that time were probably extinguished. Driven off the land, kept out of the schools and forced into either the lowest paying jobs or a cyclical migratory life, Chicanos did not have the economic or educational stability that makes possible full-scale literary development. In order for literature to flourish and sustain itself, it must have a readership, printing presses, and means of dissemination. Chicano writers of the past 124 years have never enjoyed the advantages of these minimal conditions.

Yet the societal structure could not stop the influx and influence of Mexican intellectual thought and literature as successive waves of Mexican immigrants came to the United States. Nor could it halt the establishment of Chicano newspapers that sprang up throughout the Southwest, the volantes that passed from hand to hand, the legends told and retold around the dinner table, the pastorelas at Christmas, the variedades in the urban centers, and the corridos that are essentially descriptive accounts of the composer's experience.

Another factor to consider in the treatment of Chicano literature is the unique historic circumstance of Chicanos with respect to Mexico. The Spanish-speaking population in this country was linguistically, culturally, and literarily bound first to Spain, then to Mexico. By 1848 they already had a firmly established set of oral and written literary traditions including, in poetry, the décima, redondillas, the nascent corridos, the sonnet; in prose, autobiographical accounts, satire, the picaresque novel, cuadros de costumbre, legends, fantastic fiction; and finally, liturgical and religious literature in all genres.

The War of 1848 brought about a transfer of political power that did not immediately alter the way in which people perceived themselves culturally and linguistically. The arbitrary border between the United States and Mexico was not recognized. At first the people did not consider themselves separated from their origins, and communication with Mexico and her institutions did not cease with the Treaty of Guadalupe Hidalgo. Thus people remained free to nourish the vitality of their ties as those who could afford it continued to send their children to Mexico to be educated. Those who couldn't afford a Mexican education for their children, having no recourse to education in the United States, instructed them in Spanish at home or relied on oral tradition of song, poetry, and legend to transmit knowledge. For these people, then, literature was already a part of their lives; there was no need to create a new literature.

While there was unabated communication with Mexico, it seems to have been a one-way communication. Major works by Mexican authors, published in Mexico, and treating a Mexican, not a Chicano reality, circulated in the Southwest. While Chicanos may have viewed Mexico as a model, there seems to have been little corresponding interest from Mexico, as her writers dealt with Mexican themes and remained aloof from the Chicano problems in the United States. Chicano writers were faced with two alternatives, neither of which was adequate:

1. If they adhered to Mexican models in order to publish in Mexico, their writing would have to be directed to a Mexican readership; therefore they could not reflect the Chicano experience.

2. If they wanted to write and be published in the United States, they would have to relinquish the Spanish language and the attendant conceptual and philosophic orientation inherent in language. This would have meant surrendering many of their own values. The dilemma for Chicano authors of one way communication with Mexico and no communication with Anglo society served to cut off the normal avenues by which they might have expected their creative expression to find an outlet.

We do not know if and at what point Chicano writers, responding to this dilemma, consciously chose to struggle to retain the Spanish language and the expression of a non-Anglo reality and experience. But the present scarcity of published Chicano literature would appear to be mute testimony to the fact that if what was written was in Spanish, and if it treated a non-Anglo reality, publication in the traditional sense was rarely achieved.

Like all literatures, Chicano expressive writing has undergone stages of growth and transformation. More than most, it has had to struggle for survival in a hostile environment. Survive it has, as is evident in the texts we have selected for this anthology.

Many questions of literary history, of periodization, of definition of styles, of identification of movements, remain open, inviting inquiry and interpretation by Chicano students. Similarly a valuable contribution can be made by searching out texts which lie unknown, either in old Chicano newspapers and journals, in dusty barrio librerías, in private collections, or in the inherited folk wisdom of our viejecitos.

To sum up, our anthology presents Chicano literature, which is born out of the confluence of two cultural traditions, and evolves toward an original synthesis of literary expression. Its vigor derives from the strength of the people *de acá de este lado.*

LITERATURA CHICANA

Analizando, Satirizando, Reclamando:
La Protesta Social

Enfrentando La Realidad: Ayer, Hoy, Siempre
Los Meros Meros: Figuras Populares
El Plan: The Call for Action and Change

ANALIZANDO, SATIRIZANDO, RECLAMANDO—LA PROTESTA SOCIAL

A two-fold purpose underlies the section which follows. First is the effort to show the rich Mexican literary tradition which is an important cultural heritage of the Mexican American. The second purpose is to demonstrate how the Mexican American has interpreted his experience in the United States, "de acá de este lado," with vitality and originality, while at the same time not forgetting the legacy of the past.

One quality shared by Mexicans and Chicanos alike is the capacity to face reality with a critical perspective. Some of their literary expression analyzes and questions the nature of society; other texts point out injustice, or aim sharp barbs of satire at oppressive individuals and institutions. The form and the tone of this critical perspective may vary. Sometimes it expresses the tragedy of present-day happenings, as in Omar Salinas' poem on Vietnam. At other times it may extol the bravery of those who resist tyranny such as Jacinto Treviño, Reies López Tijerina, or Emiliano Zapata. Less direct, but still sharp in critical perspective is Salinas' "Crazy Gypsy" as it mourns the spiritual "malnutrition" of Chicano youth in a hostile society. Another variant is found in Alurista, who rejects standard American stereotypes in order to substitute new formulations and images of Chicano identity.

The clearest form of protest is the call for change, as in the "Plan de Ayala" or the "Plan de Santa Bárbara." But in one way or another— "analizando, satirizando, reclamando"—each of these texts demonstrates that general critical perspective. Across the years, Chicano literary expression has been oriented toward understanding, interpreting, and changing the hard realities of existence.

3

I

enfrentando la realidad:
ayer, hoy, siempre

In this section, the first of three comprising the present unit, we present texts showing the quality of "critical perspective." We find this quality in Chicano expression in the United States, and before that in Mexican antecedents, including Mayan and Aztec thought. The organization of this first section is chronological, from pre-Hispanic times to the present.

The section below reflects the Mayan view of the Conquest, comparing
life before and after. It is from the *Book of Chilam Balam,* a Mayan narrative
which was set down in writing after the Spaniards arrived.

EL LIBRO DE CHILAM BALAM

No sabían que esperaban a los *Dzules,* ni a su cristianismo. No sabían
lo que era pagar tributo. Los espíritus señores de los pájaros, los espíritus
señores de las piedras preciosas, los espíritus señores de las piedras labradas,
los espíritus señores de los tigres, los guiaban y los protegían. ¡ Mil seiscientos
años y trescientos años más y habría de llegar el fin de su vida! Porque
sabían en ellos mismos la medida de su tiempo.

Toda luna, todo año, todo día, todo viento, camina y pasa también.
También toda sangre llega al lugar de su quietud, como llega a su poder
y a su trono. Medido estaba el tiempo en que alabaran la magnificencia
de Los Tres. Medido estaba el tiempo en que pudieran encontrar el bien
del Sol. Medido estaba el tiempo en que miraran sobre ellos la reja de las
estrellas, de donde, velando por ellos, los contemplaban los dioses, los dioses que están aprisionados en las estrellas. Entonces era bueno todo y
entonces fueron abatidos.

Había en ellos sabiduría. No había entonces pecado. Había santa de-
voción en ellos. Saludables vivían. No había entonces enfermedad; no había dolor de huesos; no había fiebre para ellos, no había viruelas, no había
ardor de pecho, no había dolor de vientre, no había consunción. Rectamente
erguido iba su cuerpo, entonces.

No fue así lo que hicieron los *Dzules* cuando llegaron aquí. Ellos
enseñaron el miedo; y vinieron a marchitar las flores. Para que su flor
viviese, dañaron y sorbieron la flor de los otros...

THE BOOK OF CHILAM BALAM

They did not know that they were awaiting the *Dzules,* and their
Christianity. They did not know what it was to pay tribute. The spirits
who were lords of the birds, of precious stones, of hand-carved jewels, the
spirits who were lords of the tigers, guided and protected them. One thousand six hundred years, and three hundred years more, and the end of
their life would arrive! Because they knew within themselves the measure
of their time.

Every month, every year, every day, every wind travels on and passes
away. Likewise every blood lineage arrives at its place of stillness, just as
it reaches power and the throne. Measured was the time in which they

would praise the magnificence of the Three. Measured was the time in which they would be able to know good from the Sun. Measured was the time in which they would have looking down upon them the grate of the stars, from which, watching over them, the gods observed them, the gods who are imprisoned in the stars. Then all was good, and then they were defeated.

There was wisdom in them. There was no sin then. There was holy devotion in them. Healthy were their lives. There was no sickness then; there were no pains of the bones; there was no fever for them, nor smallpox, nor burning chest pains, nor stomach ailments, nor consumption. Then their body walked straight and alert.

It was not thus that the *Dzules* were when they arrived here. They taught fear; and they came to make the flowers wither. So that their flower might live, they harmed and sucked the life of the flower of others...

The best known examples of Aztec poetry from pre-Hispanic times are usually either philosophical—treating themes such as the brevity of human life; or lyrical—finding beauty in flower and song. Here is the work of an Aztec poet who was critical of fatalism, preferring to face life head on.

POEMA AZTECA

Pero, aun cuando así fuera,
si saliera verdad, que sólo se sufre,
si así son las cosas en la tierra,
¿se ha de estar siempre con miedo?
¿habrá que estar siempre temiendo?
¿habrá que vivir siempre llorando?

Porque se vive en la tierra,
hay en ella señores,
hay mando, hay nobleza,
hay águilas y tigres.

¿Y quién anda diciendo siempre
que así es en la tierra?
¿Quién trata de darse la muerte?
¡Hay afán, hay vida,
hay lucha, hay trabajo!

Except for those texts for which a specific translator is indicated by name, the translations in this volume are the work of the editors.

AZTEC POEM

But even if it were so,
if it were true that suffering is our only lot,
if things are this way on earth,
must we always be afraid?
Will we always have to live with fear?
Must we always be weeping?

For we live on earth,
there are lords here,
there is authority, there is nobility,
there are eagles and tigers.

And who then goes about always saying
that this is the way it is on earth?
Who is it that forces death upon himself?
There is commitment, there is life,
there is struggle, there is work!

The outstanding poet in Mexico during its three centuries of existence as a colony of Spain was a woman, the nun Sor Juana Inés de la Cruz. The following verses, written during the late seventeenth century, are redondillas aiming critical barbs at the paradoxes of male arrogance toward women. A Chicana of today may find many of her concerns articulated here.

ARGUYE DE INCONSECUENCIA EL GUSTO Y LA CENSURA DE LOS HOMBRES, QUE EN LAS MUJERES ACUSAN LO QUE CAUSAN

sor juana inés de la cruz

Hombres necios que acusáis
a la mujer sin razón,
sin ver que sois la ocasión
de lo mismo que culpáis:

Redondillas are stanzas of four lines each, with each line composed of eight syllables, following a strict consonant rhyme pattern: a b b a. (Consonant rhyme occurs when words sound alike in both the vowels and consonants of their endings—from the last accented syllable to the end of the word; e.g. recata, ingrata.)

si con ansia sin igual
solicitáis su desdén,
¿por qué queréis que obren bien
si las incitáis al mal?

¿Qué humor puede ser más raro
que el que, falto de consejo,
él mismo empaña el espejo
y siente que no esté claro?

Con el favor y el desdén
tenéis condición igual,
quejándoos, si os tratan mal,
burlándoos, si os quieren bien.

Opinión, ninguna gana;
pues la que más se recata,
si no os admite, es ingrata,
y si os admite, es liviana.

Siempre tan necios andáis
que, con desigual nivel,
a una culpáis por cruel
y a otra por fácil culpáis.

Dan vuestras amantes penas,
a sus libertades alas,
y después de hacerlas malas
las queréis hallar muy buenas.

¿Cuál mayor culpa ha tenido,
en una pasión errada:
la que cae de rogada,
o el que ruega de caído?

¿O cuál es más de culpar,
aunque cualquiera mal haga:
la que peca por la paga,
o el que paga por pecar?

¿Pues para qué os espantáis
de la culpa que tenéis?
Queredlas cual las hacéis
o hacedlas cual las buscáis.

Dejad de solicitar,
y después, con más razón,

acusaréis la afición
de la que os fuere a rogar.

Bien con muchas armas fundo
que lidia vuestra arrogancia,
pues en promesa e instancia
juntáis diablo, carne y mundo.

AGAINST THE INCONSEQUENCE OF MEN'S DESIRES AND THEIR CENSURE OF WOMEN FOR FAULTS WHICH THEY THEMSELVES HAVE CAUSED

juana inés de la cruz

Ah stupid men, unreasonable
In blaming woman's nature,
Oblivious that your acts incite
The very faults you censure.

If, of unparalleled desire,
At her disdain you batter
With provocations of the flesh,
What should her virtue matter?

What sight more comic than the man,
All decent counsel loathing,
Who breathes upon a mirror's face
Then mourns: "I can see nothing."

Whether rejected or indulged,
You all have the same patter:
Complaining in the former case,
But mocking in the latter.

No woman your esteem can earn,
Though cautious and mistrustful;
You call her cruel, if denied,
And if accepted, lustful.

Inconsequent and variable
Your reason must be reckoned:
You charge the first girl with disdain;
With lickerishness, the second.

Let loved ones cage their liberties
    Like any captive bird; you
Will violate them none the less,
    Apostrophising virtue.

Which has the greater sin when burned
    By the same lawless fever:
She who is amorously deceived,
    Or he, the sly deceiver?

Or which deserves the sterner blame,
    Though each will be a sinner:
She who becomes a whore for pay,
    Or he who pays to win her?

Are you astounded at your faults,
    Which could not well be direr?
Then love what you have made her be,
    Or make as you desire her.

I warn you: trouble her no more,
    But earn the right to visit
Your righteous wrath on any jade
    Who might your lust solicit.

This arrogance of men in truth
    Comes armoured with all evil—
Sworn promise, plea of urgency—
    O world, O flesh, O devil!

                                (trans. Robert Graves)

This anonymous décima (1796) in the form of a mock prayer, is an example of how popular poetry conveyed the people's attitudes toward Spanish colonial rule.

POEMA ANÓNIMO

¡Oh, Dios mío! Ponnos en paz,
y nuestras quejas acalla,

Décimas are poetic units of ten lines each, with each line composed of eight syllables. The rhyme is consonant and the rhyme scheme is usually abba ac cddc.

líbranos de esta canalla
y al reino no vengan . . . . *más,*
ni vea por acá jamás
ninguno de ellos, de quien
jamás tenemos un bien;

Líbranos de mal en fin
y de todo gachupín,
por siempre jamás . . . . *Amén.*

This section is from the opening pages of Mexico's (and Latin America's) first novel, *El periquillo sarniento* (1816) by José Joaquín Fernández de Lizardi. The author's warning to his children to keep his manuscript out of the hands of certain people is a clue to his socical attitudes. He was highly critical of corruption in high society, the military, the professions, and the church.

Lizardi is important in Mexican letters because he passes on the tradition of social criticism which he learned from Spanish and French literature. His character, "El periquillo," is a pícaro descended from the Spanish picaresque novel which was born almost 300 years before Mexican independence.

Mexicans freed themselves from the tyranny of Spain, but retained, along with the language, a number of positive cultural features. Just as the corrido was a Mexican adaptation of Spanish popular poetry, the Mexican novel is indebted from its birth to Cervantes, Quevedo, and Alemán, whose writings sharpened the satirical cutting edge of *El periquillo sarniento*.

This satirical tradition is maintained today in Chicano culture : for example, in choteos and relajos that are part of barrio debates.

EL PERIQUILLO SARNIENTO

josé joaquín fernández de lizardi

Ultimamente, os mando y encargo, que estos cuadernos no salgan de vuestras manos, porque no se hagan el objeto de la maledicencia de los necios o de los inmorales; pero si tenéis la debilidad de prestarlos alguna vez, os suplico no los prestéis a esos señores, ni a las viejas hipócritas, ni a los curas interesables, y que saben hacer negocio con sus feligreses vivos y muertos, ni a los médicos y abogados chapuceros, ni a los escribanos, agentes, relatores y procuradores ladrones, ni a los comerciantes usureros, ni los albaceas herederos, ni a los padres y madres indolentes en la educación de su familia, ni a las beatas necias y supersticiosas, ni a los jueces venales, ni a los corchetes pícaros, ni a los alcaides tiranos, ni a los poetas y escritores remendones como yo, ni a los oficiales de la guerra y soldados fanfarrones y hazañeros, ni a los ricos avaros, necios, soberbios y tiranos de los hombres, ni a los pobres que lo son por flojera, inutilidad o mala conducta, ni a los mendigos fingidos; ni los prestéis tampoco a las muchachas que se alquilan, ni a las mozas que se corren, ni a las viejas que se afeitan, ni...pero va larga esta lista. Basta deciros, que no los prestéis ni por un minuto a ninguno de cuantos advirtiéreis que les tocan las generales en lo que leyeren; pues sin embargo de lo que asiento en mi prólogo, al momento que vean sus interiores retratados por mi pluma, y al punto que lean alguna opinión, que para ellos sea nueva o no conforme con sus extraviadas o depravadas ideas, a ese mismo instante me calificarán de un necio, harán que se escandalizan de mis discursos, y aun habrá quien pretenda quizá que soy hereje, y tratará de delatarme por tal, aunque ya esté convertido en polvo. ¡Tanta es la fuerza de la malicia, de la preocupación o de la ignorancia!

EL PERIQUILLO SARNIENTO (THE ITCHING PARROT)

josé joaquín fernández de lizardi

Finally, I command and charge you that these pages shall not leave your hands, so that they may not become the object of evil criticism by stupid or immoral people. But if you do weaken and lend them out some time, I beg you not to lend them to that type of person, nor to hypocritical old ladies, nor to selfish priests who know how to turn a profit from their parishioners, alive and dead, nor to rude doctors and lawyers, nor to thieving clerks, agents, clerks or attorneys, nor to interest-charging businessmen, nor to executors of estates who end up inheriting them, nor to fathers and mothers who are lazy in educating their families, nor to fanatically religious women who are stupid and superstitious, nor to crooked judges, nor to conniving cops, nor hard-hearted wardens, or ragged poets and writers like myself, or bragging soldiers and army officers, or selfish rich men, who are haughty and cruel to others, nor to poor people who are poor because of laziness, uselessness, or bad conduct, nor to phony beggars; and don't lend them either to girls who are for rent, or can be chased, or to old women who shave themselves, or to...but this list is getting long. Let me just say that you should not lend them even for a minute to anyone who in general sounds like those I have described; for despite what I may say in my prologue, the moment they see themselves described by my pen, or they read some opinion that is new to them, or different from their deformed or distorted ideas—that very instant they will call me a fool, will pretend to be shocked by my writing, and there will even be some who will claim that I may be guilty of heresy, and will try to accuse me of it even though by then I will be turned into dust. Such is the strength of malice or meanness or ignorance!

This example of popular poetry dates from the period around 1900, just before the Mexican Revolution of 1910. It provides a glimpse of campesino resentment of poverty. In its ending it affirms, through an expressive image, the peasant's right to the land.

DEJA DE ARAR, CAMPESINO

Deja de arar, campesino
echa los bueyes al monte
quema el arado de palo
y quedas igual de pobre.

Ya no asegundes la milpa
ni cultives la esperanza,
que de todos los elotes
a ti no te toca nada.

Campesino, campesino,
ya se va a venir la pizca,
mejor entierra la hoz
para no cortar la milpa.

Ya no hagas tú la cosecha
para que suba el patrón,
la tierra es para los hombres
como para el mundo el sol.

Popular poetry has no clear author, and tends to circulate anonymously. In the Spanish-speaking world, the most common form it takes is eight-syllable lines, with assonant rhyme between even numbered lines, and no rhyme between the first and third lines of each stanza. (Assonant rhyme occurs when the final vowels of two words sound alike, from the last accented syllable to the end; e.g. monte, pobre.)

This fragment is from the famous novel of the Mexican Revolution, *Los de abajo* (1916), by Mariano Azuela. The novel itself is pessimistic, interpreting the Revolution from an essentially middle-class point of view. Azuela depicted the Mexican and his Revolution as defeated by a combination of human immorality, cultural flaws, and political opportunism. Despite these basic limitations, the author displayed a new degree of national consciousness in his stress on the Mexican experience as his basic thematic raw material, in his use of popular language, popular characters, and folk poetry and song. Thus, with *Los de abajo*, the Mexican novel of this century comes into its own.

In the section below, the main character, Demetrio Macías, recalls how life was in the days before the Revolution. He conveys the peasant's resentment against the patrón who, through the action of the meddling police, interfered even with his social life. Demetrio's militant reaction matches the spirit of the anonymous author of the poem on the preceding page, "Deja de arar, campesino."

LOS DE ABAJO

mariano azuela

—Yo soy de Limón, allí muy cerca de Moyahua, del puro cañón de Juchipila. Tenía mi casa, mis vacas y un pedazo de tierra para sembrar; es decir, que nada me faltaba. Pues, señor, nosotros los rancheros tenemos la costumbre de bajar al lugar cada ocho días. Oye uno su misa, oye el sermón, luego va a la plaza, compra sus cebollas, sus jitomates y todas las encomiendas. Después entra uno con los amigos a la tienda de Primitivo López a hacer las once. Se toma la copita; a veces es uno condescendiente y se deja cargar la mano, y se le sube el trago, y le da mucho gusto, y ríe uno, grita y canta, si le da su mucha gana. Todo está bueno, porque no se ofende a nadie. Pero que comienzan a meterse con usté; que el policía pasa y pasa, arrima la oreja a la puerta; que al comisario o a los auxiliares se les ocurre quitarle a usté su gusto... ¡Claro, hombre, usté no tiene la sangre de horchata, usté lleva el alma en el cuerpo, a usté le da coraje, y se levanta y les dice su justo precio!

Mire, antes de la revolución tenía yo hasta mi tierra volteada para sembrar, y si no hubiera sido por el choque con don Mónico, el cacique de Moyahua, a estas horas andaría yo con mucha priesa, preparando la yunta para las siembras.

LOS DE ABAJO (THE UNDERDOGS)

mariano azuela

"I'm from Limón, over there close to Moyahua, right in the canyon of Juchipila. I had my house, my cows, and a piece of land to farm; in other words, I was doing all right. Well, sir, we rancheros, it was our custom to go down into town every week. You hear mass, you listen to the sermon, then you go to the plaza, you buy your onions and tomatoes and other things you need. Then with your friends you go over to Primitivo López' place for a little enjoyment. You take a drink; once in a while you feel pretty generous and you let him pour you a few extra, you begin to feel it, you feel pretty good, so you laugh and shout and sing if you happen to feel like it. That's all to the good, because you're not bothering anybody. But then they start butting in—the policeman passes by and then passes again, he puts his ear to the door; or the constable or his auxiliary police take a notion you're having too much fun... Well sure, you have the blood of a man, not melon juice, in your veins, you have your own soul in that body, all this stuff makes you mad—so you finally get up and tell them where to go!

"Listen, before the revolution I even had the ground turned, ready to seed, and if it hadn't been for that fight with don Mónico, the chief of Moyahua, why right now I'd be in a big hurry to get my oxen ready for planting."

This real-life story of one Mexican's travels and experiences is from the same general period as the previous two selections—before and during the Revolution. It tells of one man who migrated to the United States and then returned, at a time when many others migrated and stayed.

The narration was gathered by Manuel Gamio, one of Mexico's most distinguished anthropologists, author of a pioneering study in 1930 on Mexican immigration to the United States.

Within the sequence of texts in this first section, the narration below marks the transition between the Mexican experience and that of the Mexican American.

NARRACIÓN PERSONAL DE ELÍAS GARZA

recopilada por manuel gamio

(Elías Garza es nativo de Cuernavaca, Morelos.)

—Mi vida es una historia interesante, especialmente lo que he pasado aquí en los Estados Unidos, en donde lo vuelven a uno loco con tanto trabajo. Lo exprimen a uno aquí hasta que queda inútil y entonces tiene uno que regresar a México para ser una carga para sus paisanos. Pero lo malo es que eso no solamente sucede aquí, sino también allá. Es un favor que le debemos a don Porfirio: el habernos quedado tan ignorantes y tan torpes que solamente servimos para el trabajo más rudo. Yo comencé a trabajar cuando tenía 12 años de edad. Mi madre era sirvienta y yo trabajaba en uno de esos viejos ingenios que muelen caña de azúcar. Me encargaba de dirigir a los bueyes. Me llamaban El Cochero. Esto fue en el pueblo de La Piedad, en Michoacán. Creo que me pagaban 25 centavos al día y yo tenía que darle vueltas al molino de sol a sol. Mi madre, lo mismo que yo, tenía que trabajar, pues mi padre murió cuando yo era muy pequeño. Seguí en ese trabajo hasta que tenía como 15 o 16 años y entonces me dediqué a plantar maíz a medias. Los dueños nos daban la semilla, la tierra y los animales, pero resultaba que cuando se levantaba la cosecha no quedaba nada para nosotros, aunque hubiéramos trabajado muy duro. Era terrible. Esos terratenientes eran ladrones. En esa época me enteré de que había buenos trabajos aquí en los Estados Unidos y que podía ganarse bastante dinero. Nos juntamos varios amigos y fuimos primero a la ciudad de México y de ahí a Ciudad Juárez. Después pasamos a El Paso y ahí aceptamos un *renganche* para Kansas. Trabajamos en las vías, poniendo y quitando rieles, quitando los durmientes viejos y poniendo nuevos y toda clase de trabajos rudos. Nos pagaban solamente 1.50 dólares y nos explotaban sin misericordia en el campo del comisario, pues nos vendían todo muy caro. No obstante, como en esa época las cosas eran generalmente baratas, logré reunir algún dinero con el que me fui a La Piedad, para ver a mi madre. Ella murió poco después y esto me dejó muy triste. Decidí regresar a los Estados Unidos y vine a Los Angeles, California. Aquí me casé con una muchacha mexicana y entré a trabajar en una cantera. Yo colocaba la dinamita y hacía los trabajos que requerían cuidado. Me pagaban 1.95 dólares por día, pero trabajaba 10 horas. Posteriormente trabajé en una estación ferrocarrilera. Trabajaba como remachador y manejaba una máquina de presión para remachar. Por ese trabajo ganaba 1.50 dólares al día por nueve horas, pero era muy duro. En esa época murió mi esposa. Después conseguí trabajo en una empacadora. Comencé ganando 1.25 dólares al día por nueve horas de trabajo y llegué a ganar 4 dólares al día por ocho horas de trabajo.

—Aprendí a matar las reses y a despellejarlas. El trabajo era muy duro. Posteriormente me casé con una mujer de San Antonio, Texas. Era joven, hermosa y blanca, y tenía dos niños que fueron mis entenados. Juntos nos fuimos a México. Tomamos un barco en San Pedro que nos llevó a Mazatlán y de ahí nos fuimos a Michoacán. Vimos que las cosas andaban mal allá, pues era en 1912 y ya habían comenzado los desórdenes de la revolución, por eso regresamos a los Estados Unidos, por la ruta de Laredo, Texas. En San Antonio nos contratamos para la pizca de algodón en un campo del Valle del Río Grande. Fuimos a pizcar un grupo de paisanos, mi esposa y yo. Cuando llegamos al campo, el dueño nos dió un viejo jacalón que había sido gallinero para que viviéramos a la intemperie. Yo no quise vivir ahí y le dije que si no nos daba una casita que fuera un poco mejor, nos iríamos. Nos dijo que nos fuéramos y ya nos íbamos mi esposa y yo con mis hijos, cuando nos cayó el comisario. Me llevó a la cárcel y ahí el dueño de la plantación declaró que yo quería irme sin pagarle mi pasaje. Me cobró el doble de lo que costaba el transporte, y aunque al principio traté de no pagarle y después de pagarle solamente el precio justo, no pude lograr nada. Las autoridades solamente le hacían caso a él, y como estaban confabuladas con él, me dijeron que si no pagaba se llevarían a mi esposa y a mis hijitos a trabajar. Entonces les pagué. De ahí nos fuimos a Dallas, Texas, donde trabajamos en las vías hasta El Paso. Seguí en el mismo trabajo hasta Tucson, Arizona, y después hasta Los Angeles. Desde entonces he trabajado aquí en las plantas empacadoras, en el cemento y en otros trabajos, hasta como jornalero en el campo. A pesar de tanto trabajo solamente he podido ahorrar un poco de dinero para este automóvil y algunas ropas. Ahora he decidido ir a trabajar en la colonia en México y no regresar a este país en el que he dejado lo mejor de mi juventud. He aprendido un poco de inglés de tanto oírlo. Puedo leerlo y escribirlo, pero no quiero tratos con esos *bolillos,* pues lo cierto es que no quieren a los mexicanos.

PERSONAL NARRATION OF ELÍAS GARZA

collected by manuel gamio

(Elías Garza is a native of Cuernavaca, Morelos.)
"My life is a real story, especially here in the United States where they drive one crazy from working so much. They squeeze one here until one is left useless, and then one has to go back to Mexico to be a burden to one's countrymen. But the trouble is, that is true not only here but over there also. It is a favor that we owe Don Porfirio [President Porfirio Díaz] that we were left so ignorant and so slow minded that we have only been fit for rough work. I began to work when I was twelve years old. My mother was a servant and I worked in one of those old mills which ground sugar cane. I took charge of driving the oxen. They called me the driver. This was on the estate of La Piedad, Michoacán. I think that they paid me $0.25 a day and I had to go round and round the mill from the time the sun rose until it set. My mother, as well as I, had to work, because my father died when I was very small. I went on in that way until when I was fifteen or sixteen I planted corn on my own account on shares. The owners gave us the seed, the animals and the land, but it turned out that when the crop was harvested there wasn't anything left for us even if we had worked very hard. That was terrible. Those land-owners were robbers. At that time I heard that there were some good jobs here in United States and that good money could be made. Some other friends accompanied me and we went first to Mexico City and from there we came to Ciudad Juárez. We then went to El Paso and there we took a renganche for Kansas. We worked on the tracks, taking up and laying down the rails, removing the old ties and putting in new, and doing all kinds of hard work. They only paid us $1.50 and exploited us without mercy in the Commissary camp, for they sold us everything very high. Nevertheless, as at that time things generally were cheap, I managed to make a little money with which I went back to La Piedad to see my mother. She died a little later and this left me very sad. I decided to come back to the United States, and I came to Los Angeles, California. Here I married a Mexican young lady. I went to work in a stone quarry. I placed the dynamite and did other work which took some care. They paid me $1.95 a day but I worked 10 hours. Later I worked at a railroad station. I worked as a riveter, working a pressure gun for riveting. At that work I earned $1.50 a day for nine hours, but it was very hard. My wife died at that time. I then got work in a packing plant. I began by earning $1.25 a day there for nine hours of work and I got to earn $4.00 a day for eight hours' work. I learned to skin hogs there

and slaughter them also. The work was very hard. Later I was married to a woman from San Antonio, Texas. She was young, beautiful, white, and she had two little children who became my step-children. We went to Mexico together. We boarded ship at San Pedro and from there went to Mazatlán until we got to Michoacán. We saw that things were bad there, for that was in 1912, and the disorders of the revolution had already started; so we came back to the United States by way of Laredo, Texas. In San Antonio we were under contract to go and pick cotton in a camp in the Valley of the Río Grande. A group of countrymen and my wife and I went to pick. When we arrived at the camp the planter gave us an old hovel which had been used as a chicken house before, to live in, out in the open. I didn't want to live there and told him that if he didn't give us a little house which was a little better, we would go. He told us to go, and my wife and I and my children were leaving when the sheriff fell upon us. He took me to the jail and there the planter told them that I wanted to leave without paying him for my passage. He charged me twice the cost of the transportation, and though I tried first not to pay him, and then to pay him what it cost, I couldn't do anything. The authorities would only pay attention to him, and as they were in league with him they told me that if I didn't pay they would take my wife and my little children to work. Then I paid them. From there we went to Dallas, Texas, from where we worked on the tracks as far as El Paso. I kept on at the same work towards Tucson, Arizona, until I got to Los Angeles. I have worked in the packing plants here since then, in cement and other jobs, even as a farm laborer. In spite of it all I have managed to save some money with which I have bought this automobile and some clothes. I have now decided to work in the colony in Mexico and not come back to this country where I have left the best of my youth. I learned a little English here from hearing it so much. I can read and write it, but I don't even like to deal with those bolillos for the truth is that they don't like the Mexicans.

trans. Robert C. Jones

Unlike the travels of Elías Garza, the migration of Aurelio Pompa, who is the hero of this popular anonymous corrido, was a one way trip to Los Angeles. His tragic story dates from the same period as the narration of Garza.

VIDA, PROCESO, Y MUERTE DE AURELIO POMPA

Voy a contarles la triste historia
de un mexicano que allá emigró
Aurelio Pompa así se llamaba,
el compatriota que allí murió.

Allá en Caborca, que es de Sonora
el pueblo humilde donde nació,
"Vámonos madre," le dijo un día
que allá no existe revolución.

"Adiós, amigos, adiós María,"
dijo a la novia con gran dolor,
yo te prometo que pronto vuelvo,
para casarnos, mediante Dios.

Adiós, Aurelio, dijo la novia,
que sollozando se fue a rezar,
cuídalo mucho, Virgen María,
que yo presiento no volverá.

El señor cura y sus amigos
junto a la novia fueron a hablar,
a suplicarle al pobre Aurelio
que no dejara el pueblo natal.

Fueron inútiles tantos consejos
también los ruegos de su mamá,
vámonos, madre, que allá está el *dollar*
y mucho, juro, que he de ganar.

El mes de mayo de hace cuatro años
a California fueron los dos

Corridos vary, but most tell a story, and are meant to be sung. Most have four-line stanzas (the length varies) with rhyme in the second and fourth lines, whether assonant or consonant. The freedom of form and length makes the corrido more adaptable when passing from one singer to another, and definitely more extendable.

This corrido is unusual because it has lines of ten syllables, instead of the usual eight. But the rhyme scheme is fairly consistent, and of course it narrates a dramatic and meaningful story.

y por desgracia en la misma fecha
en una cárcel allá murió.

Un carpintero que era muy fuerte,
al pobre joven muy cruel golpeó,
y Aurelio Pompa juró vengarse
de aquellos golpes que recibió.

Lleno de rabia contó a la madre
y la pobre anciana le aconsejó
por Dios, olvida, hijo querido,
y el buen Aurelio le perdonó,

pero una tarde, que trabajaba,
con tres amigos en la estación,
el carpintero pasó burlando
y al pobre Pompa le provocó.

Los tres amigos le aconsejaban
que lo dejara y fuera con Dios,
y el carpintero, con un martillo
muy injurioso lo amenazó.

Entonces, Pompa, viendo el peligro,
en su defensa le disparó
con un revólver y cara a cara,
como los hombres a él lo mató.

Vino la causa, llegó el jurado,
y el pueblo Yanqui lo sentenció.
"Pena de muerte," pidieron todos,
y el abogado no protestó.

Veinte mil firmas de compatriotas
perdón pidieron al gobernador,
toda la prensa también pedía
y hasta un mensaje mandó Obregón.

Todo fue inútil, las sociedades
todas unidas pedían perdón.
La pobre madre, ya casi muerta,
también fue a ver al gobernador.

Adiós, amigos, adiós mi pueblo,
Querida madre, no llores más,
dile a mi raza que ya no venga,
que aquí se sufre, que no hay piedad.

El carcelero le preguntaba:
español eres? y él contestó,
"Soy mexicano y orgullo serlo,
aunque me nieguen a mí el perdón."

Esta es la historia de un compatriota
que hace cuatro años allí llegó,
y por desgracia en la misma fecha
en una cárcel muy mal murió.

Los Angeles, California.

LIFE, TRIAL, AND DEATH OF AURELIO POMPA

I am going to tell you the sad story
of a Mexican who emigrated out there—
Aurelio Pompa, so he was called,
our countryman who died there.

Back in Caborca, which is in Sonora,
the humble village where he was born,
"Come on, mother," he said one day,
over there are no revolutions.

"Goodbye, friends, goodbye, María,"
he said to his sweetheart very sadly,
I promise you that I will return soon,
so we can get married, God willing.

Goodbye, Aurelio, said the girl,
and she went sobbing to pray.
Look after him, Virgin Mary,
I feel a foreboding he won't return.

The priest and his friends
along with his sweetheart went to talk
and to beg poor Aurelio
not to leave his native village.

All this advice was useless
and so were the pleas of his mother,
Let's go, mother, that's where the dollar is,
and I swear I'll earn a lot of them.

Four years ago in the month of May
the two of them went to California

and, unhappily, on that very same date
there he died in prison.

A carpenter who was very strong,
very cruelly struck the poor young man,
and Aurelio Pompa swore he'd avenge
those blows he had received.

Filled with rage, he told his mother,
and the poor old woman advised him,
por Dios, forget it, dear son,
and Aurelio, good man, forgave him,

but one afternoon, when he was working
with three friends at the railroad station,
the carpenter came by, mocking at him
and managed to provoke poor Pompa.

His three friends advised him
to leave him alone and go his way,
and then the carpenter, with a hammer,
very insultingly threatened him.

Then Pompa, seeing the danger,
fired in self-defense
with a revolver and face to face,
like a man, he killed him.

The case came to court, the jury arrived,
and the Yankee people sentenced him.
"The death penalty," they all demanded,
and the lawyer did not object.

Twenty thousand signatures of compatriots
asked the governor for his pardon,
the entire press requested it too
and even Obregón sent a message.

But all proved useless; the societies,
all united, asked his pardon;
his mother, half dead already
went too to see the governor.

Farewell, friends, farewell, my village,
Dear mother, cry no more,
tell *la raza* not to come here,
for here they will suffer; there is no mercy.

The jailer asked him:
Are you Spanish? And he answered,
"I am a Mexican and proud of it,
although they deny me a pardon."

This is the story of our countryman
who four years ago arrived,
and, unhappily, on that same date
died an unfortunate death in prison.

Los Angeles, California.

(trans. Margaret P. Redfield)

The fragment below is from a long poem, "Sinfonía de combate," written in 1904 by a poet from Laredo, Texas. It was published in Los Angeles that same year in a cuadernillo entitled, *El cancionero libertario*, and sold at La Librería Mexicana on San Fernando Street, Los Angeles.

By today's poetic standards, Santiago de la Hoz sounds rhetorical, but actually he follows the Latin American tradition of neoclassical poetry. Poets in this vein praised the glories of fighting for the ideals of freedom, usually in the abstract. Frequently they referred to figures from ancient times, like Nero of Rome, and to warriors fighting with sword in hand. The form too, the silva, was a favorite of neoclassical poets of the nineteenth century in Latin America.

The terms and images of his poem may be lofty, but de la Hoz made a poetic statement which can be brought down to earth.

SINFONÍA DE COMBATE

santiago de la hoz

¡Pueblo, despierta ya! Tus hijos crecen
Y una herencia de oprobio no merecen,
Vuelve ya en tí de esa locura insana:
¡Si siguen criando siervos tantas madres,
Tus hijos, los esclavos de mañana,
Renegarán del nombre de sus padres!
Levántate y medita

The silva is a poem combining eleven-syllable and seven-syllable verse, with a flexible rhyme and stanza pattern.

En los grandes problemas de tu suerte,
Pon en salvo tu cuerpo que gravita
Sobre un abismo de afrentosa muerte;
Y piensa, con orgullo noble y bravo
Que no has nacido para ser esclavo;
Que la tierra en que hoy gimes cual cautivo
Que la tierra en que hoy eres pordiosero,

Mañana que te yergas redivivo
Y te hagas respetar con el acero,
Y de malvados tu camino alfombres,
Será lo que te anuncian tus Mesías:
La tierra donde no haya tiranías
Y en dulce comunión vivan los hombres!

¡Tuyo ha de ser el reino de mañana!
Que si esta sociedad estulta y vana
Hoy se halla dividida
En el hombre de arriba y el de abajo,
Cuando fulgure tu cabeza erguida
Y a Nerón y al burgués lleves al tajo,
Medidos con la vara del trabajo
Todos serán iguales en la vida!

¡Pueblo, piensa y combate! El pueblo debe
Combatir y pensar; el pensamiento
Siempre ha de ser un ala que lo eleve;
Y si sabe luchar a todo viento
Con la pluma y la espada y el rugido,
O con la cruz de mártir sobre el hombro,
Ha de ver que del trono demolido,
Sobre el humeante escombro,
Se levantan su gloria y su ventura
Radiantes de pureza y de hermosura!

This text is highly literary in its manner of communicating expressively what life was like in Crystal City, Texas before World War II. The writer shows a clear entendimiento of the facts of social and political life. Through the flavor of her language we can glimpse the strength of personality of the writer, una señora del pueblo.

CRÓNICA PERSONAL DE CRISTAL, PRIMERA PARTE

irene castañeda

Nenita,

Tu papá horita está todo nerbioso con sus dolores y no se acuerda de nada. El dice que mui joben se salió de su casa y más bien se crió solo. Pero según él platica ellos no sufrieron dise que tenían panadería y tenían muchos ranchos y casas—ya bes el no dise mucho de su gente. Ya te digo de todo lo que yo me acuerde de Cristal, si quieres saber del nombre de los abogados el cherife y dueño del banco y otros que mandaban en ese tiempo, escribe a Concha mi hermana a Cristal. Ella se acuerda mejor que llo. Ahora disen que está muy bien porque lo están gobernando puros mejicanos. Según dise Concha que el abogado de los mejicanos en ese tiempo hera papá. Cuando lo nesesitaban le ablaban para intérpete. En esos tiempos el mejicano no tenía bos ni boto, asían muchas injustisias, por una que no entendían el ydioma y no querían que la aprendieran para que no se pudieran defender. Si estaba par-

ado un mejicano en la banqueta y no se
quitaba para que pasaran ellos, lo pucha-
ban lo abentaban en el suelo en el charco
de agua el mejicano siempre bibió suba-
jado. En Cristal no les almetian en los
restaurantes. Si querian comer algo lo
sentaban en la cosina hafuera le daban
su plato. Las personas que lababan en
las casas de la gente blanca les daban
su platito afuera, si no no abía comida.
Algunos llebaban algo de su casa. Bueno,
esta para que comienses tu historia.

Por eso, yo más bien dicho, tube que
peliar a capa y espada como disen
el dicho, que no quise quedarme en Cristal
para que ustedes no fueran a quedarse
burritos como nosotros. Siquiera que se
pudieran defender. Pedia a dios con
mis brasos abiertos que me sacara de
ese pueblo tan ignorante y tan perdido-
puras cantinas puro mugrero.

PERSONAL CHRONICLE OF CRYSTAL CITY, PART ONE

irene castañeda

Nenita,

Right now your father is all upset from his pains and he doesn't recall too much. He says he left home when he was very young and more or less raised himself. But according to what he says, they didn't have it too bad-he says they had a bakery and several farms and houses-you know-he never says much about his people. I'll tell you what I remember about Crystal City-if you want to know the names of the lawyers, the sheriff, the owner of the bank, and others who ran the town in those times, write my sister Concha in Crystal City. She remembers better than I do. They say things are all right now because it's all Mexicans in the government. According to Concha, the lawyer for the Mexicans was my father. When they needed him, they'd call him to be interpreter. At that time Mexicans had neither voice nor vote-many injustices were committed against them-on the one hand, because they didn't understand the language, and the whites didn't want them to learn it-that way they couldn't defend themselves. If a Mexican was standing on the sidewalk and wouldn't move to let them pass, they'd shove him on the ground or in a mudhole-

the Mexican has always been put down. In Crystal City he wasn't allowed in the restaurants. If he wanted to eat something they'd sit him in the kitchen or they'd give him his plate outside. The women who cleaned house for the white people got their meals outside, or else there was no food. Some of them would bring something from home. Well, so much for the beginning of your story.

That's why we, or I rather, had to fight with cloak and sword—as the saying goes, because I didn't want to stay in Crystal City, so you wouldn't stay ignorant like us. So at least you could defend yourselves. I begged God with open arms to get me out of that town—so ignorant, so wretched, full of taverns, full of filth.

The Chicano today is examining many of the stereotyped images of mainstream society, and questioning how these images apply to him. The Anglo-American tradition has appropriated the cowboy image, opposing it to the Indian. Alurista, contemplating his Chicano heritage, reaffirms the positive values of both the charro and the Indian. In the final nine lines, he synthesizes, rather than opposes, the two traditions.

WE'VE PLAYED COWBOYS

alurista

We've played cowboys
    not knowing
nuestros charros
    and their countenance
con trajes de gala
    silver embroidery
on black wool
    Zapata rode in white
campesino white
    and Villa in brown
y nuestros charros
    parade of sculptured gods
on horses
    —of flowing manes
proud
    erect
they galloped
and we've played cowboys
    —as opposed to indians
when ancestors of mis charros abuelos
indios fueron
    de la meseta central
and of the humid jungles of Yucatán
    nuestros MAYAS
if we must
    cowboys play
—con bigotes
      y ojos negros
      negro pelo
de firmeza y decisión
of our caballeros tigres.

let them be
let them have the cheekbones

This poem is an example of *free verse*. The poet, free from the limits of rhyme and uniform length of line, can concentrate on imagery and poetic patterns, like the three-part structure seen above.

Written by a prisoner in a federal penitentiary, this letter is notable for the device of parallel constructions, used to sharpen ironic thrust, and thereby to express the writer's view more forcefully. Pintos are an integral part of today's total Chicano consciousness.

LETTER TO SOCIETY

tony "chato" estrada

You tell me that I am a criminal. You say what I am is no good. That I should be like you so that I may be a good citizen.

I have been told these things all my life. My teacher doesn't want me to speak Spanish because it is no good. I should not be a Catholic because it is no good. I should not have brown skin because it is no good. I should not be so loyal to my friends because it is no good. I should not be so clannish because it is not the American way.

I now speak only English, I am no longer a Catholic, I have quit being loyal to my friends, and I am no longer clannish. I have changed everything but the color of my skin. And what have I become; a brown man who has no belief in God, cannot speak his parents' language, who has become a traitor to his friends and an outcast of my people.

I have tried to be like you and now you tell me that I am a criminal. Isn't this what you wanted, or is it because I couldn't change the color of my skin that I am still no good?

Lyricism, bitterness, and anger are fused together in a young poet's examination of past and present. The careful selective use of rhyme and wordplay, together with the many direct and implied references to time, deepen the sense of rage and protest. For the Chicano poet, Jesús Maldonado, the poem distills the experiences of his youth in Texas, as seen later from the vantage point of the Chicano movement in the Northwest, where he now resides.

UNDER A NEVER CHANGING SUN

jesús maldonado("el flaco")

> La mañana
> > fresca
> > duerme todavía
> La brisa
> > corre aprisa
> > por los surcos
> Mis pasos
> > lentos
> > slowly kiss the dirt
> Y me voy
> > solito
> > al filo de algodón
> Las chicharras
> > en los mesquites
> > cantan
> Y segundea
> > la tortolita
> > con su coo-coo-coo
> El algodón cae
> > torpe
> > on pavement ground
> Y mi espalda
> > arde
> > under hot Azteca sun
> > > reflecting grains of sand
> > que caen
> > > through tick-tock hour-glass
> Ayer
> > mi padre también salió
> > solito
> > and crawled a gatas

on burning sands of time
    algodón piscando
    y al sol la cara dando
    como si rezando
        a un Dios Todopoderoso
Antier
    mi abuelito
        con su burrito
        al mercado fue
        con sus jarritos
        y jarrotes
        pa' ganar unos centavitos
La pinche vida
    que a tirones la vivimos
        under a never changing sun
    nos sigue jodiendo.

The novel *Pocho* by José Antonio Villarreal was written more than a decade ago. To many readers today it seems outdated. But there are moments, as in the scene below, when the young boy's experiences in California are told from a point of view which strikes a modern note of consciousness.

POCHO

josé antonio villarreal

Richard couldn't help laughing at Thomas' grin, but suddenly he stopped, because the bell rang again and he knew he was in for it. Right away, Thomas hit him in the stomach, and Richard bent over, and there it was—he just kept right on going, and landed on his head and took the count there curled up like a fetus. He didn't have to fight any more, and Thomas was very happy as he helped him up, and Thomas kept saying how he was like Fitzsimmons and that his Sunday punch was a right to the solar plexus. "I hit you in the solar plexus, Richard," he said over and over again, but Richard wasn't really listening to him, because he was sneaking looks at the people, and finally decided he had made it look pretty good.

The referee and the professional came over to see him. "Nice faking, kid," said the referee. "How'd ya like to be a fighter?"

"Uh-uh," he said, pulling at the laces with his teeth. The man took his gloves off.

"You don't know how to fight, but you got a punch for a kid and you're smart," he said.

"I not only can't fight, but I'm scared to fight, so you don't want me," he said.

"How old are ya, kid?"

"I'll be thirteen soon."

"I thought you was older," he said. "But, hell, I can teach ya a lot, and in a year I can put you in smokers. Make five or ten bucks a night that way."

"Not me, Mister. I don't need five or ten bucks."

"How about me?" said Thomas. "I'm the guy that won. You saw me hit him in the solar plexus." Now Richard knew why Thomas had been so anxious to fight.

"Yeah, I can use you, too," said the man, "but I want this other kid."

"Oboyoboy!" said Thomas. He had a trade now.

"How about it, kid?" asked the man. "I'm giving ya the chance of your life—it's the only way people of your nationality can get ahead."

"I'm an American," said Richard.

"All right, you know what I mean. Mexicans don't get too much chance to amount to much. You wanna pick prunes the rest of your life?" Richard didn't say anything, and he said, "Look, I'll go talk it over with your old man, and I'll bet he'll agree with me. I'll bet he knows what's good for you."

"You better not do that, Mister. You don't know my old man. He's already been in jail for knifing three guys."

Richard could tell he was dumb, and, like a lot of people, believed that Mexicans and knives went together. He thought he had finished with him, but the man said, "All right, we won't tell 'im anything, and when you start bringing money home, he'll come and see *me*."

"Listen," Richard said. "He'll come and see you all right, but it won't make any difference. My old man don't feel about money the way some people do. So leave me alone, why don't you?"

But the man kept insisting, and said, "I gotta line up a smoker for the Eagles, and if you and the Jap kid here put 'em on, I'll give ya each a fin. Then, when your old man sees the dough, he'll be in the bag. What do you say?"

"Okay with me," said Thomas, "but don't call me no Jap." Richard was walking away by then, and the man followed him. "I'll give ya seven-fifty and the Jap a fin."

"No, thanks." He kept walking. They would never be able to make him do anything like that. He was sure he could be no more than a punching bag, because, hell, everybody in the neighborhood could beat him, and besides he was afraid.

The guys caught up to him, but he wasn't talking. He thought how funny the guy back there was—the fight manager. He felt that the manager was the kid and he was the grownup. *Amount to something!* Jesus! Everybody was telling him what he should make of himself these days, and they all had the same argument, except that this guy was thinking of himself. At least the little old lady who was so nice and let him read the Horatio Alger books was thinking of him when she told him he should work hard to be a gardener and someday he could work on a rich person's estate; she was sure he would be successful at that, because she had known of some Mexicans who held very fine places like that. . . . Funny about her, how the Horatio Alger books meant as much to her as the Bible meant to Protestants. . . . And the adviser in the high school, who had insisted he take automechanics or welding or some shop course, so that he could have a trade and be in a position to be a good citizen, because he was Mexican, and when he had insisted on preparing himself for college, she had smiled knowingly and said he could try those courses for a week or so, and she would make an exception and let him change his program to what she knew was better for him. She'd been eating crow ever since. What the hell makes people like that, anyway? Always worried about his being Mexican and he never even thought about it, except sometimes, when he was alone, he got kinda funnyproud about it.

In this recent poem which Omar Salinas published in 1970, he develops the contrast which the Chicano poet feels between his Mexican and Aztec heritage, on the one hand, and his hostile social surroundings, on the other.

AZTEC ANGEL

luis omar salinas

I

I am an Aztec angel
    criminal
        of a scholarly
           society
I do favors
      for whimsical
          magicians
where I pawn

             my heart
                for truth
             and find
                my way
          through obscure
                streets
             of soft spoken
                   hara-kiris

II

I am an Aztec angel
    forlorn passenger
       on a train
    of chicken farmers
       and happy children

III

I am the Aztec angel
    fraternal partner
    of an orthodox
       society
    where pachuco children
       hurl stones
    through poetry rooms
    and end up in a cop car
       their bones itching
       and their hearts
    busted from malnutrition

IV

I am the Aztec angel
    who frequents bars
 spends evenings
       with literary circles
    and socializes
       with spiks
    niggers and wops
       and collapses on his way
          to funerals

V

                Drunk
                  lonely
                    bespectacled
                    the sky
                          opens my veins
                          like rain
                          clouds go berserk
                            around me
                          my Mexican ancestors
                                chew my fingernails
            I am an Aztec angel
                offspring
                of a woman
                who was beautiful

The selection below is from a series of essays entitled *Pensamientos* (1969). Eliu Carranza participates affirmatively in the ongoing process of Chicano self-definition.

THE MEXICAN AMERICAN AND THE CHICANO

eliu carranza

Octavio Paz in his book *The Labyrinth of Solitude* tells us what he believes to be a realistic perspective regarding the Mexican: "The Mexican is always a problem, both for other Mexicans and for himself."[1] And what does this mean? There is nothing simpler, he writes, "than to reduce the whole complex group of attitudes that characterize us—especially the problem that we constitute for our own selves—to what may be called the "servant mentality," in opposition to the "psychology of the master" and also to that of modern man, whether proletarian or bourgeois."[2]

Suspicion, dissimulation, irony, the courtesy that shuts us away from the stranger, all of the psychic oscillations with which, in eluding a

[1] Paz, Octavio. *The Labyrinth of Solitude: Life and Thought in Mexico,* translated by Lysander Kemp. New York: Grove Press, Inc., 1961, p. 70.
[2] Idem

strange glance, we elude ourselves, are traits of a subjected people who tremble and disguise themselves in the presence of the master. It is revealing that our intimacy never flowers in a natural way, only when incited by fiestas, alcohol or death. Slaves, servants and submerged races always wear a mask, whether smiling or sullen. Only when they are alone, during the great moments of life, do they dare to show themselves as they really are. All their relationships are poisoned by fear and suspicion: fear of the master and suspicion of their equals. Each keeps watch over the other because every companion could also be a traitor. To escape from himself the servant must leap walls, get drunk, forget his condition. He must live alone, without witnesses. He dares to be himself only in solitude.[3]

Such a view may have been or may be true of the Mexican, but it is no longer true of the Chicano. And this is the essence of the Chicano Cultural Revolution. A confrontation and a realization of worth and value through a brutally honest self-examination has occurred and has revealed to Chicanos a link with the past and a leap into the future, a future which Chicanos are fashioning, a future that has validity for Chicanos because Chicanos are the agents, i.e., the creators and the builders of their destiny. This is called Self-determination; its implementation—the Movement; Chicano determination—la Causa; the benefactors—la Raza; and the agents—Chicano militants. For the Chicano has shown his face at last! He has shed the "servant mentality" and denied the validity of the "psychology of the master." He no longer shuts himself away from the stranger nor does he seek to disguise himself when faced by a stranger. His intimacy reveals itself no longer exclusively in "fiestas, alcohol or death," but in confrontation with the oppressor. He has removed the mask and seen himself for what he is: a human being! He dares now to show himself as he really is—publicly. He is creating new relationships by destroying or modifying old ones. He no longer seeks to escape from himself by forgetting his condition and his link with the past. He *continually reminds himself of that condition by calling himself a Chicano.* He refuses to live alone, i.e., without witnesses, but lives with *la Raza*—his witness. He dares to be himself in solitude and with his fellowman. He confronts his despair— which he also recognizes in the look of the poor, the weak and the oppressed. In short, the Chicano is a Cultural Revolution. Whether one accepts it or denies it is irrelevant. Whether one judges it to be a sign of health or a symptom of sickness is another question. This Cultural Revolution means a significant change in the Chicano's world view. He recognizes that change is an ordeal, an agony for most Anglo-whites, and an ecstasy for the Chicano, but an ordeal for both; nevertheless, an ordeal the Chicano has embraced with the passion of life itself.

[3] Ibid., pp. 70–71.

Only recently has the Chicano taken time to examine carefully what he has for many years been burdened with: an unexamined cultural "Mexican American bag" made heavy by a blending in varying proportions of the educational system and his cultural heritage. Heretofore, the Chicano has been an unwilling, although a resigned victim of a systematic stereo-typification which had developed and is still perpetuating the development of emasculated Mexican Americans: these human beings who frighten many because they dare to want to heal themselves and dare to want to prevent the crippling of their brothers and sisters and other human beings.

Paz states that the Mexican neither wants nor dares to be himself. The Chicano not only wants but has dared and will continue to dare to be himself because he cares, where no one else has cared; he demands, when others plead; he reaches out, while others shrink inwardly; he dares to look up, while others bend their necks; and he speaks out, when others remain silent. In short, he dares to be a human being in an age of infrahumanity and robots. He will not tolerate dehumanization by anyone or anything!

This, then, is one aspect of an emerging Cultural Revolt. The Chicano has transcended that Mexican described by Paz as "a man aspiring to communion," for the short history of the individual Chicano is that of a man already in communion with himself and with his people. The Cultural Revolution, in a wider sense, is an open invitation to communion in an attempt to create a social order that will not be violated by the oppressor. Such a social order must permit man to express and to realize himself. Chicanos seek to free themselves completely from the restrictive philosophy of the *proper chain of command,* of *status according to title,* of *worth according to salary,* etc., each of which is expressive of the heavy emphasis on the material over and against the human, the impersonal over the personal, and the group over and against the individual.

At the same time, Chicanos realize that the establishment will welcome confrontation, especially with the more militant students, and under the now popular banner of *law and order* attempt to wipe them out. They are aware of the secret yearning in the hearts of many of their fellow citizens to have done with them once and for all. Chicanos know and remember the pachuco; they are witnesses to the violent reaction against the Hippie. The price they have had to pay cannot be measured by current traditional standards. Nor can the price Mexican Americans have had to pay be measured by the weights and balances of the current value system of the dominant society. The Mexican American price was an act of self-immolation, a rejection of his heritage and culture, falsely construed as necessarily an infrahuman culture of "spics" and "greasers", since it did not conform to the Anglo-white standard of civilized children of the Lord. This rejection was at one time reinforced by the Mexican American's sense of inferiority and the deep frustration brought about by a system of education that has continually put him down as lazy, therefore unmotivated; or quaint and friendly but not too bright; or mañana-oriented and therefore unambitious; or passive and therefore other-directed; or fieldworker types and therefore more like the burro; or drunkards, and therefore undependable, etc. This stereotypification of the Mexican American forced him to a new kind of despair—the selling of his soul for the promise of the "gringo" dream.

What I have tried to do above is to paint for you a picture of human life and the changes that are emerging as a result of a Cultural Revolt. This Cultural Revolt has at least three phases:

(1) an examination of the Mexican American's heritage and traditions to attempt to determine the origins of his attitudes, fears, and suspicions.

(2) an honest self-examination to determine what in his heritage and tradition must be cast aside, and what is of value in this time, and

(3) a striking out boldly in a new direction—one that no longer depends upon Anglo promises, values, or system of rewards, but one that holds fast to the principle of self-determination toward a new humanism.

What the Chicano Cultural Revolution has shown is the value of a little honesty. The task is to practice a little bit of honesty by first confronting yourself with the question: What are my values? and engaging yourself in an honest process of self-examination and secondly, once aware of your biases and prejudices to permit that honesty to carry you into your own Cultural Revolution. Perhaps your "trip" will be easier than the "Brown Trip," or it may prove to be an agonizing re-evaluation of all of your values; whatever, you will have engaged upon a truly human enterprise, one that may just bring us together without a computer making all of the arrangements. Incidently, I believe the Anglo-white is in need of his own Cultural Revolution; moreover, a description of that project is available: *Attack Upon Christendom* by Soren Kierkegaard.

This is a picture of human life. Through the long ages where time dwells heavy and barely moveable, for generation after generation Mexican Americans have been driven according to the horse's conception of driving. They have been governed, trained, and educated according to the Anglo-white's conception of what it is to be a man. Chicanos know what has come from that! Anglo-whites have set standards that deny both Chicano and non-Chicano spiritual growth. Both suffer from a poverty of the spirit which Chicanos will not resign themselves to. It follows from this that they can endure so little, that they impatiently use the means of the moment, impatiently want to see instantaneous rewards for their labors which for this very reason become of secondary importance.

Leonardo da Vinci once wrote, "Seek what you are capable of, and be capable of what you seek." Chicanos are the seekers. They have expressed what they seek and have found their humanity. They are also capable of what they seek because what they seek is the humanity of man. Somewhere I have read that the Mexican has shown us how to die; the Chicano, I believe, will show us how to live.

The experience of World War II made this unnamed poet question with his mind and his heart the validity of the American dream.

TO BROTHERS DEAD CROSSING THE RAPIDO RIVER...194?

in a day
        in an afternoon
                in a night
                        in years of fury
and tears
        alone and far from home
                        away from familiar sounds
                                        tender arms
        you fell on the earth of italy
                        blood of Mexico
                                blood of the northern
                                        deserts
blood of the bitter border
                spilled on earth of italy
                                on the earth of italy
hope of america
                the vain hope of america
                                never realized hope of america
against a wall of teuton steel
                        you waded the chilling river
                                waters tasting of death
far from home
                tasting of sudden death
                                left your dead on the river banks
tears of mothers on the river banks
                        hopes of sweethearts on the river banks

left tomorrows on the river banks
$$\text{bitter yesterdays on the river banks}$$
for a hope
$$\text{vain hope}$$

Omar Salinas strikes a deep note of despair and mourning as he touches the meaning of war and what that meaning holds for the Chicano community.

DEATH IN VIETNAM

luis omar salinas

the ears of strangers
$$\text{listen}$$
fighting men tarnish the ground
$$\text{death has whispered}$$
$$\text{tales to the young}$$
and now choir boys are ringing
$$\text{bells}$$
$$\text{another sacrifice for America}$$
$$\text{a Mexican}$$

comes home
his beloved country
$$\text{gives homage}$$
and mothers sleep
$$\text{in cardboard houses}$$

let all anguish be futile
tomorrow it will rain
and the hills of Viet Nam
resume
$$\text{the sacrifice is not over}$$

By way of introduction to Chicano theatre, we present an article recently published by Tomás Ybarra-Frausto, one of the co-editors of this anthology.

TEATRO CHICANO: PUNTO DE PARTIDA

tomás ybarra-frausto

The bourgeois conception of art, with its stress on rationalism, materialism and frequent escapism runs counter to the life style of the Chicanos, the second largest ethnic minority within the United States. As Chicanos assess and absorb their history, they are less willing to accept the cultural patterns of a racist society; they no longer tolerate American traditions which fail to acknowledge them as generators of and contributors to those traditions. They no longer believe in art forms that toy with philosophies of revolution but are too tepid to be examples of change. La Causa, the Chicano struggle for self-determination, is the action in life which is reflected in the Chicano theatre.

Chicano theatrical history is one of the oldest in the continent, with roots which date back to the pre-hispanic indigenous dramas like the *Rabinal Achí.* After the conquest, theatre in the European sense was inaugurated in Mexico in the 1500s with performances of plays like *Coloquio de la nueva conversión y bautismo de los cuatro últimos reyes de Tlaxcala en la Nueva España.* Of special significance were the rituals and ceremonies of the Christian church which were transformed into public fiestas and in effect became a people's theatre.

From the mid-sixteenth to the mid-eighteenth centuries, the major form of theatrical expression was the allegorical mime dramas of the *mascaradas.* Paralleling the fantastic plots and staging of the *mascaradas* was the historical drama of the exploration and colonization of what is now the American Southwest.

Juan de Oñate in 1588 enacted this first real life drama in our country on the shores of the Río Grande. Later as the Indo-Hispano people of the Southwest developed settlements, traditions and a way of life, they maintained a rich and varied tradition of religious and secular drama. *Pastorelas, posadas,* and *autos sacramentales* furnished didactic and poetic experience. Although theatre companies from Mexico crossed the .border in the latter half of the nineteenth century, performing the standard repertoire for Chicano audiences along the *frontera,* the most vital expression was provided by the roving bands of *carpas y maromeros.* These raggle-taggle troupes performed brief topical sketches and condensed versions of folk drama, intermingled with poetic recitations, music, and dance.

In the urban *barrios,* the *Chicanada* was entertained in the early part of this century by *tandas de variedad* performed by musical theatre companies. Great vaudevillians like El Chaflán and La Chata Nolesca acted out tales embodying the pain and beauty of Pocho life in the urban jungle. Dialogue was a hybrid, beautiful mixture of English, Spanish, and Pachuco *caló*; the style was fluid, improvisational and spontaneous, content was mordantly satirical, often poking fun at the mechanical inhuman world of the *Gavacho,* the automaton-like white man. Integral parts of the *tandas* were indigenous folk singers like Lydia Mendoza and Chelo Silva, who sang songs of life and protest to Chicano audiences from Texas to Nueva York.

Within this long-standing and vibrant theatrical tradition, El Teatro Campesino was founded in 1965 by Luis Valdez as an adjunct to the Farmworker's labor movement. Whether performing in dusty, agricultural communities of California and Texas, or world capitals like New York and Paris, it has carried the human message of the Chicano as he re-affirms himself and his historical destiny.

Just as La Causa encompasses a multi-faceted, contradictory people with multiple histories, leaders and ideologies, so does El Teatro Campesino reflect diverse orientations. It is a theatre of social protest that becomes ritual theatre, it is guerrilla theatre destroying established theatrical custom, while at the same time maintaining and re-defining the tenets of Chicano dramatic traditions. It examines the contemporary reality of the Chicano by mining the rich vein of mythology and archetypal memory of La Raza.

El Teatro Campesino has spawned a whole generation of *teatros* throughout the country: from El Teatro del Piojo in the state of Washington to El Teatro Bi-lingüe in Texas. Like individual pieces of a larger resplendent mosaic, the *teatros* in their confrontations with art are maintaining the militancy of the Chicano and are a vital, even indispensable component of La Causa.

This acto is one of the classics in the repertory of *El Teatro Campesino*. It has served to educate thousands of farmworkers, as well as members of general audiences, in the issues that underlie the historic grape strike at Delano: exploitation and racism.

The acto is successful as theatre because in the first place it probes skilfully and satirically into an area of painful human experience. But indispensable in this probe is the impact of theatrical techniques. Luis Valdez has shown genuine mastery in his handling of language, caricature, and role reversal. The result is a play generating the kind of laughter which cuts deep with its social satire, laying bare the inconsistencies in the patrón's (and society's) flimsy justification of their power over the campesino.

LAS DOS CARAS DEL PATRONCITO
1965

luis valdez

CHARACTERS: ESQUIROL
PATRONCITO
ARMED GUARD
FIRST PERFORMANCE: The Grape Strike, Delano,
California on the picket line.

In September, 1965, six thousand farm workers went on strike in the grape fields of Delano. During the first months of the ensuing Huelga, the growers tried to intimidate the struggling workers to return to the vineyards. They mounted shotguns in their pickups, prominently displayed in the rear windows of the cab; they hired armed guards; they roared by in their huge caruchas, etc. It seemed that they were trying to destroy the spirit of the strikers with mere materialistic evidence of their power. Too poor to afford La Causa, many of the huelgistas left Delano to work in other areas; most of them stayed behind to picket through the winter; and a few returned to the fields to scab, pruning vines. The growers started trucking in more esquiroles from Texas and Mexico.

In response to this situation—especially the phoney "scary" front of the rancheros, we created *Dos Caras*. It grew out of an improvisation in the old pink house behind the Huelga office in Delano. It was intended to show the "two faces of the boss."

LAS DOS CARAS DEL PATRONCITO

A FARMWORKER ENTERS, CARRYING A PAIR OF PRUNING SHEARS.

Farmworker: (TO AUDIENCE) Buenos días! This is the ranch of my patroncito, and I come here to prune grape vines. My patrón bring me all the way from Mexico here to California—the land of sun and money! More sun than money. But I better get to jalar now because my patroncito he don't like to see me talking to strangers. (THERE IS A ROAR BACKSTAGE) Ay, here he comes in his big car! I better get to work. (HE PRUNES)

THE PATRONCITO ENTERS, WEARING A YELLOW PIG FACE MASK. HE IS DRIVING AN IMAGINARY LIMOUSINE, MAKING THE ROARING SOUND OF THE MOTOR.

Patroncito: Good morning, boy!
Farmworker: Buenos días, patroncito. (HIS HAT IN HIS HANDS)
Patroncito: You working hard, boy?
Farmworker: Oh, sí, patrón! Muy hard! (HE STARTS WORKING FURIOUSLY)
Patroncito: Oh, you can work harder than that, boy. (HE WORKS HARDER) Harder! (HE WORKS HARDER) Harder! (HE WORKS STILL HARDER) HARDER!
Farmworker: Ay, that's too hard, patrón!

THE PATRONCITO LOOKS DOWNSTAGE THEN UPSTAGE ALONG THE IMAGINARY ROW OF VINES, WITH THE FARMWORKER'S HEAD ALONGSIDE HIS, FOLLOWING HIS MOVEMENT

Patroncito: How come you cutting all the wires instead of the vines, boy? (THE FARMWORKER SHRUGS HELPLESSLY, FRIGHTENED AND DEFENSELESS) Look, lemme show you something. Cut this vine here. (POINTS TO A VINE) Now this one. (FARMWORKER CUTS) Now this one. (FARMWORKER CUTS) Now this one. (THE FARMWORKER ALMOST CUTS THE PATRONCITO'S EXTENDED FINGER) HEH!
Farmworker: (JUMPS BACK) Ay!
Patroncito: Ain't you scared of me, boy? (FARMWORKER NODS) Huh, boy? (FARMWORKER NODS AND MAKES A GRUNT SIGNIFYING YES) What, boy? You don't have to be scared of me! I love my Mexicans. You're one of the new ones, huh? Come in from. . .
Farmworker: México, señor.
Patroncito: Did you like the truck ride, boy? (FARMWORKER SHAKES HEAD INDICATING NO) What?!
Farmworker: I loved it, señor!
Patroncito: Of course you did. All my Mexicans love to ride in trucks! Just the sight of them barreling down the freeway makes my heart feel good; hands on their sombreros, hair flying in the wind, bouncing along happy as babies. Yes sirree, I sure love my Mexicans, boy!
Farmworker: (PUTS HIS ARM AROUND PATRONCITO) Oh, patrón.
Patroncito: (PUSHING HIM AWAY) I love 'em about ten feet away from

me, boy. Why, there ain't another grower in this whole damn valley that treats you like I do. Some growers got Filipinos, others got Arabs, me I prefer Mexicans. That's why I come down here to visit you, here in the field. I'm an important man, boy! Bank of America, University of California, Safeway stores—I got a hand in all of 'em. But look, I don't even have my shoes shined.

Farmworker: Oh, patrón, I'll shine your shoes! (HE GETS DOWN TO SHINE PATRONCITO'S SHOES)

Patroncito: Nevermind, get back to work. Up, boy, up I say! (THE FARM-WORKER KEEPS TRYING TO SHINE HIS SHOES) Come on, stop it. STOP IT!

CHARLIE "LA JURA" OR "RENT-A-FUZZ" ENTERS LIKE AN APE. HE IMMEDI-ATELY LUNGES FOR THE FARMWORKER.

Patroncito: Charlie! Charlie, no! It's okay, boy. This is one of MY Mexicans! He was only trying to shine my shoes.

Charlie: You sure?

Patroncito: Of course! Now you go back to the road and watch for union organizers.

Charlie: Okay.

CHARLIE EXITS LIKE AN APE. THE FARMWORKER IS OFF TO ONE SIDE, TREMBLING WITH FEAR.

Patroncito: (TO FARMWORKER) Scared you, huh boy? Well lemme tell you, you don't have to be afraid of him, AS LONG AS YOU'RE WITH ME, comprende? I got him around to keep an eye on them huelguistas. You ever heard of them, son? Ever heard of Huelga? Or Cesar Ch'vez?

Farmworker: Oh sí, patrón!

Patroncito: What?

Farmworker: Oh no, señor! Es comunista! Y la huelga es puro pedo. Bola de colorados, arrastrados, huevones! No trabajan porque no quieren!

Patroncito: That's right, son. Sic'em Sic'em, boy!

Farmworker: (REALLY GETTING INTO IT) Comunistas! Desgraciados! Mendigos huevones!

Patroncito: Good boy! (FARMWORKER FALLS TO HIS KNEES, HANDS IN FRONT OF HIS CHEST LIKE A DOCILE DOG; HIS TONGUE HANGS OUT. PATRONCITO PATS HIM ON THE HEAD) Good boy.

THE PATRONCITO STEPS TO ONE SIDE AND LEANS OVER: FARMWORKER KISSES HIS ASS. PATRONCITO SNAPS UP TRIUMPHANTLY.

Patroncito: Atta' baby! You're OK, Pancho.

Farmworker: (SMILING) Pedro.

Patroncito: Of course you are. Hell, you got it good here!

Farmworker: Me?

Patroncito: Damn right! You sure as hell ain't got my problems, I'll tell

you that. Taxes, insurance, supporting all them bums on welfare. You
don't have to worry about none of that. Like housing: don't I let you
live in my labor camp—nice, rent-free cabins, air-conditioned?

Farmworker: Sí señor, ayer se cayó la puerta.

Patroncito: What was that? ENGLISH.

Farmworker: Yesterday, the door fell off, señor. And there's rats también.
Y los escusados, the restrooms—ay, señor, fuchi! (HOLDS FINGERS TO
HIS NOSE)

Patroncito: AWRIGHT! (FARMWORKER SHUTS UP) So you gotta rough
it a little—I do that every time I go hunting in the mountains. Why,
it's almost like camping out, boy. A free vacation!

Farmworker: Vacation?

Patroncito: Free!

Farmworker: Qué bueno. Thank you, patrón!

Patroncito: Don't mention it. So what do you pay for housing, boy?

Farmworker: NOthing! (PRONOUNCED NAW-THING)

Patroncito: Nothing, right! Now what about transportation? Don't I let
you ride free in my trucks? To and from the fields?

Farmworker: Sí, señor.

Patroncito: What do you pay for transportation, boy?

Farmworker: NOthing!

Patroncito: (WITH FARMWORKER) Nothing! What about food? What do
you eat, boy?

Farmworker: Tortillas y frijoles con chile.

Patroncito: Beans and tortillas. What's beans and tortillas cost, boy?

Farmworker: (TOGETHER WITH PATRÓN) Nothing!

Patroncito: Okay! So what you got to complain about?

Farmworker: Nothing?

Patroncito: Exactly. You got it good! Now look at me: they say I'm
greedy, that I'm rich. Well, let me tell you, boy, I got problems. No
free housing for me, Pancho. I gotta pay for what I got. You see that
car? How much you think a Lincoln Continental like that costs?
Cash! $12,000! Ever write out a check for $12,000, boy?

Farmworker: No, señor.

Patroncito: Well, lemme tell you, it hurts. It hurts right here! (SLAPS HIS
WALLET IN HIS HIND POCKET) And what for? I don't NEED a car
like that. I could throw it away!

Farmworker: (QUICKLY) I'll take it, patrón.

Patroncito: GIT YOUR GREASY HANDS OFFA IT! (PAUSE) Now,
let's take a look at my housing. No free air-conditioned mountain
cabin for me. No sir! You see that LBJ Ranch Style house up there,
boy? How much you think a house like that costs? Together with the
hill, which I built? $350,000!

Farmworker: (WHISTLES) That's a lot of frijoles, patrón.

Patroncito: You're tellin' me! (STOPS, LOOKS TOWARD HOUSE) Oh yeah, and look at that, boy! You see her coming out of the house, onto the patio by the pool? The blonde with the mink bikini?

Farmworker: What bikini?

Patroncito: Well, it's small but it's there. I oughta know—it cost me $5,000! And every weekend she wants to take trips—trips to L.A., San Francisco, Chicago, New York. That woman hurts. It all costs money! You don't have problems like that, muchacho—that's why you're so lucky. Me, all I got is the woman, the house, the hill, the land. (STARTS TO GET EMOTIONAL) Those commie bastards say I don't know what hard work is, that I exploit my workers. But look at all them vines, boy! (WAVES AN ARM TOWARD THE AUDIENCE) Who the hell do they think planted all them vines with his own bare hands? Working from sun-up to sunset! Shoving vine shoots into the ground! With blood pouring out of his fingernails. Working in the heat, the frost, the fog, the sleet! (FARMWORKER HAS BEEN JUMPING UP AND DOWN TRYING TO ANSWER HIM)

Farmworker: You, patrón, you!

Patroncito: (MATTER OF FACTLY) Naw, my grandfather, he worked his ass off out here. BUT I inherited, and it's all mine!

Farmworker: You sure work hard, boss.

Patroncito: Juan...?

Farmworker: Pedro.

Patroncito: I'm going to let you in on a little secret. Sometimes I sit up there in my office and think to myself: I wish I was a Mexican.

Farmworker: You?

Patroncito: Just one of my own boys. Riding in the trucks, hair flying in the wind, feeling all that freedom, coming out here to the fields, working under the green vines, smoking a cigarette, my hands in the cool soft earth, underneath the blue skies, with white clouds drifting by, looking at the mountains, listening to the birdies sing.

Farmworker: (ENTRANCED) I got it good.

Patroncito: What you want a union for, boy?

Farmworker: I don't want no union, patrón.

Patroncito: What you want more money for?

Farmworker: I don't want—I want more money!

Patroncito: Shut up! You want my problems, is that it? After all I explained to you? Listen to me, son, if I had the power, if I had the POWER...wait a minute, I got the power! (TURNS TOWARD FARMWORKER, FRIGHTENING HIM) Boy!

Farmworker: I din't do it, patrón.

Patroncito: How would you like to be a Rancher for a day?

Farmworker: Who me? Oh no, señor. I can't do that.

Patroncito: Shut up. Gimme that. (TAKES HIS HAT, SHEARS, SIGN)
Farmworker: No, patrón, por favor, señor! Patroncito!
Patroncito: (TAKES OFF HIS OWN SIGN & PUTS IT ON FARMWORKER)
Here!
Farmworker: Patrón...cito. (HE LOOKS DOWN AT PATRONCITO SIGN)
Patroncito: Alright, now take the cigar. (FARMWORKER TAKES CIGAR) And
the whip. (FARMWORKER TAKES WHIP) Now look tough, boy. Act
like you're the boss.
Farmworker: Sí, señor. (HE CRACKS THE WHIP & ALMOST HITS HIS FOOT)
Patroncito: Come on, boy! Head up, chin out! Look tough, look mean.
(FARMWORKER LOOKS TOUGH & MEAN) Act like you can walk into
the governor's office and tell him off!
Farmworker: (WITH UNEXPECTED FORCE & POWER) Now, look here,
Ronnie! (FARMWORKER SCARES HIMSELF)
Patroncito: That's good. But it's still not good enough. Let'see. Here take
my coat.
Farmworker: Oh no, patrón, I can't.
Patroncito: Take it!
Farmworker: No, señor.
Patroncito: Come on!
Farmworker: Chale.

PATRONCITO BACKS AWAY FROM FARMWORKER. HE TAKES HIS COAT AND
HOLDS IT OUT LIKE A BULLFIGHTER'S CAPE, ASSUMING THE BULLFIGHTING
POSITION.

Patroncito: Uh-huh, toro.
Farmworker: Ay! (HE TURNS TOWARD THE COAT AND SNAGS IT WITH AN
EXTENDED ARM LIKE A HORN)
Patroncito: Ole! Okay, now let's have a look at you. (FARMWORKER PUTS
ON COAT) Naw, you're still missing something! You need something!
Farmworker: Maybe a new pair of pants?
Patroncito: (A SUDDEN FLASH) Wait a minute! (HE TOUCHES HIS PIG
MASK)
Farmworker: Oh, no! Patrón, not that! (HE HIDES HIS FACE)

PATRONCITO REMOVES HIS MASK WITH A BIG GRUNT. FARMWORKER LOOKS
UP CAUTIOUSLY, SEES THE PATRON'S REAL FACE & CRACKS UP LAUGHING.

Farmworker: Patrón, you look like me!
Patroncito: You mean...I...look like a Mexican?
Farmworker: Sí, señor!

FARMWORKER TURNS TO PUT ON THE MASK, AND PATRONCITO STARTS PICK-
ING UP FARMWORKER'S HAT, SIGN, ETC. AND PUTTING THEM ON.

Patroncito: I'm going to be one of my own, boys.

FARMWORKER, WHO HAS HIS BACK TO THE AUDIENCE, JERKS SUDDENLY AS HE PUTS ON PATRONCITO MASK. HE STANDS TALL AND TURNS SLOWLY, NOW LOOKING VERY MUCH LIKE A PATRÓN.

Patroncito: (SUDDENLY FEARFUL, BUT PLAYING ALONG) Oh, that's good! That's...great.

Farmworker: (BOOMING, BRUSQUE, PATRÓN-LIKE) Shut up and get to work, boy!

Patroncito: Heh, now that's more like it!

Farmworker: I said get to work! (HE KICKS PATRONCITO)

Patroncito: Heh, why did you do that for?

Farmworker: Because I felt like it, boy! You hear me, boy? I like your name, boy! I think I'll call you boy boy!

Patroncito: You sure learn fast, boy.

Farmworker: I said SHUT UP!

Patroncito: What an actor. (TO AUDIENCE) He's good, isn't he?

Farmworker: Come 'ere boy.

Patroncito: (HIS IDEA OF A MEXICAN) Sí, señor, I theeenk.

Farmworker: I don't pay you to think, son. I pay you to work. Now look here—see that car? It's mine.

Patroncito: My Lincoln Conti- Oh, you're acting. Sure.

Farmworker: And that LBJ Ranch Style house, with the hill? That's mine too.

Patroncito: The house too?

Farmworker: All mine.

Patroncito: (MORE & MORE UNEASY) What a joker.

Farmworker: Oh, wait a minute. Respect, boy! (HE PULLS OFF PATRONCITO'S FARMWORKER HAT) Do you see her? Coming out of *my* house, onto *my* patio by *my* pool? The blonde in the bikini? Well, she's mine too!

Patroncito: But that's my wife!

Farmworker: Tough luck, son. You see this land, all these vines? They're mine.

Patroncito: Just a damn minute here. The land, the car, the house, hill, and the cherry on top too? You're crazy! Where am I going to live?

Farmworker: I got a nice, air-conditioned cabin down in the labor camp. Free housing, free transportation—

Patroncito: You're nuts! I can't live in those shacks! They got rats, crockroaches. And those trucks are unsafe. You want me to get killed?

Farmworker: Then buy a car.

Patroncito: With what? How much you paying me here anyway?

Farmworker: Eighty five cents an hour.

Patroncito: I was paying you a buck twenty five!

Farmworker: I got problems, boy! Go on welfare!

Patroncito: Oh no, this is too much. You've gone too far, boy. I think you better gimme back my things. (HE TAKES OFF FARMWORKER SIGN & HAT, THROWS DOWN SHEARS, AND TELLS THE AUDIENCE) You know that damn Cesar Chavez is right? You can't do this work for less than two dollars an hour. No, boy, I think we've played enough. Give me back—

Farmworker: GIT YOUR HANDS OFFA ME, SPIC!

Patroncito: Now stop it, boy!

Farmworker: Get away from me, greaseball! (PATRONCITO TRIES TO GRAB MASK) Charlie! Charlie!

CHARLIE THE RENT-A-FUZZ COMES BOUNCING IN. PATRONCITO TRIES TO TALK TO HIM.

Patroncito: Now listen, Charlie, I—

Charlie: (PUSHING HIM ASIDE) Out of my way, Mex! (HE GOES OVER TO FARMWORKER) Yeah, boss?

Patroncito: This union commie bastard is giving me trouble. He's trying to steal my car, my land, my ranch, and he even tried to rape my wife!

Charlie: (TURNING AROUND, AN INFURIATED APE) You touched a white woman, boy?

Patroncito: Charlie, you idiot, it's me! Your boss!

Charlie: Shut up!

Patroncito: Charlie! It's me!

Charlie: I'm gonna whup you good, boy! (HE GRABS HIM)

Patroncito: (CHARLIE STARTS DRAGGING HIM OUT) Charlie! Stop it! Somebody help me! Help! Where's those damn union organizers? Where's Cesar Chavez? Help! Huelga! HUELGAAAAAA!

CHARLIE DRAGS OUT THE PATRONCITO. THE FARMWORKER TAKES OFF THE PIG MASK AND TURNS TOWARD THE AUDIENCE.

Farmworker: Bueno, so much for the patrón. I got his house, his land, his car—only I'm not going to keep 'em. He can have them. But I'm taking the cigar. Ay los watcho. (EXIT)

FIN

Roberto Vargas, of Nicaraguan background, has been raised in the schools and the barrios of San Francisco's Mission district. His deep sense of "La Raza" has led him to participate in the Chicano movement, to identify with it, to reflect it in his creative writing. As might be expected, the San Francisco background shows in several ways. One is the Third World context in which the theme of "la huelga" is treated. A second is the rapid flow of images and changing rhythms. And a third is the incorporation of strong urban street language to deepen poetic impact.

HOMENAJE A LA TERCERA MARCHA DE DELANO; MANIFESTACIÓN CONTRA LA UVA GORDA Y BLANCA, DOMINGO 8 DE SEPTIEMBRE, 1968, SAN FRANCISCO, CALIFAS

roberto vargas

"primer canto"

Domingo . . . .
En el sol del medio día
Old prayers chant to notes
of New Guitar Strings
Air . . . . Heavy incense
Proud Sonrisas of Young Brown Berets
Adding to the richness and splendor
De este Domingo
En el sol del medio día/

The "Huelga" Banners (Black and Red)
Point silent proud fingers
To the witness clouds. . .
That softly glance by

Picket signs que reclaman
En espectáculo silencioso las injusticias
A nuestra RAZA. . .on this Domingo
Y miles y miles pasados

5000 Bodies melting in human ether
singing/breathing/dancing of oneness
5000 Minds crying. . .of truth and lies
                crying. . .of death and rebirth
                crying. . .of newfound awareness

5000 heartbeats marching death
                    to the American Dream
5000 Guides marching in
                    the new order of consciousness
FEET STEP FEET STEP
EYES MEET EYES THEY KNOW
                    THEY KNOW

> Vanguard of Proud Blacks/on chrome and
> iron camels roaring in the lead
> they know...Goddamn they know

Gentle fluttering Indio Feathers
Dancing Red in Sunday unison
Dancing away forked tongues
and BROKEN TREATY/PROMISES
Heralding the Coming of the Buffalo
They know...verdad...they know

> Asian Brothers and Sisters
> in half somber songstep
> keeping cadence
> With Hiroshima thoughts
> in their hearts and wise eyes
> and they know...por Dios...they know

"segundo canto"

> Ay Raza Vieja
> Raza nueva y orgullosa
> Sun bronzed and arrogant
> Con el Espíritu de Che y Sandino
> Con el ardor de Malcolm X y Zapata
> Now Marching Against Exploitation
> Now Marching Against Shit and Frustration
> Now Marching Against the Bastard Grape
> Grapes of Wrath/Grapes of Paradox
> and bittersweet madness
> grapes of big white houses
> That mold or destroy
>   the innocent lives of our children
> Children that starve
>   while pigs feed off their backs
> children of brown eyes in Delano

Delano the epitome of America
Delano of César el santo
    who fasts in their consciences
Delano of the 10 o'clock Mexican Curfew
Delano the mississippi of California
Delano of the 3 thousand year Huelga
        Huelga that Rings in Hunger's own belly
        huelga Que Inspira Revolución
        y descubre al vendido
Hoy Sí mis hermanos

This is the year of the last stolen banana
And the Rape of Coffee Beans must cease
This is the year of the bullet (and frenzied Pigs)
that Run with Grape Stuffed mouths
And they know .... Shit yes *They* know

    EN ESTE DÍA DOMINGO
    BAJO TODOS LOS SOLES
    QUE SIGUEN/

II

los meros meros:
figuras populares

This second group of texts, Mexican and Mexican American, focuses on the popular leaders who were singled out because of their special meaning to the people. Most of the compositions are in the form of the corrido.

Mexicans, adapting the Spanish tradition of the romance to their own experience, developed the rich art of the corrido. Most often corridos were sung, and would pass on from one singer-guitarrista to another, sometimes changing in the process. Frequently corridos sang the praises of popular figures who embodied what the people saw as admirable qualities, such as defending the poor, or resisting unjust authority. The difference between historical accuracy, legend, and myth is not as important as the real significance that these popular figures had in shaping national consciousness.

The corrido has become an established form for Chicano popular poets throughout the Southwest. Further, as the following texts show, the tradition of capturing the qualities of popular figures in poetic verse has been maintained in the past by Mexican Americans, and continues to undergo new adaptations today.

Pancho Villa, from *Artes de México,* número
45, año XI, p. 24. (Los 60 años de Leopoldo
Mendez, texto de Elena Poniatowska.)

The anonymous poet sings of the exploits of Pancho Villa in a range of
tones that includes comedy and satire.

LA PERSECUCIÓN DE VILLA

En nuestro México, Febrero veintiocho
dejó Carranza pasar americanos;
diez mil soldados, 600 aeroplanos
buscando a Villa por todo el país.
   ¡Ay! Carranza les dice afanoso
si son valientes y lo quieren perseguir,
concedido les doy el permiso
para que así se enseñen a morir.
   Comenzaron a echar expediciones,
los aeroplanos comenzaron a volar
con distintas y varias direcciones
buscando a Villa, queriéndolo matar.
   Los soldaditos que vinieron allá de Tejas
los pobrecitos comenzaron a temblar,

muy fatigados de ocho horas de camino;
los pobrecitos se quieren regresar.
   Los de a caballo no pueden sentarse,
más los de a pie ya no pueden caminar
entonces Villa les pasa en aeroplano
y desde arriba les dice "good by"
   Pancho Villa ya no anda a caballo
ni su gente tampoco andará,
Pancho Villa es dueño de aeroplanos
y los alquila con gran comodidad.
   Cuando supieron que Villa estaba muerto
todos gritaban con gusto y afán;
ahora sí, queridos compañeros,
vamos a Tejas cubiertos de honor.
   Mas no sabían que Villa estaba vivo
y con él nunca van a poder,
hay si quieren hacerle una visita
está en Parral, lo pueden ir a ver.
   Comenzaron a echar expediciones
Pancho Villa también se transformó
se vistió de soldado americano
toda la gente también se transformó.
   Mas cuando vieron que flotaba
la bandera que Villa les pintó
se equivocaron también los pilotos,
se bajaron y prisioneros los cogió.
   Pancho Villa les dice en su mensaje
que en Carrizal seiscientos les mató,
que agradezcan a don Venustiano
los prisioneros él fué quien se los salvó.
   ¡Ay! Carranza les dice afanoso
si son valientes y lo quieren perseguir
yo les extiendo amplio permiso
para que así se enseñen a morir.
   Toda la gente allá en Ciudad Juárez
toda la gente asombrada se quedó
de ver tanto soldado americano
que Pancho Villa en los postes colgó.
   Qué pensarían estos americanos
que combatir era un baile de carquís
con su cara llena de vergüenza
regresaron otra vez a su país.
   Como saben que en México se mata
y que de diario se mueren por acá,

con un solo soldado mexicano
nuestra bandera en sus manos flotará.

Cuando entraron los gringos a Chihuahua
todos pensaban que nos iban a asustar;
pensarían que iban para Nicaragua,
muy asustados pudieron regresar.

Emiliano Zapata, from *Artes de México,*
número 45, año XI, p. 24. (Los 60 años de
Leopoldo Mendez, texto de Elena Poniatowska.)

This corrido is by an individual poet who was following the popular
tradition. Through imagery of animals and flowers, he expresses the close
identification of the Zapata movement with nature and the land.

CORRIDO DE LA MUERTE DE EMILIANO ZAPATA

armando liszt arzubide

Escuchen, señores,
oigan el corrido
de un triste acontecimiento:
pues en Chinameca
fue muerto a mansalva
Zapata, el gran insurrecto.

Abril de mil novecientos
diecinueve, en la memoria
quedarás del campesino
como una mancha en la Historia.

Campanas de Villa Ayala
¿Por qué tocan tan doliente?
Es que ya murió Zapata
era Zapata un valiente.

El buen Emiliano
que amaba a los pobres
quiso darles libertad;
por eso los indios
de todos los pueblos
con él fueron a luchar.

De Cuautla hasta Amecameca
Matamoros y el Ajusco,
con los pelones del viejo
don Porfirio se dio gusto.

Trinitaria de los campos
de las vegas de Morelos,
si preguntan por Zapata
dí que ya se fue a los cielos.

Le dijo Zapata
a don Pancho Madero
cuando ya era gobernante:
—Si no das las tierras,
verás a los indios
de nuevo entrar al combate.

Se enfrentó al señor Madero,
contra Huerta y a Carranza,
pues no le querían cumplir
su plan que era el Plan de Ayala.

Corre, corre, conejito
cuéntales a tus hermanos
—¡Ya murió el señor Zapata,
el coco de los tiranos!...

Montado con garbo
en yegua alazana
era charro de admirar;
y en el coleadero

era su mangana
la de un jinete cabal.

Toca la charanga un son
de los meros abajeños;
rueda un toro por la arena,
pues Zapata es de los buenos.

Una rana en un charquito
cantaba en su serenata:
—¿Dónde hubo un charro mejor
que mi general Zapata?

Con mucho entusiasmo
aplaude la gente
y hartas niñas concurrieron,
que el jefe Zapata y sus generales
dondequiera se lucieron.

Con jaripeo celebraba
su victoria en la refriega,
y entre los meros surianos,
que es charro, nadie lo niega.

Camino de Huehuetoca
preguntaba así un turpial:
—Caminante, ¿que se hizo
del famoso caporal?

Nació entre los pobres,
vivió entre los pobres
y por ellos combatía.
—No quiero riquezas,
yo no quiero honores.
A todos así decía.

En la toma de Jojutla
dice a un mayor de su gente:
—¡Tráete al general García
que le entre conmigo al frente!

A la sombra de un guayabo
cantaban dos chapulines:
—¡Ya murió el señor Zapata,
terror de los gachupines!

Fumando tranquilo se pasea sereno
en medio de los balazos,
y grita: —¡Muchachos,

a esos muertos de hambre
hay que darles sus pambazos!

Cuando acaba la refriega
perdona a los prisioneros,
a los heridos los cura
y a los pobres da dinero.

Estrellita que en las noches
te prendes de aquellos picos,
¿Dónde está el jefe Zapata
que era azote de los ricos?

—Cuando yo haya muerto,
dice a un subalterno,
les dirás a los muchachos:
con l'arma en la mano
defiendan su ejido
como deben ser los machos.

Dice a su fiel asistente
cuando andaba por las sierras:
—Mientras yo viva, los indios
serán dueños de sus tierras.

Amapolita olorosa
de las lomas de Guerrero,
no volverás a ver nunca
al famoso guerrillero.

Con gran pesadumbre
le dice a su vieja
—Me siento muy abatido:
pues todos descansan,
yo soy peregrino,
como pájaro sin nido.

Generales van y vienen
dizque para apaciguarlo;
y no pudiendo a la buena
un plan ponen pa' engañarlo.

Canta, canta, gorrioncito,
dí en tu canción melodiosa:
—Cayó el general Zapata
en forma muy alevosa.

Don Pablo González
ordena a Guajardo

que le finja un rendimiento,
y al jefe Zapata
disparan sus armas
al llegar al campamento.

Guajardo dice a Zapata:
—Me le rindo con mi tropa,
en Chinameca lo espero,
tomaremos una copa.

Arroyito revoltoso,
¿Qué te dijo aquel clavel?
—Dice que no ha muerto el jefe,
que Zapata ha de volver...

Abraza Emiliano
al felón Guajardo
en prueba de su amistad,
sin pensar el pobre,
que aquel pretoriano
lo iba ya a sacrificar.

Y tranquilo se dirige
a la hacienda con su escolta;
los traidores le disparan
por la espalda a quemarropa.

Jilguerito mañanero
de las cumbres soberano,
¡Mira en qué forma tan triste
ultimaron a Emiliano!

Cayó del caballo
el jefe Zapata
y también sus asistentes.
Así en Chinameca
perdieron la vida
un puñado de valientes.

Señores, ya me despido,
que no tengan novedad.
Cual héroe murió Zapata
por dar Tierra y Libertad.

A la orilla de un camino
había una blanca azucena,
a la tumba de Zapata
la llevé como una ofrenda...

Joaquín Murrieta, from *Fulgor y muerte de Joaquín Murrieta* by Pablo Neruda.

Joaquín Murrieta, for the anonymous poet and the people of California, was a man whose independence and sense of justice pitted him against what was supposed to be the law in the years right after the Gold Rush of 1848. In presenting this corrido, we have preferred to retain the spelling that best reflects the flavor of popular tradition.

CORRIDO DE JUAQUÍN MURRIETA

Yo no soy Americano
Pero comprendo el inglés
Yo lo aprendí con mi hermano
Al derecho y al rebés
Y a cualquier Americano
Lo hago temblar a mis pies.

Cuando apenas era un niño
Huérfano a mí me dejaron
No tuve ningún cariño
A mi hermano lo colgaron

Carmelita tan hermosa
Cobardes la asesinaron.

Yo me vine de Hermosillo
En busca de oro y riquesa
Al indio noble y sencillo
Lo defendí con fieresa
Cien mil pesos los cherifes
Pagaban por mi cabeza.

Ahora salgo a los caminos
A matar Americanos
Tu fuistes el promotor
De la muerte de mi hermano
Lo agarrastes indefenso
Desgraciado Americano.

Las pistolas y las dagas
Son juguetes para mí
Balasos y puñaladas
Carcajadas para mí
Y hora por medias cortadas
Ya se asustan por aquí.

A los ricos y abarientos
Yo les quité su dinero
A los humildes y pobres
Yo me quitaba el sombrero
Hay, que leyes tan injustas
Voy a darme a bandolero.

Bonito pueblo de Estocton
Con sus calles aliniadas
Donde paseaba Murrieta
En su silla muy plateada
Con su pistola repleta
Y su gente alborotada.

Yo no soy gringo ni extraño
En este suelo en que piso
De México es California
Por que Dios así lo quiso
Y en mi sarape terciado
Traigo mi fe de bautiso.

Ya me voy de retirada
Todos vamos al cuartel
Con bastante caballada

Cien mil pesos en papel
También me llevo a Tres Dedos
Mi compañero más fiel.

Soy paseado en California
Desde el año del cincuenta
Con mi rifle treinta-treinta
Y mi pistola repleta
Yo soy aquel Mexicano
De nombre Juaquín Murrieta.

Renowned in Texas legend for his bravery in standing up to the "rinches" (Texas Rangers), Jacinto Treviño in a larger sense is a symbol of pride in Mexican heritage, as seen in this anonymous poem.

JACINTO TREVIÑO

Ya con esta van tres veces
que se a visto lo bonito
La primera fue en McAllen,
en Brownsville y en San Benito

En la cantina de Béjar
se agarraron a balazos
por donde quiera volaban
botellas echas pedazos

Esta cantina de Béjar
al momento quedó sola
nomás Jacinto Treviño
de carabina y pistola

Entrenle rinches cobardes
que el pleito no es con un niño,
querían conocer su padre
yo soy Jacinto Treviño

Decía Jacinto Treviño
que arrastraba de risa,
a mí los rinches me hicieron
los puños de la camisa.

Decía el cherife mayor,
como era un americano,

Ay, que Jacinto Treviño,
no niega ser mexicano.

Ya con esta me despido,
aquí a presencia de todos,
si me quieren conocer,
los espero en Matamoros.

Reies López Tijerina, from *Con Safos,* Number
7, Winter, 1971, p. 12.

It would be interesting to trace, in the poetry and art of New Mexico, and even of Mexico and Spain, the tradition of the popular figure conquering the devil. Pedro Padilla does more in his poem than make a magical hero of Reies López Tijerina. He also continues, with creativity, an old folk tradition which is rich in legend, fantasy, and imagination.

SEPULTURA DEL DIABLO ATREVIDO

pedro padilla

Ya murió el diablo atrevido
que todo hacía con malicia
le dió muerte Tijerina
con la voz de la justicia
lo quemó con leña verde
y no quedó ni ceniza.

Salió el grupo de valientes
de la Alianza Federal
todos con picos y palas
a enterrar a Satanás
diciendo, miren no más
que terrible funeral.

Número uno es el primero
Número dos el segundo
¿cómo lo sepultaremos
para que no vuelva al mundo?

Haremos el pozo hondo
aunque nos cuesta trabajo
lo clavamos de cabeza
le tiramos de fregaso
para si quiere salirse
que se vaya más abajo.

La cola quede de fuera
que sirva de monumento
y venga el mundo contento
a contemplar cosa fea
diciendo el Rey de este mundo
ya ni la cola menea.

Número uno es el primero
Número dos el segundo

¿cómo lo sepultaremos
para que no vuelva al mundo?

Reies López Tijerina
Nunca se dió por vencido
con el diablo Satanás
y dijo el diablo "¡No más!
Aquí me doy por vencido."

Daremos gracias a Dios
y al valiente Tijerina
Porque nos quitó de encima
Al que nos tenía oprimidos
diciendo aquí se acabó
el diablo cruel y atrevido.

César Chávez, from *Con Safos,* Number 7, Winter, 1971, p. 12.

This movement song focuses on the people and their struggle. Rather than treat César Chávez individually, setting him apart, the poet presents him as part of a larger context. The song captures the flavor and tone of the farm workers' campaigns, and has been sung at meetings in towns and cities and camps. It has elements of historical background, of humor, and of social analysis, all of which function both to educate and to move people to participation.

VIVA HUELGA EN GENERAL

Hasta México ha llegado
la noticia muy alegre
que Delano es diferente

Pues el pueblo ya está en contra
los rancheros y engreídos
que acababan con la gente

Y como somos hermanos
la alegría compartimos
con todos los campesinos

Viva la Revolución
Viva nuestra Asociación
Viva Huelga en general

El día 8 de septiembre
de los campos de Delano
salieron los Filipinos

Y después de dos semanas
para unirse a la batalla
salieron los Mexicanos

Y juntos vamos cumpliendo
con la marcha de la historia
para liberar al pueblo

Viva la Revolución
Viva nuestra Asociación
Viva Huelga en general

Viva la huelga en el fil
Viva la Causa en la historia
La Raza llena de gloria
La victoria va cumplir

Nos dicen los patroncitos
que el trabajo siempre se hace
con bastantes esquiroles

Y mandan enganchadores
pa' engañar trabajadores
que se venden por frijoles

Pero hombres de la raza
se fajan y no se rajan
mientras la uva se hace pasa

Viva la Revolución
Viva nuestra Asociación
Viva Huelga en general

Ya saben los contratistas
que ni caro ni barato
comprarán nuestros hermanos

Pero como es bien sabido
que pa' mantener familias
más sueldos necesitamos

Ya está bueno compañeros
como dice César Chávez
esta huelga ganaremos

Abajo los contratistas
Arriba nuestros huelgistas
que se acabe el esquirol

Viva la Huelga en el fil
Viva la Causa en la historia
La Raza llena de gloria
La victoria va cumplir.

Confinement in a prison has not limited, but sharpened raúlsalinas' perspective. His poem projects a panoramic view of some of today's diverse themes, styles, and popular figures. Taken together in their plurality, they comprise, as the poet sees it, the Chicano movement.

LOS CAUDILLOS

raúlsalinas
written from
aztlán de leavenworth

Stifling
　　　Crystal City
　　　　　　heat
rouses Texas sleepers
　　　the long siesta finally over
at last, at long, long last
　　　Politics wrested from
tyrannical usurpers' clutches
　　　fires are stoked
　　　　　　　　flames are fanned
Conflagrating flames
　　　of socio-political awareness
Rich Dago vineyards
　　　Chávez doing his pacifist thing
　　　　　"lift that crate
　　　　　　　　& pick them grapes"
stoop labor's awright——with God on your side
　　　Califas gold not ours to spend, baby
Small wonder David Sánchez
　　　impatient & enraged in East L.A.
dons a beret, its color symbolizing
　　　　　　Urgent Brown

Voices raised in unison
　　　in Northern New México hills,
　　　　　"¡esta tierra es nuestra!"
cached clutter: invalid grants- unrecognized treaties
their tongues are forked,
　　　Tijerina,
their decks are marked
　　　Indo-Hispano

you're our man
Denver's Corky boxing lackeys' ears back
    let them live in the Bottoms for awhile
        see how they like a garbage dump
for a next-door neighbor
José Angel Gutiérrez: MAYO's fiery vocal cat
    the world does not love energetic noisemakers
        or so says papa henry b. (the saviour of San Anto)
        who only saved himself

In Eastern Spanish Ghettos
    Portorro street gangs do
            Humanity
Young Lords: (Cha-Cha, Fi & Yoruba)
    burglarize rich folks' antibiotics
        rip off x-ray mobile units/hospital
    —become medics for the poor—
ghetto children must not die
    of lead poisoning & T.B.
Latin Kings: (Watusi Vález & the rest)
    if you're doing social service
        how can you be on
terrorizing sprees (with priest accompanist)
    in near Northside Chicago?
            Ubiquitous? We're everywhere!
Arise! Bronze people,
    the wagon-wheels gather momentum...

III

el plan:
the call for action
and change

Another tradition shared by Mexicans and Chicanos, but interpreted by each in the light of differing circumstances, is that of *El Plan*—a sort of manifesto, announcing a movement, with its program, and calling on the people for support. The texts which follow are interesting not only as historical documents, but also because each is different in use of language, in rhetorical style, and in tone.

The sequence of manifestos—"los planes"—explain the word "reclamando" in the title of this unit. Mexicans and Chicanos both inherit a history of translating analysis and criticism into programs of action.

A most historic summons to action for Mexicans was the famous *Grito de Dolores*, delivered by Father Hidalgo on September 16th, 1810. This brief section conveys the flavor of his call to arms in the struggle for Mexican independence. Portions of this address are heard every year in Chicano communities during the fiestas patrias.

EL GRITO DE DOLORES

padre miguel hidalgo y costilla

"—Mis amigos y compatriotas: no existe para nosotros ni el rey ni los tributos. Esta gabela vergonzosa, que sólo conviene a los esclavos, la hemos sobrellevado hace tres siglos como signo de la tiranía y servidumbre; terrible mancha que sabremos lavar con nuestros esfuerzos. Llegó el momento de nuestra emancipación; ha sonado la hora de nuestra libertad; y si conocéis su gran valor, me ayudaréis a defenderla de la garra ambiciosa de los tiranos. Pocas horas me faltan para que me veáis marchar a la cabeza de los hombres que se precian de ser libres. Os invito a cumplir con este deber. De suerte que sin patria ni libertad estaremos a mucha distancia de la verdadera felicidad. Preciso ha sido dar el paso que ya sabéis, y comenzar por algo que ha sido necesario. La causa es santa y Dios la protegerá. Los negocios se atropellan y no tendré por lo mismo, la satisfacción de hablar más tiempo ante vosotros. ¡Viva, pues, la Virgen de Guadalupe, Viva la América, por la cual vamos a combatir!"

EL GRITO DE DOLORES

father miguel hidalgo y costilla

"My friends and fellow patriots—no longer do we accept the king or his tributes. This shameful burden, which is fitting only for slaves, has been carried by us for three centuries, as a sign of tyranny and servitude, a terrible stain that we will wash away through our own efforts. The moment of our emancipation has arrived; our hour of liberty is here, and if you understand how precious it is, you will help me defend it from the selfish grasp of the tyrants. Within a few hours you will see me leading those men who are proud to be free. I invite you to meet your responsibility. For without a country, without freedom, we will be far away from true happiness. It has been necessary to take the step, as you know, to begin to fulfill our needs. Our cause is holy, and God will protect it. Pressures are mounting, and for this reason, I will not be allowed the satisfaction of speaking to you at length. Long live, then, the Virgin of Guadalupe! Long live America, the cause for which we will struggle!"

Emiliano Zapata, dissatisfied with the unwillingness of President Madero to distribute land to the campesinos of the state of Morelos, issued his famous Plan de Ayala in 1911. It extended Madero's earlier Plan de San Luis Potosí, and became the rallying point for the Zapatista movement.

PLAN DE AYALA

emiliano zapata

Plan libertador de los hijos del Estado de Morelos afiliados al Ejército Insurgente que defiende el cumplimiento del Plan de San Luis, con las reformas que ha creído conveniente aumentar en beneficio de la Patria Mexicana.

Los que suscribimos, constituidos en Junta Revolucionaria para sostener y llevar a cabo las promesas que hizo al país la revolución del 20 de Noviembre de 1910, próximo pasado; declaramos solemnemente ante la faz del mundo civilizado que nos juzga y ante la Nación a que pertenecemos y llamamos, los propósitos que hemos formulado, para acabar con la tirania que nos oprime y redimir a la Patria de las dictaduras que se nos imponen, las cuales quedan determinadas en el siguiente Plan:

4°. La Junta Revolucionaria del Estado de Morelos manifiesta a la Nación bajo formal protesta: que hace suyo el Plan de San Luis Potosí, con las adiciones que a continuación se expresan, en beneficio de los pueblos oprimidos y se hará defensora de los principios que defienden hasta vencer o morir.

5°. La Junta Revolucionaria del Estado de Morelos no admitirá transacciones ni componendas hasta no conseguir el derrocamiento de los elementos dictatoriales de Porfirio Díaz y de Francisco I. Madero, pues la Nación está cansada de hombres falsos y traidores que hacen promesas como libertadores y al llegar al poder se olvidan de ellas y se constituyen en tiranos.

adiciones al "plan de san luis potosí"

6°. Como parte adicional del Plan que invocamos, hacemos constar: que los terrenos, montes y aguas que hayan usurpado los hacendados, científicos ó casiques a la sombra de la justicia venal, entrarán en posesión de esos bienes inmuebles desde luego, los pueblos o ciudadanos que tengan sus títulos correspondientes a esas propiedades, de las cuales han sido despojados por mala fe de nuestros opresores, manteniendo a todo trance con las armas en las manos la mencionada posesión, y los usurpadores que se consideren con derecho a ellos lo deducirán ante los tribunales especiales que se establezcan al triunfo de la revolución.

expropiación de tierras, montes y aguas

7°. En virtud de que la inmensa mayoría de los pueblos y ciudadanos mexicanos no son más dueños que del terreno que pisan, sufriendo los horrores de la miseria sin poder mejorar en nada su condición social ni poder dedicarse a la Industria o a la Agricultura, por estar monopolizadas en unas cuantas manos, las tierras, montes y aguas; por esta causa se expropiarán previa indemnización, de la tercera parte de esos monopolios a los poderosos propietarios de ellos, a fin de que los pueblos y ciudadanos de México, obtengan egidos, colonias, fundos legales para pueblos o campos de sembradura ó de labor y se mejore en todo y para todo la falta de prosperidad y bienestar de los mexicanos.

8°. Los hacendados, científicos ó casiques que se opongan directa o indirectamente al presente Plan, se nacionalizarán sus bienes y las dos terceras partes que a ellos les correspondan, se destinarán para indemnizaciones de guerra, pensiones de viudas y huérfanos de las víctimas que sucumban en la lucha del presente Plan.

llamamiento al pueblo

15. Mexicanos: considerad que la astucia y mala fe de un hombre está derramando sangre de una manera escandalosa, por ser incapaz para gobernar; considerad que su sistema de gobierno está agarrotando a la Patria y hoyando con la fuerza bruta de las bayonetas nuestras instituciones; y así como nuestras armas las levantamos para elevarlo al Poder, las volvemos contra él por faltar a sus compromisos con el pueblo mexicano y haber traicionado la revolución iniciada por él; no somos personalistas, ¡somos partidarios de los principios y no de los hombres!

Pueblo mexicano; apoyad con las armas en las manos este plan y haréis la prosperidad y bienestar de la Patria.

Libertad, Justicia y Ley. Ayala, Estado de Morelos, Noviembre 25 de 1911.

General en Jefe, Emiliano Zapata, Rúbrica.

Within a decade after the Treaty of Guadalupe Hidalgo (1848), Mexicans who had become American citizens by its provisions were finding it necessary to struggle for their rights as citizens. One example, in 1859, was the uprising led by Juan N. Cortina in Cameron County, Texas. As Cortina's proclamation indicates in the paragraphs presented below, the essential goals were self-preservation, dignity, freedom as guaranteed by the Constitution, and retention of land.

JUAN CORTINA PROCLAMATION

An event of grave importance, in which it has fallen to my lot to figure as the principal actor since the morning of the twenty-eighth instant, doubtless keeps you in suspense with regard to the progress of its consequences. There is no need of fear. Orderly people and honest citizens are inviolable to us in their persons and interests. Our object, as you have seen, has been to chastise the villainy of our enemies, which heretofore has gone unpunished. These have connived with each other, and form, so to speak, a perfidious inquisitorial lodge to persecute and rob us, without any cause, and for no other crime on our part than that of being of Mexican origin, considering us, doubtless, destitute of those gifts which they themselves do not possess.

To defend ourselves, and making use of the sacred right of self-preservation, we have assembled in a popular meeting with a view of discussing a means by which to put an end to our misfortunes.

Our identity of origin, our relationship, and the community of our sufferings, has been, as it appears, the cause of our embracing, directly, the proposed object which led us to enter your beautiful city, clothed with the imposing aspect of our exasperation. . . .

The unfortunate Viviano García fell a victim to his generous behavior; and with such a lamentable occurrence before us on our very outset, we abstained from our purpose, horrified at the thought of having to shed innocent blood without even the assurance that the vile men whom we sought would put aside their cowardice to accept our defiance.

These, as we have said, form, with a multitude of lawyers, a secret conclave, with all its ramifications, for the sole purpose of despoiling the Mexicans of their lands and usurp them afterwards. This is clearly proven by the conduct of one Adolph Glavecke, who, invested with the character of deputy sheriff, and in collusion with the said lawyers, has spread terror among the unwary, making them believe that he will hang the Mexicans and burn their ranches, etc., that by this means he might compel them to abandon the country, and thus accomplish their object. This is not a supposition—it is a reality; and notwithstanding the want of better proof, if this threat were not publicly known, all would feel persuaded that of this, and even more, are capable such criminal men as the one last mentioned, the marshal, the jailer, Morris, Neal, etc. . . .

...All truce between them and us is at an end, from the fact alone of our holding upon this soil, our interests and property. And how can it be otherwise, when the ills that weigh upon the unfortunate republic of Mexico have obliged us for many heart-touching causes to abandon it and our possessions in it, or else become the victims of our principles or of the indigence to which its internal disturbances had reduced us since the treaty of Guadalupe? When, ever diligent and industrious, and desirous of enjoying the longed-for boon of liberty within the classic country of its origin, we were induced to naturalize ourselves in it and form a part of the confederacy, flattered by the bright and peaceful prospect of living therein and inculcating in the bosoms of our children a feeling of gratitude towards a country beneath whose aegis we would have wrought their felicity and contributed with our conduct to give evidence to the whole world that all the aspirations of the Mexicans are confined to one only, *that of being freemen;* and that having secured this ourselves, those of the old country, notwithstanding their misfortunes, might have nothing to regret save the loss of a section of territory, but with the sweet satisfaction that their old fellow-citizens lived therein, enjoying tranquility, as if Providence had so ordained to set them an example of the advantages to be derived from public peace and quietude; when, in fine, all has been but the baseless fabric of a dream, and our hopes having been defrauded in the most cruel manner in which disappointment can strike, there can be found no other solution to our problem than to make one effort, and at one blow destroy the obstacles to our prosperity.

It is necessary. The hour has arrived. Our oppressors number but six or eight. Hospitality and other noble sentiments shield them at present from our wrath, and such, as you have seen, are inviolable to us.

Innocent persons shall not suffer—no. But, if necessary, we will lead a wandering life, awaiting our opportunity to purge society of men so base that they degrade it with their opprobrium. Our families have returned as strangers to their old country to beg for an asylum. Our lands, if they are to be sacrificed to the avaricious covetousness of our enemies, will be rather so on account of our own vicissitudes. As to land, Nature will always grant us sufficient to support our frames, and we accept the consequences that may arise. Further, *our personal enemies shall not possess our lands until they have fattened it with their own gore.*

We cherish the hope, however, that the government, for the sake of its own dignity, and in obsequiousness to justice, will accede to our demand, by prosecuting those men and bringing them to trial, or leave them to become subject to the consequences of our immutable resolve.

Rancho Del Carmen,
County of Cameron, September 30, 1859

Simultaneously with the triumph of the Mexican Revolution, Chicanos in Texas planned an uprising. This document, available only in its English translation, is probably not the only one of its kind. It is a rather dramatic refutation of the myth of the "passive" Mexican American.

PROVISIONAL DIRECTORATE OF THE PLAN OF SAN DIEGO, TEXAS.
PLAN OF SAN DIEGO, TEXAS, STATE OF TEXAS JANUARY 6TH, 1915.

We who in turn sign our names, assembled in the REVOLUTION-ARY PLOT OF SAN DIEGO, TEXAS, solemnly promise each other, on our word of honor, that we will fulfill, and cause to be fulfilled and complied with, all the clauses and provisions stipulated in this document, and execute the orders and the wishes emanating from the PROVISIONAL DIRECTORATE of this movement, and recognize as military Chief of the same, Mr. Augustin S. Garza, guaranteeing with our lives the faithful accomplishment of what is here agreed upon.

1. On the 20th day of February 1915, at two o'clock in the morning, we will arise in arms against the Government and country of the United States of North America, ONE AS ALL AND ALL AS ONE, proclaiming the liberty of the individuals of the black race and its independence of Yankee tyranny which has held us in iniquitous slavery since remote times; and at the same time and in the same manner we will proclaim the independence and segregation of the States bordering upon the Mexican Nation, which are: TEXAS, NEW MEXICO, ARIZONA, COLORADO, AND UPPER CALIFORNIA, OF WHICH States the Republic of MEXICO was robbed in a most perfidious manner by North American imperialism.

2. In order to render the foregoing clause effective, the necessary army corps will be formed, under the immediate command of military leaders named by the SUPREME REVOLUTIONARY CONGRESS OF SAN DIEGO, TEXAS, which shall have full power to designate a SUPREME CHIEF, who shall be at the head of said army. The banner which shall guide us in this enterprise shall be red, with a white diagonal fringe, and bearing the following inscription: "EQUALITY AND IN-DEPENDENCE" and none of the subordinate leaders or subalterns shall use any other flag (except only the white flag for signals). The aforesaid army shall be known by the name of: "LIBERATING ARMY FOR RACES AND PEOPLES."

3. Each one of the chiefs shall do his utmost by watever means possible to get possession of the arms and funds of the cities which he has beforehand been designated to capture, in order that our cause may be

provided with resources to continue to fight with proper success. The said leaders each being required to render account of everything to his superiors, in order that the latter may dispose of it in the proper manner.

4. The leader who may take a city must immediately name and appoint municipal authorities, in order that they may preserve order and assist in every way possible the revolutionary movement. In case the Capital of any State which we are endeavoring to liberate be captured, there will be named in the same manner superior municipal authorities, for the same purpose.

5. It is strictly forbidden to hold prisoners, either special prisoners (civilians) or soldiers; and the only time that should be spent in dealing with them is that which is absolutely necessary to demand funds (loans) of them; and whether these demands be successful or not, they shall be shot immediately without any pretext.

6. Every stranger who shall be found armed and who cannot prove his right to carry arms, shall be summarily executed, regardless of his race or nationality.

7. Every North American over sixteen years of age shall be put to death; and only the aged men, the women, and the children shall be respected; and on no account shall the traitors to our race be spared or respected.

8. THE APACHES of Arizona, as well as the INDIANS (RED SKINS) of the Territory, shall be given every guarantee; and their lands which have been taken from them shall be returned to them to the end that they may assist us in the cause which we defend.

9. All appointments and grades in our army which are exercised by subordinate officers (subalterns) shall be examined (recognized) by the superior officers. There shall likewise be recognized the grades of leaders of other complots which may not be connected with this, and who may wish to cooperate with us; also those who may affiliate with us later.

10. The movement having gathered force, and once having possessed ourselves of the States above alluded to, we shall proclaim them an IN-DEPENDENT REPUBLIC, later requesting (if it be thought expedient) annexation to MEXICO, without concerning ourselves at that time about the form of Government which may control the destinies of the common mother country.

11. When we shall have obtained independence for the negroes, we shall grant them a banner, which they themselves be permitted to select, and we shall aid them in obtaining six States of the American Union, which States border upon those already mentioned, and they may form from these six States a Republic that they may, therefore, be independent.

12. None of the leaders shall have power to make terms with the enemy, without first communicating with the superior officers of the army,

bearing in mind that this is a war without quarter; nor shall any leader enroll in his ranks any stranger, unless said stranger belong to the Latin, the negro or the Japanese race.

13. It is understood that none of the members of this COMPLOT (or any one who may come in later), shall, upon the definite triumph of the cause which we defend, fail to recognize their superiors, nor shall they aid others who, with bastard designs, may endeavor to destroy what has been accomplished by such great work.

14. As soon as possible, each local society (junta) shall nominate delegates who shall meet at a time and place beforehand designated, for the purpose of nominating a PERMANENT DIRECTORATE OF THE REVOLUTIONARY MOVEMENT. At this meeting shall be determined and worked out in detail the powers and duties of the PERMANENT DIRECTORATE, and this REVOLUTIONARY PLAN may be revised or amended.

15. It is understood among those who may follow this movement that we will carry as a singing voice the independence of the negroes, placing obligations upon both races; and that, on no account will we accept aid, either moral or pecuniary, from the Government of Mexico, and it need not consider itself under any obligations in this, our movement.

"EQUALITY AND INDEPENDENCE"
San Diego, Texas, Jan. 6, 1915.

President,
Signed, L. Farrigno.
Signed, Augustin S. Garza, Com.

Signed, Manuel Flores
Signed, B. Ramos, Jr.

Secretary,
Signed, A. Gonzales, Lawyer
Signed, A. A. Saenz,
          Saloon Keeper
Signed, E. Cisneros
Signed, A. C. Alamraz.

A historic moment in recent Chicano experience was the conference at Denver, in 1969, which put forth this well known declaration.

EL PLAN ESPIRITUAL DE AZTLÁN

En el espíritu de una Raza que ha reconocido no sólo su orgullosa herencia histórica, sino también la bruta invasión gringa de nuestros territorios, nosotros los Chicanos habitantes y civilizadores de la tierra norteña de *AZTLAN,* de donde provinieron nuestros abuelos sólo para regresar a sus raíces y consagrar la determinación de nuestro pueblo del sol, declaramos que el grito de la sangre es nuestra fuerza, nuestra responsabilidad y nuestro inevitable destino. Somos libres y soberanos para señalar aquellas tareas por las cuales gritan justamente nuestra casa, nuestra tierra, el sudor de nuestra frente y nuestro corazón.

AZTLAN pertenece a los que siembran la semilla, riegan los campos, y levantan la cosecha, y no al extranjero europeo. No reconocemos fronteras caprichosas en el Continente de Bronce.

El carnalismo nos une y el amor hacia nuestros hermanos nos hace un pueblo ascendiente que lucha contra el extranjero gabacho, que explota nuestras riquezas y destruye nuestra cultura. Con el corazón en la mano y con las manos en la tierra, declaramos el espíritu independiente de nuestra nación mestiza. Somos la Raza de Bronce con una cultura de bronce. Ante todo el mundo, ante Norteamérica, ante todos nuestros hermanos en el Continente de Bronce, somos una nación, somos una unión de pueblos libres, somos *AZTLAN.*

Conferencia de Denver, marzo, 1969

THE SPIRITUAL MANIFESTO OF AZTLÁN

In the spirit of a new people that is conscious not only of its proud historical heritage, but also of the brutal "gringo" invasion of our territories, we, the Chicano inhabitants and civilizers of the northern land of Aztlán, from whence came our forefathers, reclaiming the land of their birth and consecrating the determination of our people of the sun, declare that the call of our blood is our power, our responsibility, and our inevitable destiny.

We are free and sovereign to determine those tasks which are justly called for by our house, our land, the sweat of our brows and by our hearts. Aztlán belongs to those that plant the seeds, water the fields, and gather the crops, and not to the foreign Europeans. We do not recognize capricious frontiers on the bronze continent.

Brotherhood unites us, and love for our brothers makes us a people whose time has come and who struggles against the foreigner "gabacho" who exploits our riches and destroys our culture. With our heart in our hands and our hands in the soil, we declare the independence of our mestizo nation. We are a bronze people with a bronze culture. Before the world, before all of North America, before all our brothers in the bronze continent, we are a nation, we are a union of free pueblos, we are AZTLAN.

Denver Conference, March, 1969

There are many phases and many sectors in the Chicano movement today. One very important area is the university campus. Chicano students and faculty from the various branches of the University of California came together in 1968 and hammered out this statement of principles, which they called, "El plan de Santa Bárbara."

PLAN DE SANTA BÁRBARA

manifesto

For all people, as with individuals, the time comes when they must reckon with their history. For the Chicano the present is a time of renaissance, of renacimiento. Our people and our community, el barrio and la colonia, are expressing a new consciousness and a new resolve. Recognizing the historical tasks confronting our people and fully aware of the cost of human progress, we pledge our will to move. We will move forward toward our destiny as a people. We will move against those forces which have denied us freedom of expression and human dignity. Throughout history the quest for cultural expression and freedom has taken the form of a struggle. Our struggle, tempered by the lessons of the American past, is an historical reality.

For decades Mexican people in the United States struggled to realize the "American Dream." And some—a few—have. But the cost, the ultimate cost of assimilation, required turning away from el barrio and la colonia. In the meantime, due to the racist structure of this society, to our essentially different life style, and to the socio-economic functions assigned to our community by anglo-american society—as suppliers of cheap labor and a dumping ground for the small-time capitalist entrepreneur—the barrio and colonia remained exploited, impoverished, and marginal.

As a result, the self-determination of our community is now the only acceptable mandate for social and political action; it is the essence of Chicano commitment. Culturally, the word Chicano, in the past a pejorative and class-bound adjective, has now become the root idea of a new cultural identity for our people. It also reveals a growing solidarity and the development of a common social praxis. The widespread use of the term Chicano today signals a rebirth of pride and confidence. Chicanismo simply embodies an ancient truth: that man is never closer to his true self as when he is close to his community.

Chicanismo draws its faith and strength from two main sources: from the just struggle of our people and from an objective analysis of our community's strategic needs. We recognize that without a strategic use of education, an education that places value on what we value, we will not realize our destiny. Chicanos recognize the central importance of institutions of higher learning to modern progress, in this case, to the development of our community. But we go further: we believe that higher education must contribute to the formation of a complete man who truly values life and freedom.

For these reasons Chicano Studies represent the total conceptualization of the Chicano community's aspirations that involve higher education. To meet these ends, the university and college systems of the State of California must act in the following basic areas:

1. admission and recruitment of Chicano students, faculty, administrators and staff
2. a curriculum program and an academic major relevant to the Chicano cultural and historical experience
3. support and tutorial programs
4. research programs
5. publications programs
6. community cultural and social action centers

We insist that Chicano students, faculty, administrators, employees, and the community must be the central and decisive designers and administrators of those programs. We do so because our priorities must determine the nature and development of such programs. Only through this policy can the university and college systems respond efficiently and justly to a critical reality of this society. Through such a policy universities and colleges will truly live up to their credo, to their commitment to diversification, democratization, and enrichment of our cultural heritage and human community.

We assume the sacrifices and responsibilities inherent in our commitment. It was in this spirit that we met in Santa Bárbara in mid-April: over one hundred Chicano students, faculty, administrators, and community delegates representing the northern, central, and southern regions of La Alta California, Aztlán. Away from the sensationalism of the mass media, and from the alarms of self-seeking politicians, we set out to formulate a Chicano plan for higher education.

Workshops on recruitment, support programs, campus organizing and the curricular and institutionalizing aspects of Chicano Studies produced analyses and recommendations. We never lost sight of the simple fact that these programs will be effective only to the extent that we can influence decision-making within and without the university and college systems. What follows, El Plan de Santa Bárbara, reflects one critical dimension of the Chicano struggle.

The destiny of our people will be fulfilled. To that end, we pledge our efforts and take as our credo what José Vasconcelos once said at a time of crisis and hope:

> At this moment we do not come to work for the university, but to demand that the university work for our people.

IV

to sum up ...

No prose essay can sum up the ideas and the spirit of a body of literature in terms as meaningful as a poem. We have chosen two selections—a Mexican corrido and parts of Rodolfo Gonzales' epic poem, "I am Joaquin"—because they reflect with vitality the spirit of protest in all its forms and levels. Further, they translate that spirit into an affirmative attitude, an attitude of determination to endure and to move forward. They seem to remind us of the words of the Aztec poet:

> "¡ Hay afán, hay vida,
> hay lucha, hay trabajo!"

LO QUE DIGO LO SOSTENGO

LO QUE DIGO DE HOY EN DIA
LO QUE DIGO, LO SOSTENGO,
YO NO VENGO A VER SI PUEDO,
SINO PORQUE PUEDO VENGO.

Vamos, vamos no se aplomen
esos que tanto gritaban
y le prometían al pueblo
que en la lucha lo ayudaban.

Echales bien la lazada
a esa punta de . . . . panzones,
que se van quedando atrás
a gozar de los millones.

Prepara tu carabina
que ya se nos van quedando
los políticos gallinas
que siempre se andan rajando.

!Qué desgraciados serán
esos que entran al gobierno,
nomás a robar dinero
que tanto le cuesta al pueblo!

También, ustedes, soldados,
mantenidos del gobierno,
yo no vengo a ver si puedo,
sino porque puedo vengo.

Ya verán como se mueren,
ricos hijos del . . . . dinero.
Yo no vengo a ver si puedo,
sino porque puedo vengo.

Ya verán monjas y curas
que se mantienen del pueblo,
yo no vengo a ver si puedo,
sino porque puedo vengo.

YA LOS PUEBLOS SE PREPARAN
A VIVIR DE OTRA MANERA,
CON SU FUERZA ORGANIZADA
QUE PROMETE NUEVA ERA.

YA CON ESTA ME DESPIDO
Y ¡AY! TRAIDORES, LES PREVENGO.

YO NO VENGO A VER SI PUEDO,
SINO PORQUE PUEDO VENGO.

I AM JOAQUÍN

rodolfo "corky" gonzales

...Here I stand
                    before the Court of Justice
                              Guilty
for all the glory of my Raza
                    to be sentenced to despair.
Here I stand
        Poor in money
        Arrogant with pride
                    Bold with Machismo
                    Rich in courage
                              and
                    Wealthy in spirit and faith.
My knees are caked with mud.
My hands calloused from the hoe.
I have made the Anglo rich
                              yet
        Equality is but a word,
            the Treaty of Hidalgo has been broken
        and is but another treacherous promise.
My land is lost
                    and stolen,
My culture has been raped,
                    I lengthen
            the line at the welfare door
and fill the jails with crime.
            These then
are the rewards
            this society has

For sons of Chiefs
                    and Kings
                    and bloody Revolutionists.
Who
gave a foreign people
            all their skills and ingenuity
to pave the way with Brains and Blood
for

those hordes of Gold starved
                              Strangers
Who
changed our language
and plagiarized our deeds
                    as feats of valor
                    of their own.
They frowned upon our way of life
  and took what they could use.
            Our Art
            Our Literature
            Our music, they ignored
so they left the real things of value
and grabbed at their own destruction
                by their Greed and Avarice
They overlooked that cleansing fountain of
            nature and brotherhood
  Which is Joaquin.
            We start to MOVE.
    La Raza!
Mejicano!
  Español!
    Latino!
      Hispano!
      Chicano!
or whatever I call myself,
            I look the same
            I feel the same
            I cry
                  and
            Sing the same

I am the masses of my people and
I refuse to be absorbed.
            I am Joaquin
The odds are great
but my spirit is strong
                  My faith unbreakable
                  My blood is pure
I am Aztec Prince and Christian Christ
            I SHALL ENDURE!
            I WILL ENDURE!

Lo Mero Principal

LO MERO PRINCIPAL

Chicanos maintain, in oral tradition, a famous corrido from the time of Pancho Villa which contains this stanza:

> Que pensarán los "bolillos" tan patones
> que con canoñes nos iban a asustar;
> si ellos tienen aviones de a montones,
> aquí tenemos lo mero principal.

What is *lo mero principal*? One answer—it is the set of qualities and capacities that have allowed the Chicano to endure more than a century of anguish and oppression: the migrations, lynchings, deportations, barrio riots—the mutilation of mind and body. In another perspective, it is the essence of Chicano culture as it has evolved.

By this essence we mean the series of values and attitudes and goals that have been forged out of experiences which Chicanos have shared— the knowledge of one's Mexican roots and of society's disdain for lo mexicano; the socio-economic exploitation that began on the border and followed Chicanos wherever they migrated; the racism that has become an entrenched feature of this nation's culture; the myriad problems, in education and politics, for example, encountered when defending a language other than the official one. The Chicano response has been to elaborate beliefs and norms of behavior, drawing on the Mexican heritage but adapting to the new circumstances. These beliefs and norms—whether about God, life, and death; about language and life style; about justice and human compassion, or good and evil—have provided a reservoir on which the people could draw as they faced reality head on.

In this sense, culture has been an armament, a means of defense against dehumanization, and of drawing people together in combative response. Projecting to the future, it will continue to be a resource in the struggle for self-determination.

From the many elements contributing to this inner strength, *lo mero principal*, this unit will explore the literary manifestations of four concrete components: la llorona, la comida, el humor, and el barrio.

Man sometimes creates literature as he seeks explanations of the unknown, and understanding of life's mysteries. The familiar legend of "la llorona", etched into the subconscious of most Chicanos, is more than a scary tale told by a viejito in a campo or barrio. As it tells of orphanhood, eternal search, and of loss and pain, Chicanos can understand its message from within their similar reality.

La llorona is a good example of how change can occur within tradition. Each narration localizes the story, yet the story-line remains the same whether in Mexico, Arizona, or Minnesota. Carried to remote parts of the country during the great migrations, the legend is yet another element giving sustenance to Chicanos of all generations. A seemingly simple narration, it serves as a connective bond to Mexican reality. As it is told and retold in barrios and colonias, it becomes part of that shared experience which is *lo mero principal.*

Another facet of the Chicano's enduring spirit is food, one of the most important bases for man's relation to his physical environment. In the many years of movement, whether enforced or voluntary, as Chicanos accommodated themselves to new realities, as they resisted or adapted, accepted or created, one thing remained constant: los frijoles en la olla hirviendo.

The texts in the food section attest to the permanence of the indigenous culinary tradition in Chicano culture. Some of the same dishes prepared for the great Aztec king Moctezuma Xocoyotzin are still created and placed before his descendants seated around a crude table in a campesino's kitchen.

The simple act of eating one of the indigenous foods takes on, then, a larger meaning. First, it is an affirmation of our values; the staples in our common diet—chile, frijoles, and maíz—are symbols of resistance to cultural imperialism. Further this act renews the ties with our past. In a very real sense, when we eat our traditional foods, we are also digesting our history.

From the beginning, the Chicano has been able to surmount his hostile circumstance and maintain his humanity through various responses. Among them is humor, a phenomenon which has much in common with literature. Both require original use of language, both involve the play of the imagination, and both provoke an emotional response.

Humor depends on man to generate from within himself the capacity to apply a distorting lens to daily experience, so that suddenly its relations and its proportions seem changed or reversed. The result not only produces laughter, it also clarifies the real set of relations in question. Most importantly, having summoned the ability to perceive reality in a different perspective, man has improved his chance of transcending it.

The Chicano's very unique ties to the barrio are in the first place defined in terms of space—some call it turf. But the ties are much more complex, taking in many intangible emotive relations—the people in the barrio (guisanderas, chavalas, pachucos, viejitos); the special physical features (graffitti-covered walls, dusty cemetery crosses, imposing presence of an empty Catholic church); the sensations remembered (fragrance of pan dulce freshly baked, yerbabuena and istafiate smells of a hierbería).

If we see the barrio, its people, places and sensations, as a tapestry, the design on this tapestry is the network of human relations that define its unique style.

The four representative elements—la llorona, la comida, el humor, and el barrio—embody a set of values. But values do not stand alone; they need man to give them life. It is you, then, carnal, on whom they depend . . . YOU, CARNAL, ARE *LO MERO PRINCIPAL*.

I

la llorona

La Llorona
is in town
by the river
or so the people
say.

Luis Omar Salinas

Chicanos are haunted by the image of la llorona. She runs screaming through our uncapped skulls looking for her lost progeny. Are we her lost children? ¿Los olvidados hijos de dos sangres enemigas?

From preconquest days to the present, the myth of la llorona has been passed on by oral tradition among La Chicanada.

Some of our viejecitos say that she is the Aztec goddess Matlacíuatl (the woman with the net), a vampire-like creature who stalks desolate places preying and feeding on men. Others bring forth versions saying that she is Ciuapipiltin, a goddess who ventured forth at midnight dressed in flowing robes, carrying an empty cradle, looking and lamenting for her lost child. Ciuacóatl, a pre-Columbian earth goddess, is also mentioned as the prototype of this anguished vision. And many claim that la llorona is La Malinche, the Indian mistress of Cortés, who eternally laments the betrayal of her people.

La llorona appears in many shapes and places throughout Aztlán In the innermost recesses of our minds, like a distant echo, Chicanos hear her voice. Like a blurred, cracked photograph her image is retained. She is etched in the very center of our consciousness.

The maintenance of this vision repeated and embellished from generation to generation demonstrates one aspect of *lo mero principal*: tradition within change.

As we have changed, we have nevertheless adhered to some traditional forms, styles, and structure in our fiestas, our food patterns, and our stories and songs. But ours is not a static continuation of dead forms. El cora del pueblo sifts each tradition through the sieve of experience. What remains are traditions that have the piquete of life, that reflect contemporary realities without losing continuity with the past.

La llorona is a good example of this process. In Texas, California, Minnesota, or wherever Chicanos live, her ancient story is told and re-told. In many instances the narrative has been localized, adding a sense of immediacy and truth so that the myth becomes blurred with reality.

In that magical space between fantasy and reality, she is poised, always alert for her release. Through time and space, la llorona looms as a central archetype in the memory of La Raza.

> The origin of la llorona is lost in antiquity. After the fall of Mexico-Tenochtitlán, various Spanish chroniclers collected and preserved indigenous narrations telling her story. In these two examples, la llorona seems to foretell the collapse of the Aztec nation.

TEXTO DE LA LLORONA

bernal díaz del castillo

...se oyó de noche en el aire una voz de mujer que decía: "¡oh, hijos míos, ya nos perdemos!" algunas veces decía: "¡oh hijos míos, adónde os llevaré!" (Bernal Díaz del Castillo, *Historia de las cosas de Nueva España*.)

LA LLORONA TEXT

bernal díaz del castillo

At night, in the wind, a woman's voice was heard. "Oh my children, we are now lost!" Sometimes she said, "Oh my children, where shall I take you?"

TEXTO DE LA LLORONA

diego muñoz camargo

Dios...comenzó con su inmensa bondad de enviar mensajeros y señales del cielo para su venida, las cuales pusieron gran espanto a este Nuevo Mundo, y fué que diez años antes que los españoles viniesen a esta tierra ...muchas veces y muchas noches se oía una voz de mujer que a grandes voces lloraba y decía, anegándose con mucho llanto y grandes sollozos y suspiros: "¡Oh, hijos míos! del todo nos vamos ya a perder..." y otras veces decía: "¡Oh, hijos míos, adónde os podré llevar a esconder!..." (Diego Muñoz Camargo, *Historia de Tlaxcala.*)

LA LLORONA TEXT

diego muñoz camargo

God...in his immense goodness began to send messengers and signals from heaven, foretelling their coming. These caused great fear in this New World, for ten years before the Spaniards came to this land...many times and many nights one heard a woman's voice that wept loudly and drowned her speech in cries, sobs and sighs "Oh my children! We shall be completely lost"...and other times she would say: "Oh my children, where can I hide you?"

The story below, a contemporary folk version collected in Mexico City, is interesting for several reasons; first, because it clearly identifies La Malinche as la llorona. Further, it reverses the commonly held concept of betrayal. Here the stress is on Cortés as betrayer, not La Malinche.

LA LLORONA EN MÉXICO

maría del refugio

Según nuestros antepasados, existió una historia llamada La Llorona. Esto fué en tiempo de la Colonia o mejor dicho en el tiempo de la Conquista, cuando a México aún le llamaban la Nueva España, cuando Hernán Cortés...En ese tiempo Cortés tenía como intérprete entre los indios a una bella y hermosa mujer de raza india; su verdadero nombre era Marina, pero por apodo le decían La Malinche. Como era tan bonita, al transcurrir el tiempo, Cortés llegó a fijarse en ella; tanto le llamó la atención, que entre ellos nació un amor, y al poco tiempo tuvieron un hijo, el cual al llevarlo a las aguas bautismales llevó por nombre Hernando. Así siguió el tiempo, el niño creció y cuando Cortés no tenía nada qué hacer, él tenía que volver a España, pero no quería dejar a su hijo, por el cual tuvo muchos contratiempos. Tanto luchó, que lo único que consiguió fué que la Malinche (como así le decían) empezó a sentirse enferma, de la pena que su hijo sería llevado a España. La antes mencionada se volvió loca y fué puesta bajo calabozo, y bien vigilada. Pero como su enfermedad fué temporánea, muy pronto recuperó su salud y fué puesta en libertad. Cortés siguió su intento, pero nunca tuvo éxito porque él a ella no la quería para esposa: siempre fué su amante. El quería a su hijo por su sangre; sabía que por sus venas corría sangre española. El no podía llevar consigo a Marina por ser india. Cuando el niño tenía la edad de siete años, Cortés no pudo esperar más, y dijo que a la buena o a la fuerza se lo llevaría. Entonces ella, no sabiendo qué hacer, tomó a su hijo en sus brazos, lo sacó al balcón, de su seno sacó un cuchillo de oxidiano, (sic) pero antes le dijo a Cortés: "Si quieres a tu hijo, aquí está; pero no te lo llevarás con vida", y sepultando el filoso cuchillo en el pecho del niño, atravesóle el corazón. Después que estuvo segura que su hijo era muerto, lo sepultó en el suelo, quedando madre e hijo tendidos en el suelo. Después su espíritu se fué escapando de su cuerpo, del cual salió un grito que decía: "¡Aaaayyy!". Según cuenta la historia, que desde entonces por las noches su espíritu vaga por todos lados, llamando la atención de la gente por su grito tan lastimoso. La gente le llama "la llorona".

(Informante: María del Refugio
nativa de Chihuahua, Chih.)

LA LLORONA IN MEXICO

maría del refugio

According to our ancestors, there existed a story called la llorona. This was during colonial times, or rather during the conquest, when Mexico was still called New Spain, when Hernan Cortés...

During that time, for his work among the Indians, Cortés had as an interpreter a beautiful Indian woman. Her real name was Marina but she was nicknamed La Malinche. As time passed, Cortés began to notice her since she was so beautiful. She attracted him so much that love blossomed between them and soon they had a son, who was baptised with the name

of Hernando. Time passed, the child grew, and when Cortés had no further business here, he wanted to return to Spain, but he didn't want to
abandon his son who had caused him so many difficulties. He insisted so
much that La Malinche (as she was called) got ill from worrying that her
son would be taken to Spain. She became insane and was put away in a
well-guarded dungeon. Since her malady was only temporary, she soon
regained her health and was set free. Cortés continued with his plan but
he was never successful because he didn't want her for a wife; she was
always his mistress.

He wanted his son, knowing that Spanish blood ran in his veins. Cortés
couldn't take Marina with him since she was an Indian. When their son
was seven years old, Cortés couldn't wait any longer. He said that he would
take the child through agreement or by force. Marina not knowing what to
do, took their child in her arms and brought him to the balcony. From her
breast she withdrew an obsidian knife and told Cortés: "If you want your
son, here he is, but you shall not take him alive." And she plunged the
sharp knife into the child's breast, piercing his heart. After making sure
that her son was dead, she stabbed herself, mother and child lying in a
heap on the floor. Afterwards her soul escaped from her body issuing a
lament... "¡Aaayyy!"

According to history, from that time, her spirit roams everywhere at
night, catching people's attention by her painful lament. People call her
"la llorona."

This scene from a contemporary Mexican play by Carmen Toscano
presents several aspects of the "llorona" story: (a) the archetypal figure
floating through time and space, (b) the anguished wailing of the apparition
reverberating in the inner-self of all who encounter her, (c) the attempt to
decipher her origins. Was she created through love or hate? Is she an omen
for the living or a sign from the dead?

LA LLORONA

carmen toscano

TODAVÍA A OSCURAS, UN RELOJ COMIENZA A SONAR. DAN LAS DOCE. HAY UN
FONDO DE MÚSICA EXTRAÑA. DESPUÉS SE ESCUCHA EL LÚGUBRE GRITO DE
LA LLORONA.

La Llorona Ayyy...tristes de mis hijos...los pobrecitos...mis desdichados
hijos...

SE ILUMINA LA CRUZ Y HACIA ELLA VAN LLEGANDO VARIAS MUJERES SO-
BRECOGIDAS, EN UN MOVIMIENTO DE DANZA MODERNA.

Mujer Primera   Es ella.

Mujer Segunda   Dios nos ampare (SE SANTIGUA).

Mujer Tercera   Casi la sentí el otro día junto a mí, como si me hubiera
rozado las carnes... un frío sudor invadió mi cuerpo.

Mujer Primera   Y al mismo tiempo dicen que se la ve en San Angel...
y se la ve en el Portal... y en la Quemada, en Mercaderes y allá por
los Indios Verdes...

Mujer Cuarta   Qué inclemente destino la arrastra por las calles silenciosas
y por las veredas más escondidas, por donde quiera su blanco espectro
hace temblar los corazones, por donde quiera se escucha su espantoso
lamento.

Mujer Primera   Su llanto ha corrido por los campos, ha invadido las
montañas, se tiende sobre los valles, su sombra suele desaparecer entre
las aguas, y los tenues velos de su vestidura parecen flotar entre las
nubes.

Mujer Cuarta   Cruza por los caminos blanqueados de luna y su voz se
cuela entre las ramas de los árboles en los bosques, choca contra las
peñas, ondula por las serranías...

Mujer Quinta   Al caer la noche, su largo, su agudo lamento hace estre-
mecer al más fuerte... yo he visto caerse de las manos los rosarios de
muchas atemorizadas mujeres, al escuchar el lúgubre gemido.

Mujer Segunda   No es un llanto humano, pero así nos resuena en la
conciencia, invade el caracol de nuestro oído...

Mujer Primera   Y parece que llevara consigo y adentro, las voces de
muchas mujeres...

Mujer Segunda   Más allá, mucho más allá del tiempo.

Mujer Cuarta   Malos augurios acarrea el oírla.

Mujer Primera   Dicen que su grito más doliente lo lanza al llegar a la
Plaza Mayor, que allí se arrodilla... y, vuelta hacia donde estaban los
viejos teocallis de los indios, besa el suelo y clama con angustia y
llena todo de aflicción.

Mujer Segunda   Cuentan que amó intensamente...

Mujer Cuarta   Que fue abandonada...

Mujer Tercera   Que cometió un horrible crimen...

Mujer Quinta   Que hizo correr la sangre de los suyos...

Mujer Primera   De todos modos, habrá sufrido mucho, pobre mujer...
¿por qué no puede descansar aún?

LA LLORONA

carmen toscano

WHILE THE STAGE IS STILL DARK, A CLOCK BEGINS TO CHIME. IT STRIKES TWELVE O'CLOCK. WEIRD BACKGROUND MUSIC IS PLAYED. AFTERWARDS, ONE HEARS THE MOURNFUL WAILING OF LA LLORONA.

La Llorona   Ayyy...my sorrowful progeny...my poor dears...my unfortunate children...

THE CROSS IS ILLUMINATED, SEVERAL STARTLED WOMEN ADVANCE TOWARDS IT WITH MODERN DANCE MOVEMENTS.

First Woman   It's her.

Second Woman   May God protect us (SHE MAKES THE SIGN OF THE CROSS).

Third Woman   I almost felt her next to me the other day, as if she had brushed against my skin...a cold shiver invaded my body.

First Woman   They say one can see her at San Angel, and at the same time in El Portal and at La Quemada, at Mercaderes, and way over by Los Indios Verdes.

Fourth Woman   What merciless destiny drags her through the silent streets, and over the most hidden paths. Everywhere, her white spectre makes hearts tremble, everywhere one can hear her hideous lament.

Second Woman   What horrible sin could that condemned soul have committed?

First Woman   Her weeping has run through the fields, it has invaded the mountains, it spreads out over the valleys, her shadow often disappears among the waters, and the tenuous veils of her gown seem to float among the clouds.

Fourth Woman   She crosses roads dappled in moonlight, and her voice filters among the tree branches in the woods, it reverberates against the rocks, weaves among the mountains.

Fifth Woman   At nightfall, her long, shrill lament makes the hardiest person shudder...I have seen the rosary fall from the hands of many frightened women as they hear her mournful wail.

Second Woman   It's not a human cry, but it resounds in our consciousness, it invades the inner coils of our hearing.

First Woman   It seems that she carries with her, inside of herself, the voices of many women.

Second Woman   Far away, beyond time.

Fourth Woman To hear her is a bad omen.

First Woman They say that her most doleful cry is uttered when she gets to la Plaza Mayor...That she kneels down there...Turning towards the ancient temples of the Indians, she kisses the ground and wails in anguish and fills everything with sorrow.

Second Woman They say that she loved passionately.

Fourth Woman That she was abandoned...

Third Woman That she committed a horrible crime.

Fifth Woman That she spilled the blood of her loved ones.

First Woman One thing we know, she must have suffered greatly...poor woman. Why can't she find any rest?

Alurista, a contemporary Chicano poet, creates a chilling picture of suffering and loss of identity. This poem is a double lament. La llorona as ever cries for her lost children. And they, in the grip of oppressive modern society, can no longer draw strength and sustenance from her as a cultural symbol.

MUST BE THE SEASON OF THE WITCH

alurista

Must be the season of the witch
 la bruja
 la llorona
she lost her children
 and she cries
en las barrancas of industry
 her children
devoured by computers
 and the gears
Must be the season of the witch
 I hear huesos crack
in pain
 y lloros
la bruja pangs
 sus hijos han olvidado
la magia de Durango
 y la de Moctezuma
 —el Huiclamina

Must be the season of the witch
La bruja llora
sus hijos sufren; sin ella

Infanticide punished by eternal damnation is a common motif in la
llorona tales. This Chicano folk narration gathered from oral tradition in Los
Angeles, California presents one version of this theme.

LA LLORONA EN CALIFORNIA

De la llorona solamente sé que era una señora que tuvo tres hijos. Y
que...los mató para seguir ella su vida libre. Y cuando ella...ya se murió,
que fue a dar las cuentas a Dios, entonces El le dijo solamente que ella le
llevara sus hijos, que dijera qué había hecho con sus hijos. Ella le dijo que
...uno echó al excusado, otro echó al mar,...y que el otro lo había echado
en...en un río. Entonces Dios le dice que para...poderla...perdonar, que
se fuera a buscar sus hijos. Y desde entonces la señora anda en busca de
sus hijos. Y por eso dice con ese grito: —Ay, mis hijos.

LA LLORONA IN CALIFORNIA

About "la llorona," I only know that she was a woman who had
three children. And that...she killed them in order to continue her wild
life. And when she...had died, when she went to settle her accounts with
God, well, He asked her to bring Him her children, to tell Him what she
had done with them. She told Him that...she had thrown one down the
toilet...another had been thrown into the sea...and that she had thrown
the other one into...a river. Then God told her that in order to...be able
to pardon her, that she should go look for her children. And since then, the
woman has been searching for her children. And that's why she utters that
cry...Ay, my children.

Other variations in the vast llorona lore are legends that depict her as a beautiful, tantalizing siren, a temptress who seduces men and entices them to destruction.

LA LLORONA EN TEXAS

Un hermano mío vio la llorona. Iba pasando un río...y el caballo, luego que la vio, se paraba de manos y no quería caminar. Porque le daba miedo. Y...y luego la, la siguió mi hermano. Sacó la pistola y...él dijo: —Hora la voy a matar. Y cuando pensó hacerlo se le cayó la pistola en el río...de la mano. Y...y luego, dice que...cuando ya salió del río que ...el, el caballo bufaba y bufaba y...y luego,...él no quería voltear, y volteó una vez así para atrás [imitating the movement], y se veía una mujer con...el pelo largo, y como, como una sábana...cubierta. Pero no le vio la cara. No más el..., y hacía: —Aaayyy...

LA LLORONA IN TEXAS

One of my brothers saw la llorona. He was fording a river...and the horse, when he saw her, stood on his hind legs and didn't want to move. Because he was afraid. And...and then my brother followed her. He took out his pistol and told her: "Now I'm going to kill you." And when he thought of doing it, his pistol fell out of his hand into the river. And then, he says that, when he got out of the river, that the horse whined and whined and then...he didn't want to turn around, but he turned around once [imitating the movement], and he could see a woman with...long hair, and covered with something like a sheet. But he didn't see her face. Nothing but her...and she wailed...Aaayyy...

The cycle of llorona tales closes with the following versions collected by Soledad Pérez in Austin, Texas. In a simple, direct way, they attest to the vitality of the folk imagination.

At night in the rural campos and the urban barrios of Aztlán, somewhere, someone remembers her tale . . .Por ay anda la llorona, or so the people say.

THE WEEPING WOMAN

soledad pérez

Do you know why La Llorona appears near the Colorado River? Well, La Llorona was a woman who lived here in Austin. She had two children, but she didn't love them. One day she took them to the river and drowned them. She never repented, and that is why she appears there and cries for her children.

My son, Rodolfo, was ten or eleven years old when he and some other boys decided to spend the night out near the river. They went in a little cart and took some blankets.

At night they spread the blankets out on the ground and went to sleep. He says that after midnight all of them woke up at the same time and saw a shadow flit across them. Then they heard the piercing wail of La Llorona. They got up and came home immediately. My son was very frightened when he got home.

THE WEEPING WOMAN

soledad pérez

My brother had a very good friend who was a shoemaker. The two were heavy drinkers, and they liked to go out together to eat and drink.

Well, one night my brother went to see his friend about twelve-thirty and prevailed on him to go out to drink with him.

Shortly after the two had started out for their favorite saloon, they noticed that a very attractive woman was walking just ahead of them. They decided to follow her. The two followed for a long time, but they couldn't catch up with her. When it seemed that they were coming up even with the woman, she suddenly seemed to get about half a block ahead of them. Finally, my brother and his friend decided to turn back, but as a parting gesture they said, "Good-by, my dear!"

At the same time that the two said, "Good-by, my dear!" the attractive woman whom they had followed turned around. She had the face of a horse, her fingernails were shiny and tin-like, and she gave a long, piercing cry. It was La Llorona.

My brother would have run, but his friend had fainted, and he had to revive him. The two reformed after that encounter with La Llorona.

II

la comida:
de anáhuac a aztlán

Lo Chicano is many things to many people. For some it is a militant commitment to social change, for some it is loyalty to the values of La Raza, while others seek the creation of a new cultural synthesis. Within this framework, the premise of this unit is that no one index such as food, dress, or language is sufficient to define *lo mero principal*: the enduring spirit of La Raza.

In Aztlán today, a culturally varied world, the Chicano has developed multiple life styles, which include food and its preparation. Our texts focus on one particular style, the indigenous, which we show in its pre-Hispanic and its Chicano forms. While attempting to exemplify the many positive values generated by this way of relating to food, we are not implying that it is the only valid cultural pattern, or that other patterns lack similar positive sets of values.

The delights and pleasure of eating and of food have been recorded in many ways by our people. Literary expression ranges from tomes on table etiquette and comportment written by the wise men, or *tlamantini*, in pre-Cortesian times, to the wondrous and detailed crónicas of the exotic new food of America compiled by the Spanish frailes during the conquest, to a robust and abundant popular expression in canciones, dichos, and refranes circulated throughout Aztlán.

Within our homes, many of us are constantly educated and our Chicanismo is repeatedly re-enforced by the food we eat. The chocolate we drink for ceremonial occasions like bodas y bautismos links us to the indigenous civilizations of Mesoamerica where cacao was highly valued. Mole, that supreme creation of our alta cocina, has baroque sensibility in the intricacy of its preparation and its hierarchy of spices, herbs and condiments.

In many barrios and colonias the neighborhood tortillerías daily manufacture thousands of tortillas de harina y de maíz, the panaderías fill the air with the delicate aromas of el pan dulce de cada día, the corner tiendita de Don Fulanito sells hojas for tamales, chorizo, barbacoa, carnitas, chicharrones, and chile of infinite varieties. Dulcerías fill their vitrinas with hundreds of varieties of candies, los restaurantes típicos serve the traditional dishes like mole and menudo, often featuring local antojitos like panocha in Nuevo México, atole azul in Colorado, and cabrito in Texas.

One of our viejecitos has said, "nosotros los Chicanos debemos educarnos en el chile que comemos." It is our native food that daily relates us to our history. In a very real sense, the holy trinity of chile, frijoles, and maíz has not only nourished our body but sustained our spirit for thousands of years.

The Chicano also has the option of eating in the style of what one of our poets calls "crackers con salsa." El refín, like all aspects of culture, is adaptive and continually creative. We take gringo weiners and fry them a la Chicana. If there is no tortilla, bread and frijoles make a taco muy de aquellas! French fries con nopalitos, spam con fideo, the list is endless.

As we open the bags con "el mandado" we often see canned goods, hamburger patties, and t.v. dinners packed next to hojas pa' los tamales, cilantro pa' los frijoles and posole pal menudo. Economic realities and culinary tradition fuse to create a true Chicano gastronomy.

Perhaps it is the capirotada which is the culinary counterpart of our real life complexity and diversity as a people. Capirotada, a dessert or main dish, is often prepared during Lent. It is a seemingly random amalgamation of bread, cheese, raisins, nuts, milk and countless other ingredients. Each guisandera follows the unwritten recipe that "cada cabeza es un mundo." The result is that the capirotada of each cook is singular and unique though created from a common base. This diversity within unity is analogous to the Chicano experience : Todos Unidos . . . Todos Diferentes.

Moctezuma was served elaborate dishes prepared from foods carried from throughout his far flung and bountiful empire. The luxury and splendor of his meals and the rituals of his eating attest to the elaborate court culture that the Aztec elite had developed.

It is important to note however, that as in all class structured societies, the bounty enjoyed by the Lords of such a court was the fruit of the labor of thousands of people.

DE LA COMIDA DE MOCTEZUMA

bernardino de sahagún

El emperador comía solo. El pavimento de un gran salón perfectamente tapizado de esteras era cubierto con centenares de platillos. Algunas veces Moctezuma mismo, pero más de ordinario su mayordomo, designaba los platillos que debían servirle, y los cuales se conservaban calientes en braseros. Los manjares consistían en animales domésticos y cazados en los bosques más lejanos, y de pescados que el día antes se movían todavía en el golfo de México. Estaban preparados de varias maneras, porque como ya lo hemos dicho, los artistas aztecas habían penetrado profundamente en el arte culinario. La mesa era servida por nobles que se resignaban aun al bajo oficio de presentar al monarca las mancebas que por su gracia y belleza eran de su real agrado. Para ocultarle de las miradas del vulgo durante la mesa, lo rodeaban con un biombo de madera ricamente dorado y esculpido. Sentábase en un cojín, y la comida se servía en una mesa baja cubierta con finos manteles de algodón. Los platos o escudillas eran de barro fino de Cholula, teniendo además una vajilla de oro que sólo se usaba en días de fiesta religiosa; y en verdad que ni sus pingües rentas hubieran bastado para servirse siempre con oro, porque la vajilla que había servido no volvía ya a servir y era regalada a los criados. El salón era iluminado con antorchas hechas de una madera resinosa que al quemarse esparcía un suave olor y probablemente no poco humo. Acompañábanle durante la comida cinco o seis nobles consejeros, que se mantenían a una respetuosa distancia, respondían a sus preguntas, y de vez en cuando gustaban de los platillos con que se dignaba obsequiarles desde su mesa.

A los platillos sólidos seguían los postres y pasteles en cuya confección contaban con los importantes requisitos de la harina de maíz, huevos y azúcar de áloe. Eran los cocineros aztecas muy famosos. Dos mancebas se empleaban allá en el rincón más apartado de la sala, en preparar durante la comida, hermosas tortillas con las que de tiempo en tiempo cubrían la mesa. El emperador no tomaba más potage que el chocolate sazonado con vainilla y otras especias, y preparado de tal manera que estaba reducido a una especie de espuma de la consistencia de miel, que se disolvía poco a poco en la boca. Este brebaje, si así se le puede llamar, era servido en copas de oro con cucharillas del mismo metal o de concha de tortuga, primorosamente trabajadas. Al emperador le gustaba con pasión, si hemos de juzgar por la cantidad que consumía diariamente, que no bajaba de cincuenta tazas, además de las cuales se preparaban más de dos mil para los de su servidumbre.

La disposición de la comida en general, no difiere mucho de la usada por los europeos; pero no hay en Europa príncipe que en cuanto a la esplendidez de los postres se pueda comparar con Moctezuma, porque éste podía reunir las producciones de los más opuestos climas: los de la templada región en que habitaba, y las sabrosas frutas de los trópicos que arrancadas el día anterior de los verdes bosques de la tierra caliente, eran mandadas a la capital por medio de correos con la velocidad del vapor. ¡Es como si un cocinero nuestro sirviese en nuestros banquetes las especias que un día antes estaban todavía creciendo en una de las cálidas islas del remoto mar de Indias!

Después de satisfacer el apetito, le lavaban las mujeres en bandejas de plata, de la misma manera de que se había hecho antes de comenzar; porque los aztecas eran más exactos en la ceremonia de la ablución que ninguna de las naciones de Oriente. Traíanle en seguida pipas de madera ricamente doradas y labradas, con las cuales respiraba por las narices y algunas veces por la boca, el humo de una yerba embriagante llamada tabaco, mezclada con liquidámbar. Mientras duraba la grata ocupación de fumar, se divertía el monarca con ver a sus saltimbancos y jugladores, de los que había una compañía perteneciente a palacio.

At many meals, el chile occupies the place of honor in the center of the Chicano table. Majestically waiting in the concave, cool hollow of the molcajete, el gran señor shimmers quietly like a dormant volcano ready to erupt in a piquant fury when sprinkled on the food.

Chile is such a basic component of the Mexican world view that outsiders to the culture are often judged by their reactions to it. Here is the homage to this king of spices by the noted Mexican writer and cronista, Salvador Novo.

EL CHILE

salvador novo

Pero a todo señor, todo honor. Rindamos al chile el merecidísimo homenaje de rastrear sus andanzas desde nuestra cocina prehispánica hasta las mesas universales.

Conforme los europeos se adentraban a aculturarse en las fértiles tierras americanas, descubrían que los chiles se daban en todas las formas y tamaños imaginables: redondos, cónicos, largos, torcidos: en forma de botoncillos (chile piquín), de zanahoria, de pera; verdes, anaranjados, escarlata, amarillos, casi blancos; algunos tan feroces (generalmente, los más pequeños son los más picantes) que comerlos equivalía a ingerir plomo derretido; otros, cuyo mayor tamaño parece comportar su mayor dulzura.

Se descubrió, asimismo, que los chiles se hibridizan con facilidad, lo cual ha multiplicado y desarrollado en todo el mundo nuevas formas y "picores", al exportarse a otros Continentes, y aclimatarse en ellos, las semillas de los chiles mexicanos. Su diseminación en Asia y en Africa ocurrió en un tiempo tan corto, que durante muchos años, los europeos creyeron que los chiles serían originarios del Oriente.

Al lado del tomate —con el cual se desposa en amplia gama de gustosos sabores— el "pimiento" de Colón y los legos conquistadores: el chilli o ají de los nahuas, ha sido una de las más importantes contribuciones del México prehispánico a la cultura gastronómica universal. Rico en ácido ascórbico, las variadas cocinas regionales de nuestro país y de buen comer aprovechan con imaginación en moles y salsas la riqueza de sus sabores, colores, grados distintos de picor que la pimienta reduce a uno solo.

We have omitted certain sections of the text in order to focus on certain ideas.

Alfonso Reyes contributes further elements to the mythology of el mole, the most poetic, the most baroque (complex, elaborate, varied), the most resplendent and succulent of our national cuisine. Reyes, who died in 1959, was an outstanding Mexican intellectual.

EL MOLE DE GUAJOLOTE

alfonso reyes

Pero el sentido suntuario y colorista del mexicano tenía que dar con ese lujoso plato bizantino, digno de los lienzos del Veronés o mejor, los frescos de Rivera; este plato gigantesco por la intención, enorme por la trascendencia digestiva, que es abultado hasta por el nombre: "mole de guajolote", grandes palabras que sugieren fieros banquetes.

El mole de guajolote es la pieza de resistencia en nuestra cocina, la piedra de toque del guisar y el comer, y negarse al mole casi puede considerarse como una traición a la patria. ¡Solemne túmulo del pavo, envuelto en su salsa roja-oscura, y ostentando en la bandeja blanca y azul de fábrica poblana por aquellos brazos redondos, color de cacao, de una inmensa Ceres indígena, sobre un festín silvestre de guerrilleros que lucen sombrero faldón y cinturones de balas! De menos se han hecho los mitos. El mole de guajolote se ha de comer con regocijo espumoso, y unos buenos tragos de vivo sol hacen falta para disolverlo. El hombre que ha comulgado con el guajolote —totem sagrado de las tribus— es más valiente en el amor y en la guerra, y está dispuesto a bien morir como mandan todas las religiones y todas las filosofías. El gayo pringajo del mole sobre la blusa blanca tiene ya un pregusto de sangre, y los falsos y pantagruélicos bigotes del que ha apurado, a grandes bocados, la tortilla empapada en la salsa ilustre, le rasgan la boca en una como risa ritual, máscara de grande farsa feroz.

guajolote en mole poblano

A un guajolote, cuarenta chiles pasillas tostados y remojados, cuatro piezas de pan y unas tortillas tostadas en manteca, dos cuarterones de chocolate, una poca de semilla de chile tostada; de todas especias, poquitas; y ajonjolí, también tostado; todo esto bien molido se deslíe en agua y se fríe en manteca; se acaba de sazonar con un polvo de canela, tantito vinagre y un terroncito de azúcar. Estando sazonado, se le agrega el guajolote, hecho cuartos.

Para llegar al mole de reglamento, ya se ve, nos está faltando la almendra; y ya el chocolate es aditamento de lujo. Pero aquí la iniciativa y el temperamento personal tienen su parte, que es la función del libre albedrío dentro de las normas del destino. Hay recetas que traen nuez moscada, pepitas de calabaza, chile ancho, clavo, un diente de ajo, cebolla desflemada, perejil molido, comino, pimienta, cacahuates, rebanadas de naranja agria, laurel, tomillo, y hasta ciruelas y perones, y algún cuartillo de Jerez (las cocineras mexicanas dicen siempre: "Vino-Jerez"); porque el pavo se ha de servir entre un resplandor cambiante de aromas y sabores, como otra nueva cola tornasolada a cambio de la que ha perdido en el trance.

In the tradition of the moral precepts that the ancient *tlamantini* recited in the school of arts and sciences called the *Calmecac,* the following selection defines the qualities that make a good cook.

The art and secrets of cookery are still maintained by our guisanderas. Every campo, colonia, and barrio has several noted experts who create the traditional dishes like mole for the grand and ceremonial occasions of our communities.

Aside from what it reveals about food, this text gives a revealing glimpse of the role of women in Aztec society. Some of the basic assumptions of this role are being questioned by contemporary Chicanas.

GUISANDERAS

bernardino de sahagún

La mujer que sabe bien guisar tiene por oficio entender en las cosas siguientes: hacer bien de comer, hacer tortillas, amasar bien, saber echar la levadura, para todo lo es diligente y trabajadora; y sabe hacer tortillas llanas y redondas y bien hechas, o por el contrario hácelas prolongadas y hácelas delgadas, u hácelas con pliegues, o hácelas arrolladas con *ají*; y sabe echar masa de los frijoles cocidos en la masa de los tamales, y hacer tamales de carne, como empanadillas, y otros guisados, que usan. La que es buena en este oficio, sabe probar los guisados si están buenos, o no, y es diestra y experimentada en todo género de guisados, entendida y limpia en su oficio, y hace lindos y sabrosos guisados.

La que no es tal no se le entiende bien el oficio, es penosa y molesta porque guisa mal, es sucia y puerca, comilona, golosa, y cuece mal las tortillas, y los guisados de su mano están ahumados, o salados o acedos, y tal que en todo es grosera y tosca.

COOKS

bernardino de sahagún

The woman who is a good cook knows the following as part of her craft: She must know how to cook, to make tortillas, to knead the dough, how to use leavening—and is a diligent and hard worker in everything; she knows how to form flat, round, well-made tortillas. On the other hand, she must also know how to make large thin tortillas, or form them with fluting or combined with ají; and further she must know how to fold the paste of mashed beans into the dough for tamales and how to make meat tamales like turnovers and other common dishes. The good cook can taste whether a dish is well cooked or not, and she is adept and experienced in preparing all sorts of dishes, well behaved and clean in her calling and she prepares beautiful and savory dishes.

A cook without these attributes does not understand her calling. She is distressing and bothersome since she does not cook well, she is dirty and filthy, a glutton, and makes bad tortillas, and the dishes she prepares are burned or too salty or too rancid and she is gross and coarse in everything.

Among the half remembered, muffled sounds of memory, Chicanos recall the tlac . . . tlac . . . tlac . . . of the palote as mamá made tortillas de harina, or the plat, plat, plat of her two hands as she gently patted the masa into round little cakes, yellow like the sun.

In this evocative fragment, the Mexican writer Elena Poniatowska captures the essence of that ephemeral art of making tortillas, and pays tribute to women as creators and maintainers of this fine art.

LA TORTILLA

elena poniatowska

Las manos recogen una bolita de masa, la aplanan y luego palmean una y otra vez *rociándola* con el agua de cal. La tortilla va y viene —vuelo pequeño de una mano a la otra— y cuando está delgadita, en su punto va a dar al comal para cocerse en pan nuestro de cada día. El palmoteo resuena en todas las calles, en todos los pueblos, en todas las ciudades, como un lenguaje secreto cuyas sílabas van condensándose en pequeños mundos. Las tortillas, pequeñas lunas de maíz, calientes como soles, porque también allí se han amasado sus rayos, redondas, círculos que comienzan y terminan en todos sus puntos, son la vida y el rescoldo del hogar. Al engendrarlas, suavizándolas entre sus palmas, las mujeres amasan su propia gallardía, su recia mansedumbre.

THE TORTILLA

elena poniatowska

Skillful hands retrieve a small dough ball, they press and palm it once and again "sprinkling" it with lime water. The tortilla comes and goes—a short flight from one hand to the other—and when light and thin, is placed on the cooking earthen plate (comal) to be baked into our daily bread. The hand palming sounds are heard throughout the streets, throughout the "pueblos," throughout all cities as a secret language whose syllables condense each other into small worlds. The round tortillas, small moons of corn, hot as suns, as in them the sun's rays have been massed, round, infinite circles which begin and end at all their points are the life and source of home. When giving them life and shape, ever so softly, between their hands, women mass their own pride and their gentle stoutness.

(trans. by *Artes de México*)

El comal le dijo a la olla . . . Escucha lo que te voy a contar. Here is a representative group of refranes from the popular oral tradition of La Chicanada. Most of us are attuned to these versitos, because from childhood we have heard their counterparts.

LOS REFRANES DE LA COCINA

El mexicano ciento por ciento,
vive de maíz, arroz, frijol y pimiento.

Los muchachos de
estos
tiempos
Son como el atole
frío. . .
Perdidos de
enamorados
Y el estómago
vacío.

Las muchachas de
estos
tiempos
Son como las
aceitunas :
Las que parecen más
verdes
Suelen ser las más
maduras.

Almuerza bien, come
más.
cena poco y vivirás.

Al que nace pa'
tamal
del cielo le caen las
hojas.

Cuando andes a
medios chiles
búscate medias
cebollas.

Sólo las ollas saben
los hervores de su
caldo.

Mañanita de San
Juan
Cuando la gente no
ayuna.
El que con vino se
acuesta
Con agua se desayuna.

The "prietito molcajete" lovingly described in this poem is so indispensable en las cocinas de Aztlán that it is almost considered a part of the family. When their eldest daughter marries, some Chicana mothers maintain the custom of giving them el molcajete de la familia.

From time immemorial, this concave, pudgy lava-stone mortar has been the source of magic. In it are ground the condiments and spices that turn simple meals into feasts.

By paying homage to an ordinary kitchen utensil, the poet finds beauty in our daily reality. El palote y la tabla for making tortillas de harina, la olla pa' los frijoles and the molcajete for preparing chile all serve to define and affirm our Chicanismo. In daily encounters with them, we build understanding of our cultural selves. In this sense we say . . . Power to the guisanderas!

ODA AL MOLCAJETE

jesús maldonado (el flaco)

> Piedra mágica de tres patitas pachoncitas
>   en culequillas te sientas
>   Majestuosamente
>   vientre salpicado
>   mueles tu magica diaria
> casting spells
>   on comidas humildes
>   ¡Aaaamaasísate!
> En tu vientre asoliado
>   nace la sabrosa fuerza
>   el piquete mexicano
>   de la Raza Noble
>   mi linda Raza Bronce
> El clas-clas——clas-clas musical
>   el pardo son que cantas
>   baña cocinas morenitas
>   con aromas cariñosas
>   ¡Ajúa!
> En tu vientre bronceado
>   se casan los cominos
>   con las pimientas
>   y el pardo ajo
>   bendice
>   la Bronce Boda alcaweta
> Se besan, se abrazan
>   y mezclan sangres cafecitas

chores tapones, gordos, flacos,
weras, morenas, prietas, renegridas
¡ Dale gas!
Y logo en el sartén
tu luna de miel
siembras besos picosos
¡ Aaamacita!
Allí naces otra vez
magia sin nombre
magia hechicera
magia de Aztlán
magia Tejana
magia de Nuevo
magia de Arizona
magia de Colorado
magia de Califas
magia del Magic Valley
magia del Yakima Valley
magia Chicana
Tus bewitching brujerías
prietito molcajete
son el chile de nuestra vida
el pilón Azteca
el carnalismo
que corre en nuestras venas
Tu choco vientre beso
y canto hoy mis versos bronces
por tu magia diaria
de estómago lleno
corazón contento.

Midst the affluence of this society, many Chicanos do not have enough to eat. Often, as a family gathers for a meal, the mother will admonish each youngster to be sparing as he serves himself . . . "Faltan los demás" she will say or "no nomás tú eres." . . . for the poor there is never enough.

Within this framework of frugality and want, the poet speaks joyfully of the vitality and goodness of the simple yet nourishing foods which are the daily diet de muchos Chicanos : el arroz, los frijoles, y las benditas tortillas !

FALTAN LOS DEMÁS O NO NOMÁS TÚ ERES

jesús maldonado (el flaco)

Dorado arroz,
Al hambre atroz
Matas. . .sofocas
Y lo arrojas
Contra mil rocas,
Quebrantándolo,
Derrotándolo.

Bendito arroz,
No eres feroz
Mas con tus tropas
Llenas diez bocas,
Aunque pocas,
Amparándolas,
Consolándolas.

LOA AL FRIJOL

jesús maldonado (el flaco)

Frijolito pinto,
Frijolito lindo,
Rico caldudito
Traes el apetito

Frijolito chico,
Frijolito rico,
Reinas cuando frito
Matas hambrecito.

EL TRÍO MEXICANO

jesús maldonado (el flaco)

Tortillas con mantequilla
Parientes de Pancho Villa,
Bistec de los mexicanos
De placeres soberanos.

El rico café saluda,
A matar hambres ayuda.
Sabroso humilde trío
Me contentas cuando frío.

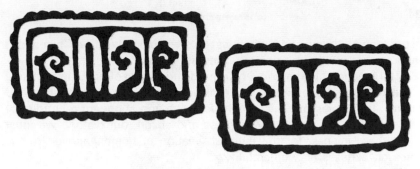

III

el humor

The survival kit of La Raza has many components, but humor above all others has been the indispensable companion of endurance. Amidst all the suffering and mutilation, at the zenith of oppression, the cleansing sound of laughter contributed to that profound inner strength of our people, *lo mero principal.*

Daily confrontations with the most depressing realities have allowed the Chicano to poke fun, to ridicule and laugh at his own condition and thus to surmount his circumstance . . . no se agüite compadre, es puro pedo!

In the barrios, humor has been ritualized by the vatos into tournaments of wit within the group. Sardonic sarcastic jokes, word plays and allusions, often of a sexual nature, named albures, jibe opponents into submission. At times this form of humor functions as a coping mechanism, enabling the jester to project through humor the hostilities he has built up in the course of interaction with his environment. While frequently this humor is creative, it is not always constructive. For example, many albures focus on proving masculinity by means of linguistic virtuosity.

In rural areas La Raza maintains the tradition of "la sesión de tallas". These are all-night joke sessions usually attended by members of a particular organization or profession—like a talla session for curanderos.

A number of the texts present humor in sophisticated terms. For example, the scholarship of Américo Paredes analyzes folk humor in order to show its conceptual basis. Even as he does this, Professor Paredes, with the tone of his own language, shows himself to be a part of the tradition he is discussing. The texts by Steve Gonzales and Celso de Casas are based on intellectual irony, as differentiated from folk humor.

Relajos, choteos, chistes, burlas, vaciladas, and multiple other forms

of spontaneous humor and wit attest to the humanity of la Chicanada:
cuando ya no puede uno llorar, se permite reír.

The function of humor in a colonized situation is of prime importance
for it allows the oppressed to strike back symbolically, to annihilate and
vanquish the oppressor. Chicanos have a rich and abundant repertoire of
humor about los güeros. As we assess and absorb our history, we must
project these images, for the cultural weapon of humor, applied to the
oppressor, exposes his vulnerability.

This section devoted to humorous literary expression captures
diverse manifestations of that vital perspective, in its different tonalities—
the satiric, the sardonic, the joyous—which have helped make survival
possible. The range includes Mexican and Chicano texts in both poetry
and prose.

This joyous yet ephemeral form of awareness is a reflection of our
spiritual condition . . . Let laughter be an index to our humanity!

Here is a Mexican's view of the modern Anglo-American value system, including such basic questions as materialism, technology, and the family.
Appropriately, Juan José Arreola chose a form characteristic of the U.S.A., the advertisement.

BABY H. P.

juan josé arreola

Señora ama de casa: convierta usted en fuerza motriz la vitalidad de sus niños. Ya tenemos a la venta el maravilloso Baby H.P., llamado a revolucionar la economía hogareña.

El Baby H.P. es una estructura de metal muy resistente y ligera que se adapta con perfección al delicado cuerpo infantil, mediante cómodos cinturones, pulseras, anillos y broches. Todas las ramificaciones de este esqueleto suplementario recogen cada uno de los movimientos del niño, haciéndolos converger en una botellita de Leyden que puede colocarse en la espalda o en el pecho, según necesidad. Una aguja indicadora señala el momento en que la botella está llena. Entonces usted, señora, debe desprenderla y enchufarla en un depósito especial, para que se descargue automáticamente. Este depósito puede colocarse en cualquier rincón de la casa, y representa una preciosa alcancía de electricidad disponible en todo momento para fines de alumbrado y calefacción, así como para impulsar alguno de los innumerables aparatos que invaden ahora los hogares.

De hoy en adelante usted verá con otros ojos el agobiante ajetreo de sus hijos. Y ni siquiera perderá la paciencia ante una rabieta convulsiva, pensando en que es una fuente generosa de energía. El pataleo de un niño de pecho durante las veinticuatro horas del día se transforma, gracias al Baby H.P., en unos útiles segundos de tromba licuadora, o en quince minutos de música radiofónica.

Las familias numerosas pueden satisfacer todas sus demandas de electricidad, instalando un Baby H.P. en cada uno de sus vástagos, y hasta realizar un pequeño y lucrativo negocio, trasmitiendo a los vecinos un poco de la energía sobrante. En los grandes edificios de departamentos pueden suplirse satisfactoriamente las fallas del servicio público, enlazando todos los depósitos familiares.

El Baby H.P. no causa ningún trastorno físico ni psíquico en los niños, porque no cohibe ni trastorna sus movimientos. Por el contrario, algunos médicos opinan que contribuye al desarrollo armonioso de su cuerpo. Y por lo que toca a su espíritu, puede despertarse la ambición individual de las criaturas, otorgándoles pequeñas recompensas cuando sobrepasen sus récords habituales. Para este fin se recomiendan las golosinas azucaradas, que devuelven con creces su valor. Mientras más calorías se añadan a la dieta del niño, más kilovatios se economizan en el contador eléctrico.

Los niños deben llevar puesto día y noche su lucrativo H.P. Es importante que lo lleven siempre a la escuela, para que no se pierdan las horas preciosas del recreo, de las que ellos vuelven con el acumulador rebosante de energía.

Los rumores acerca de que algunos niños mueren electrocutados por la corriente que ellos mismos producen son completamente irresponsables. Lo mismo debe decirse sobre el temor supersticioso de que las criaturas provistas de un Baby H.P. atraen rayos y centellas. Ningún accidente de esta naturaleza puede ocurrir, sobre todo si se siguen al pie de la letra las indicaciones contenidas en los folletos explicativos que se obsequian en cada aparato.

El Baby H.P. está disponible en las buenas tiendas en distintos tamaños, modelos y precios. Es un aparato moderno, durable y digno de confianza, y todas sus coyunturas son extensibles. Lleva la garantía de fabricación de John P. Mansfield & Sons, de Atlanta, Ill.

BABY H. P.

juan josé arreola

Lady of the house: convert your children's vitality into motor power. We now have on sale the marvelous Baby H.P. which has revolutionized household economy.

Baby H.P. is made of a very light resistant metal that adapts itself perfectly to the infant's delicate body by means of comfortable belts, bracelets, rings, and brooches. The ramifications of this supplementary skeleton catch each one of the child's movements, converting them into a Leyden bottle that can be placed on the back or the chest, depending on necessity. A needle pointer indicates when the bottle is full. Then, Madam, you can unhook it and plug it into a special outlet, so that it will discharge automatically. This deposit can be placed in any corner of the house and represents a precious store of electricity ready at any moment for light and heating, as well as for any of the innumerable gadgets that invade our homes nowadays.

From now on you will feel differently about the exhausting activities of your children. And you will not even lose patience at a convulsive tantrum, when you remember that it is a generous source of energy. The kicking of a nursing baby during the twenty-four hours of the day is now transformed, thanks to Baby H.P., into some useful seconds of electric blending or into fifteen minutes of radio music.

Large families can satisfy all their electrical demands by installing a Baby H.P. on each of their offspring, and even realize a small and lucrative business by transmitting a little of the extra energy to their neighbors. Big apartment buildings can satisfactorily supply electricity when there are failures in the public service by hooking up all the family deposits together.

Baby H.P. causes no physical upset or psychic disturbance in children, because it doesn't hamper or disturb their movements. On the contrary, some doctors are of the opinion that it contributes to the harmonious development of their bodies. As for their spirits, it can awaken children's individual ambition, by giving them rewards when they exceed their usual record. With this end in mind, candies and sweets are recommended, because they repay their cost many times over. The more calories added to the child's diet, the more kilowatts are stored up in the electric computer.

Children should keep their lucrative H.P. on night and day. It is important for them always to wear it to school, so the precious recess period won't be wasted, and they will return home with the accumulator overflowing with energy.

Rumors that some children die electrocuted by the current they themselves generate are completely irresponsible. The same must be said of the superstitious fear that youngsters provided with a Baby H.P. attract lightning bolts and sparks. No accident of this nature can occur, especially if the directions in the explanatory pamphlets which are given out with each apparatus are followed to the letter.

Baby H.P. is available in good stores in different sizes, models, and prices. It is a modern, durable, trustworthy apparatus, and you can hook up extensions to all its parts. It carries the factory guarantee of J.P. Mansfield & Sons of Atlanta, Illinois.

(trans. by
George Schade)

Like Arreola, the Chicano author Steve Gonzales uses the grating style and vocabulary of the advertising media to create a humorous parody. He succeeds in exposing the absurdity of the numerous stereotypic images of the Mexican American. Our laughter is not at the stereotypes but at the society that created them.

THE ADVERTISEMENT

steve gonzales

The following advertisement originally appeared in the September 6 issue of The White Liberal's Digest, *and the September 9 issue of* The Southwestern Journal of Cultural Engineering. *It is being brought to you as a public service.*

American Ethnic Supply Company, a Division of I.B.M. (Intergalactic Business Machines, Inc.), is proud to present the latest model in its popular "Other Minorities" line—the all-new Mark IV MEXICAN-AMERICAN!! Superbly crafted and made of only the finest foamium, chromium and tacomium, the Mark IV has been expertly engineered and computer-programmed to efficiently serve all your Mexican-American needs.

Far ahead of the field with its advanced design, the Mark IV MEXICAN-AMERICAN is the first model to offer you that long-hoped-for engineering breakthrough—Multipox Stereotypification—a literal triumph of American ingenuity and technology! Produced after ten years of intensive Social and Cultural Engineering research by our team of dedicated Industrial Anthropologists and Cybernetic Sociologists, the Multipox Stereotypification system allows you by the simple turning of a dial to select the particular MEXICAN-AMERICAN you need to suit your particular purpose:

(1) a familially faithful and fearfully factional folk-fettered fool
(2) a captivating, cactus-crunching, cow-clutching caballero
(3) a charp, chick-chasing, chili-chomping cholo
(4) a brown-breeding, bean-belching border-bounder
(5) a raza-resigned, ritual-racked rude rural relic
(6) a peso-poor but proud, priest-pressed primitive
(7) a grubby but gracious, grape-grabbing greaser

A second significant design feature of the Mark IV is its Instantaneous Convertibility. With this engineering innovation, you'll never again have to worry about being caught in an embarrassing position with your MEXI-

CAN-AMERICAN; when the need arises for him to disappear, a simple utterance of the verbal command "Civil Rights" will instantaneously convert the MEXICAN-AMERICAN into an inconspicuous muted-brown teatray, complete with service for six.

The all-new Mark IV is truly revolutionary in terms of safety design —it is the first one-hundred percent guaranteed safe MEXICAN-AMERICAN!! If at any time the Mark IV should begin behaving in a contrary, threatening, or subversive manner, a clear enunciation of the verbal command "Traditional Culture" will immediately initiate the self-destruct mechanism, culminating in the Mark IV committing full harikari with the blunt end of an original 1914 Edition of William Madsen's *The Mexican-Americans of South Texas*. In the event of this, of course, you will be immediately furnished another MEXICAN-AMERICAN at no cost to you by the American Ethnic Supply Company.

For complete specifications and a full description of the many quality features of the Mark IV, send for our free illustrated brochure, or better yet, visit your local dealer and try out a MEXICAN-AMERICAN for yourself. Upon purchase of the Mark IV, the American Ethnic Supply Company will furnish, at no extra cost to you, your MEXICAN-AMERICAN'S lifetime supply of American Grease Pellets—the very latest in easy insertion! And remember, when it comes to the MEXICAN-AMERICAN —"Only your Supplier Knows For Sure!"

> The whimsical aspect of humor is internalized by most adults, for we all remember childhood rhymes and stories where man, beast, and fowl cavorted with abandon in impossible relationships.
> In this amusing poem, an infinite number of animal creatures are involved in human situations, making fun of man's foibles by comically assuming human attributes. They romp through a never-never land of the imagination.

LOS ANIMALES

i

Señores les contaré
lo que son los animales:
Entre tejidos huacales
y entre huacales hilachas,

las urracas enojadas
me pelan tamaños dientes,

como son tan relucientes
que parecen de marfil

les conté más de diez mil
aparte de los colmillos;
los pericos amarillos
regañando a un comején,

un zancudo y un jején
con una rana cantando
y un chapulín arando,
uncidos dos jabalines,
el sapo con sus botines
iba a montar a caballo;

también vi pelear un gallo
con un osito garcino,
también vide beber vino
a un chango en una taberna;

y una criatura de pecho
enamorando a una viuda
¡ah, qué dicha de criatura
que antes de nacer habló!

ii

Por el pie de una ladera
dió estampida una manada,
me fui yo a ver qué era
y topé una liebre ensillada

con un toro mancornada,
la liebre al toro cornando,
diciendo, "Yo 'esesperando,"
diciendo, "Cómo me ofendes,"
que andaban piojos y liendres,
que andaban deschaparrando.

iii

Iba llegando un coyote
a la gran Ciudad de León
cuando llega un zopilote
que andaba de comisión

y le dice en la calzada,
"Oiga amigo, ¿a dónde va
con esa mujer casada?
¡ahora me la pagará!"

Se lo llevó con el juez
al darle vuelta a una esquina,
éste era un gato montés
que estaba en una cocina;

una pobre golondrina,
al saber lo acaecido,
se fue volando del nido
derecho para la plaza
en busca de una torcaza
porque no tenía marido.

iv

Descalzo y con un huarache
llegaron apareaditos
una ardilla y un tlacuache,
llegaron con sus hijitos;

de verlos tan peladitos
toda la gente reía,
pues de ver que en ese día
se fueron para el Parián
a comerse una sandía
un zancudo y un alacrán.

v

"En esto no cabe duda
que todo tiene su maña,"
así dijo la tortuga
a la hormiga y a la araña;

"vámonos todos mañana
con el amigo coyote."
Luego les dice el jicote,
"Yo también los acompaño
porque me gusta el mitote,
nomás me aguardan un año."

vi

Luego llega un pinacate
con su botella en la mano,
de guante con un mayate
con su sombrero jarano;

todos llegaron temprano,
siempre en buscas del coyote,
luego llegó el guajolote,
pero convertido en mole,
en tranvía llegó al trote
un cochino hecho pozole.

vii

"Me junto con la reunión
hasta no verles el fin,"
así dijo un chapulín
de sorbete y de bastón;

cuando le di la canción
a un tordo y un armadillo,
se fueron al baratillo
a comprar unos anteojos
para espulgar al zorrillo
porque tenía muchos piojos.

viii

Como decentes personas
llegaron todos en coche,
un sensontle, una paloma,
un gorrión y un huitlacoche;

todos llegaron de noche,
hicieron un gran fandango,
una lechuza y un chango
bailaban purito schotis
cuando les dice el coyote,
"¡Ay qué gusto se andan dando!"

Colleges and universities are today being confronted with the task of creating relevant curriculum for Chicano students.

Generally, these institutions are not responsive, the result being that academic success is predicated on the Chicano's adaptability and acceptance of the norms of established academic tradition.

This essay, written by a young university student, is a lampoon of the pseudo-intellectual posturing, the pedantry and false palaver that students have to digest and regurgitate in search of academic legitimacy.

The intellectual gymnastics and empty verbiage of the essay are in the humorous tradition created by the great Mexican comic, Cantinflas. A special element of his humor is the dazzling pyrotechnical display of verbal double-talk.

AND ANOTHER PIECE OF LITTER IS
THROWN ON THE JUNK HEAP

celso a. de casas

preface

As everything must be placed in a perspective approximating its original conditions, it is necessary to preface my introduction to the history of philosophy with a few words regarding the dysfunctionality and inapplicability of such traditional forms of academia. It is incumbent (and wholly binding) upon the reader that he empathize with the author's lack of formal, classical education. In addition to personal considerations regarding the particular environmental and essentially historical indicators that influence one's personality (a term to be defined and elaborated upon within the body of this work) and predilection to behave in a certain manner (observable by others through their respective and individually dynamically different sensing mechanisms and data collators), there are interpersonal considerations, which are much like or resembling those considerations mentioned previously (considerations still being the topic of discussion and not necessarily what the mind prefers to dwell on at this moment in the past, present, or future time) which are basically similar to or like, though varying in intensity, the relationships between and among the aforementioned factors (whether single or grouped, clustered or individual, paired or multiplied, makes a difference in the end product) which can be said to resemble but not be exactly as, transpersonal and essentially inexplicable characteristics (entities being a synonym capable of being substituted for the construct used throughout the initial explanation of the phenomena) which shall be the subject or object (depending upon the inclinations of the parties involved) of the ensuing discussion in order that the substantive knowledge of those eschewing the values of a materialistic system may at least be altered quantitatively (if not significantly or measurably) and spiritually. With this in mind, the reader may proceed.

contents

INTRODUCTION

NOTE: The above will be available in a hard-bound volume or as an album, depending on whether the author decides to sell out to the school system or the media.

introduction

The subject of this pseudo-intellectual work is intended as a basis for the beginnings of a course in the historical philosophy of the world. The course (no catalogue number or course code will be required for registration), will deal with the History of Philosophy, consisting in three distinctive yet similar approaches encompassing the Spaniard, the Indian and the

Mestizo (being the dialectic of the Chicano) and the respective contributions to the sum total of this reality in its entirety as it prepares to do away with itself.

That is to say, the above three components appear as the rational elements that can be seen as alternatives or combinations of possibilities for expression of man's view of the world (the material and spiritual elements being the only two recognizable spheres in the eyes of those whose understanding is limited to that universe) in which he exists at once solid and also void (not only of the physical but of the spatial) of the spirit enabling him to glance at true and pure knowledge of the unknowable that begs for understanding as it rebuffs the seeker (though not intentionally cruel, its unobtainable nature makes it appear so at times, to the perceiver) who approaches with all humility and genuine desire to witness the beauty of the knowledge that what he is looking for is not there, nor anywhere, but everywhere.

Bearing the preceding in mind, the reader can proceed and find comfort in the knowledge (or faith) that the writer has even less of an idea of what all this means.

Not wishing to compromise the standards of this university and the academic excellence for which it stands, it has been decided that the body of this essay shall follow the example of the greatest of American traditions. That is, it shall be written on the installment plan, with more to come in irregular intervals.

questionnaire
****

Answers will be kept in the strictest of confidence and will not be filed in any data bank, FBI office file or Unamerican Activities Committee dossier. If categories are vague, ambiguous, not applicable, etc., please continue as if they made sense.

1. Libraries are: a drag——— substitutes for sleeping pills——— exciting——— sexually stimulating——— other, explain———
2. My research is: meaningless——— irrelevant——— important for the betterment of mankind——— important for the betterment of my career——— other, explain———
3. I find Stanford: depressing——— exciting——— challenging ——— by turning left on University Drive, heading North on El Camino——— other, explain———
4. This questionnaire: bores me——— is stupid——— is stupid and irrelevant——— is scientifically unreliable, invalid, methodologically deficient and uncalled for——— is a ploy to cover up for

the academic shortcomings of its author——— other, explain ———

5. I think Chicanos are: a bunch of crazies——— a crazy bunch——— an animal——— a mineral——— a vegetable——— reactionary ——— radical——— racists——— earthy——— phoney——— on their way out———

6. This has been: the worst event of the day——— an uncalled for and silly interruption of my day——— a recording——— fun——— insane——— other, explain———

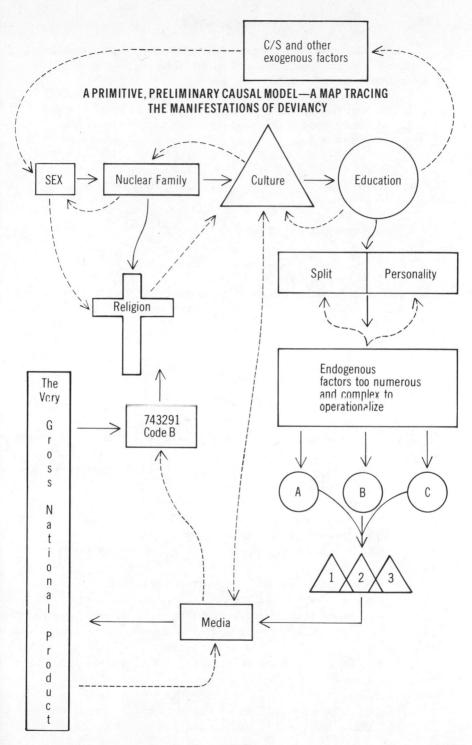

A PRIMITIVE, PRELIMINARY CAUSAL MODEL—A MAP TRACING
THE MANIFESTATIONS OF DEVIANCY

Leonor Barrientes, a young Chicana from the Northwest, transforms a traditional children's story into a contemporary Pachuco fairy-tale muy de aquellas!

The narration is fast-paced and rib-tickling, the humor being generated by the expressive qualities of the Pachuco caló. The characters are exaggerated and the simple plot, repeated in the story, follows in the tradition of children's tales.

LA MANO NEGRA

leonor correa barrientes

Una vez hace muchos años, había tres chavalas que se llamaban Julieta, Linda y Nora. Las dos chavalas mayores eran muy malas y pinches. La más chica sufría de frecuentes regañadas injustas. Esta era muy bonita, cariñosa y dadivosa.

Un día la chavala mayor andaba dando la vuelta cuando se trompezó con una anciana. La gente decía que ella era una bruja, pos era tan horrible. Bueno, como sea, se pusieron a periquear las dos. La bruja le invitó a su cantón.

Cuando estaban ahí le dijo, "Mira, quiero que te refines esta mano negra; si te la refinas te doy lo que se te antoje. ¿Okay maguey?"

La chavala no estaba tan tapada y le contestó, "Bueno pos enséñeme cómo es."

Entonces la bruja le mostró una mano negra muy greñuda con uñas largas y mugrosas. Se escamó la chavala pero no se rajó y le dijo, "¡Está de aquellas, esa! Me la refino antes de que vengas del chancle."

Al irse la bruja, Julieta se dijo a sí misma, "¡Ni de mensa me trago esa vaisa! ¡Ya la tengo, la escondo debajo de la cama!"

Cuando se acabó el chancle la bruja llegó a su casa y le preguntó que si se la había refinado.

"Simón, esa. ¿Pos qué cree, que no puede la llanta?"

La bruja se calentó todita, pos no le gustaba como se mandaban las rucas de esta nueva generación. Esta le dice, "¡Si no te la comiste, te mato!" Con una voz muy misteriosa dice, "¿Mano negra, mano negra, dónde 'tas?"

Después de unos minutos silenciosos contesta una voz, "Aquí 'toy debajo de la cama. ¡Esta ruca no me refinó!"

Lo que le pasó a la chavala por mentirosa no voy a decir.

Mientras tanto sus carnalitas estaban preocupadas. Linda decidió ir a buscarla. Durante su busca la bruja la ve.

"¿Qué andas haciendo?" le pregunta.

"Pos ando buscando a Julieta. Se me hace que anda en una movida chueca, pos no regresó al cantón anoche."

"¿Por qué no tomas una quebrada y vas a mi chante?"

Linda por ser mitotera le dijo que estaba suave.

"¿Sabes qué?" Yo tengo una mano negra y 'toy tratando de deshacerme de ella. Si tú te la refinas, te doy lo que pidas."

En dos por tres, Linda se olvidó de Julieta y le dijo a la bruja que ella se la comía. Con esta respuesta, la bruja se descontó. Al ver la mano negra, a Linda le dio asco.

"¡Jíjole de su——! ¡'Ta bien monstra esta madre! Ni de tonta me la refino. A ver. A la mejor esta vieja bomba no se fija detrás de la puerta cuando barre. Simón, ahí la escondo."

Cuando llegó la bruja, Linda hizo como que estaba muy llena, y le dice, "¡Chingao, esa madre estaba pero bruta!"

La bruja se puso sospechosa y por vez segunda pregunta, "¿Mano negra, mano negra, dónde 'tas?"

"Aquí 'toy detrás de la puerta, pos esta ruca le dio asco comerme."

Linda siguió el destino de Julieta.

'Pa este tiempo a Nora se le habían volado las tapas, pos Julieta y Linda no le habían ayudado con las vasijas por dos días ya.

Se puso sus tramados y salió al pueblo en busca de sus dos carnalas. La bruja había estado espiándola y le cayó cuando Nora andaba en busca.

"¿Qué pasó esa? ¿Por qué andas tan caliente?" le pregunta la bruja.

"Ando en busca de mis carnalas que no han ido a ayudarme con las vasijas."

"Cálmala un rato en mi chante."

Después de tomarse una taza de café, la bruja empieza a decirle sus problemas. Al preguntar cuál era su problema más chingón, se entera que la bruja tiene una mano que da mucha mucha lata.

"No se agüite, esa. Yo me la refino aquí mero. ¿No sabe que yo soy de aquellas con todo el mundo?"

No le tuvo que decir dos veces a la bruja. Le trajo la mano a Nora antes de que se rajara. Nora se escamó cuando la vio y pensó, "¡Chingao, qué cosa tan más fea! Bueno pos, aquí va, aummmmmmmmmmmmm." Con una mordida (mentiras, fueron dos), se comió la mano latosa.

La bruja estaba tan agradecida que le dijo, "¿Qué deseas?"

"Pos por lo tanto, quisiera encontrar a mis carnalas pa' que me ayuden con las vasijas. Luego quiero dinero pa' comprarme géneros y moldes para hacerme unos vestidos. Después quiero una casa para recibir a toda la gente pobre."

Al oír eso la bruja la llevó a un cuarto donde estaban sus carnalas hechas paletas. Las derritió a las dos. En dos por tres la bruja le dio lo que

Nora había pedido. No nomás eso, también le dio un pilón. . . . .
. . . . .una dishwasher.

The momentous events of the campesino struggle for economic and
social justice in California are personalized and humanized through the
gentle humor of this letter.

Interweaving images, people, and events of la causa, the letter informs and
pokes fun at certain ideological currents of the evolving struggle. One
technique is that of personification—attributing human qualities to concepts,
such as la causa, and movements, such as el boicoteo.

CARTA A LA RAZA

Fresno, California
26 Mayo 1969

Querida Raza

Te escribo las siguientes líneas deseando
que te encuentres en buena salud, pues aquí
todos estamos bien gracias a huitzilopachtli.
te manda saludos tu hijita la causa que
nació muy peleonera, pues tú lo sabes que
se agarraba con cualesquiera persona que la
miraba sospechando que estaban burlándose de
ella, ahora empiesa ha hagarrar juicio y
sigue creciendo día tras día. Ya sabes que la
niña está llendo a la jai escul ahora y
sigue haciendo muy buen trabajo. trae a todos
los maestros y bien enojados. ¿Pero qué pueden
hacer ellos? La causa va ha crecer aunque
se disgusten y salten de rabia. A demás
está organizando a todos los chicanitos
y muchos de los jóvenes se han enamorado
de ella. De su brabura, belleza, estilo de
vibir. y ahora andan diciendo que hasta

*por ella morirán si es necesario. la huelga
también sigue bien. aunque pobrecita aveses
le duele que se casó con un gabacho. A tenido
un hijo que lo nombró el boycoteo pero
aquí todos le dicen el "boicot" pues sabrá
diosito como irá salir el muchacho entre
tantos americanos. Ojalá que no olvide
su propria gente. bueno, comadre, ya me
despido porque se me están quemando los
frijoles. sin más.*

*con cariño
la historia*

Américo Paredes, the noted Chicano folklorist and scholar, analyzes the conceptual framework of humor. Examining prose narrative and songs within a historical sequence, he shows the formation and dissemination of Mexican and Chicano attitudes toward the Anglo-American. Chicanos are seen not only as transmitters of Mexican views, but as generators of attitudes which travel from the United States into Mexico.

The following excerpts treat folk humor from a sophisticated and critical perspective, and at the same time demonstrate the author's personal identification with his material.

THE ANGLO-AMERICAN IN MEXICAN FOLKLORE

américo paredes

There are at least three different kinds of Mexican folk groups in the United States: the regional groups, such as those centered in New Mexico and South Texas; the rural or semirural immigrant groups, made up of braceros who have migrated from central Mexico into areas not occupied by the regional groups; and the urban groups, concentrated in cities like Los Angeles, San Antonio and East Chicago and composed of displaced persons from the regional areas, the more ambitious braceros, and the type of immigrant who has abandoned Mexico either to better himself or to seek political asylum. Of these three, the rural immigrant groups obviously are the least acculturated.

This "México de Afuera" (Mexico Outside), as Mexicans sometimes call it, is continually interacting with the parent stock in the Mexican Republic, a condition made possible by the fact that the regional groups are divided from Mexico only by an imaginary line that is most easily crossed, legally or otherwise. Mexican folklore, then, does not recognize political boundaries; not only is there a continuing influence by Mexican oral tradition on Mexican-American folklore but influences also may move in the opposite direction. Nowhere is this truer than in the folklore reflecting attitudes toward the United States. I wish to suggest that Mexican attitudes toward the Anglo-American (or North American, as he is more likely to be called within the political boundaries of Mexico) tend to move from north to south, from the Mexican-American and border areas toward the interior of Mexico.

 Attitudes may be expressed in every genre of folklore, with names deserving some mention even in an abbreviated treatment of the subject such as this. If one is to judge by names and epithets, little attention was paid the Anglo-American as a person in the folklore of central Mexico during the early days of conflict between Mexico and the United States. Even the occupation of Mexico City by Scott's forces seems to have produced no dirtier name for the invaders than "yanqui" (Yankee). Meanwhile, along the Rio Grande, where cultural conflict was a vivid and personal thing, names like "gringo" (foreigner), "patón" (bigfoot), and "gademe" (goddam) are reported by the time of the Mier Expedition. "Gringo" and "patón" appear in the folklore of central Mexico near the end of the Díaz regime. Resentment in Mexico seems to have been much stronger originally against the French troops that supported Maximilian. Names like "güero" (fairhaired) and "bolillo" (French bread), now used by Mexican-Americans and northern Mexicans for the Anglo-American, originally were used in Mexico for the French. Most interesting is "gabacho," said to come from *gave,* a torrent in the Pyrenees. The name was first used by the Spanish against the troops of Napoleon I who occupied Spain during the Peninsular War; Mexicans applied the same epithet to the troops of Napoleon III supporting Maximilian in Mexico during the 1860's. In the 1930's "gabacho" reappeared, not in Mexico or Spain but among urban Mexican-Americans and applied not to Frenchmen but to Anglo-Americans. Though I questioned folklorists from Mexico about the use of "gabacho" for North American as late as the 1950's, they had not heard it so used. But in the early 1960's it began to be reported as part of the slang of Mexico City adolescents, by observers who being unfamiliar with the word accepted it as newly coined.

 Names are very important in revealing attitudes, as are proverbs, riddles, customs, beliefs, and particular uses made of items of material culture—to name but a few possible sources. In this paper, however, I will deal mostly with prose narrative with some consideration of song as well. Tales and songs, because of their greater complexity, are good indicators of customs, beliefs, names, and other folklore. And because they are performed in formalized situations, they correspond quite closely to audience attitudes. I will offer as part of a working hypothesis an oversimplification which I believe useful. Mexican attitudes toward Anglo-Americans from the period of the first armed clashes in the 1830's down to the present time may be seen as going through three stages clearly evident in Mexican folklore—though I do not suggest that each of these stages is strictly confined to a definite historical period. First there is an attitude of open hostility principally expressed in song and legend, especially in the *corrido.* Next there is an attitude of veiled—often thinly veiled—hostility, principally expressed in an escapist type of jest featuring dream situations in which the Mexican bests the Anglo-American. Finally there is an attitude of self-satire, principally expressed in jests which are at best mildly masochistic and at worst frankly self-degrading.

Open hostility toward the Anglo-American is most clearly expressed in the heroic *corrido,* in the legend which often accompanies it, and to a lesser degree in other songs and tales criticizing American customs. In the *corrido* the American is The Enemy, seen in the heroic terms. He may have his faults but he is a formidable foe and rarely is ridiculous. Faceless and nameless, he is more of an idea than a man; when he is singled out in the narrative he will be nothing more than the Major Sheriff or the Chief of the Texas Rangers, very much a stock type. The Anglo-American will run when the battle goes against him, he always attacks in large numbers; but though he is capable of cruelty and treachery he may also exhibit generosity. When not cruel and treacherous, he may be rich, fat, and soft, and addicted to a strange, almost sybaritic habit—that of the ham sandwich. A folk poet on the Mexican side of the Rio Grande satirizes a friend who has gone to live in central Texas in a series of *décimas* advising him to "sink those Mexican teeth of yours all the way down to the gums into the legs of pigs." In a *corrido* Jacinto Treviño holds off a crowd of Texas Rangers while taunting them about their ham-eating habits. "Come on, you cowardly Rangers, always trying to take advantage! This isn't the same as eating white bread with slices of ham!"

The legends about Villa and General Pershing stress the softness of the American soldier, who needs cots and kitchens and mosquito nets, not to mention ham and white bread, in order to fight. The Mexican guerrilla is superior because he is a tough man living on a tough diet of tortillas, jerked beef, and mesquite beans. But though he is soft, the Anglo-American wins most of the time because there are great numbers of him and because he is sly and farsighted. Consider the case of little Tomás Alba. He was a Mexican boy who showed extraordinary brilliance at an early age. But his parents were too poor to send him to school, while the Mexican government did nothing for him. Along came an American couple who realized the boy's genius, adopted him, and took him to the United States. The couple's name was Edison, and everybody has heard of the great Thomas Alva Edison.

Anglo-Americans have odd customs, according to the *corrido* legendry, such as that of giving away convicted prisoners to pretty girls at Christmastime if the girls will marry them. Rito García, Gregorio Cortez, and other *corrido* heroes are said to have got out of the penitentiary in this way. Usually, though, the hero refuses to marry an American girl because he does not want to become like the Anglo-Americans, who are ruled by their women. American men have their good points, but little can be said in favor of American women. Though it may be admitted that there are *some* good ones, the average American woman is seen as licentious and lewd. Hers is a historical immorality, as can be seen by the story about Virginia, the first Anglo-American ever to be born. In the first English colony to be established in America there were 240 men and 64 women, so the women slept with all the men in turn. This is a habit they have preserved to this day. Finally one of them, Virginia Smith, became pregnant. When asked who was the father of her child she could not tell. So when a little girl was born to her, the child was named Virginia Virginia. That is why there are two states named Virginia in the United States. But this is what you could expect of people who eat ham to excess.

Psychologically, the attitudes expressed in the *corrido* and the *corrido* legend are related to the Mexican cult of manliness, which is part of the *corrido* tradition and as such is a natural and basically wholesome expression of a nascent cultural and national identity. There are analogues in the United States of early frontier times in the "ringtailed roarer" type who by virtue of his ability to whip all men, love all women, and outface all foreigners was the image of the manly and local values of his audience. Historically the types of Mexican folklore expressing open hostility toward the Anglo-American occur along the Texas-Mexican border by the 1850's in the *corridos* about Juan Nepomuceno Cortina, the first border raider. They reach their peak during the Mexican Revolution, when Mexican ideals of manliness, feelings of national identity, resentment against the United States, and the *corrido* tradition all coincide in one great climax that changes the very bases of Mexican life.

Attitudes of veiled hostility, released in pointedly derisive humor, rarely are expressed in song, being most common in a type of anecdote in which the Anglo-American plays the simpleton within a framework of slapstick or low comedy. This stage in the Mexican's attitudes may be related to situations in which open conflict no longer is possible, with the Mexican finding himself in a disadvantageous economic or social position. The dream situations of this kind of jest serve as compensation for a strong sense of frustration and inferiority which was not so keen when open conflict pre-supposed a possible victory for the Mexican. The pattern is a simple one with two main characters, a stupid American and a smart Mexican. Through the Mexican's guile or the American's stupidity, the Mexican gets the best of the Anglo-American and makes the Anglo look ridiculous, beats him, relieves him of his money, seduces his wife, or uses the American himself as the passive partner in sexual intercourse.

The Stupid American jest is given a somewhat different twist among the regional groups. The Anglo plays the newcomer to the region, the tenderfoot. The tales, told mostly in all-male groups, rarely end with the beating of the American, who is more likely to lose face, money, or wife if he is not used sexually himself. Similar variants are common in urban lore and among the folk groups in northern Mexico that are complimentary to the Mexican-American regional groups. As this type of jest moves into the interior of Mexico, the boss or the tenderfoot is replaced by that international image of the United States, the American tourist. Stupid American tales very much like those of the regional groups are told in Mexico City, with the gullible tourists in the title role. And in this case perhaps, the jests are less of a dreamlike character and correspond more closely to the actual facts of life.

Stupid American tales are bilingual and bicultural, though rarely shared with Anglo-American friends. Sometimes the American is just a fool, as when he pays ten thousand dollars for a burro that is supposed to tell the time whenever you heft his testicles. More often the American's undoing depends on a bilingual pun or on his misinterpretation of something said in Spanish, or he may be the victim of a custom which is different in Mexican and American cultures. An American who is working nights is told by his Mexican co-workers that if he goes by his house unannounced he will find "Juan Sánchez" in bed with his wife. "Juan Sánchez" is a common term for a married woman's lover or kept man, a variation on an earlier name, "sancho." The American hurries home, and sure enough; he runs into a Mexican who is leaving by the back door in a half-dressed state. "Stop!" cries the American, pointing a pistol at the man. "Is your name Juan Sánchez?"

"No," says the Mexican. "I'm Joe García."

"Okay," says the Stupid American, "you can go. But wait till I catch up with that Juan Sánchez!"

Mexicans are accustomed to say "It is yours" when something belonging to them is admired. This is simply a conventional way of saying "Thank you," with no more real meaning than the "How are you?" of the Anglo-American. It is a convention that has tripped up many an American, who then has complained of Mexican insincerity. The Stupid American jest makes use of this confusion. In a typical version an American and his wife are out hunting with a Mexican guide. When the American admires the guide's knife, the Mexican ceremoniously cleans it and offers it to the American, who accepts it. That night the American's wife is squatting some distance from the campfire, relieving herself, and the Mexican admires her buttocks shining white in the moonlight. So the American gives the Mexican his wife. In some versions the American is not cuckolded; he is just made ridiculous when the tables are turned on him, hastily returning the Mexican's gift when the Mexican expresses admiration for his wife, or for the American's own buttocks. The jest was told about the late President Kennedy, who accepts a wrist watch from Mexican President López Mateos during the visit made to Mexico by the Kennedys. Kennedy returns the watch when López Mateos expresses his great admiration for Mrs. Kennedy.

The American woman is seen as an object both of rejection and of desire. Folk belief paints her as an insipid sexual partner compared to the Mexican woman, and as physically incapable of providing proper sexual satisfaction to a man. In spite of the Mexican's scorn she offers herself to him at every opportunity. Yet the whole point of a jest may be the Mexican's possession of the American woman as a sign of victory over the American man.

Both the dollar and the American woman obviously are symbols of power and status, and their acquisition by the Mexican in the jests is without a doubt a convenient release of aggressive feelings. Aggression is even more evident in the stories that end with the victorious Mexican making sexual use not of the American's wife but of the American himself. The symbolic use of sodomy in Mexican folklore, especially in the wordplay known as the *albur,* has been the object of much comment by Mexican writers making more or less agonized appraisals of their own national character. Samual Ramos started it all back in 1934, and the chorus was taken up by many others, from the psychologist to the poet.

Consensus has it that the Mexican's use of sex as aggression is a disease peculiarly his, for which we must blame an exaggerated cult of the male commonly called *machismo.* With uncompromising Freudian logic *machismo* has been traced to oedipal conflicts arising at the moment when the first Spaniard threw the first Indian woman to the ground and raped her, thus laying the foundations of modern Mexico. Because of this primal act of sexual violence the Mexican sees sex as aggression, and assuming the role of the hated Spanish father he translates his fixation into sadism toward women and symbolic threats of sodomy toward other males. So *mestizaje*—the cross-breeding of Spanish and Indian—becomes the culprit, the underlying reason for the Mexican's spiritual ills. Expressed by a poet like Octavio Paz this can sound like something out of William Faulkner, curse of miscegenation and all.

In sum, the cult of manliness is not peculiar to the Mexican, nor does the Freudian interpretation of the Conquest explain very much. We can find all the elements of Mexican *machismo* among peoples whose ancestral mothers were never raped by Spanish conquistadors. Yet we cannot deny that in Mexican culture these elements are put together in their own special way. *Machismo* everywhere is characterized by an aggressive attitude behind which there lurks a feeling of defensiveness and insufficiency. The "ringtailed roarer" of a United States still groping for national identity is extremely proud of himself and his own, but in his xenophobia one can detect a feeling of inferiority toward the eastern seaboard and Europe. Behind Teddy Roosevelt's flamboyant pursuit of the strenuous life there is a note of self-doubt as to his ability to measure up to it. And Hemingway's hardboiled prose concealed an extremely sentimental heart. This is the same tendency, highly exaggerated, that distinguishes both Mexican *machismo* and the Mexican folklore which expresses it, especially the *albur* and the jest. Their really distinguishing feature is not the aggressive use of sexual metaphor but the careful avoidance of all female symbols or metaphors in reference to the speaker, for fear they may bring aggression directed at him.

The Mexican boy learns that nicknames and taunts are more safely put in the feminine. If he wishes to insult another boy by calling him "The Pig," he will say, "La Marrana." Should he be foolish enough to say, "El Marrano," the other boy may answer, "Yes, I'm the he-pig and you are the female," turning the insult against him. It is true that to the Mexican many words signifying coition also mean destruction, wounding, or humiliation; but the American has similar terms, the World War II SNAFU being a well-known example. The American, however, may refer to someone who nags or pesters him as "being on his ass," without fear of being the target of ridicule or humiliation. On the contrary, many would take this as a manly way of speaking. Such an expression would be unthinkable to the Mexican, who will say that someone is "irritating his penis." He must avoid all reference to his own buttocks or rectum since this will put him in a vulnerable position, open to insult and ridicule. The most popular obscene poem in Mexican tradition, corresponding to the "Diary of a French Stenographer" in the United States, is "El Anima de Sayula," about a poor man who is raped by a ghost and passes the rest of his life with a protective hand on his backside and his back toward the wall, his other hand holding a knife threateningly before him.

This attitude of truculent defensiveness—the Mexican's well-known mistrust (*desconfianza*)—is the basis of his *machismo* and the dominant feeling behind the veiled hostility of the Stupid American jest. As a symptom of a contemporary malaise, it owes more to the ever-present image of the Anglo-American than to the racial memory of the conquistador. The proponents of the Spanish father-image thesis have had to project contemporary data centuries into the past, with no real proof that the same conditions existed during colonial days, or even in Díaz's time. The cult of manliness in the grotesquely exaggerated form known as Mexican *machismo* seems to be a recent development, an ingrowing of the Revolutionary code. It is a reaction to the inescapable presence of the American and his culture, a culture which at once repels and fascinates the Mexican and which is a very real threat to his awakened sense of national identity. It is due to a kind of cross-breeding, but a cultural rather than a racial one, being the congenital disease of the new middle class, which develops along with the Revolution and which still is striving, self-conscious and insecure. That is why the Mexican middle class always looks suspiciously to the north, why it often looks upon the Mexican-American and the bracero returned from the United States as cultural Typhoid Marys who may contaminate it.

But the Mexican, alas, has been looking in the wrong direction all these years; the primary base for dissemination of United States influences has become Mexico City itself. The Mexican may seek escape by going to "charro" movies, only to find that the basic Mexican symbols have become Hollywoodized. If he turns on the TV he will watch Mexican imitations of Elvis Presley, the Beatles, and Jackie Gleason. And if he takes a walk along any busy city street, he may enjoy the spectacle of Indian girls with their hair bleached a strawy blond, so sadly reminiscent of the American Negro's attempt to straighten out his hair. Thus the Mexican, on guard against the United States, finds that while he has been facing north in a posture of defense he has been outflanked and taken from behind.

It would appear that the attitudes of the Mexican middle class in regard to Anglo-American culture no longer are radically different from those of the Mexican-American, in spite of the fact that to the Mexican the very existence of the Mexican-American may be another cause for resentment against the United States. But the Mexican-American also is a living dilemma. The same strong sense of national identity, interpreted in personal terms, makes him try at all costs to preserve his Mexican self even as he yields to the irresistible demands of the majority culture which surrounds him. One way out for both is the thinly veiled hostility of *machismo* and the Stupid American jest. Another way is the satire of the self-directed anecdote, although this third stage in Mexican attitudes toward the Anglo-American may be expressed in other forms of folklore such as bilingual songs, proverbial expressions, and epithets. At its best the self-directed anecdote is a vehicle for wisdom and insight into the Mexican's predicament vis-à-vis the American, a mechanism which helps him accept the world as it is. Two *compadres* in Mexico are discussing the United States and the sensitive question of Mexican territory lost to the United States.

"These Gringos are terrible people," says one. "Cheaters, liars and robbers."

"Sure, *compadre*," says the other, "Look what they did in '46. They took half our national territory."

"Yes, *compadre*," says the first, "and the half with all the paved roads."

Fully to appreciate the satire it is necessary to know that the phrase "half our national territory" has been a common one with Mexican orators denouncing American manifest destiny. In Texas the two *compadres* may be found in a rundown beer joint in the Mexican section of Kingsville. All of a sudden one of them yells, "Yoo-hoo-ee, *compadre!* I think I'll just go out and sell the King Ranch!"

"Quit your fooling, *compadre*," says the other one. "You know I don't want to buy it."

The tendency among some Mexican-Americans to call themselves "Latins" or "Spanish" rather than Mexicans and the exaggerated sexuality of *machismo* are satirized in the story about the boy who in New York City was known as "The Passionate Spaniard" but who was just a fuckin Mexican back home in Texas.

Machismo is more pointedly attacked in another story about some Mexicans visiting a fancy nightclub. The cigarette girl is calling out, "Candy, chewing gum, cigarettes. Candy, chewing gum, cigarettes." But when she passes their table she says, "Bird seed, condoms, boxing gloves." A Mexican follows her and demands an explanation. "Because when you Mexicans get drunk," she says, "all you want to do is sing, fuck, and fight."

A belief taken seriously in the *corrido* legend, that Mexican ingenuity can more than compensate for North American technology, is satirized in jests where a Mexican is called in to solve in his own way a problem that has baffled the scientists or philosophers of the world. The question may be a very esoteric one, such as establishing what General Custer's last thoughts were at Little Big Horn. Stories ridiculing Mexican technology are closer to outright masochism, but they also satirize well-known foibles and vanities. There is the tale about the Japanese gun crew in World War II, urgently told by their commander not to shoot at a Mexican plane flying overhead. "It will fall down all by itself," says the Japanese officer. This again is a satire on *machismo*, the Japanese shown as apparently too scared to rile a Mexican, but it touches gently on another point, the once friendly relations between Japan and Mexico broken by Mexico's alliance with its traditional enemy, the United States. Fun is also poked at Mexico's great pride over its 201st Squadron, its only combat unit in the war.

Still other jests show little except an urge for self-degradation. Several nations compete in designing the submarine which will stay longest under water, and Mexico wins. Its submarine never comes up. Then there is the story that a Mexican named Manuel rode on a space-ship with an American astronaut. After having answered a call of nature the astronaut was heard to say, "I am now going to put it on Manuel (manual)."

The self-critical jest is told in all Mexican folklore areas, but more than the *corrido* or the jest of veiled hostility it can be identified with the direct influence of United States culture. Some jests of this type are popular with Anglo-Americans, among whom they form part of a corpus of "ethnic" jokes along with stories about Negroes, Jews, or Irishmen. Many undoubtedly were evolved by Mexican-Americans, who as individuals caught between two cultures were more apt to look with a critical and ridiculing eye now at the American, now at the Mexican. Many others no doubt have originated in Mexico, in the more cosmopolitan circles, most likely during recent decades. It is my own experience that some 35 years ago this kind of jest was restricted almost entirely to Mexican-Americans, who might have imperiled life or limb by telling them on the Mexican side of the border. Now the self-critical jest is current throughout Mexico, though the Mexican prefers to tell it on himself rather than hearing it on the lips of the Anglo or the Mexican-American.

It is not only the Mexican who in these times faces a world that is more than man can cope with, and therein lies the appeal of the self-directed jest. We find the same thing in an American tradition of a more literary sort. In American frontier humor the protagonist resembles the Mexican hero of the jest of veiled hostility: the Davy Crockett type who is his own main character, coarse, full of bumptiousness and xenophobia, bulling his crude way through situations in which the laugh seems to be on him but which in the end falls on the foreigner or the Eastern dude. We have seen how the Mexican folk hero goes from confidence and violence to an ineffectual state in which he realizes his insignificance in a complicated and incomprehensible world. The same thing may be seen in American humor, where Davy Crockett has become James Thurber. The Thurber humor uses the same patterns, the same devices of frontier humor, changing little except the nature of the protagonist, who no longer is crude and self-confident but has become a lonely little figure lost in the mazes of his own inadequacy. And perhaps we see here as well the hero of modern fiction contrasted with the champions of a more heroic age. We do not need to be reminded that Charles Chaplin on the screen and Charlie Brown of the "Peanuts" comic strip are but variant aspects of the same figure, or that Prufrock is a more serious equivalent of the same. Thus the Mexican works through a series of attitudes in regard to the inescapable actuality which the Anglo-American represents for him, not only moving toward greater wit and wisdom but attaining a kind of universality as well. His humor becomes part of a general *Weltansicht* rather than a cry expressing nothing more than his own particular pain.

IV

los barrios de aztlán

A common denominator in the life of most Chicanos is the fact of having lived in a barrio, whether in a rural or urban locale. More than a geographic reality, barrios are spiritual zones where the dynamics and vitality of the Chicano experience are formed, defined, and distilled.

Separated from the alien, non-Chicano world by invisible yet formidable walls, los barrios are like urban villages, each one having its particular heroes and traditions, its personal code of ethics, its singular vision, and at times even its own vocabulary and aesthetic. As distinct as each barrio is, they all harbor people who have shared and endured a heritage of oppression.

La Raza today lives largely in urban centers. The largest barrio concentrations are found on the West Coast (Los Angeles), the Midwest (Chicago, Kansas City), and the Southwest (San Antonio, El Paso). Barrios also exist in innumerable rural communities, from Wisconsin and Michigan to Washington, Idaho, and Oregon.

The historical process of urbanization has two major aspects. In some areas the Chicanos established the urban centers (Santa Fe, New Mexico; San Antonio, Texas), and in other places they migrated into the cities from rural areas (Seattle, Washington; Minneapolis, Minnesota). Apart from the migrations into the metropolis, the Chicanos who come into the barrios maintain a constant out-migration, a phenomenon not shared by other ethnic groups.

Suffering several decades of exploitation and dehumanization, the barrios have resisted and endured. Paradoxically, some of the very values and institutions that oppressed the Chicano became the vehicles for group identity and solidarity. As the people were forced to withdraw into the circle of their own kind, they elaborated a communal consciousness of

151

allegiance to themselves, and resistance toward those outside the invisible walls of the barrio.

This relative personal freedom within the boundaries of the ghetto freed the energies and creative spirit of the inhabitants, culminating in the preservation of Chicano cultural traditions, and the creation of new expressive forms peculiar to the urban scene. In art, the special cholo calligraphy and graffiti, and the artistic elaboration evolved in stylizing individual ranflas (automobiles), are examples of new creative manifestations. In language, a similar new expressiveness was achieved with the development of Pachucano (Pachuco caló), which allows barrio poets and authors multiple choices of language in which to convey the complexity of barrio experience.

In folklore, traditional tales of la llorona, espantos, and ánimas are augmented with the deeds of Don Cacahuate, a barrio rogue. Musical and literary versions of corridos and Pachuco texts, together with short stories and novels that reflect life in the barrio, can also be found.

The material collected in this section concentrates on feelings and attitudes toward the barrio, the people who live there, and the experiences they share in common.

"My Loma of Austin
My Rose Hill of Los Angeles
My Westside of San Anto
My Quinto of Houston
My Jackson of San Jo
My Segundo of El Paso
My Barelas of Alburque
My Westside of Denver

Flats, Los Marcos, Maravilla, Calle Guadalupe, Magonilia, Buena Vista, Mateo, La Seis, Chiquis, El Sur, and all Chicano neighborhoods that now exist and once existed; somewhere . . . someone remembers . . ."

Recognizing their mortality and the illusionary character of life, our indigenous ancestors created the aesthetic conception of flor y canto. Flor y canto are metaphors for the creative, humanistic spirit of man which enables him to transcend his reality through art and literature.

In this poem, Temilotzin, a famous pre-Columbian poet, sings of his two-fold mission: to create flower and song and to seek brotherhood and roots within his community.

In contemporary terms this love for our barrio and loyalty to our amigos are best exemplified in the Chicano concept of carnalismo. The bonds of spiritual brotherly love conceived in our comunidades re-affirm that we are "en préstamo los unos a los otros."

POEMA DE TEMILOTZIN

He venido, oh amigos nuestros:
con collares ciño,
con plumajes de tzinitzcan doy cimiento,
con plumas de guacamaya rodeo,
pinto con los colores del oro,
con trepidantes plumas de quetzal enlazo
al conjunto de los amigos.
Con cantos circundo a la comunidad.
La haré entrar al palacio,
allí todos nosotros estaremos,
hasta que nos hayamos ido a la región de los muertos.
Así nos habremos dado en préstamo los unos a los otros.

Ya he venido,
me pongo de pie,
forjaré cantos,
haré que los cantos broten,
para vosotros, amigos nuestros.
Soy enviado de Dios,
soy poseedor de las flores,
yo soy Temilotzin,
he venido a hacer amigos aquí.

THE POEM OF TEMILOTZIN

Oh my friends, I have come;
with necklaces do I gird you,
with plumes of the tzinitzcan I bind you together,
with feathers of the parrot I surround you,

I paint with colors made of gold,
with vibrating *quetzal* feathers I tie together
the whole group of my friends.
With song I encircle the community.
I shall have all enter the palace,
there we shall all be together
until we have gone to the region of the dead.
So shall we give ourselves in trust, one to another.

I have come,
on my feet I stand,
I shall fashion songs,
I shall make songs burst forth
for you, our friends.
I have been sent by God,
I am the master of flowers,
I am Temilotzin,
I have come here to make friends.

"While the term 'Chicano' is the short way of saying Mexicano, it is the long way of referring to everybody," says the narrator of this story set in Tucson, Arizona in the late 1940s. This is an early literary expression of some of the qualities which today give meaning to the word Chicano.

The people of El Hoyo, sustained by that intangible spirit of brotherhood or carnalismo, show the solidarity and sentido de lucha that comes from sharing oppression. They sustain one another in their daily tribulations and tragedies. Although linked in community each member of the barrio is free to create his personal life-style.

EL HOYO

mario suárez

From the center of downtown Tucson the ground slopes gently away to Main Street, drops a few feet, and then rolls to the banks of the Santa Cruz River. Here lies the sprawling section of the city known as El Hoyo. Why it is called El Hoyo is not clear. It is not a hole as its name would imply; it is simply the river's immediate valley. Its inhabitants are *chicanos* who raise hell on Saturday night, listen to Padre Estanislao on Sunday morning, and then raise more hell on Sunday night. While the term *chicano* is the short way of saying *Mexicano*, it is the long way of refering to every-

body. Pablo Gutiérrez married the Chinese grocer's daughter and acquired
a store; his sons are *chicanos*. So are the sons of Killer Jones who threw
a fight in Harlem and fled to El Hoyo to marry Cristina Méndez. And so
are all of them—the assortment of harlequins, bandits, oppressors, oppressed,
gentlemen, and bums who came from Old Mexico to work for the Southern
Pacific, pick cotton, clerk, labor, sing, and go on relief. It is doubtful that
all of these spiritual sons of Mexico live in El Hoyo because they love each
other—many fight and bicker constantly. It is doubtful that the *chicanos*
live in El Hoyo because of its scenic beauty—it is everything but beautiful.
Its houses are built of unplastered adobe, wood, license plates, and abandoned car parts. Its narrow streets are mostly clearings which have, in time,
acquired names. Except for the tall trees which nobody has ever cared to
identify, nurse, or destroy, the main things known to grow in the general
area are weeds, garbage piles, dogs, and kids. And it is doubtful that the
chicanos live in El Hoyo because it is safe—many times the Santa Cruz
River has risen and inundated the area.

In other respects living in El Hoyo has its advantages. If one is born
with the habit of acquiring bills, El Hoyo is where the bill collectors are
less likely to find you. If one has acquired the habit of listening to Señor
Perea's Mexican Hour in the wee hours of the morning with the radio on
at full blast, El Hoyo is where you are less likely to be reported to the
authorities. Besides, Perea is very popular and to everybody sooner or later
is dedicated The Mexican Hat Dance.

If one has inherited a bad taste for work but inherited also the habit
of eating, where, if not in El Hoyo, are the neighbors more willing to lend
you a cup of flour or beans? When Señora García's house burned to the
ground with all her belongings and two kids, a benevolent gentleman conceived the gesture that put her on the road to solvency. He took five
hundred names and solicited from each a dollar. At the end of the week
he turned over to the heartbroken but grateful señora three hundred and
fifty dollars in cold cash and pocketed his recompense. When the new
manager of a local business decided that no more Mexican girls were to
work behind his counters, it was the *chicanos* of El Hoyo who acted as
pickets and, on taking their individually small but collectively great buying
power elsewhere, drove the manager out and the girls returned to their
jobs. When the Mexican Army was enroute to Baja California and the
chicanos found out that the enlisted men ate only at infrequent intervals,
they crusaded across town with pots of beans, trays of tortillas, boxes of
candy, and bottles of wine to meet the train. When someone gets married,
celebrating is not restricted to the immediate families and friends of the
couple. The public is invited. Anything calls for a celebration and in turn
a celebration calls for anything. On Armistice Day there are no fewer than
half a dozen fights at the Tira-Chancla Dance Hall. On Mexican Independ-

ence Day more than one flag is sworn allegiance to and toasted with gallon after gallon of Tumba Yaqui.

And El Hoyo is something more. It is this something more which brought Felipe Ternero back from the wars after having killed a score of Germans with his body resembling a patch-work quilt. It helped him to marry a fine girl named Julia. It brought Joe Zepeda back without a leg from Luzon and helps him hold more liquor than most men can hold with two. It brought Jorge Casillas, a gunner flying B-24's over Germany, back to compose boleros. Perhaps El Hoyo is the proof that those people exist who, while not being against anything, have as yet failed to observe the more popular modes of human conduct. Perhaps the humble appearance of El Hoyo justifies the discerning shrugs of more than a few people only vaguely aware of its existence. Perhaps El Hoyo's simplicity motivates many a *chicano* to move far away from its intoxicating *frenesí,* its dark narrow streets, and its shrieking children, to deny the bloodwell from which he springs, to claim the blood of a conquistador while his hair is straight and his face beardless. Yet El Hoyo is not the desperate outpost of a few families against the world. It fights for no causes except those which soothe its immediate angers. It laughs and cries with the same amount of passion in times of plenty and of want.

Perhaps El Hoyo, its inhabitants, and its essence can best be explained by telling you a little bit about a dish called *capirotada.* Its origin is uncertain. But it is made of old, new, stale, and hard bread. It is sprinkled with water and then it is cooked with raisins, olives, onions, tomatoes, peanuts, cheese, and general leftovers of that which is good and bad. It is seasoned with salt, sugar, pepper, and sometimes chili or tomato sauce. It is fired with tequila or sherry wine. It is served hot, cold, or just "on the weather" as they say in El Hoyo. The Garcías like it one way, the Quevedos another, the Trilos another, and the Ortegas still another. While in general appearance it does not differ much from one home to another it tastes different everywhere. Nevertheless it is still *capirotada.* And so it is with El Hoyo's *chicanos.* While many seem to the undiscerning eye to be alike it is only because collectively they are referred to as *chicanos.* But like *capirotada,* fixed in a thousand ways and served on a thousand tables, which can only be evaluated by individual taste, the *chicanos* must be so distinguished.

This evocative vision of the barrio as a honeycomb of memories establishes a sad mournful mood. The first image of graffiti on a wall slowly being eradicated is elaborated in views of encapsulated people who live breathing the presence of death. Dust is the central image, linking the dehumanizing aspects of the barrio to the stillness and solitude of the inhabitants.

NUESTRO BARRIO

alurista

Nuestro barrio
    en las tardes de paredes grabadas
    los amores de Pedro con Virginia
    en las tardes
        barriendo
Dust about
    swept away in the wind of our breath
el suspiro de dios por nuestras calles
    gravel side streets of solitude
    the mobs from the tracks are coming
en la tarde
    mientras Don José barre su acera
    mientras dios respira vientos secos
        en el barrio sopla la vejez de Chon
    y la juventud de Juan madura
en la tarde de polvo
    el recuerdo de mi abuelo
    —de las flores en su tumba
        of dust
        polvorosas flores
blowing free to powdered cruces

One way of understanding the barrio is to be both participant and observer. As John Rechy, a Chicano novelist and journalist from the Southside of El Paso, describes the constantly changing patterns of life in this border town, he himself varies his point of view. There are moments when he depicts Chicano values with irony as in the episode of the movie scenario, and times when he identifies warmly within the Chicano culture. An example is the passage recalling the preparations and celebrations of Christmas with his family. Rechy's double vision recreating and evaluating Chicano barrio experience from inside and outside the culture projects an analytical and critical focus on both the barrio and the larger society.

The fluid, impressionistic sketches of people and events in that "México de afuera" along the border capture the pulsating tempo, the tawdry gaiety, the wretchedness and strength: el cora del barrio. The following are excerpts from a longer narration written in 1958.

EL PASO DEL NORTE

john rechy

This is about El Paso (and Juárez: the Southwest), which so long was just a hometown to me and which now is different from any other section in America.

El Paso and Juárez are in the middle of the Texas, New Mexico, and Mexico white, white desert surrounded by that range of mountains jutting unevenly along the border. At sundown the fat sun squats on the horizon like a Mexican lady grandly on her frontporch. Appropriately.

Because only geographically the Rio Grande, which in the Southwest is a river only part of the time and usually just a strait of sand along the banks of which sick spiders weave their webs, divides the United States from Mexico. Only geographically. The Mexican people of El Paso, more than half the population—and practically all of Smeltertown, Canutillo, Ysleta— are all and always and completely Mexican, and will be. They speak only Spanish to each other and when they say the Capital they mean Mexico DF.

Oh, but, once it was not so. When the War came, Christ, the Mexicans were American as hell. The youngmen went to war wearing everything that was authorized, sometimes even more. Huge stars appeared on the south-side tenement and government-project windows. *Our son is serving America.* My mother wore my brother's Purple Heart to Mass and held it up when the Priest gave his blessing.

Outside El Paso City, giant machines dig into the mountains for ores (Smeltertown), and beyond that (where I used to climb poetic as hell) is a tall beautiful mountain.

The Mountain of Cristo Rey.

Huge processions go up this holy mountain. The people of El Paso, Ysleta, Canutillo, of Smeltertown and of Juárez march up climbing for hours, chanting prayers. The procession starts downtown in El Paso, outside the churches, and the groups join each other in the streets, kneeling at intervals on inspiration, carrying placards of the Virgin, Saints in colors. Small bands jazz solemnly, crying dissonant sounds. The shawled ladies of the Order of Saint Something grip rosaries and mumble and feel—as rightly so as anyone in the world—Holy. The priests in bright drag lead them up. They carry sadfaced saints. The small bands stay behind at the foot of the mountain, the musicians wiping the sweat off their dark faces, and drinking cool limonada and mingling with the sellers of coca-cola, religious medals. The procession winds up the mountain slowly past the crude weatherbeaten stations of the cross along the path. And at the top, finally—where they say Mass, the people kneeling on the rocks in the blazing white sun—is The Statue.

It is a primitive Christ.

Fifty-feet tall. And it looks like a Mexican peasant. Mr. Soler made it. I think he was a kind of semi-atheist who didnt believe in God but believed in the Virgin Mary.

But the poor Mexican Christ, what it has to look down on—the line of desperate ants, as the Magazine (I think it was *Time,* or if it wasnt they would have) called it, of mustached, strawhatted men, braceros invading America.

Because the Rio Grande, no matter what you think, is usually dry, as I said, just sand and scrawny spiders and fingery indentations where water should be or was. Sometimes it is very full, though, and beautiful, and then the Rio Grande is like a dirty young black animal full of life rushing along the sand, swallowing the bushy dry banks. And I would walk along its bank, to the mountains. But usually it is so dry that the wetbacks can enter Sacred Country by merely walking across the River.

On their way to Georgia?

Well, Ive heard that from I dont know how many people. They say, for some strange reason, that Georgia is a kind of heaven where all good spiks go—some crossing into the country illegally, others standing at the Santa Fe Bridge lined up all rags and cloth bags and wooden and cardboard boxes and holy amulets, whiskers, waiting to be inspected by the Customs-gods. The Magazine also said, well, wasn't it natural, those wetbacks wanting to come into America?—Christ, they heard about sweet-tasting tooth-paste. It really said that. And if sweet-tasting American toothpaste aint enough to make a man face the Border Patrol (as Bad as L.A. fuzz) and the excellent labor conditions in progressive Georgia, well, man, what is? The Magazine said it was sad, all those displaced wetbacks, but all that happened though was that they were sent back, but they tried to come across again and again and again.

(I remember a dead bracero near the bank of the Rio Grande, face down drowned in the shallow water, the water around him red, red, red. Officially he had drowned and was found, of course, by the Border Patrol. And his wife will go on thinking forever he made it with a beautiful blonde Georgia woman—loaded with toothpaste—and so, therefore, never came back to her and the even-dozen kids.)

Which brings me to this—

The hatred in much of Texas for Mexicans. It's fierce. (They used to yell, Mexicangreaser, Mexicangreaser, when I went to Lamar Grammar School, and I thought, well, yes, my mother did do an awful lot of frying but we never put any grease on our hair, and so it bothered me—if God was Mexican, as my mother said, why did He allow this?) Many of them really hate us pathologically, like they hate the Negroes, say, in Arkansas. Here, it's the bragging, blustering bony-framed Texan rangers/farmers/ ranchers, with the Cadillacs and the attitude of Me-and-god on My ranch. It has nothing to do with the Alamo any more. It's just the full-scale really huge (consistent with everything Big in Texas—and Alaska wont change anything) Texan inferiority complex. Dig: the Texas rancher strutting across San Jacinto Plaza, all bones and legs, getting kicks from sitting, later, booted-feet propped getting a shine from the barefoot spik kid, tipping him 50 cents—not just sitting like you and I would get a shine but sitting Grandly, and strutting across the Border owning the streets, I hope he gets rolled. They dont really dislike Mexicans in Texas if theyre maids and laborers.

So the Mexicans live concentrated on the Southside of El Paso largely, crowded into tenements, with the walls outside plastered with old Vote-for signs from years back and advertisements of Mexican movies at the Colon— the torn clothes just laundered waving on rickety balconies along Paisano Drive held up God knows how. Or if not, in the Government projects, which are clean tenements—a section for the Mexicans, a section for the Negroes. Politely. Row after row of identical boxhouses speckled with dozens and dozens of children.

So this, the Southside, is of course the area of the Mean gangs. The ones on the other side are not as dangerous, of course, because they are mostly Blond and mostly normal Anglo-American kiddies growing up naturally and what can you expect? Like the ones from Kern Place—all pretty clean houses at the foot of Mount Franklin—and if those kiddies carry switchblade knives, at least they keep them clean, and when they wear boots, they are Cowboy Boots.

The southside gangs—that's a different thing. Theyre blackhaired. And tense. Mean and bad, with Conflict seething. El Paso's southside (the

Second Ward) gave birth to the internationally famous Pachucos. (Paso—
Pacho.) They used to call them boogies, marijuanos, the zoot-suits—and
the baggy pants with the pegged ankles were boogiepants, and, man, those
tigers walked cool, long graceful bad strides, rhythmic as hell, hands deep
into pockets, shoulders hunched. Much heart. They really did wear and
still sometimes do those hats that Al Capp draws—and the chains, too,
from the belt to the pocket in a long loop.

And sitting talking Mexican jive, *mano,* under the El Paso streetlamps
along Hill and Magoffin and Seventh, around Bowie High School and next
to the Palace Theater digging Presley and Chuck Berry and Fats Domino,
outside the dingy 40-watt-bulb-lighted Southside grocery stores, avoiding
la jura, the neo-Pachucos with dreamy junk eyes and their chicks in tight
skirts and giant pompadours and revealing 1940-style sweaters hang in the
steamy El Paso nights, hunched, mean and bad, plotting protest, unconscious
of, though they carry it, the burden of the world, and additionally, the
burden of Big Texas.

Well, look. In East Texas. In Balmorhea, say. In Balmorhea, with its
giant outdoor swimming pool (where that summer the two blond tigers
and I went swimming, climbed over the wall and into the rancid-looking
night water) there were signs in the two-bit restaurant, in Balmorhea-town
then, that said *We do not serve mexicans, niggers or dogs.* That night we
went to the hick movie, and the man taking the tickets said, You boys be
sure and sit on the right side, the left is for spiks. So I said I was on the
wrong side and walked out. Later at Kit's aunt's ranch, the aunt waited
until the Mexican servant walked out and then said, miserably, Ah jaist caint
even eat when they are around. And because earlier had made me feel
suddenly a Crusader and it was easy now, I walked out of the diningroom
and said well then I shouldnt be here to louse up your dinner, lady.

And you never know it—to look at that magnificent Texas sky.

At Christmas is when Mexican El Paso is magnificent. I dont mean
the jazz at San Jacinto Plaza (trees and lights and Christmas carols and
Santa Claus). I mean the Southside Christmas. A lot of them—most of
them, in fact—put up trees, of course, but many of them put up nacimientos.
My father used to start putting ours up almost a month before Christmas
when we lived on Wyoming Street. It's a large boxlike thing—ours was,
anyway—about six-feet wide, six-feet tall, eight-feet deep, like a room
minus the front wall (the minus faces the windows, which are cleaned to
sparkle), and inside is a Christmas scene. Ours had the manger and the
Virgin of course and St Joseph, and angels hanging from strings floating on
angelhair clouds. To the sides of the manger were modern-looking California miniature houses, with real lights in them—some had swimming pools.
And stone mountains. On one was the Devil, red, with a wired neck so
that the slightest movement made it twitch, drinking out of a bottle. Christ

was coming, and naturally the Devil would be feeling low. My father painted an elaborate Texas-like sky behind the manger, with clouds, giant moon, the works—lights all over, and he enclosed the boxlike nacimiento with Christmas-tree branches, and then, one year, he had a real lake—that is, real water which we changed daily. The wisemen on their way. Christmas lights, bulbs, on top. He moved the wise men each night, closer to the manger. The Christchild wasnt there yet—He wast born. Then on Christmas Eve everyone came over. My mother led the rosary. We all knelt. Someone had been chosen to be the padrino—the godfather—of the Christchild to be born that night. He carried the Child in his hands, everyone kissed it ("adored" it), and then finally He was put into the manger, in the hay. We prayed some more. *Dios te salve, María, llena eres de Gracia.* . . . At the stroke of midnight, the Child was born. Then there was a party— tamales, buñuelos, liquor.

The Patron of Mexico is the Virgin of Guadalupe. The story says She appeared to Juan Diego, one day, and in order to make the incredulous know that he had indeed seen Her, She stamped Herself on his shawl, and that is the one you see in Mexican churches, all stars and blue robe. Oh, how tenderly they believe in the Virgin of Guadalupe (*even the Priests!*), and how they love Her, the Mother of all Mexico.

How they Respect mothers because of it. Mothers are a Grand Mexican thing. They belong sacredly in Mexico and the Mexican Southwest.

Dig: a serious Mexican movie. The favorite theme. The son goes away. The little Old Mexican Mother stands at the dingy door with her black shawl sheltering her from the drizzling rain. Christ. The son goes away, and forgets about her. He becomes a Great Matador, lured by women like Maria Bonita before the President's wife—and this is only gossip— chased her out. Wow! The Little Mother in the Black Shawl wanders over Mexico, working for harsh people—like sewing in a factory where, she's so old, poor thing, she cant keep up with the heftier ladies. She comes at last into a very rich home in Mexico City. Of course. It is her son's home. But he doesnt recognize her, and she decides not to tell him who she is so he wont be ashamed of her. She'll just be satisfied to be near him. He is gruff. "Old woman, look how much dust has accumulated on this my favorite table." "Yes, sir." She wipes it. He is cruel, yells at her despite the pitiful black shawl. She takes it, and this is true. Mexican mothers and wives do take It—not Americans, and this is what grips a Mexican audience. Loyalty. One day the Big Corrida comes on. The wife is digging it on television (she cant bear to go it live). The matador is gored. The shawled Mother screams, MI HIJO!!!! The wife knows now, and being Mexican herself and on the way to becoming a Mexican Mother, she hugs the Old Lady. They run out, get a cab, go to the bullring. There he is. Unconscious. Dying. The beautifully dressed wife pulls the shawl off the little old Mother and proclaims to the dying matador, "Die if God wills it—but not without knowing that—This—Is—Your—Mother!!!!" Everyone is crying, the unnatural son repents (as he must), and all three live happily ever after.

This is real. Mexicans really love Mothers. Americans dont. I dont have a single American acquaintance whose mother faints everytime he comes home and again when he leaves. Mine does. The Mexican mother-love has nothing to do with sex, either. You can imagine an American wanting to make it with his mother. She is slick. She looks almost as young and bad as he does. But can you imagine making it with your mother if she wears a Black Shawl, and, even if she doesnt, if she acts all the time like she is wearing One?

Mexican religion is a very real thing, not lukewarm at all, nor forbidding and awesome. Mexican Catholics (and this, again, includes the Priests)believe in a God with two hands, two feet, eyes—the works. The Devil has horns, a tail, and he is most certainly red. Each church in the Mexican sections of the Southwest, and all of them in Juárez have Real patron saints, who guard them. On their days, they have kermesses—this is like a fair. On the really big days (for example, in May, the month of the Virgin Mary), the Indians (who are Catholics although their religion is still magnificently pagan, having room in it for Mayan, Aztec, other legends —witchcraft—right along with the story of Jesus) come into the City. The matachincs (they used to scare me, like the beggars I will tell you about later) are Indians dressed in all kinds of feathers, painted all over, making dance marathons, dancing for hours. Some Indians—I think the Tarahumaras—run all the way from somewhere like Chihuahua City to Juárez, offering I suppose that amount of exerted energy to the Virgin. In religious frenzy, they burn an effigy of Satan—a kind of man-shaped catherine wheel. They light him up, and the bastard burns shooting fire straight from hell. The people yell up a storm, and the Politicians and Gangsters shoot real bullets into the air in this tribute to the Virgin Mary.

And cockfights!

And witches—lots of them.

They hold a position in the Mexican Southwest almost as respected as that of the priests. There's a kind of hierarchy among them, headed by Don Ben (the Pope of El Paso's witches). A problem too big for an ordinary witch is referred finally to Don Ben, a root-twisted old, old man. (He wont die—he'll shrink.) I remember when I was a kid, an *espíritu maligno* kept bugging us, misplacing my father's glasses. We ended up going to Don Ben. He fell into a dramatic trance, and when he woke, he said, My *tata Dios* (daddy God) is so busy right now He suggests we call Him later. We called later, and *tata Dios* said to leave the *espíritu* alone and it would go away.

My second-aunt ("she of the blue hair and the deer eyes—ahhh!"—
Don Ben's description of her) has had a picture of her husband, inverted
in a glass of strange liquid, behind her bedroom door, for years. About 40
years ago, he left her—and this will bring him back some day.

And why should devout Mexican Catholics (as they are) consult
witches (as they do)? For the same reason that a man with a sick ear goes
to an ear specialist. . . .

And bullfights.

But they dont get the best bullfighters at the Juárez arena, although
sometimes they do. The real sight—when the bullfight aint good—are the
Americans in huge Mexican hats being so Mexican, and the inevitable
cluster of Mexicans around them, the fawning ones glorifying the grand
American—these are the sick ones—and then the opportunists, hoping the
money will rub off and willing to see to it that it does.

At dawn, on a lady's birthday—even now and in El Paso—five or
six men gather outside her window, singing and playing their guitars. The
sun is about to come out. They sing softly,

> Estas son las mañanitas
> Que cantava el Rey David.
> A las muchachas bonitas
> Se las cantava él así. . . .

Now the lady comes coyly to the window, standing there until they
have finished the soft dawn singing. Now all the neighbors' windows are
up and everyone is listening. (No one thinks of calling the police.) Then
the lady invites the serenaders inside, and they all have early-morning
coffee, *pan de dulce, menudo.* Then the sun is up in the sky.

The Southwest sky. Beautiful and horrifying. And therefore Wonderful.

Because in all the blunder and bluster of Texas about the wrong
things, one thing is really so. The sky.

When it is beautiful it is depthless blue. The sky in other places is
like an inverted cup, this shade of blue or gray or black or another shade,
with limits, like a painted room. Not in the Southwest. The sky is really
millions and millions of miles deep of blue—and in summer, clear magic
electric blue.

(How many stars are there in the sky? was our favorite six-year-old
children riddle. The answer: *cincuenta.* Which means fifty, but also:
countless. And it's true, so true.)

Before the summer storms, the clouds mass and roll twisting in the
sky clashing fiercely, sweeping grandly across the sky. Then giant mush-
rooms explode. The sky groans, opens, it pours rain.

But before the windstorms, everything is calm, and then a strange ominous mass of gray gathers in the horizon. Then swiftly, in a moment it seems, blowing with the wind, the steel clouds cover the sky, and youre locked down here, so lonesome suddenly youre cold. The wind comes. The tumbleweeds rush with it.

And always there's the fearful wailing.

This excerpt from the life story of a Vato, is a straightforward account of daily barrio reality as seen by a young person. The narration includes elements which have been seen as negative by those who have formulated stereotypes of the Pachuco.

More important is the focus on authentic facets of the barrio life-style and value system. Aspects of carnalismo, mutual protection and defense, creation of language and a sense of struggle, pervade the selection and provide a vivid community view.

EXCERPTS FROM THE LIFE STORY
OF A VATO:

This is the story of life in a Mexican barrio, the barrio is called "San Fer". The kids, so called Pachucos, run this barrio; life in this barrio is rough, harsh. The boys learned early to carry can openers and knives. As soon as they got a little older they graduated to switchblades, lengths of chain and guns, if they could get hold of them.

The boys joined together, to form street gangs and some of them sported the Pachuco's brand between the thumbs and forefingers fo their left hands. They formed a closely knit group that regarded the Anglos as their natural enemies. You find these Pachucos mostly in the barrio—Kalisher street— in streets, corners, alleys, and inside dark streets; it is the largest barrio in San Fernando Valley, compared to other barrios.

This gang is the stuff of life as the Pachuco knows it. For it he will undertake the most fantastic stunts to prove a great deal, he will risk life and freedom to maintain his growing reputation as a tough fighter, a rugged guy, at the young age they enter the "front of life". They find conflicts so perplexing and so full of both cultures—that of their parents and that of America—and create their own world of Pachuquismo; the Vatos have created their own language, Pachucano; their own style of dress; their own folklore, and behavior patterns.

The Vatos have developed a barrio group spirit that has resulted in the establishment of a few-score areas and territories. One of these territories is "Borrego Valley". The Vatos in this territory are from O'Melveny St. to Laurel Canyon Blvd. These Vatos hang out in the center of Acala Ave., a dark street, and in the alleys around that area. These Vatos in this area are better organized and a little tighter due to the fact that it is a smaller group, and therefore, all the Vatos participate in the activities planned by them. Everybody shows and brings anything that will be enjoyed by the group; for instance, one boy will bring beer or wine while others will bring "rifa", still others bring money for the use of activities or gas for a member's car.

This is a thing that goes on every night with usually something different every night that can be called a "dead kick". This is a neighborhood that never looks for any trouble but is always full of excitement.

Freeing himself from accepted standards of literary expression, the Pachuco developed an elaborate system of symbols that are today maintained as graffiti on the walls of the barrio. Like cabalistic signs, they are the hieroglyphics of barrio consciousness. They are secret symbols, the use of which rejects the accepted norms of conventional society. Through this language, an in-group based on shared barrio experience generates its own values. Their version of what is good and bad, what is accepted and what isn't forms the basis of a barrio morality.

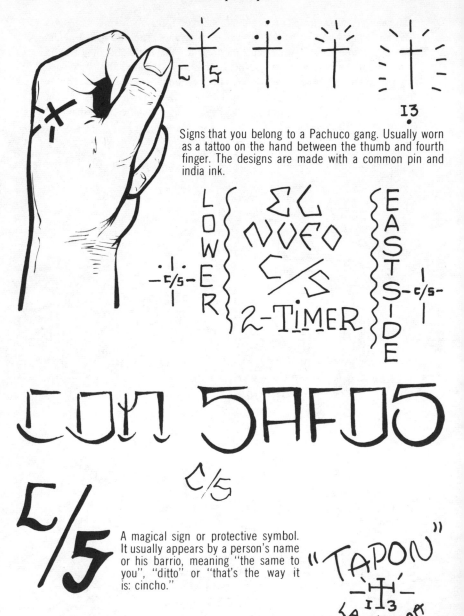

Signs that you belong to a Pachuco gang. Usually worn as a tattoo on the hand between the thumb and fourth finger. The designs are made with a common pin and india ink.

CON SAFOS

c/s

C/S

A magical sign or protective symbol. It usually appears by a person's name or his barrio, meaning "the same to you", "ditto" or "that's the way it is: cincho."

"TAPON"
LA LOMA
I3

PV

POR VIDA: usually added to message of love.

RIFAN

RIFAN: a sign of control meaning, "the best" or "the toughest."

13: the thirteenth letter of the alphabet means yesca, mota, cannibus, marijuana.

We now turn our focus on the people of the barrio. The story below highlights the qualities and values of those who have achieved the rank and title of maestro—an honorary designation meaning that they are masters of a "trade, art, or folly."

Gonzalo Pereda the protagonist, an expert trainer of fighting cocks, exemplifies the values of a true maestro : complete dedication and devotion to his craft. By maintaining standards of excellence he achieves personal dignity and community respect.

Writing in the 1940s Mario Suárez was pessimistic about the survival of the values and language of the maestros. Re-examining this idea today, we see that those very values have not only survived but provide some of the vitality of our new maestros : Chicano craftsmen, poets, teachers, and community leaders.

MAESTRÍA

mario suárez

Whenever a man is referred to as a *maestro* it means that he is master of whatever trade, art, or folly he practices. If he is a shoemaker, for example, he can design, cut, and finish any kind of shoe he is asked for. If he is a musician he knows composition, direction, execution, and thereby plays Viennese waltzes as well as the *bolero*. If he is a thief he steals thousands, for he would not damn his soul by taking dimes. That is *maestría*. It is applied with equal honor to a painter, tailor, barber, printer, carpenter, mechanic, bricklayer, window washer, ditchdigger, or bootblack if his ability merits it. Of course, when a man is greying and has no apparent trade or usefulness, out of courtesy people may forget he is a loafer and will call him a *maestro*. Whether he is or not is of no importance. Calling him a *maestro* hurts no one.

During the hard times of Mexico's last revolution many *maestros* left Mexico with their families with the idea of temporarily making a living north of the Río Grande. But the revolution lasted for such a long time that when it finally came to an end the *maestros,* now with larger families, remained here in spite of it. During the hard times of the last depression they opened little establishments on West Broad Street and North Pike where they miraculously made a dollar on some days and as many as two or three on others—always putting on, because they were used to hard times, a good face. When good times returned, most of the *maestros* closed up their little establishments and went to work for the larger concerns which came back in business. Some left for the increasing number of factory jobs in California. But some, enjoying their long independence and believing that it is better to be a poor lord than a rich servant, kept their little establishments open.

Gonzalo Pereda, for example, was a *maestro* who kept a little saddle shop open on West Broad Street. Being a great conversationalist he was not against having company at all hours. Being easy with his money he was always prey for those that told him of need in their homes. And easier prey still for those that often talked him into closing up his establishment, so that they might gossip of old times over a bottle of beer. Being a good craftsman, therefore, had never helped to give the *maestro* more than enough with which to provide for his family.

But if there were men in the world who worried about their work after being through for the day, as far as the *maestro* was concerned they deserved to die young. It certainly was not so with Gonzalo Pereda. Life, he figured, was too short anyway. When he closed up in the afternoon he rid his mind completely of jobs pending and overhead unpaid. He simply hurried home to feed his stable of fighting roosters and to eat supper with his family. Even before taking off his hat he made his way to the back yard to see that his roosters had fresh water and that their cages were clean. That the *maestro* did all of this before going in to greet his family does not mean that he liked the roosters better. But the family, now grown up and with its own affairs, could wait. The roosters, dependent on his arrival for their care, could and should not.

One day when the *maestro* came home, he found a little cage in his back yard. Attached to the top of it was a tag which read, "A present from your friend Bernabé Lerda. Chihuahua, México." In the cage was a red rooster. The *maestro* stuck his finger through an opening and had to jerk it out immediately when the rooster picked at it with a bill which seemed to be made of steel. The *maestro* took a thin leather strip from his pocket, opened the cage, and tied it to the rooster's leg. Then he took the rooster out in order to examine him carefully. The *maestro* looked closely at the rooster's long thick legs, at his tail, which by its length might have belonged to a peacock, at the murder in both of his eager eyes; and the *maestro* knew that this rooster would assassinate any unfortunate fowl pitted against him.

After gazing around a bit the little rooster stretched and strutted. He flapped his wings a few times and then he crowed. The *maestro* was amazed. How could it be, he asked himself, that an animal could possess such pomp? How was it that he knew he was a better rooster than any other that had ever emerged from a hen's egg and therefore strutted about like a race horse confident of winning the Kentucky Derby? How did he know he was such a handsome example of chicken-hood that he, without doubt, could be the Valentino of any chicken yard? Well, it was unbelievable, but it was so. And the *maestro* was sure that this rooster, being from Mexico no less, would slash his way to thirty victories once they put him in the pit. A few minutes later, when one of the *maestro's* sons saw the rooster, both decided that he must have a worthy name: they decided to call him *Killer*.

So great a stir did Killer cause that the *maestro* forgot all about eating supper that night. While he watched admiringly, Killer took his time about eating his grain and drinking his cool water. One would have thought that the *maestro* could aliment himself by merely gazing at the conceited rooster as he strutted about. The *maestro* said, "The minute he goes into the pit the other rooster will drop dead from fright. Just look at the beautiful creature."

And so it was. The following Sunday afternoon the *maestro* burst in through the front door with Killer. Killer was still hot under the wings from having chased the other rooster and then having slashed it to ribbons. He was still kicking inside the cage as if asking for all the roosters who ever sported a gaff to take him on. "You should have seen him," said the *maestro* to his wife. "Killer is the greatest rooster that ever lived." Then he took Killer to the back yard to cool off.

During the night there was a big commotion in the yard. Killer had gotten out of his cage and was attacking the other roosters through the wire fronts of their cages. Already, in a minute or so, there was blood in front of the cage belonging to a rooster named General, who had retreated to the back of his cage for safety. Killer was squaring off, with his neck leathers ruffled, at another cage, in an effort to pick out the eyes of a rooster named Diablo. "He is really cute, isn't he?" asked the *maestro*. Then he took Killer and holding him said, "Well, I guess it is only natural for him to want to fight. He had no competition this afternoon." When Killer was put in another cage, the *maestro* and his son went back to bed.

After the Killer's second fight, the following Sunday, the *maestro* once again came in through the front door with Killer. This time Killer had disposed of his adversary in less than two minutes. The *maestro* was happy. "I am convinced," he said, "that Killer is a butcher if there ever was one." And in victory the *maestro* brought Killer through the front door after the third, fourth, and fifth fight. Now, of course, Killer traveled to and from the pit in style. His was a big cage, made and designed to give him a lot of comfort, with letters reading, "Killer."

On the Sunday that Killer won his sixth fight the *maestro* was so happy when he brought Killer through the front door for his wife to admire that tears came from his eyes as he said, "Every rooster that sees this champion can say that the Devil has taken him." And on that day Killer established himself firmly as the best rooster that had ever come to fall in the *maestro's* possession. This Sunday, after all, had been a great one for the *maestro*, financially speaking and otherwise.

The following Sunday the *maestro* got up very early. Before his daughter left for church he had her take out the camera in order to photograph Killer. The picture that came out best would be sent away to *Hook and Gaff*, a magazine dedicated to cockfights and poultry. They photographed Killer from various angles. In the arms of the *maestro*. Perched on top of a pole. Looking into a hen roost.

But that afternoon, after the fight, the *maestro* did not storm through the front door to tell how Killer had all but peeled and removed the entrails from the opposing rooster. The *maestro* hurried around the side of the house to the back yard with Killer in his hands. Killer, the invincible one, had met its match. After six battles had come his Waterloo. The reason that Killer was not dead was because the *maestro* had stopped the fight and forfeited his bet. But Killer seemed more dead than alive. His bill was open as if to force breath into his lungs. One of his wings was almost torn off. His back was deeply gashed. One of his eyes was closed. The *maestro* worked frantically to keep Killer alive. He put flour under the torn wing. He took a damp rag and wiped the blood off Killer's head. The *maestro* looked as though he had lost his best friend.

For many days the Killer did not eat. He only stood, and weakly, on his long, thick legs. The *maestro* came home many times to take care of him. He brought Killer some baby-chicken feed in order that he might eat something when he recuperated enough to open his eyes. But to no avail. The *maestro's* gladiator still seemed close to death.

Then, of a sudden, Killer got better. He began to pick at the baby-chicken feed. And the *maestro* was overwhelmed with joy. Killer did not strut as before, or crow, or flap his wings; but he would, in time. Many things, the *maestro* often said, were fixed by time alone.

Towards the end of Killer's convalescence the *maestro* felt proud of the job he had done in rescuing the Killer from death. As a finishing touch he decided to give the rooster, who was beginning to act somewhat like the Killer of old, some little pieces of liver. These would give him more blood. So, while the *maestro's* son opened Killer's bill, the *maestro* pushed a little piece of liver down Killer's throat. But the second piece caused Killer to gurgle, to kick momentarily, and then suddenly to die in the *maestro's* hands. With tears in his eyes the *maestro* stroked his beloved Killer, bit his lip as he wrapped the limp body of his Spartan in a newspaper, and tenderly put it in the garbage can. Then, without supper, the *maestro* went to bed. His beloved Killer was gone.

Like Killer's plight, it might be added, is the plight of many things the *maestros* cherish. Each year they hear their sons talk English with a rapidly disappearing accent, that accent which one early accustomed only to Spanish never fails to have. Each year the *maestros* notice that their sons' Spanish loses fluency. But perhaps it is natural. The *maestros* themselves seem to forget about bulls and bullfighters, about guitars and other things so much a part of the world that years ago circumstance forced them to leave behind. They hear instead more about the difference between one baseball swing and another. Yes, perhaps it is only natural.

Ofttimes when *maestros* get together they point out the fact that each year there are less and less of their little establishments around. They proudly say that the old generation was best; that the new generation knows nothing. They point out, for example, that there are no shoemakers any more.

They say that the new generation of so-called shoemakers are nothing but repairers of cheap shoes in need of half soles. They say that the musicians are but accompanists who learned to play an instrument in ten lessons and thus take money under false pretenses. Even the thieves, they tell you, are nothing but two-bit clips. The less said about other phases of *maestría,* they will add, the better.

When one of the *maestros* dies all the other *maestros* can be counted upon to mourn him. They dust off the dark suits they seldom wear, and offer him, with their calloused hands folded in prayer, a Rosary or two. They carry his coffin to and from the church. And they help fill his grave with the earth that will cover him thereafter. Then they silently know the reason why there are not so many of the little establishments as before. Perhaps it is natural. There are not so many *maestros* any more.

This prose-poem is a lyrical lament on the death of a Pachuco. On one plane it provides information about people, places and events in a Chicano barrio. On another level, it projects the fantasy life of the Pachuco protagonist, which may have been the only salida he could find from social oppression.

The merging of his daily reality with the fantasy of his role-playing, creates the illusion by which Louie lived his life.

In counterpoint with this illusion is the poet's sober evaluation of Louie's reality.

EL LOUIE

josé montoya

> Hoy enterraron al Louie
>
> And San Pedro o sanpinche
> are in for it. And those
> times of the forties
> and the early fifties
> lost un vato de atolle.

Kind of slim and drawn,
there toward the end,
aging fast from too much
booze y la vida dura. But
class to the end.

En Sanjo you'd see him
sporting a dark topcoat
playing in his fantasy
the role of Bogard, Cagney
or Raft.

Era de Fowler el vato,
carnal del Candi y el
Ponchi—Los Rodríguez—
The Westside knew 'em
and Selma, even Gilroy.

48 Fleetline, two-tone—
buenas garras and always
rucas—como la Mary y
la Helen...siempre con
liras bien afinadas
cantando La Palma, la
que andaba en el florero.

Louie hit on the idea in
those days for tailor-made
drapes, unique idea—porque
Fowler no era nada como
Los, o'l E.P.T. Fresno's
westside was as close as
we ever got to the big time,

But we had Louie and the
Palomar, el boogie, los
mambos y cuatro suspiros
del alma—y nunca faltaba
the gut-shrinking love-
splitting, ass-hole-up
tight-bad news—
        Trucha, esos! Va 'ber
        pedo!
        Abusau, ese!
        Get Louie

No llores, Carmen, we can
handle 'em.
    Ese, 'on tal Jimmy?
    Hórale, Louie
    Where's Primo?
    Va 'ber catos!

En el parking lot away from
the jura.

    Hórale!
    Trais filero?
    Simón!
    Nel!
    Chale, ese!
    Oooooh, este vato!

And Louie would come through—
melodramatic music, like in the
mono—tan tan tarán! —Cruz
Diablo, El Charro Negro! Bogard
smile (his smile as deadly as
his vaisas!) He dug roles, man,
and names—like blackie, little
Louie...

Ese Louie...
Chale, call me "Diamonds", man!
Y en Korea fue soldado de
levita con huevos and all the
paradoxes del soldado raso—
heroism and the stockade!

And on leave, jump boots
shainadas and ribbons, cocky
from the war, strutting to
early mass on Sunday morning.

Wow, is that el Louie

Mire, comadre, ahí va el hijo
de Lola!

Afterward he and fat Richard
would hock their bronze stars
for pisto en el Jardín Canales
y en el Trocadero.

At barber college he came
out with honors. Después
empeñaba su velardo de la
peluca pa' jugar pócar serrada
and lo ball en Sanjo y Alvizo.

And "Legs Louie Diamond" hit
on some lean times...

Hoy enterraron al Louie.

Y en Fowler at Nesei's
pool parlor los baby chooks
se acuerdan de Louie, el carnal
del Candi y el Ponchi—la vez
que lo fileriaron en el Casa
Dome y cuando se catió con
La Chiva.

Hoy enterraron al Louie.

His death was an insult
porque no murió en acción—
no lo mataron los vatos,
ni los gooks en Korea.
He died alone in a rented
room—perhaps like a
Bogard movie.

The end was a cruel hoax.
But his life had been
remarkable!

     Vato de atolle, el Louie Rodríguez.

The uniqueness of this corrido is that it is a recording of artistic expression about art. Collected in the village of San Antonio, New Mexico, more than forty years ago, it sings the praises of a famous Matachín dancer.

The Matachines are presentations combining music, dance, drama, and pantomime. As a form of sacred theatre, they are still performed in a few Chicano communities during religious holidays such as December twelfth—the feast of our Lady of Guadalupe. The Matachines are one part of the rich and varied tradition of Chicano folk theatre.

José Apodaca, a famous dancer in real life, was another maestro del barrio. This corrido composed and sung in his honor demonstrates the positive attitudes which Chicanos hold toward the creative person. Whether the artist be a good singer, carver of santos, or a guisandera, he or she is respected and remembered.

CORRIDO DE JOSÉ APODACA

Señores voy a cantar
Lo que traigo en mi memoria
De un hombre que fué notable.
Voy a cantarles la historia.

Del pueblo de San Antonio
Nació un hombre muy brillante,
Y con el tiempo llegó
A ser el mejor danzante.

Esta dichosa carrera
Circunstancia mucho abarca,
Y con el tiempo llegó
A ser el mejor Monarca.

José Apodaca era el hombre
De tan grande corazón.
Siempre lleva en su mente
De servirle a su patrón.

Con su guajito y su palma
Y aquel cupil de diamantes
Se enfrentava de San Antonio
Con un grupo de danzantes.

CORRIDO OF JOSÉ APODACA

Gentlemen, I am going to sing you
That which I carry in my memory
Of a man who was notable.
I am going to sing the story.

In the village of San Antonio
Was born a very brilliant man,
And with the passage of time
He came to be the best dancer.

This distinguished career
Was favored by circumstances,
And with the passage of time
He came to be the best *Monarca*.[1]

José Apodaca was a man
With a very great heart.
Always he carried in his mind
The thought of service to his Lord.

With his *guajito* and his *palma*[2]
And his headdress of diamonds
He presented himself before San Antonio
With a group of dancers.

[1] The *Monarca* is the leader of the Matachines dancers.
[2] The *guajito* is a rattle and the *palma* is a three-forked stick often carved and colored.

Con aquel cupil dorado
Le nació del corazón
Y la Malinche a su lado
Bailándole a su patrón.

Vestido de mil colores
En nuestra iglesia se alegraba,
Y el pueblo lleno de gusto
Cuando Apodaca bailaba.

Quedó triste San Antonio
Con grande luto se vía;
Tan pálido y tan sereno
Como una aurora del día.

En su tumba está grabado
Con letras interesantes
Con un letrero que dice:
Viva el rey de los danzantes.

Nos despedimos, señores.
Aquí termina la historia.
Y Apodaca está en el cielo
Gozando de Dios y gloria.

With this gilded headdress
He touched his heart
And with the *Malinche*[3] at his side
He danced before his patron.

In vestments of a thousand colors
In our church he danced,
And the entire village rejoiced
When Apodaca danced.

San Antonio was left sad
And appeared in deep mourning;
Pale and so serene
Like the dawn of the day.

On his tomb is engraved
In interesting letters
An inscription which says:
"Long live the king of the dancers."

Now farewell, gentlemen.
This is the end of the story.
And Apodaca is in heaven
Rejoicing with God in his glory

---

[3] The *Malinche* is a little girl in white who dances with the matachines dancers.

In the barrios of Aztlán no contemporary figure has caught the popular imagination like the Pachuco or his latter day prototype, the Bato Loco. Maligned as social outcasts or mythified as archetypal vanguards of the Chicano movement, the Pachucos left a cultural legacy which is now in the process of evaluation.

The birth of Pachucano, a caló of the barrio, allowed the Pachuco to express his feelings, and his creative spirit. Since for him English and Spanish offered only anemic vocabularies, he forged new words, new idioms, and new usage, making the languages respond to his social reality.

In this text we present a Spanish and a Pachuco version of a traditional corrido.

EL HIJO DESOBEDIENTE

Un domingo estando herrando,
Se encontraron dos mancebos,
Echando mano a sus fierros
Como queriendo pelear.

Cuando se estaban peleando,
Pues, llegó el padre de uno,
Hijo de mi corazón
Ya no pelees con ninguno.

Quítese de aquí, mi padre,
Que estoy más bravo que un león
No vaya a sacar mi espada
Y le traspase el corazón.

Hijo de mi corazón,
Por lo que acabas de hablar,
Antes de que raye el sol,
La vida te han de quitar.

Lo que le encargo a mi padre
Que no me entierre en sagrado,
Que me entierre en tierra bruta,
Donde me trille el ganado.

Con una mano de fuera
Y un papel sobre dorado,
Con un letrero que diga:
Felipe fué desgraciado.

A PACHUCO VERSION OF "EL HIJO DESOBEDIENTE"

Un domingo entrando a lunes
Se encontraron dos pachucos
Metiendo mano a sus filas
Como quieriendo forjear.

Cuando se estaban forjeando,
Pues, llegó el jefe de uno,
"Hijo de mi corazón
Ya no forjees con ninguno."

"Quítese de aquí, mi jefe,
Que estoy más bravo que burro.
No vaya sacar la fila
Y le traspase el menudo."

"Hijo de mi corazón
Por lo que acabas de hablar
Antes que raye el sol
La vida te he de quitar."

"Lo que le encargo a mi jefe
Que no me entierre en Califa
Que me entierre en Arizona
Con tres costales de grifa."

"Con una vaisa de fuera
Y un picotazo en el brazo
Yo ya no quero morfina,
Ahora quiero cosa fina."

Medicine sold under the trade-name "Don Pedrito" with a picture of Don Pedrito Jaramillo and the legend ". . . supplier of herbs and roots" on the container, is available in many boticas and hierberías of Chicano barrios.

Don Pedrito Jaramillo was a folk healer who died at Paisano, Star County, Texas on July 3, 1907. He is an authentic hero in the mythology of the barrio throughout the Southwest. In many cases he has achieved the status of folk sainthood.

In the direct, declarative narrations which follow, his feats are recounted. The stories are not embellished but are direct and expressive. It is these qualities that reflect the spirit of the people.

REMEDIES OF DON PEDRITO JARAMILLO

presented by ruth dodson

nosebleed

When Simón Valdez was a boy, he lived on a ranch in the country of Duval. One day Don Pedrito was there giving remedies to those who wanted them. Simón's grandmother asked for a remedy for nosebleed, from which Simón suffered frequently.

The curandero told the grandmother that as a remedy she should put clean clothes on her grandson and not change them for nine days. During this time, every night she should pour a bucket of water over the boy until he was thoroughly wet, and he should sleep that way. Simón said that he didn't feel cold at night with the wet clothes on, although it was in the winter. He was cured of nosebleed from that time on.

three leaves of prickly pear

It was told that a señora suffered with severe pains in her stomach, which at times caused her to take to her bed. Her husband had called doctors to her at various times when she had these attacks. And not until he was sure that the doctors were not going to cure her of this sickness did he take her to Don Pedrito.

When the woman explained her sickness to the curandero, as the doctors had diagnosed the case, he said, "No, that is not your trouble; it is in your kidneys."

He prescribed that when she had the pains her husband should roast three leaves of prickly pear cactus, slice them through the middle and scrape the pulp out as quickly as possible so as not to lose the heat. Of this warm pulp he should make three poultices, placing the pulp between pieces of muslin. Then he should fix a poultice over each kidney and a third one over the stomach, so that the one over the stomach was in line with the ones over the kidneys.

This señora was entirely cured, it was said.

a vaquero who failed to follow directions

One time when a vaquero was running some horses through mesquite brush, a limb struck him in the face with such force as to hurt his eyes very badly. He doctored his eyes with different home remedies in vain. Then he sent to ask Don Pedrito for a remedy.

The remedy that Don Pedrito prescribed was that this vaquero should do hard work for nine successive days; that he work with an ax every day, from early in the morning until night; that he take no siesta, nor rest during the day; and that he make no charges for his work.

The vaquero followed directions until Sunday came; but instead of continuing the work on this day also, he rested. The consequence was that he was blind the rest of his life.

various cures

At times a man suffered from headache until he took to his bed. The remedy for him was that for three mornings he should get up at the same hour and drink a glass of water. He recovered in three days.

For a sick girl, the remedy with which she was cured was that she take a bath every night for nine nights, washing her head well with soap; then that she eat as much as she should want of a can of fruit of whatever kind was available and place the remainder where only the chickens could find it.

The prescription for a certain woman was to dip her head into a bucket of water as she was ready to go to bed. The next morning she was to put half a can of tomatoes into each shoe, then put the shoes on and wear them that way all day, *sin verguenza*—without shame.

A case of particular interest, it was said, was that of a Colonel Toribio Regalo who was brought from the city of Torreón, Mexico. He was so violently insane that he was kept tied. Don Pedrito prescribed a can of tomatoes every morning for nine mornings. The man was confined at Los Olmos while he took the remedy. At the end of nine days he was well, and his friends took him back to Mexico.

A man had a very fine horse that got sick. Don Pedrito told the man to tie the horse to a chinaberry tree at twelve o'clock sharp, and at one o'clock sharp to take him away from the tree. With this the horse would get well and the chinaberry tree would die.

borrowed shoes

A man who didn't have much faith in Don Pedrito as a healer asked him for a remedy for the malady from whcih he suffered. The curandero gave him such a simple prescription that the man doubted his power still more. He asked him, "Are you sure this remedy will cure me?"

Don Pedrito assured him, "I am as sure that this remedy will cure you as I am that you are wearing borrowed shoes."

The man was convinced because he *was* wearing borrowed shoes. And all doubt left him when the remedy took effect.

Confined in prison, the poet elaborates the complex images and experiences of el barrio captive in his memory. Like a majestic litany of life, the people, language, art, customs, and paradoxes of existence in La Loma become symbolic of all Chicano barrios that "... now exist or once existed".

Part of the deeper meaning of the poem lies in the paradox of a barrio which is the root and regenerative source of Chicanismo but also represents spiritual and physical violence, the exploitation and death of many of its inhabitants. The barrio for Salinas forms and degrades, creates and destroys, debilitates and sustains. It leaves indelible tattoos in the mind and spirit of all who share its experience.

A TRIP THROUGH THE MIND JAIL

raúlsalinas

for ELDRIDGE

[A Trip Through the Mind Jail is dedicated by a Chicano poet, raúlsalinas, from his little room at Leavenworth, to his camarada wherever he is, El Eldridge (Leroy) Cleaver de Rose Hill, barrio de Con Safos]

la loma

Neighborhood of my youth
    demolished, erased forever from
    the universe.
    You live on, captive, in the lonely
    cellblocks of my mind.
Neighborhood of endless hills
    muddied streets—all chuckhole lined—

that never drank of asphalt.
Kids barefoot/snotty-nosed
playing marbles, munching on bean tacos
(the kind you'll never find in a café)
2 peaceful generations removed from
their *abuelos'* revolution.
Neighborhood of dilapidated community hall
. . .Salón Cinco de Mayo. . .
yearly (May 5/Sept. 16) gathering
of the familias. Re-asserting pride
on those two significant days.
Speeches by the elders
patriarchs with evidence of oppression
distinctly etched upon *mestizo* faces.
"Sons of the Independence!"
Emphasis on allegiance to the *tri-color*
obscure names: Juárez & Hidalgo
their heroic deeds. Nostalgic tales of war
years under Villa's command. No one listened,
no one seemed to really care.
Afterwards, the dance. Modest Mexican
maidens dancing polkas together
across splintered wooden floor.
They never deigned to dance with boys!
The careful scrutiny by curbstone sex-perts
8 & 9 years old. "Minga's bow-legged,
so we know she's done it, huh?"
Neighborhood of Sunday night *jamaicas*
at Guadalupe Church.
Fiestas for any occasion
holidays holy days happy days
'round and 'round the promenada
eating snow-cones. . .raspas. . .& tamales
the games—bingo   cake walk   spin the wheel
making eyes at girls from cleaner neighborhoods
the unobtainables
who responded all giggles and excitement.
Neighborhood of forays down to Buena Vista—
Santa Rita Courts—Los projects—friendly neighborhood
cops n' robbers on the rooftops, sneaking peeks
in people's private night-time bedrooms
bearing gifts of Juicy Fruit gum for
the Projects girls/chasing them in adolescent heat

causing skinned knees & being run off for the night
disenchanted walking home affections spurned
stopping stay-out-late chicks in search of
Modern Romance lovers, who always stood them up
unable to leave their world in the magazines pages.
Angry fingers grabbing, squeezing, feeling,
french kisses imposed; close bodily contact, thigh &
belly rubbings under shadows of Cristo Rey Church.
Neighborhood that never saw a school-bus
    the cross-town walks were much more fun
    embarrassed when acquaintances or friends or relatives
    were sent home excused from class
    for having cooties in their hair!
    Did only Mexicans have cooties in their hair?
        Qué gacho!
Neighborhood of Zaragoza Park
    where scary stories interspersed with
    inherited superstitions were exchanged
    wating for midnight and the haunting
    lament of La Llorona...the weeping lady
    of our myths & folklore...who wept nightly,
    along the banks of Boggy Creek,
    for the children she'd lost or drowned
    in some river (depending on the version)
    i think i heard her once
    and cried
    out of sadness and fear
    running all the way home nape hairs at attention
    swallow a pinch of table salt and
    make the sign of the cross
    sure cure for frightened Mexican boys.
Neighborhood of Spanish Town Cafe
    first grown-up (13) hangout
    Andres,
    tolerant manager, proprietor, cook
    victim of bungling baby burglars
    your loss: Fritos n' Pepsi-Colas...was our gain
    you put up with us and still survived!
    You too, are granted immortality.
Neighborhood of groups and clusters
    sniffing gas, drinking muscatel
    solidarity   cement hardening
    the clan   the family   the neighborhood   the gang

Nomás!
Restless innocents tattoo'd crosses on their hands
"just doing things different"
"From now on, all troublemaking mex kids will
be sent to Gatesville for 9 months."
Henry home from *la corre*
khakis worn too low...below the waist
the stomps, the *greña* with duck-tail
—Pachuco Yo—
Neighborhood of could-be artists
who plied their talents on the pool's
bath-house walls/ intricately adorned
with esoteric symbols of their cult:

the art form of our slums
more meaningful & significant
than Egypt's finest hieroglyphics.
Neighborhood where purple clouds of *Yesca*
smoke one day descended & embraced us all.
Skulls uncapped—Rhythm n' Blues
Chalie's 7th. St. Club
loud funky music—wine spodee—odees—barbecue—grass
our very own connection man: big black Johnny B......
Neighborhood of Reyes' Bar
where Lalo shotgunned
Pete Evans to death because of
an unintentional stare,
and because he was *escuadra*,
only to end his life neatly sliced
by a prison barber's razor.
Durán's grocery & gas station
Guero drunkenly stabbed Julio
arguing over who'd drive home
and got 55 years for his crime.
Ratón: 20 years for a matchbox of weed. Is that cold?

No lawyer no jury no trial i'm guilty.
          Aren't we all guilty?
Indian mothers, too, so unaware
of courtroom tragi-comedies
folded arms across their bosoms
saying, *"Sea por Dios."*
Neighborhood of my childhood
          neighborhood that no longer exists
          some died young—fortunate—some rot in prisons
          the rest drifted away to be conjured up
          in minds of others like them.
          For me: only the NOW of THIS journey is REAL!
Neighborhood of my adolescence
          neighborhood that is no more
          YOU ARE TORN PIECES OF MY FLESH!!!
          Therefore, you ARE.
LA LOMA...AUSTIN...MI BARRIO...
                    i bear you no grudge
          i needed you then...identity...a sense of belonging.
          i need you now.
          So essential to adult days of imprisonment,
          you keep me away from INSANITY'S hungry jaws;
                    Smiling/Laughing/Crying.

                    i respect your having been:
                         My Loma of Austin
                         my Rose Hill of Los Angeles
                         my West Side of San Anto
                         my Quinto of Houston
                         my Jackson of San Jo
                         my Segundo of El Paso
                         my Barelas of Alburque
                         my Westside of Denver

Flats, Los Marcos, Maravilla, Calle Guadalupe, Magnolia,
Buena Vista, Mateo, La Seis, Chiquis, El Sur and all
          Chicano neighborhoods that now exist and once
          existed; somewhere....., someone remembers.....

                                        raúlrsalinas
                                        14, Sept.—'69

Dejando Huellas:
Caminos de la Migración

Desde siglos atrás...
Cuando vino el alambre vino el hambre...
De acá de este lado...
Hacia lo nuestro...

DEJANDO HUELLAS...
CAMINOS DE LA MIGRACIÓN

Migration—the movement of people from one place to another through time and space—is a pattern known to mankind throughout the centuries. The motives for such movement varied, as people have been uprooted by climate, by war, by political or religious persecution, by economic necessity, or by a desire to seek a new life.

As we view the Mexican/Chicano migratory experience in a universal context, and consider the specific human problems it engenders, we are confronted with questions about its fundamental meaning. Is the meaning to be found in the goals and ideals that people formed? For example, has it been a search for a final "place"? Or is the meaning to be found in what they have become and what they have created during this process of continual journey?

This unit attempts to present the Mexican/Chicano answer to those questions. In letters, corridos, poetry, novelas, crónicas, and other literary forms, their voices express the scope and depth of the meaning of their migrations.

As seen through their literature, the essence of the Mexican/Chicano response is that throughout the process of migration their "place" is where they are—or wherever they have been. They have invested part of their lives wherever they have existed, have left part of themselves in each place—whether in the form of a new colonia with a family or two, a newly dug grave where a parent is buried, or tejidos en las ventanas de un campo de labor—and therefore claim the right to call each place "theirs." And although people have been dispersed, displaced, and relocated, they have never been separated. For in spite of severe economic deprivation and social injustice—indeed because of it—the people have maintained identity with one another; they have adapted, innovated, and created new forms to meet new realities. The cry of greeting "Ya llegaron los Martínez!" "Vienen de McAlan!" and similar greetings heard yearly in communities throughout the United States, contain many implications of spiritual strength, of physical and cultural continuity. It is not only a matter of their survival, but rather, how they have survived, that is uniquely their own.

189

The literature reflects the inner personal and collective strength of a people who have not allowed themselves to be defeated by imposed physical circumstance, who through adverse economic and social conditions have retained an essential human sense of community, a sense of belonging to something beyond the immediate.

What is that essential quality? Has it been the root Mexican culture and Spanish language which survive in diverse forms in urban barrios and rural colonias throughout the United States? Has it been that inexplicable profound sense of oneness with the earth that Enriqueta Vásquez speaks of in "La Santa Tierra"? Or has it been a collective response, partly defensive in nature, forged by people banding together in mutual self-protection?

In answer to these questions we offer the following four sections recreating the Mexican/Chicano migratory experience. "Desde siglos atrás . . ." treats migration from the beginning of the mythic Aztec journey from Aztlán to the valley of Mexico, the dislocations of the colonial period, and the enforced relocations of the early nineteenth century. The second section, "Cuando vino el alambre vino el hambre", deals with the nineteenth and early twentieth centuries in the United States. These selections reflect the experience of the vaquero, el trasquilador, y los trabajadores del traque, all of whom were unique types, each representing an original adjustment to the new realities presented by the migration north. The political upheaval of the Mexican Revolution of 1910, with the resulting migration northward of ten percent of Mexico's population, the conflicts engendered by this migration, labor struggles, the indiscriminate mass deportations of the repatriation period of the 1930s, comprise the subunit "De acá de este lado . . .". The fourth and final section, "Hacia lo nuestro . . .", reflects the Chicano migratory labor experience, treating the period from 1940 to the present. The migration of single men, both braceros and those who crossed without papers, is included in this part.

Indio / Español / Mexicano / Spanish-American / Mexican-American / Pocho / Chicano—rural/urban/ suburbanite—the migrant experience is something we have all shared, if not directly, then through our parents, our grandparents, or a relative, perhaps the uncle who arrived from Mexico just last month.

The migratory experience is an ongoing process into which the Chicano has wrought change, and which has changed him. The confluence of Mexican cultural roots and the U.S. experience, the human basis of Chicano migration, is being redefined. A new set of relationships is being developed, which involves seeing ourselves differently, looking at Mexico from another perspective, and being less dependent on it as a regenerative source of cultural continuity. This awareness is nourished by an increasingly militant struggle for basic rights. The immigrants and migrants will continue to arrive from Mexico, and the migrant stream will continue to be a fact of our existence. Its long presence is part of the basis on which Chicanos today are creating the dignity of a new vision of themselves—as they continue to move . . . hacia lo nuestro.

I

desde siglos atrás

"Así lo vinieron a decir,
así lo asentaron en sus relatos,
Y para nosotros lo vinieron a
    dibujar en sus papeles
Los ancianos, las ancianas . . ."

Thus they have come to tell it,
thus they have come to record it in their narration,
and for us they have painted it in their codices,
the ancient men, the ancient women . . .

When man in his own time in history seeks to define himself, he refers to his past. What he sees, or reads, or hears about himself forms the basis from which he will determine where he is, and where he is going.

As the Chicano defines his historical position in terms of his relationship to the Mexican roots that nourish him, he must probe the meaning of that Mexican origin. This first section, treating internal migration, begins with the mythological version of the founding of Mexico, and follows different manifestations of Mexican migration up to the early twentieth century.

The Azteca-Chichimeca, a nomadic people, began their migration in search of a "promised land" to create a new life as ordained by their god Huitzilopochtli. They ended their quest by subjugating other peoples and building an empire. As history progressed, their role changed from conquerors to conquered.

The coming of the Spaniards was itself a migration across time, space, and culture. The Spanish conquest of Mexico, effected with the help of tribes warring with the Aztecs, resulted in major displacement of people, as the Spaniards systematically set about destroying all visible symbols and restructuring relationships of the existing civilization. Entire tribes were uprooted and families separated as Indians were parceled out to the conquistadores under the system of reducciones which ensured that the Spaniards would have workers for the lands and mines granted to them in the form of repartimientos. La tierra se repartió—los indios fueron reducidos.

While new social systems were being established in Mexico proper, and dislocation was being imposed on the Indian population, simultaneous migrations involving both Indians and Spaniards were taking place. They continued from the sixteenth to the eighteenth centuries. Bands of people journeyed to explore and colonize the territories to the north, which we now know as the Southwest. In land that continued the arid wastelands of northern Mexico, they founded their settlements, planting the seeds of their dual Indo-Hispano traditions.

Through the colonial period, the Wars of Independence, the U.S. war with Mexico, and into the early twentieth century, migration was generally dictated by the economic and political climate of Mexico. And the Indian population has been the most affected, suffering the greatest losses both in human terms and in terms of land.

The Tzeltal Indians in the state of Chiapas are but one example of a people dislocated from their home and forced to farm the mountainsides where the land is less fertile; then having to enter a pattern of migrating to work the lowlands coffee plantations in order to sustain themselves economically.

Another significant migration within Mexico has been that of the Yaqui Indians. Their continuing struggle for economic and cultural survival, waged against Spanish and Mexican governments, resulted, during the Porfiriato, in their being hunted and herded across Mexico— from Sonora to Yucatán—to work the henequen plantations. Their land, confiscated by the government, was then leased to North American mining interests.

After the U.S. war with Mexico of 1846–1848, in which the United States acquired half of Mexico's territory, there was a reverse migration south. Dispossessed of their land by Anglo interpretation of a legal system they did not understand, many people returned to Mexico. Others left, unwilling to relinquish their Mexican citizenship.

The Indio/Spaniard/Mestizo experience from the earliest time has known migration in all its aspects. These movements have been for reasons related to economic oppression, political persecution, and cultural survival. As a result Mexican history has been nourished by deep human experiences which have inevitably been reflected in rich and imaginative literary expression.

Most of the Aztec Codices containing the myth of origin and documenting Aztec history and thought were burned by the Spaniards during the holocaust of the conquest. Of the few that were saved, some have been translated into Spanish. In these excerpts from *Crónica Mexicayotl*, the Aztec historian Tezozómoc, writing after the conquest, relates the migration from Aztlán, the arrival and settlement in the Valley of Mexico, where the Aztecs found the "eagle perched atop a cactus."

CRÓNICA MEXICAYOTL

fernando alvarado tezozómoc

principio de la crónica

8. He aquí el comienzo de la crónica de la mexicanidad, en la cual se habla del renombre, origen y nacimiento, del mismísimo principio, partida y advenimiento de quienes vinieron aquí a la Nueva España a radicarse y a ganarse todo cuanto hay aquí de grande; y también se trata de cuando comenzó, dió principio y tuvo arraigo la ciudad de México Tenochtitlan (llámaseles mexicanos, chichimecas. gentes de Aztlan, chicomoztoquenses); empero, ya no se recuerda bien cuándo o en qué época haya sucedido.

14. Entonces salieron los chichimecas, los aztecas, de Aztlan, que era su morada, en el año uno-pedernal.

15. Por allá permanecieron entonces mucho tiempo, cuando se hallaban radicados, esparcidos allá en Aztlan los chichimecas, los aztecas: durante mil y catorce años, según resulta del cómputo anual de los ancianos; y entonces se vinieron a pie para acá.

17. El lugar de su morada tiene por nombre Aztlan, y por eso se les nombra aztecas; y tiene por segundo nombre el de Chicomoztoc, y sus nombres son estos de aztecas y mexicanos; y hoy día verdaderamente se les llama, se les nombra mexicanos; pero después vinieron aquí a tomar el nombre de tenochcas.

18. Los mexicanos salieron de allá del lugar llamado Aztlan, el cual se halla en mitad del agua; de allá partieron para acá los que componían los siete "calpulli".

19. El Aztlan de los antiguos mexicanos es lo que hoy día se denomina Nuevo México; reinaba allá el llamado Moctezuma. Este rey tenía dos hijos, y al tiempo de su muerte establece como señores a sus mencionados hijos. El nombre del primogénito, quien habría de ser el rey de los cuextecas, no se sabe bien. El menor, que era mexicano, se llamaba Mexi, era de nombre Chalchiuhtlatonac, y a él habíansele de adjudicar los mexicanos, habría de ser señor suyo el mencionado Chalchiuhtlatonac.

30. Según cuentan los ancianos, cuando los aztecas vinieron de Aztlan no se llamaban todavía mexicanos, sino que aún se llamaban todos aztecas,

y hasta después de esto que relatamos fué cuando tomaron el nombre, y se denominan mexicanos. Según esto, entonces se les dió dicho nombre: como dicen los ancianos, quien les dió el nombre fué Huitzilopochtli.

35. Bastante tiempo, así pues, vagaron los mexicanos por tierras chichimecas; cuando se asentaban en algún lugar bueno permanecían como por unos veinte años; cuando se hallaban a gusto se establecían en el sitio por dos, tres, cuatro, cinco, diez o quince años; cuando no se sentían a gusto se establecían como por veinte o cuarenta días (fueron a salír a Cuextecatl-Ichocayan y a Coatl-Icamac); por todas partes daban nombres a la tierra; por alimento y sustento venían comiendo carne, frijol, bledos, "chía", chile y jitomate.

90. Y luego de noche cuando lo vió, cuando se lo procuró al "teo-mama" de nombre Cuauhtlequetzqui o tal vez Cuauhcoatl él Huitzilopochtli le dijo: "¡oh Cuauhcoatl! pues visteis todo lo que allá yace dentro del carrizo, os maravillasteis. Y pues oídlo aún otra cosa la que todavía no veis, y al punto id vosotros, id a ver el "tenochtli", allá lo veréis, por lo que alegremente sobre, está en pie ella, el águila allá come, allá se calienta al sol, y pues por esto se satisface vuestro corazón, pues él, el corazón de Copil que arrojaste cuando allá te paraste en Tlalcocomocco, y luego allá vino a caer lo que visteis al borde del escondrijo, al borde de la cueva, en Acatza-llan, en Toltzallan, y pues allá nació el corazón de Copil, ahora lo llamamos tenochtli (tuna dura) y pues allá estaremos, guardaremos, esperaremos, nos reuniremos con la diversa gente, nuestro pecho, nuestra cabeza, nuestra flecha, nuestro escudo lo con que les veremos a todos estará nuestro poblado, Mexico Tenochtitlan, el lugar en que grita el águila, se despliega y come, el lugar en que nada el pez, el lugar en el que es desgarrada la serpiente, México Tenochtitlan, y acaecerán muchas cosas"; e inmediatamente dijo Cuauhcoatl: "Está bien, ¡oh sacerdote! Ha otorgado tu corazón: óiganlo por tanto tus padres, y los ancianos todos", y de inmediato reunió Cuauhcoatl a los mexicanos, y les notificó la plática de Huitzilopochtli, oyéndola ellos.

BEGINNING OF THE CHRONICLE

fernando alvarado tezozómoc

8. Here begins the chronicle of the Mexicans, in which mention is made of the renown, origin and birth, of the very beginning and arrival of those who came here to New Spain to live and to earn for themselves all that is good here; and also it treats of when it all commenced, when Mexico Tenochtitlán began and was settled (they have been called Mexicanos, Chichimecas, people of Aztlán, Chicomoztoquenses); however, it is not remembered when or in what epoch it happened.

14. And then the Chichimecas, the Aztecas, left Aztlán which was their home, in the year one flint.

15. There they then remained for a long time, when they found themselves established, scattered throughout Aztlán, the Chichimecas, the Aztecas; for one thousand and fourteen years according to the annual computation of the ancients. And then they set out on foot to come here.

17. Their dwelling place is called Aztlán and that is why they are called Aztecs; and the second name of their settlement is Chicomoztoc, and the peoples' names are thus Aztecs or Mexicans; and today they are truly called, they are named Mexicans; but then they came here to take the name of Tenochcas.

18. The Mexicans departed from there, from the place called Aztlán, which is found in the midst of water; from there they came here, the group that comprise the seven "Calpulli."

19. The Aztlán of the ancient Mexicans is what today is called New Mexico: He who ruled there was named Moctezuma. This king had two sons, and at the time of his death he established these sons as Lords. The name of the first born son who was to become king of the Cuextecas is not known. The youngest son who was a Mexican was named Mexi, his title was Chalchiuhtlatonac, and the Mexican had appropriated themselves to him, this aforementioned Chalchiuhtlatonac was to be their Lord.

30. According to our old people, when the Aztecs came from Aztlán they were not yet called Mexicans, but all were called Aztecs, and only after the happenings we are here describing was when they took the name and called themselves Mexicans. Accordingly such a name was given to them: As our oldsters tell it, it was Huitzilopochtli who gave them the name.

35. For a long time, the Mexicans wandered through the lands of the Chichimecas; when they established themselves in a good place they remained there for some twenty years; when they were comfortable in a site they stayed for two, three, four, ten or fifteen years. When they were not comfortable, they remained for twenty or forty days. (They left from Cuextecatl-Ichocayan and from Coatl-Icomac). Everywhere they named the land; for nourishment and sustenance they ate meat, beans and wild amaranth, "chia," chile and tomatoes.

90. And at night when he saw it, when the "teomama" named Cuauhtlequetzqui or perhaps Cuauhcoatl found it, Huitzilopochtli told him: "Oh Cuauhcoatl! If you could see everything which lies among the reeds you would be astonished. And hear something which you cannot yet see, and then go, take yourself to see the "tenochtli," there you will see it, an eagle resting on the cactus and eating, the sun is warm there and thus your heart is happy. For it is the heart of Copil which you threw away when you stopped at Tlalcocomocco and it came back to rest there at the edge of the hiding place, by the cave, in Acatzallan, in Toltzallan, and there

the heart of Copil was born, now we call it tenochtli (hard prickly pear) and there we shall all be, we shall guard it, we shall all wait, we will be reunited with our diverse peoples, our breast, our head, our arrow, our shield where we shall see everyone, our entire city, Mexico Tenochtitlán, the place where the eagle screams, where it descends and eats, the place where fishes swim, the place where the snake is torn asunder, Mexico-Tenochtitlán where many things will come to pass"; and Cuauhcoatl immediately answered: I agree oh priest. Your heart has been offered: may your parents and all the old people hear it. And immediately Cuauhcoatl assembled the Mexicans, and told them the discourse spoken by Huitzilopochtli which they heard.

Enforced migration of the Indians during the repartimientos and reducciones of the colonial period were related by Fray Bartolomé de las Casas in letters to his bishops and other church authorities. Las Casas was one of the few Spanish clerics who defended the Indians during the Spanish conquest.

DE LA REPARTICIÓN DE LOS PUEBLOS INDIOS

fray bartolomé de las casas

La segunda razón por que se impide el dicho fin y conversión de aquellas gentes, teniendo señorío y mando sobre ellas, como hasta aquí, los españoles, es porque como para cumplir con los dichos españoles, especialmente con los que se jactan de conquistadores y con otros que son amigos o deudos de los gobernadores, o que tienen de acá o de allá algún favor, les hayan de repartir los pueblos de los indios, y acaesce dar entre dos, y tres, y cuatro un pueblo, dando tantos a uno y tantos a otro, y ha acaecido llevar la mujer repartida un español, y el marido otro, y los hijos otro, como si fuesen cochinos, y cada uno ocupa los indios que le caben en una hacienda y en un tiempo, y en una parte de tierra; y el otro, por el contrario, en otra y en tiempo y partes diversas de los otros; y otros los envían cargados a las minas como bestias; otros los llevan o los alquilan por recuas, treinta, y cuarenta, y cincuenta, y ciento, y docientas leguas para llevar cargas, y esto cada día lo vemos y esperimentamos.

Y para estorbar esto no basta habelles Vuestra Majestad mandado tasar los tributos y puesto penas que no lleven ni los trabajen más, ni bastará, aunque les dijesen que habían de perder las vidas, como probaremos abajo. De donde salen y los indios padecen, sin los otros muchos, dos evidentísimos daños y que son directamente contrarios y estorbativos de poder los indios oír la palabra de Dios, ni jamás ser en cosa de nuestra sancta fe doctrinados.

El uno, que son puestos en gran captiverio, como abajo diremos. El otro, que son desparcidos y derramados por muchas partes. Los cuales ambos a dos daños e inconvenientes son más que otros de directos enemigos y condenados por la ley de Dios, como dos cosas muy eficaces que impiden la predicación y dilatación della y salvación de las ánimas; porque para cualquiera gente y pueblos o naciones oigan y reciban alguna ley y sean instruídos en ella y puedan guardalla, dos cosas, o disposiciones, de directo contrarias de los dos dichos inconvenientes necesariamente se requieren. La primera, que sea pueblo, conviene a saber, que viva la gente junta social y popularmente, porque de otra manera, si la promulgación de la ley oyeren diez no la oirán ciento ni mill; y, por consiguiente, ni tendrán obligación a guardalla, ni tampoco la podrán guardar. La segunda, que tengan libertad, porque no siendo libres no pueden ser parte de pueblo, ni tampoco, ya que les constase, no la podrán guardar, por estar al albedrío y servicio ordinario dedicados de otro.

OF THE DIVISION AND DISTRIBUTION OF INDIAN VILLAGES

fray bartolomé de las casas

The second reason for the frustration of our general aim to convert these people, over whom the Spaniards have control and authority, stems from having to comply with these same Spaniards—especially with those who boast of being conquistadores, and with others who are friends or kin of the governors, or who have some favor due them from one place or another. To these people it is necessary to distribute the Indian villages. The way it turns out, sometimes one village is given to two, three, or four Spaniards, with so many Indians distributed to one, and so many to the next. And it has happened that one Spaniard received an Indian's wife, another the husband, and a third the children, as though they were swine. And each one works the Indians that fit on his estate at the time of his need, and on the land he chooses; while the next Spaniard, on the other hand, sends them to work different land, at different times and places than the rest. Others send them to the mines loaded like beasts; others rent them out like teams of mules to carry loads for thirty, forty, even one or two hundred leagues. This we see as daily practice.

To stop this, it is not enough for Your Majesty to order that the tributes these people pay you be verified, or to assign penalties for those who abuse the Indians, nor would it be enough even to threaten the abusers with their lives, as shall be shown below. From all this come two kinds of abuses which the Indians, not others, suffer, and which directly prevent the Indians from hearing God's word or accepting indoctrination in our holy faith. One abuse is that they are kept in captivity, as we shall show below. The other is that they are dispersed and spread out over many places. Both these abuses are greater than what is meted out to direct enemies, or to those who are condemned according to God's law. They function effectively to prevent propagation of the faith and the salvation of souls. In fact, in order for any people or nation to listen to and to accept a new code of law, and to learn it and keep it, two things are required—and both are contrary to the abuses mentioned above. The first is that it be a community, that is, that the people live together socially and in good numbers. If this were not so, if the law were to be heard only by ten people instead of one hundred or one thousand, they would have no obligation to uphold it. The second requirement is that they have liberty, for if they are not free they cannot be part of their community, nor can they uphold the law, since they are at the whim and the service of someone else.

Another example of people dislocated from their homes and forced to enter a pattern of migration is that of the Tzeltal Indians in Chiapas. In *Los hombres verdaderos*, (1959), a Tzeltal narrator relates his own experience as a ten year old boy, contracting himself to an enganchador, leaving his highland home and going to work in a coffee plantation in the lowlands. The bilingual nature of the text, in Tzeltal and Spanish, reflects the strength and vitality of the Tzeltales, who in the twentieth century continue to struggle to regain their land and to reestablish an ejido system of agriculture. Another index of confidence in their own culture is the self description of the Tzeltales as "The True People."

LOS HOMBRES VERDADEROS

carlo antonio castro

Más tarde conocí a un ladino que daba dinero a quienes querían ir a las fincas. ¡Las fincas! Lugares de trabajo, lejos, allá donde yo nunca había estado, pero donde mi *tat* sufrió tanto. Sabía las cosas de asombro que era posible admirar en la tierra caliente, donde no había necesidad, según decían, de llevar siempre el chamarro, donde el aire permitía lucir la camisa del hombre verdadero; donde había enormes ríos, en los que nadaba *ayin,* el animal de las quijadas como sierras y la piel como tronco, del que pocos creían la existencia. ¡Las fincas!

Los hombres se vendían entonces para ir a trabajar a esos lugares. Y así fue como yo también me vendí, junto con dos hijos de mi *tajún,* tío paterno, hermano mayor de mi padre, ellos también mis mayores, como hermanos míos.

Pasó un mes.

Dejé mi casa y me encaminé a Oxchuc.

Los ladinos tenían allí muchas casas y el enganchador un lugar donde atendía sus negocios. Entré, saludando:

—Señor *ajwalil,* ¿cuándo vamos a partir para la finca?

Contestó a mi pregunta:

—El día cinco del mes en que sale la fiesta de los alumnos de este pueblo.

Hablaba bien el idioma verdadero.

Este ladino era *puj puj,* barrigón. Tenía barbas grandes; decían que era de un lugar muy lejano, llamado *Tusta* por los *kaxlanes* y por los jóvenes tzeltales, pero que nusetros viejos nombraban *T'ulum,* tierra de los conejos.

Los enganchadores que distraían su espera contaban lo que sabían del *puj puj kaxlán.* Que a veces pegaba mucho, cuando estaba impaciente; que en ocasiones, ofrecía a los hombres de verdad hasta bocados de su propia comida; que aunque aquí se reducía su propiedad a la del sitio en que arreglaba el enganche, allá lejos, en *T'ulum,* más allá de Jobel, en el fondo de inmensa cuesta, madre de cuestas menores, en el calentadero de los huesos, tenía casas de piedra, con huertas y animales; que era un hombre rico, *k'ulej.*

Pero apenas puedo hoy acordarme de todo esto.

Como entre sueños me parece oír su voz, cuando nos daba en la mano o nos aventaba las monedas del enganche, según estaba su corazón:

—¡Ujú...! Ya eres mío, indito... ¡Díselo a los demás!

Llegó el cinco de septiembre.

Todos cuantos habíamos pedido dinero de la finca nos reunimos en mi pueblo. Salimos de Oxchuc y caminamos día y medio, durmiendo en el monte, para llegar a San Cristóbal, a Jobel.

En los grandes zacatales permanecimos una semana, esperando a los que se habían quedado en sus chozas. Mandaron a traerlos, ya con una multa de diez pesos a cada uno. Durante los días que pasé en Jobel, tuve mucho miedo; decían que, por orden de un jefe, no nos dejarían ir a los más pequeños hasta la tierra caliente; mi edad era ya la de diez años. Pero era poca para ese jefe de quien se hablaba. No lo conocí, ni él me vio a mí; como no se dio cuenta, pude ir a la finca.

Salimos de San Cristóbal y nos dirigimos por el camino hacia Jimxol, que los ladinos llaman Teopisca; allí hicimos nuestro primer alto. No íbamos solos: había un guía, responsable de pagarnos las tortillas en cada sitio donde dormíamos.

Nueve días caminamos todos cuantos nos habíamos reunido. Yo nunca había viajado así, sólo pequeñas caminatas, con mi padre, completé años atrás, y luego había estado en el *asento* cercano a mi pueblo. Pero dar paso y paso a lo largo del día no le cayó bien a mi cuerpo: en el camino encontré dolor de pies y fiebre. Y sentí mis males cada noche, en los sitios donde dormía.

Cumplidas nueve jornadas, a las once de la mañana, llegamos un día a la finca "Unión Juárez", cerca de los mojones del terreno de Guatemala. ¡Qué extraño veía yo ese lugar! Más verde que mi propia tierra, no había palabras en mi mente para distinguir los colores de los árboles. Pequeños *chinchán*, enteramente desconocidos para mí, revoloteaban, persiguiéndonos. Zumbaba la mosca, como borracha de viento.

Pronto nos dieron nuestra herramienta. De los hombres grandes, unos recibieron machetes para limpiar el cafetal, otros azadones para calzar las matas de café.

A nosotros, los keremelik, los pequeños nos dieron machetes usados para abrirnos el paso, cuando cortáramos el grano, el fruto rojo, y sólo debíamos hacerlo allá donde más maduro estaba; teníamos nuestro caporal aparte, no nos mezclábamos con los *winiketik*, mayores.

Apenas desqués de medianoche, la que hizo terminar el día en que llegamos, vino el mayordomo a pasar lista. Nos nombró para saber qué otras herramientas recibiríamos. Desayunamos en plena oscuridad, para luego dirigirnos al trabajo.

Los caporales formaban grupos separados de gente; al recibir un grupo, lo llevaban consigo. Nosotros nos fuimos a cortar café. Era de noche todavía cuando salimos hacia el cafetal; al llegar nos dieron dos surcos a cada uno, y no se veía aún cuando recibimos las indicaciones.

Nuestro caporal nos dijo:

—¡Cortan bien, donde están maduros los cafetos! ¡Y que no se quede ni un grano en el arbolito, ni debajo de la mata!

Hablaba en *la castilla*, mandando bruscamente; una que otra palabra podía yo oír, pero otro *kerem*, algo mayor, entendía más y me lo decía en palabras verdaderas.

Respondimos, todos, según nuestro entendimiento:

—¡Está bien, señor *ajwalil!*

Y dijo más:

—¡Que no se quiebren los gajos de café!

Luego me miró directamente:

—¡Si vos quebrás uno —me dijo— lo pagarás! ¡Un peso por cada ramita: ese es el precio!

Y gritándoles a todos, terminó:

¡Ya oyeron ustedes! Les anticipo mis palabras, si alguien no cumple ¡que me vea la cara!

Eso fue lo que el *kerem* me dijo que había dicho.

El día entero fue pasando para nosotros, muy difícil de aguantar: hacía mucho frío allá porque estábamos cerca del gran cerro, la madre del temblor.

Regresamos a las cuatro de la tarde; llegamos a dormir, sobre nuestros chamarros, sin petates; mentira que el calor era grande. ¡Toda la noche bailaron mis dientes!

Y así, pasó una semana...

Siete días se escondieron. El patrón nos dio nuestra ración de carne: medio kilo recibió cada hombre en la tarde del sábado. Y aquellos de entre nosotros que quisieron manejar dinero para hacer compras en la tienda, o en el mercado, recibieron también los centavos que el patrón daba a cuenta y que apuntaba cuidadosamente en su gran libro.

Domingo por la mañana.

Había quienes tomaban su aguardiente. Los viejos, en la borrachera, decían tener un *lab* poderoso. Esto sucedía con el que estaba al frente de nuestro grupo de descanso, en el que nos encontrábamos reunidos los prójimos, emparentados por nuestra tierra y nuestro pueblo.

El jefe de cada conjunto recibía cigarros, como regalo, de parte de quienes le obedecíamos; se trataba así de evitar que la enfermedad viniera a nosotros.

—¡Aquel que no ofrece cigarros, quien no da *may,* es porque no quiere vivir sobre el mundo!

Así decían los viejos.

Yo compraba cigarros, cada domingo, para el anciano, jefe y prójimo. Por ello nunca me enfermé; cumplí con lo que me aconsejaban mis primos hermanos:

—¡Debes seguir la costumbre!

—¡Regala cigarros!

Así me habían dicho.

Y también yo comencé a quemarme las orillas de la boca.

Tres meses nos vieron pasar.

El dueño de la finca ajustó nuestras deudas para ver quién tenía ganancia y quién estaba comprometido aún. Al término de esos días había hombres que debían muchísimo; otros, como yo, apenas alcanzamos a salir parejo. ¡Qué contento me puse de que así fuera!

Estaba ya aburrido de acarrear el fruto maduro del café. ¡Qué difícil me era llenar media caja! Apenas podía levantarla porque pesaba mucho, y había, quizá, dos leguas de distancia, del sitio donde se cortaba hasta el lugar de depósito. Y sólo cerros qué caminar; ningún plano se veía en el cafetal.

Tal como lo había contratado el jefe, pasados los seis meses se hizo la cuenta total de nuestro trabajo. Todos los hombres desquitaron entonces lo que debían y pudieron regresar a sus casas. Muy felices nos pusimos al salir de la finca; ¡como si me escapara de una cárcel, así sentí cuando tomamos el camino de regreso!

El poco dinero que gané en los seis meses sumaba dieciséis pesos. Salimos, pues, todos los compañeros, yendo mis dos primos y yo por nuestro lado, y dejamos la finca en el principio del camino.

THE TRUE PEOPLE

carlo antonio castro

Later I met a *ladino* who gave money to those who wanted to go to the big farms. The plantations! Places to work, far away, where I had never been, but where my *tat* suffered so. I knew about the wonderful things to be seen in the hot country where they said you did not need to wear a *chamarro* all the time, where the warmth allowed a True Man to show off his shirt, where there were enormous rivers in which there swam the *ayín,* the beast with jaws like a saw and hide like the trunk of a tree, an animal that few people believed in. The plantations!

Men sold themselves to go and work in those places. And so I sold myself, too, along with the two sons of my *tajún,* paternal uncle, my father's older brother. These two boys were also older than me and like brothers to me.

A month passed. I left my house and went to Oxchuc. The *ladinos* had many houses there and the man who signed us up had a place where he conducted his business. I went in and said to him, "Señor *ajwalil,* when are we going to leave for the farm?"

He answered, "The fifth day of the month in which the students of this town have their fiesta." He spoke the True Language well.

This stranger was *puj puj,* pot bellied. He had a big beard; they said he was from a place a long way off, called Tusta by the *kaxláns* and the young Tzeltals, but which our old people called T'ulum, land of the rabbits.

The other agents passed away their free time telling what they knew of the *puj puj kaxlán.* That sometimes when he was impatient he beat people, that sometimes he even offered mouthfuls of his own food to the True People, that although here his only property was the place in which he made the contracts, far away, in T'ulum, beyond Jobel, beyond a huge mountain, the mother of lesser mountains, in a country that warmed one's bones, he had stone houses with fields and animals, that he was a rich man, a *k'ulej.* But today I can scarcely remember all that. I seem to hear his voice as if in a dream, when he handed or tossed us the contract money, according to his mood: "Uh-uh! Now you're mine, little Indian! Go tell the rest!"

The fifth of September arrived.

All of us who had asked for money from the plantation met in my town. We left Oxchuc and walked for a day and a half, sleeping in the woods, to get to San Cristóbal, to Jobel.

We remained for a week in the pastures waiting for those who had stayed in their huts. They sent out to get them and charged each one a ten peso fine. I spent the days in Jobel full of fear. They said that, by order of a boss, the youngest of us could not go to *tierra caliente,* the hot country. I was ten years old but that wasn't old enough for the boss they spoke of. I did not meet him, and he did not see me; as he did not know about me, I got to go to the farm.

We left San Cristóbal and went on the road to Jixmol, which the *ladinos* call Teopisca; there we made our first stop. We were not on our own; there was a leader who had the job of giving us our tortillas at every place where we slept.

All of us who had met together walked for nine days. I had never traveled like that, I had only taken short trips years ago with my father, and later I had been on the *asento* near my town. To walk and walk all day long was hard on my body; on the way I had a fever and sore feet. Every night, wherever we slept, I felt aches and pains.

After nine days' journey, at eleven in the morning, we reached the Unión Juárez Plantation, near the boundary of Guatemala. How strange that land seemed to me! It was greener than my own country; I knew no words to describe the different colors of the trees. Little *chinchán,* that I had never seen before, flew around tormenting us. Flies buzzed about, whirling drunkenly.

Soon they gave us our tools. Some of the grown men received machetes to clean up the fields, others got hoes to cultivate the coffee trees. We younger ones, the *keremetik,* were given worn machetes to clear the way for us when we cut the coffee berries, the red berries, and we were only to pick where they were the ripest. We had our own foreman and we did not mix with the *winiketik,* the men.

Shortly after midnight of the day on which we arrived, the boss came to call the roll. He checked us to know what other tools we needed. We had breakfast in the dark, and got off to work right away.

The foreman made separate groups of workers and when a group was chosen, it started off with its leader. We went out to cut coffee. It was nighttime when we set out toward the coffee field and when we arrived they gave us two rows each. It still wasn't light yet when we got our orders.

Our foreman said to us, "Cut where the coffee trees are ripe! And don't leave a single berry on the tree or under the branches!" He was giving rough commands in *castilla;* I could get an occasional word, but another *kerem,* a little older than I, understood more and he told me in the True Language.

We all replied, according to our understanding, "All right, señor *ajwalil.*"

And he added: "Don't break the branches of the trees!" Then he looked straight at me, "If you break one, you'll pay for it! A peso for every little branch; that's the price! I am telling you beforehand that if you don't do as you are told, you'll have me to deal with!"

That's what the *kerem* told me he had said.

The whole day went by and it was long and hard for us; it was very cold there because we were near the great mountain, the mother of the earthquake. We returned at four in the afternoon and slept on our *chamarros,* without straw mats. It's a lie that it was hot! My teeth chattered all night!

And so a week passed by. . .

Seven days slipped over the horizon. The boss gave us our ration of meat; each man got a half a kilo on Saturday afternoon. And anyone who wanted money to buy things at the store or in the market got some on account from the boss, who put it all down carefully in his big book.

Sunday morning. Some were drinking their liquor. The old ones were boasting in their drunkenness of having a powerful *lab.* This happened with the leader of our rest group, where we had gathered like old friends drawn together by being from the same neighborhood and from the same town.

The chief of each group was given cigarettes by those of us who followed him; that's the way we tried to keep illness away from us.

"Anyone who doesn't give cigarettes, who doesn't offer *may,* doesn't want to live long in this world!" So spoke the old man. I bought cigarettes every Sunday for the elder who was our chief. So I was never sick; I took the advice of my cousins.

"You must follow custom!"

"Give cigarettes!"

That's what they had told me. And I also began to burn the edges of my own mouth.

Three months passed by.

The owner of the farm counted up our debts to see who had earned money and who was still in debt. At the end of that time there were men who owed a great deal; others, like me, just broke even. How glad I was that it was like that for me!

I was getting tired of carrying the ripe coffee berries. It was so hard for me to fill half a box! I could scarcely lift it, it was so heavy, and it was two leagues from where the coffee was cut to the place where it was to be left. And there were always hills to climb; there was no flat ground on the coffee farm.

After six months, the boss counted up all our work as he had promised in the contract. By that time all the men had paid off what they owed and could go home. And weren't we happy to leave the plantation! I felt as if I were escaping from jail the day we set out for home.

The money I earned in six months amounted to only sixteen pesos. All our companions left the farm and my two cousins and I went our way alone.

(trans. by Mauda Sandvig)

Imposed migration is treated below as one of the elements that gave rise to the struggle for social justice, culminating in the Mexican Revolution of 1910.

In this excerpt from a modern novel by Carlos Fuentes, *La muerte de Artemio Cruz* (1962), a Yaqui soldier explains his people's struggle to maintain land and culture. This was his reason for joining the Revolution.

LA MUERTE DE ARTEMIO CRUZ

carlos fuentes

Ahora el yaqui estaba murmurando cosas en su lengua y él se fue arrastrando los pies hasta la cabecera dura, a tocar con la mano la frente afiebrada del indio y a escuchar sus palabras. Corrían con un sonsonete dulce.

—¿Qué dice?

—Cuenta cosas. De cómo el gobierno les quitó las tierras de siempre para dárselas a unos gringos. De cómo ellos pelearon para defenderlas y entonces llegó la tropa federal y empezó a cortarles las manos a los hombres y a perseguirlos por el monte. De cómo subieron a los jefes yaquis a un cañonero y desde allí los tiraron al mar cargados de pesas.

El yaqui hablaba con los ojos cerrados. —Los que quedamos fuimos arrastrados a una fila muy larga y desde allá, desde Sinaloa, nos hicieron caminar hasta el otro lado, hasta Yucatán.

—De cómo tuvieron que marchar hasta Yucatán y las mujeres y los viejos y los niños de la tribu se iban quedando muertos. Los que lograron llegar a las haciendas henequeneras fueron vendidos como esclavos y separados los esposos de sus mujeres. De cómo obligaron a las mujeres a acostarse con los chinos, para que olvidaran su lengua y parieran más trabajadores...

—Volví, volví. Apenas supe que había estallado la guerra, volví con mis hermanos a luchar contra el daño.

El yaqui rió quedamente.

THE DEATH OF ARTEMIO CRUZ

carlos fuentes

Now the Yaqui was murmuring in his Indian tongue. Artemio Cruz went to the stone ledge and put his hand on Tobías' fevered forehead and listened to his words, a soft singsong...

"What?"

"I was telling about it. How the government took our land away to give it to gringos. About how we fought to defend our land and then the Federals came and cut off men's hands and chased us though the mountains. How they captured the Yaqui chiefs in a big canyon and tied weights on them and threw them into the sea."

The Yaqui talked with closed eyes. "Those of us who were left were lined up in a long column and marched all the way from Sinaloa to Yucatán.

"We had to march to Yucatán and the women and children and old people of the tribe couldn't take it and began to die. Those who survived to get to the sisal plantations were sold as slaves. Men and their wives were separated. They made the women sleep with Chinese, to make them forget the language and breed more workers...

"I came back, I came back. As soon as I knew that a war had begun, I came back with my brothers to fight against the persecution."

The Yaqui laughed quietly.

(trans. by Sam Hileman)

II

cuando vino el alambre—
vino el hambre

By the end of the eighteenth century the Indo-Hispano migrations had increased, and settlements had been established in California, New Mexico, Texas, and Arizona. Spanish/Indian traditions and systems took firm root. The land flourished with new methods of irrigation, diverse agricultural crops, and domestic and farm animals introduced by the colonizers. Cattle, horse, and sheep raising became the major occupation of the population.

This section, covering migration in the Southwest during the nineteenth and early twentieth centuries, treats the vaquero, the trasquilador, and el trabajador del traque. The first two, seldom considered participants in the migratory experience, came with the early settlements. Their particular life style evolved out of the reality they encountered in the territory. They adapted their knowledge of the land, the skills of horsemanship and sheep raising to the demands of sustaining life in the Southwest.

The life and experiences of these men who left an indelible imprint on the early Southwest are reflected in various forms of literary expression. They had their poets, their composers, and their makers of legends whose corridos, coplas, and stories distill the essence of their experience. The basis of this literary expression was a rich vocabulary dealing with the new phenomena they constantly came upon. This linguistic legacy was appropriated by the dominant society—sin darles crédito.

"Los reenganchados a Kansas," the last selection in this part, is especially significant. For this was the time of railroad building in the Southwest. The major historic processes that would determine the course of Chicano migratory labor history were being set in motion. In the United States this was the era of consolidation of westward expansion, of prosperity generated by the new technology, and of a deepening North-South split. The motivation of the Anglos controlling Texas was to make a new slave state. Thus Mexicans who found themselves part of Texas faced incorporation into a society whose very foundations were racist. The imperialist philosophy of the United States culminated in the war with Mexico of 1846–1848. Inhabitants of the newly won territories were given one year to decide between accepting U.S. citizenship or returning to Mexico.

To the vaquero and the trasquilador the railroads meant displacement and the undermining of a way of life. Vast acres of grazing lands were fenced off and made ready to be crisscrossed by steel rails. It is one of the ironies of history that Mexicans, legally and illegally contracted to work the railroad chain gangs, receiving a lower wage than other workers, were indirectly involved in helping to displace their compatriots. Yet, these men and their families were responsible for settling many of the present barrios and colonias, especially in the midwestern states.

Also important in this period is the impact of the new technology. The advent of refrigerated railcars and the laying of rail-lines across the United States meant that perishable agricultural products could be picked, packed, and shipped long distances without loss to either producer or consumer. This immediately increased the need for arable land to meet the new demand for foodstuffs, which logically increased the need for laborers to work the crops. And the cycle began. Land was acquired through legal and extra-legal force, as Anglos dispossessed Mexican owners of the acreage guaranteed them by the Treaty of Guadalupe Hidalgo. Some hacendados returned to Mexico, participating in a reverse migration. Mexicans who remained in the Southwest were forced to live on the fringes of the rising Anglo society, which neither understood nor accepted them. Whether former small landholders, or landless peons, they were dislocated from their homes and denied participation in the new social structure, becoming unwilling prey to the increasing demand for agricultural laborers.

The meaning implicit in "cuando vino el alambre vino el hambre" is that the introduction of fencing signaled the beginning of dislocation, of migration, and of hunger for Mexicans and their progeny. Throughout the uprooting and constant movement of the migrations, the people endured—they innovated, incorporated and changed as the diversity and richness of the following selections illustrate. Their literary response was multiple. In some texts, such as "Imparcialidad de la muerte," they are clearly drawing upon the past. In others, "Songs of the vaqueros," for example, the poet responds with originality to new experiences and landscapes.

The hard life of the vaquero, the imminent presence of death, and the
dangers involved in the two-month cattle drive from Texas to Kansas are
recounted in this corrido describing the death of a young vaquero. This
poem provides an interesting literary background for study of Juan Gómez,
the historic organizer of vaqueros in the 1880s. This version of "La corrida de
Kiansas" is one variant of an early border corrido.

EL CORRIDO DE KIANSIS

anonymous

Cuando salimos pa' Kiansis
con una grande partida,
¡ah, qué camino tan largo!
no contaba con mi vida.

Nos decía el caporal,
como queriendo llorar,
—Allá va la novillada,
no me la dejen pasar.

Ibamos por el camino y
nos pescó un aguacero.
Pa' poderlos detener
les formamos un tiroteo.

En la corrida de Kiansis
(ni me quisiera acordar),
caporales y vaqueros
no más nos faltó llorar.

Llegamos al Río Salado
y nos tiramos a nado.
decía un americano
—Esos hombres ya se hogaron.

Pues qué pensaría ese gringo
que venimos a esprimintar
si somos del Río Grande,
de los buenos pa'nadar.

Eran quinientos novillos
y toditos muy livianos;
no pudieron detenerlos
ni entre treinta americanos.

Los novillos eran bravos,
no los podían separar;

THE CORRIDO OF KANSAS

anonymous

When we left for Kansas
with a very large herd
The road was so long
I couldn't even count on my life.

The foreman told us,
almost wanting to cry.
There goes the herd of young steers,
for my sake, don't let them pass.

We were on the road
caught by a strong rainstorm
We had a shooting spree
in order to contain them.

On the cattle drive to Kansas
I don't even want to remember
foremen and cowboys alike
we almost started to cry.

We got to the Salado River
and started to swim,
one American said
Those men have already drowned.

What did that gringo think
that we were yearlings,
why we are from the Río Grande
and know how to swim.

There were five hundred steers
and they were all very wild;
they couldn't be controlled
even by thirty Americans.

The steers were wild
they couldn't separate them;

gritaba el americano:
—Que se baje el caporal.

El caporal tuvo miedo
y un vaquero se arrojó
a que lo matara un toro.
No más a eso se bajó.

Llegaron diez mejicanos
y al punto los embarcaron
y los treinta americanos
se quedaron azorados.

La mujer de Alberto Flores
le pregunta al caporal:
—¿Dónde se ha quedado mi hijo,
que no lo he visto llegar?

Señora, si le dijera
se pusiera usté a llorar;
a su hijo lo mató un toro
en las puertas de un corral."

Treinta pesos alcanzó
pero todo limitado,
y trescientos puse yo
pa' haberlo sepultado.

Todos los aventureros
lo fueron a acompañar,
con sus sombreros en las manos,
a verlo sepultar.

Ya con ésta me despido
con 'l amor de mi querida.
Aquí se acaban cantando
los versos de la corrida.

one American yelled:
"Let the foreman get down."

The foreman was scared
so a cowboy volunteered
Only to be killed by a bull
Just for that he got down.

Ten Mexicans arrived
and immediately controlled the steers
and the thirty Americans
were left astounded.

The wife of Alberto Flores
comes up to ask the foreman:
"Where has my son stayed
for I have not seen him arrive?

Ma'm if I told you
you would start to weep;
your son was killed by a bull
on the doors of a corral.

Thirty pesos was his wages
but it was all owed.
and I put in three hundred
to have him buried.

All the drovers
went to accompany him,
with hats in hand
they saw him buried.

And now I say farewell
with thoughts of my beloved.
We come also to the end
of this cattle driving song.

(trans. by Paul S. Taylor)

In his book, *The Vaquero*, Arnold Rojas presents a historic treatment of the men of the range and of an era now past. With a sense for accurate documentation to correct misconceptions about these men, he traces the origin of the vaquero in the Southwest to the Moors, and distinguishes between the "buckaroo" of the Gulf Coast, rooted in African tradition, and the vaquero/cowboy of the Pacific.

His descriptions of the experiences shared on the open range with other men, of long cattle drives and lonely hours, are written with the perception, sensitivity and warmth of a man who himself lived and enjoyed life as a vaquero.

THE VAQUERO

arnold rojas

The blood of caballeros, bullfighters, Jews, Moors, Basques, and Indian heroes ran in the vaquero's veins. He was a strange mixture of races. He admired his Iberian father, but sided and sympathized with his raped Indian mother. If food was short he fed his horse before he fed his wife. Though often a strange contradiction, he was, without doubt, the most interesting man in the New World.

He was a descendant of the old conquerors, and retained the language of Spain. In living the free life of the nomad he imitated the Spaniard in the trappings of his horse, and the Indian in his abode. He spent his wealth on silver-mounted bits and spurs and often left his home destitute of necessities. He slept on the ground, but rode a silver-mounted saddle. He may not have combed his hair, but his horse's mane was trimmed, with one tuft for a colt and two for a bridle horse. He was named after the saint's day on which he was born; it was often Jesús who was the most proficient in stealing cattle.

The vaquero would lie on the ground with his saddle for a pillow even though the rain was falling, and sleep without a word of complaint, yet he would grumble when his saddle-blankets got wet. Wet saddle-blankets make a horse's back sore.

The vaquero's way of life gave him virtues which do not exist in this modern day, and at this distant time no man can judge a man of that era. His life was hard. He would stand shivering in the early morning cold, holding a cup of coffee in his shaking hand, then sit a horse all day in the driving sleet, chilled to the bone. He would ride from dawn to dusk in a cloud of alkali dust, his tongue parched and swollen, with rippling water in a mirage shimmering in the distance, with visions of all the water he had ever drunk or seen wasted haunting his memory, for memory plays queer, cruel tricks. The want of water was the vaquero's greatest hardship in the burning heat of a San Joaquin Valley summer. He often rode in a daze with visions of springs of cool water bubbling out of the pine-scented Sierra, of canals of water from which he had never bothered to drink. And when he came to drink it would more than likely be out of a reeking waterhole that contained the putrid remains of some animal. But there was another side. A matchless sky overhead. An expanse of wild flowers that spread over the great valley like a purple carpet, so vast that a day's ride would take one only to the middle of it. The bold, brooding Sierra standing in grim outline that stretched away to the northern horizon. A wild chase down a mountainside in the fall when the air is like wine and life is good. The feel of a good horse between one's knees as he sweeps and wheels around a herd of restless cattle. The evening campfire when men broil *costillas,* ribs, on chamiso root coals, and gather around to tell tales of long ago, of Murrieta, Vásquez, and García.

A mutual history of social and economic oppression, a nonwestern philosophic orientation, and kinships resulting from intermarriage are compelling reasons for Chicano and Native American solidarity. In these excerpts from the chapter on "The Indian Vaquero", Arnold Rojas, from a non-Anglo perspective, interprets the role of the Indian vaquero in the Southwest.

TODOS SOMOS INDIOS

arnold rojas

When a vaquero was especially skilled, and he was asked how he had reached such a degree of proficiency, his answer would invariably be: *"Me crié entre los Indios."* I was raised among the Indians. Or when some vaquero had performed his work with great skill, the other men would look at each other, smile approvingly, and say, *"Se crió entre los Indios pues."* Well, he was brought up among the Indians.

Contrary to a lot of false statements, a man took pride in calling himself "Indio." The Indian vaquero was highly respected for his skill and good qualities—that is, by those who knew him. And the proof is that very few of the men who have ridden on the Tejón stayed there any length of time without becoming *"Indios del Tejón,"* Tejón Indians, whatever their true race may have been.

At night around the fire a note of awe would creep into the old man's voice, as he told of hard riding Indian vaqueros who had roped grizzly bears and led wild cattle out of the Sierra, men who had become legends on the Tejón Ranch.

The vaquero or buckaroo who herded the cattle on the ranches of California was sometimes a Cahuilla, a Piute, a Mission Indian, or a member of one of the numerous tribes which populated California. Sometimes he was a Sonoreño, that is to say, a native of the state of Sonora in Old Mexico, or a descendant of Sonoreños born in California. Sometimes he was a Californian of pioneer colonial stock, like Don Jesús López. At other times he was from Baja California like Federico Lamas, and sometimes he was a gringo. Once in a while a Chilean was met among the vaquero crews.

The Indian vaquero was sparing in speech, and serene under all circumstances. He was pithy in all his expressions and often spoke in metaphor or ironically. One would have to be well acquainted with him to know his meanings. He had a knack for giving names which never failed to correspond to something risible in their owners. To a man on Tejón who rode humped up over his horse the other men applied the name *El Tacuachi*, the Possum. They would say of a man who showed much Indian blood in his makeup, *Ese no le debe ni los Buenos Días a los Españoles*— that one doesn't owe even a "good day" to the Spaniards.

> In her collections of Mexican/Chicano folklore, Jovita González has devoted several sections to the vaquero. The three love songs included in this page are brief and have only one theme: speaking to the loved one of hopes for a life together. In "La Palomita" and "Mi Querida Nicolasa", the poet weaves a song around the elements in his environment that have meaning to him—nature and his work—and offers them to his love, inviting her to share them with him. The last song, lamenting the death of the vaquero's horse, gives a sense of the bond that existed between the man and his animal.

SONGS OF THE VAQUERO

collected by
jovita gonzález

la palomita

Palomita ven pronto a mi tierra
y estaremos en gracia de Dios
subiremos del monte a la sierra
y estaremos felices los dos.
Por que quiero yo nunca dejarte
rendido adorarte
si te amo yo a ti.
Palomita ven pronto a mi tierra
y estaremos en gracia de Dios.

mi caballo bayo

Ya no vuelve a su palenque
mi fiel caballo, no vuelve, no;
ya no relincha de gozo,
como cuando alguien lo acarició.
Maldita la suerte perra
que de repente me lo llevó.
¡Ay! mi pobre caballo bayo,
cuanto he llorado
cuando él murió.

mi querida nicolasa

Ay, mi querida Nicolasa,
si te vinieras conmigo,
te llevaría hasta mi casa,
en ancas de mi rosillo.

Mi machete y mi petate,
mi rosillo y mis espuelas,
¡ay! me han de dar tu linda mano
Chatita, aunque no quieras.

Que cosa pa' mí tan buena,
esperar en el potrero,
abrazar a mi morena
detracito de un maguey.

Después ya con su chamaco,
mi querida Nicolasa
componiendo sus macetas
pa'que esté chula su casa.

la trigueña

Trigueña hermosa, mi corazón se encuentra triste
porque no sabe si en algún tiempo le correspondes
yo te aseguro que en esta vida no hallas otro hombre
que te quiera trigueñita, como yo.

The theme of death as an equalizer, irrespective of class, here treated in a vaquero legend, has a long tradition in Mexican and Chicano literature. Implicit in this ironic story is a note of criticism directed at the Church, for its inability or unwillingness to treat all believers with equality. More important, it gives evidence that life experience was being transformed into imaginative stories and legends with moral evaluations about life.

This particular legend is from a collection of Southwestern folklore in which the collector, Aurora Lucero White, gathered the material with the help of the people in small towns and villages.

This theme, extending beyond Mexico, echoes the medieval European tradition of "La danza de la muerte," which in the fourteenth century presented death in the same terms as the text below. It is one example of the reservoir of universal culture the Chicano could draw upon in confronting harsh new circumstances.

THE IMPARTIALITY OF DEATH

collected by
aurora lucero white-lea

imparcialidad de la muerte

An old man stole a rooster from a chicken coop because he was very hungry. He took it home, killed it, and put it to boil. Someone came to the door. The man did not want to go because he thought it was the owner of the bird, but the knocking continued and he could not ignore it. "Who are you and what do you want?" he asked the man standing there.

"I am God and I want something to eat."

"I am sorry but I cannot give you anything," said the man.

"Why," asked our Lord. "I smell food so I know you are not in want."

"No, I am not in want," said the man.

"Then what is the reason?" said the visitor.

"The reason is," said the man, "that I do not like to feed anyone who does not treat everyone alike. I notice that to some you give much; to others little."

"Yes, that is true," said the visitor, and departed.

Soon there came another knock at the door. A woman stood there this time. "And who are you?" said the man.

"I am the Virgin," said the woman, "and I would like something to eat."

"I am sorry," said the man, "but I cannot share my food with you."

"Why?" asked the Virgin.

"Because," said the man, "you are one of those who does not treat everyone alike. To some you give much; to others little." The Virgin had nothing to say so she left.

And now the rooster was cooked and the man was ready to sit down and eat. Another knock was heard. "I wonder who it can be this time?" said the man. At the door stood Death. She said, "I smelled your rooster and I came along to help you eat it."

"And why not?" said the man. "Aren't you one who treats everyone alike?"

"That is so," said Death. "I have no favorites. The poor, the rich, the young, the old, the sick, the well—all look alike to me."

"That is the reason you may come in and share my food," said the man. Death entered and the two had a grand feast. (Gathered by Juanita Gonzales, Pojouaque, New Mexico)

In our communities, "whenever a man is referred to as a maestro it means that he is a master of some trade, art, or folly."

José Ortega, for example, is a maestro who in himself carries a vast knowledge of one unrecorded aspect of the history of the United States—la trasquila. His hands are gnarled and his eyes have seen too much. He is wise, with the wisdom of life's experience etched in his face. To hear him tell about the trasquiladores, the vaquero, and the daily life on the open range, is to know our roots. He himself is like part of the topography of which he speaks.

Early one spring evening in 1971, I sat down with him at his home, outside Hayward, California, and heard him tell parts of his life's story, authentic examples of oral history. Tío José is the uncle of one of us, Tomás Ybarra-Frausto. Later he took me outside, through his little jardín de abuelito with chile, tomate . . . y antes de irme, me cantó una canción. Through him we learn that scattered in towns and cities there are many maestros who themselves have lived as yet untold parts of our history.

DON JOSÉ ORTEGA—TRASQUILADOR

collected by
antonia castañeda shular

Of how Mexicans were treated on the ranches.

¿Cómo trataban en los ranchos a los Mexicanos, tío José?

Tío José: Pos ya sabes—a puro tirón. Yo amansaba caballos a treinta pesos al mes—y a los vaqueros gringos les pagaban más. El mexicano nunca ha tenido ganancia.

The two trips on roundups to Kansas with his brothers.

Platíqueme de las entradas, tío José.

Tío José: Mis hermanos y yo fuimos a Kiansas dos veces—entonces no había en qué acarrear el ganado—no había tren, no había trocas—no había nada. Durábamos dos meses quince días—pasamos por Oklahoma con novilladas p'allá pa Kiansas—los dos hermanos y yo. Después en la trasquila fui otra vez dos veces p'allá pa Kiansas.

¿Y en la trasquila había muchos mexicanos?

Tío José: Sí, muchos—casi todos al principio. Trasquilaban con tijera. Yo trasquilaba cien borregas por día. Era el único trabajo que le dejaba a uno un poquito de dinero.

Of how the Mexican sheep shearer lived on the range.

Vivíamos en el campo cuando íbamos a los ranchos a la trasquila. Traíamos un güayín pa' las camas e íbamos de rancho en rancho.

En Nuevo México había un rancho donde trabajaban cien hombres—cincuenta arriba y cincuenta abajo. Era un rancho de veinte y cino a treinta mil borregas.

He tells of the journeys of the sheep shearer according to the season.

Trasquilábamos en abril, mayo en San Angel —después nos veníamos pa' Nuevo México y trabajábamos junio, julio y parte de agosto y alcanzábamos la trasquila chiquita en el Ojo Azul otra vez.

El corte grande era durante mayo y junio hasta mediados de julio. En San Angel era en abril. En Nuevo México durante mayo y junio. En Laguna de Piedra en Wyoming duraba hasta el once de agosto y veníamos a alcanzar el corte chiquito a Nuevo México.

Of his sixty years as sheep shearer, of how the men cured their ills, of the practices of his craft.

¿Cómo era el trabajo, tío José?

Tío José: Pos sabes—que era duro.

Yo trasquilaba cien borregas por día, con tijera de mano y se lastimaba mucho la mano—nos curábamos las manos usando orines sobre piedras calientes, se hacía vapor, y así se curaba uno las canillas, las mancaduras. Con el vapor ya amanecía uno bien y podía trabajar muy a gusto el siguiente día. Yo fui tacinque 60 años.

Las borregas se trasquilan cada seis meses. Se empieza por el pescuezo de mayor a menor—luego las panzea uno y le avienta el vellón de lana al lanero para que la amarre y él se la avienta al empacador.

Hay dos cortes—el corte chico son borregas de seis meses; en el corte grande, ya son mayores las borregas.

Las borregas se pelan cada seis meses.

Of the poetry, dances, and music in his life.

¿Cómo era la vida, tío José?

Tío José: Uy, pos era muy interesante. Nos divertíamos mucho. Siempre íbamos a los bailes, amansábamos caballos, cuando era muy joven jugaba mucho a la baraja y tocaba mi guitarra. También teníamos poetas que nos componían versitos. Don Ignacio Zaragoza era poeta, él componía inditas* que son cancioncitas—a mí me compusieron varias—.

Salieron doce tacinques,
entre invierno y verano,
entre ellos José Ortega,
y el capitán Don Feliciano.

A Rómulo y a mí nos compusieron estos versos; se titulaba, "Rómulo era jinete."

Rómulo dice, yo monto,
al cabo qué me he de hacer,
luego que lo vio mover,
se arrepintió muy pronto.

Porque el caballo se paraba y se daba vueltas—muy feo—

---

*"The *indita* is a combination of three elements. It is written in octosyllabic romance verse, sung to a primitive Indian rhythm, and danced like a Spanish *jota.* . . . After the introduction of the *canción popular* or popular song, the *indita* became more finished, and the *tonada* developed a more melodious character, but the oldest compositions show a very marked Indian influence." From "A Bibliography of Spanish Folklore in New Mexico," by Arthur L. Campa, in *The University of New Mexico Bulletin,* Language Series, Vol. 2, No. 3, September, 1930.

Luego, le dije, pos yo lo subo, y de allí
salió el verso de José Ortega...

Sin quedar ninguna duda,
José Ortega ya montado,
les dijo—háganse a un lado,
¡déjenle que se sacuda!

*Of mechanization and the
sheep shearer.*

Se hacía muy buen dinero—pero ya
después se empezó a acabar todo ese laberin-
que—pusieron máquinas para trasquilar. Pos
la primera vez que fuimos, nosotros no
sabíamos ni cómo se agarraban las máquinas.
Sabíamos como agarrar la borrega, pos
sabíamos qué hacer con tijera, pero no
sabíamos cómo corría el mango, ni sabíamos
qué era el mango—ni nada. Yo trasquilé
sesenta años, con tijeras y con máquina. La
primera vez que usé la máquina ya mero la
me mandaba al carajo.

*He tells of how his family
founded San Angel, Texas.*

¿Y de su familia, Tío José?

Tío José: Eramos de San Antonio, allá nací
yo—nos fuimos a San Angel—fueron fun-
dadores de San Angel—mil ochocientos
ochenta y dos. No había más que nosotros y
una familia que también eran de San Antonio
—venían a San Angel a cortar zacate pa' las
caballadas del gobierno.

También en Puerto de Conchas—los
Alderetes y los Arrellones, eran cincuenta
familias que vinieron de San Antonio a
trabajar pa'l gobierno allí. Trabajamos con
el gobierno, mi "apá' y mis hermanos. Yo
estaba muy mediano—tenía apenas siete años.
Crecía el zacate toboso, grandote, y lo
mochaban con azadón y hacían unas algüinas
muy grandes de zacate pa' los animales, los
caballos. Los mexicanos fundaron casi la
mitad de los pueblos de Tejas.

*Wherein he tells of certain
lively boyhood experi-
ences...*

Yo me mudé de mi casa muy joven—
mi padre me pidió que saliera. El tenía unos
amigos, ya señores. Yo todavía era muy joven,
de algunos diez y seis años, pero como tocaba

la guitarra, me invitaban que fuera con ellos, y yo me echaba una copita o dos. Una noche llegué a casa, mi papá estaba sentado en la mesa, esperándome—me saludó..."Buenas noches, hijo." "Buenas noches," le dije yo. Me dijo, "Váyase a descansar, hijo, mañana hablamos." Yo pensé "Algo va a pasar," y dije "Bueno," y me fui a acostar.

En la mañana—muy tempranito—me dijo "Hijo, quiero que saque su ropa, se lleve sus caballos, y que se vaya. Usted anoche vino borracho. No quiero que le diga nada a su mamá."

Yo le dije que no había venido borracho, pero él dijo que sí. Pos, hice lo que me pidió, agarré mi ropa, mi guitarra y mis caballos, y me fuí, sin decirle nada a mi mamá. Iba saliendo del pueblo cuando me encontré con una novia que tenía. Ella estaba lavando ropa a la orilla del río. Me preguntó —"¿Pa' dónde vas?" Yo le dije "Salgo de mi casa, voy pa' Arizona, ¿vamos?" Ella dijo— "Pos...vamos."

Y nos fuimos. Tenía yo diez y siete años. Ella tenía quince.

Pero luego yo me fuí a la trasquila y la dejé con una familia conocida pa' que me la cuidaran.

Of how he married, and his family.

Me casé con una mujer buena, ella me hizo hombre. Antes de casarme yo ni sabía trabajar—ella me enseñó. Tuvimos siete hijos, un varón y seis mujeres. El niño se nos murió.

Yo he hecho muchas cosas en mi vida ...por un tiempo, antes de casarme, fuí contrabandista. En esos tiempos se sembraba algodón, sandía, frijol, chile, todo lo que es labor. La gente dependía en la cosecha, a veces no bastaba la siembra y no tenían dinero con qué comprar mandado...

He recalls the deportations.

¿Pasó usted por las deportaciones, tío José?

Tío José: Oh, sí—se llevaron a muchos... dejaron a niños sin padres. A mi esposa la llevé inmediatamente para arreglar todo, porque ella nació en México. Pero como era esposa de uno de acá de este lado y ya teníamos muchos años de casados, no fue molestada. Pero a muchos sí—venían en la noche con los rinches y se llevaban a la gente sin darles razón ninguna, ni tiempo para nada—o se los llevaban de los files o de dónde estuvieran trabajando.

Of how he has more to tell.   Bueno, y por ahora, ¿hay más cosas que me quisiera contar?

Tío José: Bueno, ya te platiqué de casi todo —al rato te cuento más.

During the late 1800s approximately seventy percent of the section crews and ninety percent of the extra gangs on some railway lines were composed of Mexican laborers legally and illegally contracted by commissaries or contratistas. "Los reenganchados a Kansas" refers to the thousands of men who traveled with their families and lived in boxcars while working el traque for the Santa Fe, the Rock Island Line, the Great Northern, and the Southern Pacific. Many of the present colonias and barrios, especially in the Midwest, were originally settled by this group of migrants and immigrants that preceded the major migration of 1910.

The final stanza of the corrido presents the Mexican view of U.S. labor unions as being contradictory to their Mexicanidad. The reenganchados knew that as non-U.S. citizens they would not receive any union benefits, and that they were seen only as a means of bolstering up the numerical strength of American railway unions—not as participating members. As the corrido was sung throughout the country it served to inform all who heard it of the conditions and problems in el trabajo del traque.

LOS REENGANCHADOS A KANSAS

CONTRACTED TO KANSAS

Un día tres de septiembre,
Ay, ¡qué día tan señalado!
Que salimos de Laredo
Para Kansas reenganchados.

Cuando salimos de Laredo
Me encomendé al Santo Fuerte,
Porque iba de contrabando
Por ese lado del puente.

One day the third of September,
Oh, what an unusual day!
We left Laredo
Signed up for Kansas.

When we left Laredo
I committed myself to the strong saint,
Because I was travelling illegally
On that side of the bridge.

Uno de mis compañeros
Gritaba muy afanado:
—Ya nos vamos reenganchados
A trabajar al contado.—

One of my companions
Shouted very excitedly:
"Now we are going under contract
To work for cash."

Corre, corre, maquinita,
Por esa línea del Quiri
Anda a llevar este enganche
Al estado de Kansas City.

Run, run, little machine
Along that Katy line,
Carry this party of laborers
To the state of Kansas City.

Salimos de San Antonio
Con dirección a Laguna,
Le pregunté al reenganchista
Que si íbamos para Oklahoma.

We left San Antonio
In the direction of Laguna,
I asked the contractor
If we were going through Oklahoma.

Respondió el reenganchista:
—Calle, amigo, no suspire,
Pasaremos de Oklahoma
Derechito a Kansas City.—

The contractor replied:
"Quiet, friend, don't even sigh,
We shall pass through Oklahoma
Right straight to Kansas City."

Ese tren a Kansas City
Es un tren muy volador,
Corre cien millas por hora
Y no le dan todo el vapor.

That train to Kansas City
Is a flying train,
It travels one hundred miles per hour
And they don't give it all the steam.

Yo les digo a mis amigos:
—El que no lo quiera creer,
Que monte en el Santa Fe,
A ver dónde está al
    amanecer.—

I say to my friends:
"Let him who doesn't want
    to believe it
Get aboard the Santa Fe
Just to see where he will be by
    morning."

Al llegar a Kansas City
Nos queríamos regresar,
Porque nos dieron el ancho
Con las veras de alinear.

On arriving at Kansas City
We wanted to return,
Because they gave us a raw deal
With the aligning bars.

Decían los americanos
Con muchísimo valor:
—Júntense a los mexicanos
Para meterlos en la unión.—

The Americans said
With a great deal of bravery:
"Round up the Mexicans
So as to put them in the union."

Nosotros le respondimos:
—Lo que es la unión
    no entramos,
Esta no es nuestra bandera.
Porque somos mexicanos.

We replied to them:
"We will not join this thing
    called union,
This is not our flag
Because we are Mexicans."

(trans. by Brownie McNeil)

III

de acá de este lado

"Yo soy Mexicano
de acá de este lado.
De acá de este lado
puro Mexicano . . ."

canción popular

Estalló la revolución y mucha gente salió pa'l norte. Salieron peones, artesanos, poetas, filósofos, e intelectuales, quienes al llegar contribuyeron a forjar la compleja realidad contemporánea de la gente chicana. The vast majority migrated to the Southwest where they found a reflection of themselves in a Spanish-speaking population, essentially Mexican, living in communities very similar to those they had recently left in Mexico. While the barrios and colonias provided a welcome and familiar environment, the newcomers were immediately confronted with the contradictory socio-economic realities that produced and maintained Chicano communities as separate entities.

The corridos and ensayos in this section are an index to the literary and historical importance of this transitional period. It was an era of constant movement and constant struggle, of mass migration north, formation of large communities, labor strikes, and mass indiscriminate deportations during the 1930s.

It was a time of self-affirmation, as individuals made the decision to leave Mexico and then decided whether to remain in the U.S. or return. For those already in the Southwest, the arrival of gente de México constituted a reaffirmation of their Mexican selves. The infusion of living symbols replaced their own dying echoes, partially alleviating the sense of betrayal by Mexico in the War of 1848. The essence of this infusion was paradoxical, for even those who for one reason or another were uprooted by the Revolution, nonetheless brought with them the ideology of social change and of struggle for justice.

This transitional period, when external societal forces imposed physical limitations on barrios and colonias alike, is characterized by the complexity of the human struggle and the process of adaptive change occurring within Mexican/Chicano communities. Profound personal, familial and societal conflicts were engendered by the mass migrations north, for many who stayed in Mexico perceived immigrating as synonymous with betrayal of country and heritage. The tension created by this conflict of sentiments is reflected in the poetic interchange between two Mexicans, "Los deportados" and "Defensa de los norteños".

Once in the U.S., immigrants had to struggle to maintain cultural and linguistic identity against consuming forces of a society that would accept them only if they denied their Mexicanidad. One response was to form mutual aid, burial, and other organizations to meet social needs. These societies performed the double function of preserving community solidarity and maintaining cultural values, while also providing a vehicle for socio-political confrontation with the larger society. In addition, the people had to struggle for economic equality. They met this challenge by organizing agricultural labor unions and calling strikes, winning wage increases in some of the agricultural struggles. They also played an important role in organizations such as the Mine, Mill and Smelter Workers Union. But because unionization of the Mexican/Chicano labor force posed a threat to agricultural interests, the agrarian leadership was depleted by arrests. Many were deported during the repatriations.

As they encountered differing social, economic, and environmental realities, the people adjusted to their particular circumstance, creating new population and culture patterns in barrios that were basically similar in nature to each other, but characterized by individual styles. It was during the first four decades of this century that many of the present institutions and life styles in the barrios were formed—forged by the people in response to the realities of the United States. One example of a cultural response were the variedades. Presenting short skits of social and political life in the community, they were precursors of today's Chicano popular theatre. Anglo-American education was seldom accessible, thus many children were taught to read Spanish by their parents, using as texts community newspapers and political broadsides.

The main themes which characterize the experience of this period are those of continued uprooting, of movement, of migration, of constant struggle and adaptation to new realities. Within this process, as before, Mexicans were able to retain the values of their past, such as language and a strong sense of community, and to continue struggling with the difficulties of their present.

La llegada de los gringos and the subsequent dislocation of Mexicans, are the historical framework for this ballad collected in New Mexico in the early 1900s. The encroaching foreigner and his alien value system are scrutinized with disdain by the cantador, who views them as materialistic and greedy. The ballad emphasizes the harsh realities of the transition from a sedentary cattle and sheep raising economy to plot farming.

We have retained the spelling employed by the distinguished folklorist Aurelio Espinosa, whose effort in recording this poem was to convey the flavor of the spoken Spanish of rural New Mexico. Of further interest is the fact that the poet refers to his composition as a *cuando*.

LOS AMERICANOS

**recitado por juan chaves y garcía,
edad 52 años,
de puerta de luna, nuevo méjico.**

Año novesientos nueve,
pero con muncho cuidado,
voy á componer un cuando*
en nombre d'este condado.

Voy á cantar este cuando,
Nuevo Méjico mentado,
para que sepan los güeros
el nombre d'este condado.

Guadalup' es, el firmado
por la nasión mejicana,
madre de todo lo criado,
virgen, reina soberana.

*The cuando derives its name from the constant repetition of the word *cuando* at the end of the tenth syllable of the stanza. A good understanding of Spanish is needed to understand the subtle meaning that is often attached to these words. In form the cuando is very similar to the décima, except that there is no limitation to the number of verses. Unlike the décima, the introductory quatrain is not repeated but the word *cuando* must always end each stanza. From "A Bibliography of Spanish Folklore in New Mexico," by Arthur L. Campa in *The University of New Mexico Bulletin*, Language Series, Vol. 2, No. 3, September, 1930.

Voy á cantar estos versos,
ya comensaré 'l primero;
señores den atensión
al punto que me refiero.

Voy [á] hablar del estranjero,
y lo que digu es cerdá;
quieren tenernos d' esclavos,
peru eso no les valdrá.

Señores, pongan cuidado
á la ras' americana;
vienen a poser las tierras
las que les vendió Sant' Ana.

Cuando 'ntraron di Oklajoma
sin saber el casteyano,
entraron como los burros
á su pasu americano.

Vienen dándoli al cristiano
y hasiéndoli al lundo guerra;
vienen [á] echarnos del pais
y [á] haserse de nuestra tierra.

A todo 'l mundu abarcaron
y si hasen del bien ajeno;
ora les pregunto yo
á los que 'stán sin terreno,

y los voy á reconvenir
como un hombre jornalero:
Si han quedado como burros
no más mascándos' el freno.

Si acabaron las hasiendas
y los ganados menores;
ya nu hay onde trabajar
gu ocuparnos de pastores.

¿Qué les parese, señores,
lo que vinu á suseder?
Nu hay más que labrar la tierra
pa podernos mantener.

Es nación muy ilustrada
y afanos' en saber;
trabajan con muchu esmero
y todos quieren tener.

Su crensi' es en el dinero,
en la vaca, nel cabayo,
y ponen todo su haber
en la gaína y el gayo.

Son nasión agricoltora
que siembran toda semía;
por ser comidas de casa
siembran melón y sandía.

También siembran calabasas
raíses y de todas yerbas;
y comen de todas carnes,
peses, ranas y culebras.

Hábiles son en saber
y de grand' entendimiento;
son serujanos, dotores,
y hombres de grande talento.

¿Qué les parese, señores,
lo ilustrado que son?
hasen carritos de fierro
que caminan por vapor.

El que compusu este cuando
nu es un pueta consumado;
es un pobre jornalero,
que vive de su salario.

Mi nombre no les diré
ni les diré 'n todo 'l año;
soy un pobre pastorsito
qui apasenta su rebaño.

1. Los nuevo-mejicanos, por regla general desprecian al estranjero que desde 1846 llegó á gobernarlos. Todavía vive este desprecio, particularmente en las pequeñas aldeas donde el castellano todavía no ha sido suplantado por el inglés. Por buen ó mal nombre les dicen á los americanos, *miricanos, miricachos, mericachos, gringos, yanques ó yanquis, bolíos, paiquespiques* (del nombre del general americano Pike que nombró á cierta montaña de Colorado, Pike's Peak), *güeros, dochis* (del inglés dutch = holandés), y un sin fin más de nombres mucho menos elegantes.

2. El general Santa Ana, presidente de la república mejicana en 1846–1848, cuando por el tratado de Guadalupe-Hidalgo, la mayor parte del terreno ahora ocupado por los estados de Nuevo Méjico, Arizona y California, fué cedido á los Estados Unidos.

3. Se refiere aquí á una emigración reciente (1908 y 1909) de los habitantes de Tejas y Oklahoma á Nuevo Méjico.

A worker's perspective of how conditions were before the Revolution began in 1910 is narrated in this corrido version of the copper strike at Cananea. This historic strike is famous as an important event in which Mexican workers resisted a segment of the Porfirian power structure. Because the poet is very historically conscious, the events themselves are made clear in the text. The composer leaves us with a philosophical drawing of a final lesson in the last line of his poem.

DOBLE BOLA DE
LA HUELGA DE CANANEA
RECORDANDO LA HISTÓRICA HUELGA
DEL 2 DE JUNIO DE 1906

Fue tan injusto y tirano
el régimen porfirista,
que en sus treinta años de paz
los crímenes forman lista.

Sin entrar en los detalles,
tan sólo les cuento los hechos
y bases con los que iniciaron
los viejos obreros su lucha de clases.

Con salarios miserables
y con las cargas muy toscas,
viviendo a la sabandija
y muriendo entre las moscas;

Siempre a merced de los amos,
dueños de las minas y de las haciendas,
y concesionarios
de los ricos fundos y de las prebendas...

Año del seis de este siglo
—ya mayo se petateaba—
la cosa fue en Cananea
cuando junio principiaba.

En la lejana Sonora,
la Ley estimaba delitos mayores
que se organizaran
en sus sindicatos los trabajadores.

Los patrones eran gringos
y gringos los capataces,
y más gringos, ladrones,
como las aves rapaces.

Las demandas eran justas:
derecho al ascenso, mínimo salario,
jornada de ocho horas
y trato a los nuestros más humanitario.

Un pliego de peticiones
se presentó ante la empresa
y la empresa contestó
que le causaba sorpresa.

Los mineros se reunieron
y al verse negados con esa respuesta
lograron un mítin
y se engolillaron en recia protesta.

Pero al llegar hasta el mero
taller de carpintería,
los recibió una rechifla
de larga fusilería,

pues los cobardes mandones
con winchester dieron descarga cerrada,
cayendo los nuestros
igual que los patos al tronar l'armada,

Muertos y pilas de heridos
doblaron desde el principio;
los rengos, tras la Justicia,
jalaron p'al municipio.

Allí, dos nuevas descargas
los pies les pararon mochando sus alas;
y allí se aguantaron
balas contra piedras, piedras contra balas.

Y tanto miedo sintieron
el gobierno y el gerente,
que pidieron de Arizona
—con el carácter de urgente—

Un batallón de soldados.
Los Yanquis vinieron, mas la masa entera
del pueblo indignado
los largó de plano para su frontera.

Y fue don Rafáil Izábal,
cobarde y gobernador,
el soplón que pidió ayuda
para aplacar el furor

Del obrero organizado
¡General de paja y traidor notorio
que llamó a los yanquis
para que pisaran nuestro territorio!

¡Maldito Rafáil Izábal,
inconsciente y obediente,
pa' que otra vez se repita
el mátalos en caliente!

¡Fue más papista que el Papa,
pues sirvió a Porfirio y a ricos magnates!
¡Todo por el Amo,
su Paz y Progreso. . .hasta los tompiates!

A la larga y por su cuenta,
con las fuerzas federales,
el gobierno dominó
con puros actos bestiales.

Pero le quedó la mancha
de pedir auxilio y el mucho cinismo
de usar contra hermanos
las armas y brazos del Capitalismo.

Por fin accedió la empresa
a las muy justas demandas,
mas el Tirano no andaba
con blondas ni manos blandas;

Y pa' servir de escarmiento,
los líderes presos, Calderón e Ibarra,
Diéguez y De Lara,
de San Juan de Ulúa sufrieron la garra.

Y así se volvió la Paz,
al Orden y a los Progresos:
¡A costa de sangre y viudas
y de huérfanos y presos!

Y hasta que ganó Madero
se abrieron las rejas de aquel despotismo,
pa' los precursores
de la lucha obrera y el sindicalismo.

¡Pero esa sangre no importa
si con otro hachazo más
se logra que caiga el palo
y con él ruede la Paz!

¡Porque a la larga en la corta,
lágrimas del pueblo y lluvias del monte
llegarán al mar,
aunque monte y pueblo sufran el desmonte!

Y en este primer encuentro
la derrota fue una pausa
y el presentar resistencia,
signo de la buena Causa

Pues desde entonces se afirma
que hay que prepararse y plantear los hechos
y tomar impulsos
porque cuesta mucho conquistar derechos...

"Los deportados" and "Defensa de los norteños" present in corrido form the polemic resulting from the migrations north. From the Mexican point of view the deportados deserved little sympathy since they were lacking in patriotism and motivated by materialistic gain.

"Defensa de los norteños," the migrant's response to these accusations, cites economic need, exploitation of the working class by los ricos, and rejection of the patrón system as the motives for migration.

LOS DEPORTADOS

Les cantaré un corrido
de todos los deportados,
que vienen hablando inglés
y vienen de desgraciados.

Los tiran en donde quiera
a puro mendigar,
da lástima verlos
que no traen ni para almorzar.

Marchan para el norte
con gran gusto y afán,
trabajan en el campo
como cualquier gañán.

THE DEPORTEES

I shall sing you a song
of all who were deported,
who come back speaking English
and in wretched shape.

They are shoved around anywhere
and have to beg their way.
It's a pity to see them
with nothing to eat.

They set out for the north
with high hopes and eagerness,
but they work in the fields
like any field hand.

Se van al algodón
y dan muy mala cala,
trabajan en el traque
o en el pico o la pala.

Pues eso y más merecen
esos pobres paisanos,
sabiendo que este suelo
es para los Mexicanos.

Se tumban el vigote,
y mascan su tabaco,
parecen la gran cosa y no
cargan ni...tlaco.

Se pelan a la boston
como burros tuzados,
se van a las segundas
y compran trajes usados.

Los corren, los maltratan
los gringos desgraciados,
no tienen vergüenza
siempre allá están pegados.

Por eso yo me quedo
en mi patria querida,
México es mi país
y por él doy la vida.

They go to pick cotton
and get on very badly;
they work on the track
or with shovel or with pick,

So they deserve that and more,
those poor countrymen,
for they knew that this land
is for the Mexicans.

They lop off their mustaches
and chew their tobacco;
they seem like a big success
and they don't have a cent.

They cut their hair close
like a clipped donkey;
they go to second-hand stores
and buy worn-out clothes.

They're insulted, mistreated,
by those *gringo* wretches;
they have no shame,
they are always beaten there.

That is why I remain
in my beloved country:
Mexico is my country
and for it I give my life.

(trans. by Paul S. Taylor)

DEFENSA DE LOS NORTEÑOS

DEFENSE OF THE EMIGRANTS

Lo que dicen de nosotros
casi todo es realidad;
mas salimos del terreno
por pura necesidad.

Que muchos vienen facetos
yo también se los dijera;
por eso la prensa chica
tuvo donde echar tijera.

What they say about us
is nearly all the truth,
but we left the country
from sheer necessity.

I myself could have told you
that many come back boasting;
that is why the local press
speaks harshly about them.

Pero la culpa la tienen
esos ingratos patrones
que no les dan a su gente
ni aun cuando porte chaqueta.

But those who are to blame
are those unkind employers,
who don't give their people
enough to buy a jacket.

No es porque hablo del país:
pero claro se los digo
que muchos trabajadores
enseñan hasta el ombligo.

I'm not criticizing the country,
but I certainly tell you
that many of the laborers
are naked to their navels.

El rico en buen automóvil,
buen caballo, buena silla,
y los pobrecitos peones
pelona la rabanilla.

The rich go in automobiles,
riding a good horse and a good saddle
while the poor peones
go about half naked.

Siempre el peón es agobiado,
tratándolo con fiereza,
donde le miran los pies
quieren verle la cabeza.

The peon is always burdened,
is treated with cruelty;
the rich would like to see his head
where they see his feet.

Lo tratan como un esclavo
no como útil servidor
que derrama para el rico
hasta el último sudor.

They treat him like a slave,
not like a useful servant,
who pours out for the rich
his last drop of sweat.

Yo no digo que en el Norte
se va uno a estar muy sentado,
ni aun cuando porte chaqueta
lo hacen a uno diputado.

I don't say that in the north
one is going to be well off;
nor because one wears a suit
is he elected to Congress.

Allí se va a trabajar
macizo, a lo Americano,
pero alcanza uno a ganar
más que cualesquier paisano.

One has to work there,
hard, in the American fashion,
but one succeeds in earning
more than any of our countrymen.

Aquí se trabaja un año
sin comprarse una camisa;
el pobre siempre sufriendo,
y los ricos risa y risa.

Here one works a year
without earning enough for a shirt;
the poor man suffers always
and the rich man laughs and laughs.

Los cuarenta y el tostón
no salen de su tarifa,
no alcanza para comer;
siempre anda vacía la tripa.

Paid forty or fifty cents,
never more than that,
he can't get enough to eat,
his stomach is always empty.

Que lo digan mis paisanos,
si yo les estoy mintiendo,
porque no hay que preguntar
lo que claro estamos viendo.

Let my countrymen say
if I am telling a lie,
for it's needless to ask about
what we can clearly see.

Mucha gente así lo ha dicho:	Many people have said
dizque no somos patriotas	that we are not patriotic
porque les vamos a servir	because we go to serve
a los infames patotas.	for the accursed *patotas*.[1]
Pero que se abran trabajos	But let them give us jobs
y que paguen buen dinero,	and pay us decent wages;
y no queda un Mexicano	not one Mexican then
que se vaya al extranjero.	will go to foreign lands.
Ansia tenemos de volver	We're anxious to return again
a nuestra patria idolatrada,	to out adored country;
pero qué le hemos de hacer	but what can we do about it
si está la patria arruinada.	if the country is ruined?

(trans. by Paul S. Taylor)

[1] Literally "big feet," an uncomplimentary term applied to Americans.

¡HUEL—GA! ¡HUEL—GA!
¡Sálganse! ¡No sean esquiroles!
¡Abajo el patrón!
¡No queremos contratistas!
¿Dónde está el picket sign?

A campesino vocabulary of struggle has reverberated throughout the fields and campos of this country for several decades. Neither the words nor the struggle are new. As we read this recent essay by Ronald López, a Chicano historian, describing the El Monte berry strike of the 1930s and uncovering portions of the history of Chicano unionizing activity, we recognize the power of agribusiness and related industries used to disrupt these efforts. Just as the strike at Cananea generated its corrido, so this strike and others like it, must have generated songs, poetry, and stories, communicating the events of the struggle. This literature remains to be collected and studied.

THE EL MONTE BERRY STRIKE

ronald lópez

In the 1930s El Monte was a small community in the San Gabriel Valley with a population of approximately 16,000. El Monte proper had a population of about 12,000 and the remaining 4,000 lived in the agricultural center. The population was a mixed one comprised of Mexican, Japanese and Anglos. Mexicans accounted for approximately 20 percent of the population, Japanese about 5 percent and the remainder were Anglos. Most of the Japanese lived on farms and most of the Mexicans lived in three barrios. The largest of these barrios was Hick's Camp. Hick's Camp was a veritable shack town, located across a gulch from El Monte. It had a population of over 1,000 people most of whom were migratory laborers.

The San Gabriel Valley had between 600 and 700 acres of berries. Approximately 80 percent of the acreage was in the hands of Japanese growers who belonged to the Central Japanese Association of Southern California. The greater part of this acreage, however, was not owned by the Japanese but, rather, by Anglos. Apparently the majority of the Japanese growers were on the land in violation of the Alien Land Laws of 1913 and 1920 which, among other things, had limited land leases to three years (in 1913) and barred further leasing or transfers (in 1920) to Japanese nationals or to corporations with a majority of stock owned by Japanese nationals.

Berry picking was piece work. The pickers were paid on a crate basis and the rate per crate was set early in the season. The crate price varied with the type of berry. The growers also anticipated the market price when setting the rate. The rate had been set in 1933 at 40 cents a crate for raspberries, 20 cents for youngberries, and 20 cents for black-berries. These pay scales also took into consideration the various pickings. That is, there were normally four pickings. The first crop was light, the second heavy, and the third and fourth lighter than the first. With this scale, a skilled adult berry picker might average as high as 20 cents an hour during a ten hour day over the entire season. However, the berries were picked by women and children as well as by men and many pickers made as little as 9 cents an hour.

Towards the end of May a mixed group of about twenty people, Anglos, Mexicans, and Japanese (the group included two women) approached S. Fukami, secretary of the Japanese association and demanded higher wages. The group got no satisfaction from the secretary so they returned to Hick's Camp and began to call meetings to organize a strike. On the first of June, with some 500 to 600 present, the workers voted to strike. That day an estimated 1,500 workers went out on strike.

The next day a strike committee of sixty was formed. The committee included Mexican, Japanese, and Filipino workers from Hick's Camp, Chino, El Monte, Medina Court, and La Puente. The strike committee and the strike were controlled by C&AWIU organizers. Daily mass meetings were held in El Monte and pickets were set up in many of the surrounding camps. Plans for relief were made and organizers went to Monrovia, Las Flores, Azuza and other communities to try to spread the strike. Women and children were actively involved in the picketing and in the distribution of leaflets. The leaflets were printed in Spanish, Japanese and English and were distributed in thirteen of the surrounding communities. The leaflets at this point were probably printed or mimeographed by the C&AWIU organizers who were always prepared for such exigencies.

The growers reacted quickly to the strike. A long strike would have had a severe impact since the berries had to be picked within three days after ripening. On Sunday, June 4, they sent a representative to meet with the strike committee. The growers offered to settle for 15 cents an hour or 40 cents per crate. The strikers, however, had made an initial demand of 25 cents an hour or 65 cents per crate, so they promptly rejected the first offer. But they did lower their demands to 25 cents an hour or 50 cents per crate.

Two days later, on Tuesday, June 6, the growers raised their offer to 20 cents an hour or 45 cents per crate. The strike committee rejected the offer. This time the rejection was made as much on the basis of the growing militancy of the strikers as on the basis of the offer itself. The offer was close enough to the demands that one of the members of the strike committee decided to ask the general meeting's position. He went into the meeting hall where the strikers were awaiting the outcome of the negotiations and asked the congregation whether they wanted 20 cents an hour or 25 cents an hour. The answer was resoundingly for the latter. The spirit of the strikers was running high. This was the growers' second offer within a week from the beginning of the strike. Also the strike had already spread into some of the other crops in the area and agricultural workers from elsewhere in the surrounding area were beginning to come to the El Monte district to ask for help in organizing their own strikes.

On Wednesday the strikers discovered over 300 scabs in the fields. They increased their picketing and tried to talk the scabs into joining the strike. There had been relatively little picketing up to this point and no confrontations with the sheriffs. The sheriffs, in fact, had been on friendly terms with the strikers until they set up mass pickets and tried to draw the scabs out of the fields. The strikers accused the sheriffs of interfering with the pickets but the sheriff in charge of the intelligence unit denied having received any reports of disturbances.

Because the sheriffs were on good terms with the strikers they were able to "lure" the settlement committee to the station on the pretext that the growers were ready to make another offer. Once at the station, the committee was held there for several hours. While they were at the station, the Mexican consul, Alejandro Martínez, arrived in El Monte at the request of the chairman of the strike committee, Armando Flores. The consul denounced the C&AWIU organizers as "reds" who were not really interested in the welfare of the Mexican workers. He was successful in turning the workers against the C&AWIU organizers but when the C&AWIU organizers returned and learned what had taken place they immediately began calling mass mettings and by Friday they were again in control of the strike.

On Saturday, however, eight of the C&AWIU organizers were arrested and jailed. The Mexican consul again came on the scene and denounced the C&AWIU leadership. This time because of the arrests and because other known C&AWIU organizers were kept out of El Monte by sheriffs, the C&AWIU was unable to re-establish its leadership. The strikers, with the assistance of the consul, formed a new union along national lines. The strike was not yet two weeks old.

The new Mexican union was actually a revival of labor organizations formed in 1928 as a result of strikes among the lettuce and cantaloupe pickers in Southern California and in the Imperial Valley. The El Monte union, however, was probably a direct descendant of the Confederación de Uniones Obreras Mexicanas (CUOM) that was formed in April 1928 and included urban and rural workers. The membership in CUOM had dwindled shortly after its founding until it consisted only of about 10 locals. The leadership of CUOM, however, had the experience necessary to take charge of the El Monte strike. Besides experienced leadership, the new Mexican union also had the assistance of the consulate in Los Angeles probably in the person of vice consul Ricardo Hill.

By the end of the second week the strike had spread to the union and celery fields in Santa Monica and to Culver City. The total number of strikers was estimated at 5,000.

By the end of the third week of the strike financial contributions from Mexico had reached between $3,000 and $4,000. Locally, donations were solicited from individuals and from business establishments who dealt with Mexicans. Members of the strike committee that solicited local funds carried identification which had the seal of the Mexican consulate imprinted on it.

Mr. Ross H. Gast of the Los Angeles Chamber of Commerce Agricultural Department entered the scene on June 22 to help obtain a signed agreement from the growers and an amicable settlement of the strike. He sought to convince the growers to grant the concessions to the strikers which they had presented through U.S. Labor Commissioner Marsh and Conciliator E. H. Fitzgerald.

In the agreement that Gast had secured from the growers the strikers' demands were nearly met. They proposed a crate rate that would make it possible for the pickers to earn between 20 and 25 cents an hour for a ten hour day. The strikers' demands had called for a crate rate that would allow them to make 25 cents an hour. In spite of the fact that the growers had for all intents and purposes capitulated to the strikers' demands, the offer was rejected.

The strikers, feeling that they had the growers "on the run," decided to continue the strike and broaden it to all other agricultural industries in the area.

The strike was in its fourth week when the growers' third offer was rejected. There had been very little violence and what there had been had been restricted to fistfights. The Sheriffs had arrested some picketers, one of whom was jailed, despite the fact that there were no anti-picketing ordinances. The C&AWIU organizers who had been arrested earlier had filed suit against the head of the Sheriff's farm detail for false arrest of picketers. As a result of the suit the Sheriff had called off his men and picketing had become wide open. The strikers had around 600 active picketers daily in the district.

On June 28 Gast reported to Clements that riots had occurred in El Monte berry section the night before. Gast implied that the "riots" were somehow related to growers' attempts to bring scabs into the fields. There were no reports of the disorders in the newspapers.

The following day the growers offered berries to the public at one cent a box. The only catch was that the people had to go into the fields and pick the berries themselves. The announcement was carried in newspapers and over the radio and reportedly "hundreds of men, women, and children" responded. The strikers also responded to the call and by late morning most of the picking had stopped. There were a number of fistfights through the day and one incident, involving a striker and a deputy sheriff, ended with the striker being sent to the hospital for "repairs."

Finally on July 6, after a series of conferences that included the strike committee, the growers, the consuls of Mexico and Japan, and representatives of the State Division of Labor Statistics and Law Enforcement, a settlement was reached. The settlement called for a wage of $1.50 for a nine hour day or 20 cents an hour where the employment was steady.

The final agreement constituted a gain for the workers in the sense that the new wages were higher than those the growers had offered prior to the strike. But, the new rate was lower than the growers' second or third offer. More importantly, however, the agreement did not come until after the peak of the season had passed. Thus, although the pickers now had a guaranteed income that was far better than at the beginning of the season, there was now less work available. Also, as the berry picking season reached its conclusion, fewer pickers were required.

The growers required 500 fewer workers at the time of the settlement and estimated they would need 500 fewer pickers within a week and 500 less within a week after that. The Chamber of Commerce, the County Charities Department and the representative from the State Division of Labor Statistics and Law Enforcement consulted to determine what to do with the pickers as they became unemployed. After a brief investigation they were able to determine that over half of the pickers were citizens while the remainder were Mexican nationals. They chose to approach the problem of unemployment among the two groups in separate ways. They decided to try to find employment for the citizens in the harvests in the San Joaquin Valley and to try to induce the non-citizens to return to Mexico.

In order to effect the repatriation of the Mexicans an "undercover" man who had been placed among the workers was instructed to do what he could to persuade them to return to Mexico. Los Angeles County had had an active repatriation movement since early 1931. The Charities Department was actively engaged, not only in providing transportation for indigent Mexicans (or those they could convince, whether indigent or not) to return to Mexico, but also in developing colonizing opportunities in Mexico to make the prospect of repatriating more attractive. The idea of sending the laborers fresh from a strike was not considered without some trepidation. Reports had already been heard that the workers were not oblivious to the possibility of organizing strike activity in the San Joaquin Valley. One El Monte striker by the name of García was quoted as saying that if there had not been any strike activity in the San Joaquin yet, there would be when they (the El Monte strikers) got there.

IV

hacia lo nuestro

The decades from 1940 to the present, perhaps more than any other period in Chicano history, are best characterized by the full range of meaning implicit in the word, migration. To describe the movement of people during these years, one has to refer to both physical and psychological migration.

In physical terms, the flow of the agricultural labor stream, first swelling, then ebbing, succeeded in carrying Chicanos to the far reaches of the midwestern and the northwestern sections of the country. Arriving to often intolerable labor camps, they have responded to oppressive conditions by establishing Chicano colonias.

Paralleling the far-reaching agricultural stream was another major movement, the migration to the cities. Urban inflow was intensified during World War II, when the armed forces and the industries of the war effort exerted an uprooting effect on a large segment of the rural Chicano population. Two of the texts which follow, "Crónica personal de Cristal" and "American Me" convey with sensitivity and honesty the individual and collective strength of people—young and old—facing the rigors of migration, in both rural and urban variations.

The move to the cities in the turbulent 1940s engaged many Chicanos in a form of psychological migration. For those who achieved a minimum of economic stability and assimilated into the larger society, the migration seemed permanent. Others, in ghettos like East Los Angeles, found themselves alienated both from their families, which were still essentially Mexican, and from the Anglo-American world, as unreceptive as ever. Their response was an effort to create their own psychological "place," complete with their own verbal and visual symbols, their own social norms and code of ethics. Less painful than the identity problem of the pachucos, but just as sharp, is the awareness of contradiction experienced by the young Chicana in the story "American Me". In this story, the identity theme is carried by the language itself. Beneath the surface of Lucy's English are Spanish language patterns and vocabulary.

For the vast majority of Chicanos, this period from the 1940s to the present, so marked by the impact of migrations, has witnessed an ongoing creation of cultural values and linguistic forms. Culture and language based on a Mexican underpinning, have evolved to meet the demands of life in the United States. The diversity of texts which we have included in this section gives evidence of this evolutionary process in literature. The selections, representing different generations, also represent different forms of literary expression: poetry, essay, social manifesto, personal narrative, political interview. The dominant theme in these selections is one of assertion—assertion of dignity (José Angel Gutiérrez); assertion of cultural strength (Enriqueta Vásquez); assertion of the human validity of the Chicano past (Irene Castañeda); assertion of demands for social justice (Plan de Delano).

On another level, the richness and vitality of these texts convey further assertion—that Chicano writers, reflecting in their creative expression the spiritual condition of our people, are moving hacia lo nuestro. The migrations of the Chicano people, in all their aspects, have provided the sub-soil from which literary expression now flowers, the sub-soil of rich and painful human experience.

Sometimes we accuse our parents' generation of not having participated in movements for social change. Yet the fact that we think of ourselves as Chicanos, that Spanish is still spoken in many homes, and that we maintain certain cultural values transmitted to us by them, is visible proof of their ongoing struggle for cultural survival.

The human values threaded throughout the Crónica and communicated with an eloquent directness, include a sense of community, a sense of social responsibility and concern for those less fortunate, and emphasis on the family as the well-spring of identity.

In answer to a daughter's inquiries about her origins, Doña Irene traces the experiences of two generations, from the early 1900s to the present, and in so doing recreates the history of many Chicano families.

If we are truly to validate the experience and the expression coming from the heart of our people, then the form of their expression must be preserved. In this Crónica the very orthography authenticates the ideas. The total effect is one of depth and unadorned truth, which by our standards are a key index of literary quality.

CRÓNICA PERSONAL DE CRISTAL: SEGUNDA PARTE

irene castañeda

Bueno hija pues de lo que yo me acuerdo abía muchas familias mexicanas y salían a piscar algodón—Ganado, Tejas, Corpos Cristy, Agua Dulse, Kerney, y muchos otros pueblitos. Cuando se terminaba la pisca de algodón bolbían a sus casitas—comenzaban a cortar aselga, tomate, sebolla, sandía, melon, nabos. Después con el tiempo comensaron a biajar a menisota, nort dakota, y ohio, wisconson a desaijar betabel—los que tenían muebles traían jente en las trocas y les cobraban diez pesos por persona ho cinco—según fuera el presio del betabel. Algunos tenían casitas—nomás dos piesas—un cuarto para dormir y una cosinita pequeña. Los escuzados eran afuera o en los chaparros. Los que no podían salir a los trabajos afuera porque tenían mucha familia chica—pues tenían sus casitas de adobe—o de botes biejos, los estendían y los clababan y arreglaban un tequruchito. Dormían en el suelo o asían bancos de madera. El colchón no era mui popular en esos tiempos—no era sufisiente el medio para comprarlos.

Mis padres creo llegaron a Cristal en 1910—no abía muchas cosas todabía. No bendían solares. Todo era como un rancho—las bacas y los caballos andaban sueltos el 1910. 1911 trajeron jente de méxico, comensaron a desenrraisar. Mi papá jue el maiordomo porque era el único que podía entender el idioma inglés. Así fue que comensaron a cuardar solares y benderlos y mucha jente se quedó.

Mamá tenía una casita pequeña y una carpita. Una bes que binieron a trabajar a Tejas—papá trabajaba en el camino de fierro—ho el traque que le desían—y tubo un accidente y perdió dos dedos del pie hisquierdo, estubo en el hospital—cuando salió la companía le dió un poco de dinero y con eso regresaron al Cristal y compararon unos solares, creo que treinta pesos cada uno.

El 1913 hubo la epidemia de la biruela y mucha jente moría—la quemaban—y con el cuento del trabajo se desarrolló mucho el tuberculosis. El trabajo de la aselga es en la pura agua—se mojaban asta la sintura. Mujeres y hombres y niños—mojados—y el sol tan caliente en la cabesa. Comensaban a enfermarse de tuberculosis. El médico desía de que estaban enfermos y les ponían unas casita pequeñas afuera del pueblo y allí morían. Familias enteras se acabaron con esa enfermedad.

No había sementerio para los mexicanos. Los sepultaban en un pedaso de terreno pedregoso. Papá y otros señores juntaron sentabos—colectaron y dieron el primer abono de un terreno para formar un sementerio. Se pagaba veinte y cinco sentabos por abrir una sepultura—con eso juntaban para seguir dando el abono del lugar. El se hiso responsable de pagarlo y guardó los documentos por veinte y cinco años para que nadie tubiera derecho nomás nosotros los mexicanos.

Mamá—de ber la pobre jente morir por falta de atensión médica—quiso aser algo para alludarles y aprendió como ella pudo a traer niños—a beses en el suelo con una cobijita. Se alumbraban con una bela—ho lámpara de petrolio—nada de focos eléctricos. Ella a beses les traía almuadas ho cobijas de casa. Muchas no habían comido—les traía arroz de la casa y les daba cucharaditas. Las inyecciones era una tasa de pimienta cosida—calientita para dar fuerza que nasiera el bebé. Porque no había médico. El único tenía que recorrer barios pueblitos y cuando llegaba ya era tarde.

No había escuela para los mexicanos. Por eso nadie sabía leer. Mamá lavaba ropa ajena por un peso un buen nudote. Tenía que plancharla y almidonarla. Toda la semana ganaba cinco pesos. Cuando ella estaba lavando nos sentaba a nosotros en un lado y nos enseñó a leer el español.

Con el tiempo comensaron a salir personas para Washington a trabajar en el aspárrago, el elote, la fruta, las bodegas, y en el mentado jape. Entonces cuando se termina el trabajo ban a la costa a la pisca de fresa, después se buelben al jape al último trabajo con toda la familia. Y de Washington se ban a Aidaho a piscar papas. Comiensan a llegar a Washington en marzo y se buelben en septiembre pa Aidaho. Allí se quedan un mez más. De allí se ban a Tejas, pasan allá cuatro meses del año. Así es que los niños ban cuatro meses a la escuela en Tejas y alguno ho dos en Washington. Los sacan de la escuela allá, después los sacan de aquí y las criaturas se confunden mucho. Muchos aprenden algo—hotros no—y el

tiempo pasa y se quedan sin saber nada. Cresen y siguen lo mismo—
biajando de aquí para allá y de allá para acá y esa es la razón porqué
el mexicano no sabe nada y no puede tener un trabajo desente.

Tu papá trabajaba en una planta donde asían hielo por 15 años—
después la cerraron y se fue a trabajar como carpintero en un campo de
consentrasión en Cristal. Después se enganchó con esta companía para
Bancuber, Washington el 1944 y 45 en una construcción donde asían barcos.
Nosotros nos quedamos en Eagle Pass—allí comensaron los tres muchachos
la escuela. Se terminó la guerra el 1945 y mucha jente quedó desocupada.

Oimos el cuento de Washington—que había mucho dinero, que
pagaban mui bien y pensamos benir a Washington. No teníamos carro en
que biajar y este señor Eduardo Salinas contrataba jente y nos benimos
con el. Nomás traíamos muy poco dinero—le pagamos 25 pesos por nosotros
y 15 por cada uno de los muchachos. Era la primera bes que biajábamos. Este
señor dijo que tenía casas y todo para poner a la jente—pero no fue sierto.
Salimos el 13 de marzo de 1946 y llegamos a Toppenish el 18. En el camino
se descompuso la troca sabe cuantas beses—en Lluta tubimos que quedarnos
una noche porque estaba muy nevado el camino y no podíamos caminar.
Todos dormimos sentados y los chiquitos en los brazos porque no teníamos
dinero para rentar un motel. Beníamos como 25 personas adentro de la
troca, más los belises y las cobijas y un colchón estendido adentro de la
troca y unas llantas—paresíamos sardinas. Después se bino un aire y la
lona se rompió por enmedio—la amarraron como pudieron y la nieve
callendo—al fin salimos de la nieve y después se perdió el chofer del camino
—por tantito nos boltea a todos. Pero dios es mui poderoso y nos cuidó—
llegamos por fin a Toppenish. No tenía casa—nada—puras mentiras que
nos contó. Por fin encontró unos tecuruchos todos agujerados en Brown
Estown—como 20 millas afuera de Toppenish. Y en carpas acomodó toda
la jente—con un frío de jesucristo—con estufas de leña y la leña mojada.

Cuando se terminó el jape—vivimos siete meses allí—los muchachos
se enfermaron y a mí me dió pulmonía y tube que ir al doctor. Pues con
el susto que llebamos en el camino no nos quedaron ganas de bolber y
desidimos quedarnos en Washington. Se terminó el trabajo en Brown
Estown y benimos a Toppenish. De allí fuimos a bibir al Golding Farm,
este se componía de hileras de casitas sin puertas y todas calléndose—nomás
tenían una pared y bibía otra persona. Las casas no estaban forradas—
unas no tenían piso—y trabajábamos en el jape. A las mujeres nos pagaban
setenta y cinco centabos la hora y a los señores ochenta centavos por hora.
Pero José como era carpintero no trabajaba en la labor. Asía cajones para
mandar el jape a otros lugares y barias otras cosas. De allí fue dónde tubo
el primer accidente y tú sabes lo demás.

Como comensaste tú a bender sodas desde que tenías diez y doce
años, después en la tiendita en Granger, después en la botica para poder

tener dinero pa hir a la escuela. Y tú sabes que tus hermanos fueron al ejérsito—cómo fueron—dónde anduvieron—lo que hisieron y lo que son.

Ya escribí a María mi hermana que me diera más hideas de como comensó Cristal. Pero dise que no bibió ella mucho allí, pronto se casó y se fue a otra parte. Así es que ya te dije muchas historias. Si quieres los nombres de los mexicanos que abía allá en Cristal cuando llegó mamá a papá díme—llámame y te doy los nombres de los que yo me acuerdo.

PERSONAL CHRONICLE OF CRYSTAL CITY: PART II

irene castañeda

Well daughter as I remember there was lots of Mexican families and they'd go to pick cotton—Ganado, Texas, Corpus Cristy, Agua Dulce, Kerney, and lots of other little towns. When the cotton picking was done they'd come back to their shacks—they'd start to cut spinach, tomatoe, onion, watermelon, melon, radiches, then—in time—they started traveling to Minesota, North Dakota and Ohio, Wisconsin—to top beets—the people who had transportation would carry people in the trucks and charged $10.00 per person or $5.00—depending on the price they got paid for beets. Some of the people had houses—only 2 rooms—a room to sleep and a little kitchen. The toilets were outside or in the chaparros. The people who couldn't get out to work the crops because they had too many little kids, well they had adobe houses or houses made from old tin cans that they hamered open and nailed—they'd fix a little shack. They would sleep on the floor or make wooden benches to sleep on. Matresses weren't very common then—there wasn't enough money to buy them.

My parents—I think they got to Crystal City in 1910—there wasn't too much there then—they didn't sell lots. Everything was like a ranch, cows and horses roamed loose in 1910. 1911 they brought people from Mexico, they started to clear the land. My father was the foreman because he was the only one who could understand English—so that's how they started to make up lots and sell them and many people stayed.

Mother had a small house and a little tent. Once when they came to Texas to work, father worked on the railroad, or el traque as they called, he had an accident and lost two toes from his left foot—he was in the hospital—when he got out the company gave him a little money and with that they returned to Crystal City and bought a few lots—I think they were $35.00 each.

In 1913 there was the smallpox epidemic and many people died—they would burn the bodies. With the kind of work they did, tuberculosis was pretty common. With spinich, you worked right in the water, people would get wet clear up to their waist—women, men and children—everybody all wet and the hot sun beating down on the head—they began to get sick from tuberculosis—the doctor would say what they were sick from and they would build little shacks for them outside of town—and whole families died there from that sickness.

There was no cemetary for Mexicans. They would bury them in ground that was all rocky. My father and other men collected money—they collected and gave the first payment on a piece of ground to form a cemetary. You paid twenty-five cents to dig a grave—that's how they collected to keep making the payments on the place. He took the responsibility of paying for it and he saved the papers for twenty-five years so that no one except us Mexicans would have right to it.

Mother, from seeing the poor people die for lack of medical attention, wanted to do something to help them and she learned, as best she could, to deliver babies. Sometimes on the floor with just a small blanket. Lighting was a candle or petroleum lamp—there were no electic bulbs. Sometimes she would bring pillows or blankets from home—many of the women had not eaten—she would bring them rice from home and feed them by spoonfuls. The shots were a cup of hot pepper tea—to give strength for the baby to be born—because there was no doctor. The only one had to travel to several towns and when he arrived it was too late.

There was no school for Mexicans. That's why no one knew how to read. Mother washed other people's clothes for a dollar for a big load. She had to starch and iron it. She would earn five dollars for a week's work. When she was washing clothes she would sit us down beside her and she taught us to read Spanish.

In time people began to go out to Washington to work in asparagus, corn, warehouses, in the so-called hop. Then when that work is over, they go to the coast to pick (straw)berries, then they return to the hops—the final stage—with the whole family, and from Washington they go to Idaho in September. They stay there a month, from there they go to Texas—spending four months of the year there. So the children go to school four months in Texas and one or two in Washington. They take them out of school there then they take them out of school here and the youngsters get very confused. Many learn something—others don't—and time passes and they know hardly anything.—They grow up and keep on in the same way —journeying from here to there—from there to here—and that's the reason why the Mexican hasn't learned anything and can't have a decent job.

Your father worked for fifteen years in a plant where they made ice— then they closed it and he went to work as a carpenter in a concentration camp in Crystal City—then he contracted himself with this company to go to Vancouver, Washington in 1944 and 1945 in a construction company that made boats. We stayed in Eagle Pass—that's where the three older children started school. The war ended in 1945, many people were left unemployed.

We heard the tale of Washington—that there was lots of money, that they paid real well, and we thought about coming to Washington. We didn't have a car to travel in and this man, Eduardo Salinas used to contract people and we came with him. We didn't have much money, we paid him $25.00 for us and $15.00 for each of the children. This was the first time we had traveled. This man said that he had housing and everything for the people, but it wasn't true. We left the 13th of March of 1946 and arrived in Toppenish the 18th. On the road the truck broke down—who knows how many times. In Utah we had to stay overnight because the road was snowed in and we couldn't travel—we all slept sitting up with the little ones in our arms because we had no money to rent a motel. We were about twenty-five people in the truck, plus the suitcases and blankets and a mattress spread out inside, and some tires—we looked like sardines. Then a heavy wind came and the tarp on the truck tore in half. They tied it as best they could—and the snow falling. We finally got out of the snow and then the driver lost his way—we almost turned over. But God is powerful and he watched over us—finally we got to Toppenish. He didn't have housing—nothing—all lies that he told us. He finally found some old shacks, all full of knotholes, in Brownstown—about twenty miles outside of Toppenish—and in tents he placed all the people. It was bitterly cold—with wood stoves and wet wood.

When the hop was over, we'd lived seven months there, the boys had gotten sick, I'd gotten pneumonia and had to go to the doctor. Well—with the fright we'd had on the road, we didn't feel like returning and we decided to stay in Washington. The work ended in Brownstown and we came to Toppenish. Then we went to live at the Golding farm—this was made up of rows of shacks—without doors and all falling apart—there was only a wall between the next unit where another person lived. The houses weren't insulated—they didn't have floors, and we worked in the hop. They paid us women 75¢ per hour and 85¢ for the men. But since José was a carpenter he didn't work in the field. He made crates to ship hop to other places—he did other things too. That's where he had his first accident—and you know the rest—how from the time you were ten and twelve years old you worked selling pop, then in the little corner market in Granger, then in the drugstore to have money to go to school. And you know about your brothers—that they went into the service, how they went, where they went, what they did, and what they are.

I have already written to María, my sister, to give me more ideas about how Crystal City got started, but she says that she didn't live there very long, she married young and went to live someplace else. So now I've told you many histories—if you want the names of the Mexicans who were living in Crystal City when my mother and father arrived there, call me and I'll give you the names I remember.

Abelardo uses the analogy between migrants and swallows returning to the same place year after year to emphasize the cyclic nature of a migratory life. He answers his own question about the reasons for migrating by noting that they are victims of economic necessity. He also speaks of the love for mother earth, and with the last line reminds one of the present struggle being waged by farmworkers.

EL IMIGRANTE

abelardo

golondrinas cortando betabel,
Americanos de papel,
este México-Americano
o nomás mejicano
que migra con to'y familia
n los compos de colorado,
illinois, califa, y michigan
se me hace que no es más que puro gitano.
salmones en el desaije
con un ojo a las colonias
a las cuales muy pronto volverán,
no les voy
a decir porque lo hacen
porque la verdad ni ellos saben,
quizá el cariño a la tierra
mamado de una chichi prieta,
quizá el corazón libre
que dicta la jornada,
aunque el carro esté muy viejo
y la gasolina cara.
turistas sin un centavo
de vacación en nebraska,
aun alabama
es un descanso de tejas.
bumerangas que la mano de dios
por este mundo tiró,

gente buena,
gente honesta,
gente víctima de su necesidad de migrar,
la lechuga o la justicia es lo que van a sembrar.

In contrast to the Crónica, which was a retrospective view of migration, "American Me," dating from the mid-1940s, narrates a young girl's present experience—leaving the urban barrio during the summer months to work the crops with family and friends in surrounding agricultural areas.

Despite the harshness of her economic situation, she relates to her family, friends, and nature, with fresh innocence. As the story's title implies, she encounters a conflict between her concept of her own identity, and society's definition of her.

The sensitive use of language in describing her reaction to nature and to personal relationships makes for a warm and convincing human character.

AMERICAN ME

personal narration of a young chicana— presented by beatrice griffith

We go every July from Los Angeles to pick the fruits in the summer hills of Hanford. We lived in tents and would get up early in the grey morning when it was cold. Then we all ate outdoors over a little fire. Everybody getting up from their tents and talking and calling to each other and cooking the beans. Then we go to work and stand on our feet from seven in the morning until six at night. Gee, man, I would get so tired. You know, in the fruits you dream, sleep, walk, breathe, and talk apricots— yellow and big and soft all around you. You pick 'em, you dump 'em, you squash 'em, you peel 'em, you cut 'em, you count 'em. Everything is apricots. How many you pick? How many you peel? How much buckets or trays? Always it is to eat and smell apricots. Cause apriots is pennies and sometimes they are silver dollars after you pick them a long time. Now we get lots more money in the fruits cause there is a war, and now can go to the carnival with rich money like the boss of the ranch.

This day I tell you the boss came and paid the checks. Man, it was great. To all the working people and kids he paid them. My father and mother and me and my brother gots a hundred dollars for working three weeks, would you believe it? When I saw that check I told my mother she was fooling. The boss was just playing a game. But she said it was real money, and when I heard that I jumped up crazy I guess. I told her that check was a lot of school dresses. She said that in that check was a couch that made a bed at night for my father and brother who are tired to sleep on the little iron bed by the washing machine. And it was clothes for my brother and my father, and in it was a car. Would you believe it? A little broken car was in that check? And sure it was. Oh I tell you all was happy that night for getting money and lots clothes and food and stuff in that check.

At this camp was my new boy friend, Mokey. He was clean and handsome, not too tall—just right for me with a big smile and a handsome nose. He always looks like a movie actor in his Levis. And he walks with a swing real sure, like the Negro baseball player at school who never hurries, just reaches out and grabs the ball so slow he count the stitches on them. It was Mokey who helped Freddie and my cousin Ramón fix a good shower for us when we got to camp. They took some rubber hose and put it up high, then spread branches to spray from the water. Then they made it private with boards, and we had a shower. Sure, there was a little hole down by our legs and the boys used to look in and sing and yell.

This night of getting paid was excitement, *Jíjola!* All the kids call from the tents about going to the carnival near Fresno. My old aunt who remembers the little jamaicas in Mexico, and who is with a young heart still, comes to our fire to talk over the war, and her boy who is a prisoner in Bataan, and the long fights and revolutions of the Mexicans, with my father. My aunt is a very beautiful woman with smooth brown skin and a proud face. She knows everything, all things in the heart of a girl. She had eight with five in the grave behind the adobe house on the hill. It is like all those dead girls were making her heart sweet with their wants of living in their dark graves. She brought my father a little bottle of her old old wine this night, and he goes with her and my mother to sit by the fire, where others from the fields are sitting and eating under the trees in the night.

My cousin Ramón from Hanford has a little truck that's green and cute named Benito, that will take us to town. To get to this truck and Ramón, Mokey and me walk through the fields to the long dusty road. In the fields was sometimes little rabbits and birds, and there was always haystacks all bunched to jump on real quick and run. With Mokey, he loved those rabbits and sometimes would catch one and rub it soft on his face. Always it was like that. Sometimes he look at a little black fly, so careful how his wings is made, and his head put on by God. And he looks so long at the plants to see their little veins and how is a leaf put on that his sister tell him, "What you see in that plant, a picture of a pretty girl, a blondie maybe?" Then Mokey tell her to go lay an egg—and a big one.

Walking across the fields into the dark hills far away with Mokey was keen. He took my hand and said, "I wish Felix and Frankie could see this sky. Man, they knew this country, they worked this country."

"Mokey, you know lots, what makes wars anyway? All my brothers too are gone to war and they weren't mad at anybody—except the cops." I looked at him but he only shake his head.

"Lucy, I don't know. Sister at church says wars is from all the people's sins. But my mother says it's the big heads make 'em, and the little people slave 'em. I tell her, wars just don't happen. It's from the people bumping and pushing and getting mad at each other, I guess. Maybe they're afraid." He stopped and cut two sunflowers, then he stuck each the one in my braids. "Now let's run, I'll race you to the truck," and so we did.

Inside the truck without much paint was lots kids already. Everybody was happy and singing and calling to everybody, pushing and laughing. All the kids sit tight in the truck cause it goes to pieces lots of times and the sides all fall down. You always hit hard when you drive cause the tires go flat sometimes. Then Ramón and the boys stuff rags into the tires when they go flat so we ride lots of hitting together. Manuel, he's my cousin they call Jitterbug Sanchez, cause he's a good dancer, his picture is in the paper for the prize fight, well Manuel brings his good guitar to sing some ranchero songs and some songs for love. All sing "Soldados Rasos," and are happy for smiling and yelling, cause all are happy for living, I guess.

When we come onto the long highway that goes to Hanford this night I tell you about, two policemen in their white car stopped the truck because they see us Mexicans inside. But my cousin Ramón, who's been to high school and who is smart knowing all about maps and what means a filibuster and the United States Congress, says to that cop, "This is a free country aint' it? We can sing in this little truck if we want can't we? The man who says Mexicans can't sing for breaking the law in this truck doesn't know his country."

So the cops, seeing my cousin was smart said, "Oh, wise guy, huh? Okay, let's see your draft cards. All of you."

But only my cousin had a card from the draft, only he was eighteen. The cops look hard at his draft card and then tell us, "Okay, cholos, go on."

And so we go down the long bright highway into the streets of the town. Lots of people and kids were holding hands and walking down the streets. Little cars from the ranches and fruit camps passed us, some fast with only one light, some honking horns, but everybody was laughing and calling. Mokey waves his arms and says some dirty words to the car in back of us that gives us a big bump. The boys all pile out to look, then pile in again when they see it was nothing.

Pretty soon we come to the carnival. You know it's the place before you get there cause the music comes right through the trees and houses and into our truck. And you can see high up in the pink sky the ferris wheel going swing around the stars. And the voice of the ticket man you can hear a little, just like the radio from the boss's house in the night on the ranch. Only sometimes you cannot hear it with the crickets, like it went around the posts and cars and barns to get to us who were listening.

At the carnival everything was excitement, and all the kids pile out. First thing I see is my cousin Danny. My cousin Danny, I tell you, was fun like Cantinflas in the Mexican movies.

The flying baskets with skirts and legs swinging in the sky stopped, and Mokey and me got in a gold basket. Adelita and Manuel sit in a red one, and soon the music begin and we are whizzing in the sky with all the stars falling around and down down to the ground. Then we jerked up high almost to a pink cloud, and Mokey held me tight, with the air whirring around us like a dive bomber. There was little screams coming from around like they was whistles that got stuck, but it was only the girls liking the hugging I think.

When we got out from the gold basket Mokey and me was still hugging like in the movies. All the peoples and tents and music and little screams was going around dancing in my head like a jitterbug. Up the streets some kids was riding on the merry-go-round and yelling and laughing to catch the gold ring from the horses and lions. Mokey and me watched Felix showing how strong he was from working and getting hard muscles in the hay fields that summer. He hit the wood block bang with the big hammer, and hit it so hard the little bell at the top in the dark would ring. The other guys was laughing and making fun of him showing off big for Theresa, him that didn't know she was going steady with two marines.

The tin woman in the next show was laughing too, but always she is laughing. Whenever you walk or ride in that carnival, or down the near streets, you hear her big laugh, in the night or day, you always hear it.

Across the carnival street, behind the wire fence, was the place where the little green and yellow and red automobiles go bump and crash around the big floor with music and fun. In one of the automobiles was an old man with red hair waving his arms and bumping the other autos like a borrachito. He had a white duck he won in the carnival and waved that duck over his head like a flag I think.

Pretty soon down the carnival street come all the kids singing and laughing and shouting. All their arms was around each other like a chain. In the middle was Danny with his arms full of Kewpie dolls.

Danny was always like the miracle man in the circus. Always he could go to a carnival with nothing but poor money, some pennies and nickels, and come home with hams and ducks and alarm clocks and Kewpies. Only never before tonight was there so many Kewpies.

He gave a Kewpie to Mokey for some tickets to ride the little automobiles. Then he yelled us, "Come on, let's have a race!"

We all piled in the cars, red, green, yellow—all the cars that was empty gots full. Danny put all his Kewpie dolls around him and piled some more in the other cars. Then the race began. *Qué suave!* Man it was swell. My heart was pumping up and down like some jumping beans. I got scared bumping so many cars and my heart went black and my ears go clank...clank, but it was fun.

Danny banged my car, Mokey hit him, then Manuel and Adelita and Ramón and Rosie all was banging cars and yelling. Everybody got bumped, nobody got hurt and the music was loud like in the circus. The American kid bumped Mokey and laughed, and Mokey bumped him back. Then they was bumping, laughing and pushing, each car a little faster and a little harder. Pretty soon then the American guy looked away, and Mokey gave him a hard bump. Then they was getting mad for reals. The American kid called him, "Dirty Mexican, I'll fix you!"

Mokey tell him, "Who do you think you are, calling me dirty Mexican?"

The guy banged him hard and say, "Well, I'm me, American me. That's who I am!"

So Mokey banged him hard on the head with a pink Kewpie and yell him, "Yeah? Well I'm American me too. American inside, but Mexican on top!"

Danny throws a Kewpie to Mokey who jumps high in his car to catch it. Then all the kids begin to make trouble for purpose, all bunching and popping out of the cars to fight and hit. Danny throws us all his Kewpies, and the fight was on hard. The Kewpies was going over the cars hitting kids, busting on the floor with broken pieces getting smashed and run over. Everybody was mad with anger falling down and busting like a bomb in that place. The Kewpies was going zoom like big bullets. The cars was driving hard and spinning and bumping. Adelita's car she whirled in a circle, round and round. The air was thick and hot with kids. Some stand up in their cars the better to hit. The cars all jammed up in bunches. Everybody was all mixed up and tangled, hitting hard, zam the next one to him.

The manager or somebody cut off the electricity. Ramón yells, "Cops coming!"

Then it was a fight to get out that door with everybody running and tripping and getting socked. The American kids beat it out first, running through all the carnival people to where their cars was parked. We got in our truck, but before Ramón got the engine started everything was all mixed up again, with the American kids and us all yelling and hitting and pulling hair and getting socked. But we finally got going and drove bumping down the street by the popcorn man and the carnival people. Some of those kids was hanging on the truck but we banged their hands and they let go.

Ramón drove fast going down that big road in our truck. Danny turned off the lights so the cops wouldn't see our truck and we rode into the very night across the fields to the highway. Like Danny, Mokey's hands was bloody and his clothes was torn, and his breath was breathing hard—but he put his arms tight around me in that little ride.

It was quiet in the dark with the trees and fields and hills. Only could we hear the kids whispering and the car going fast like the wind, and the loud crazy laughing of the tin woman at the carnival following us down the road into the mist to our tents across the black fields.

Soon we would be in bed in our tents by the camp in the fruits, and I would put my head from under the tent and Mokey put his from his tent in the dark and stars, and we would talk and talk so long, our heads by the dark ground. All swell, until our mothers say, "Quit your talking and long gossip." And then we would go to sleep in the warm tent for morning to wake us to move on to pick the prunes.

But now, this little minute, I was sitting tight close to Mokey. I ask him, "Mokey, knowing about pushing and bumping and hating and all that, doesn't keep people from getting mad, huh?"

Mokey hugs me tighter. Then he kissed me soft soft, the first kiss. For Mokey knows that to be a gentleman means always please the lady for what she wants.

The decades between 1942–1964 witnessed yet another kind of massive Mexican migration to the United States. This time it was single men—braceros—and was the result of a series of agreements between the governments of Mexico and the United States. Theoretically a means to ensure harvesting of crops during the crisis of World War II, the Bracero Program was actually a tool by which agribusiness was able to maintain an expendable supply of cheap labor.

Underpaid and abused in the United States the bracero often experienced additional hardships upon his return to Mexico. In the Mexican novel, *La región más transparente* (1958) Carlos Fuentes uses Gabriel to represent the contradictions in the societies of both Mexico and the U.S., to express the negative cultural influence of the U.S. on the bracero, and to show how both governments exploit the laborer. Fuentes demonstrates the dehumanizing process by showing its effect on the language and vocabulary of the braceros.

LA REGIÓN MÁS TRANSPARENTE

carlos fuentes

Todo el olor a vómito, respiración pesada, sueño, se suspendió un segundo al frenar el camión. "¡Méee-ico!" eructó el chofer y se echó la gorra hacia atrás. Cagarruta de pájaro embadurnada en las ventanas, y un lento removerse de los pasajeros, de pollos en huacales, de petaquillas maltratadas y zapatos descartados. Gabriel trató de limpiar el vidrio para peinarse; se acomodó la gorra de beisbolista y descolgó su saco de cuero. ¡México! A correr, ahora sí, a gastar unos pesos en un libre, y llegar pronto a la casa. Con la mano apretada sobre la cartera, Gabriel se abrió paso hasta la puerta del camión. Unas huilas se paseaban por la plaza Netzahualcóyotl con las rodillas vendadas y los tacones lodosos. "Ahora, maje, o no me vuelves a ver". "Conmigo te acabas de criar, papacito". "Para todas traigo, putas. ¡Y pago dolaritos!" "Yes yes hazla buena pendejote sabroso". "¡Nos estuvimos mirando!" Gabriel se echó a andar por la calle, a sentir el olor punzante de las carnes morenas, a escuchar el taconeo de sus pies sobre baldosas viejas, a ver su nuevo reflejo, próspero, curtido, en los aparadores apagados de las zapaterías. Se le amontonaba la ciudad, se le hacía pedazos en la cabeza. Como que no había cielo. Pero ya volvería al campo abierto de California, cada año, a respirar piel de tomate. "¡Libre!" Calles rectas, amojonadas de basura, casas bajas, descascaradas. Se divertía leyendo los letreros, de las cantinas, de la pila de funerarias que hay por Tránsito y la Colonia Obrera: sus fachadas pintadas de blanco, y siempre los féretros enanos, para los niños, de pino blanco, en exhibición afuera. Creía oler la sangre tiesa de un niño detrás de cada puerta: en su casa, nada más, se habían muerto cuatro, tempranito, antes de poder hacer nada, ni trabajar, ni coger, ni ninguna de las cosas importantes. Gabriel castañeteaba con impaciencia los dedos. Ya mero, con el fajazo de dólares en la bolsa, y los regalos relucientes para que todos vivieran mejor. Era el primer año, y volvería todos, a como diera lugar, con la legalidad o sin ella, exponiéndose a las balas y hasta encuerado por el río. Eso, o andar de paletero en las colonias del D. F. Ya se lo decía al Tuno, cuando estuvieron juntos en la cosecha de Texas: "Y qué que no te dejen entrar a sus pinches restoranes. Voy, voy, ¿a poco te dejan entrar al Ambasader en México?" "Aquí mero; cóbrese". Tocó Gabriel la puerta de tablas, las del 28-B. "Aquí estoy con mis chivas". La mamacita con los dientes amarillos, y el viejo con su expresión de máscara de sueños, y la hermana grande, la que ya estaba poniéndose buena, y los dos niños de overol y camisetas con hoyos. "¡Grabiel, Grabiel, estás más fuerte, más hombrezote!" "Ahi les traigo a todos; anden chamacos, abran la petaca". El cuarto iluminado por velas, con las estampas junto al catre de hierro. "Para ti, Pepa, que ya te encontré tan tetona: esto que usan las gringas para detenérselos. Very fain". "Ah qué Grabiel tan curioso" repetía la madre una y otra vez. "Y otra gorra igual a la mía para ti, viejo, de los meros indios de Cleveland: ahí es donde se las pone de a cuatro Beto Avila. Y para ti, viejecita: mira nomás, para que ya no trabajes tanto". "¿Y qué clase de chingaderita es ésa, hijo?" "Ahoritita te enseño. Oigan, ¿y Fidelio?" "Anda de chamba, Grabiel, en casa de unos apretados. Pero explica este chisme". "Mira: el frasquito lo pones encima de la cosa blanca; luego metes ahi los frijoles, o las zanahorias, o lo que quieras y al rato está todo bien molido, solito, en vez de que lo hagas tú". "A ver, a ver". "No, viejecita, hay que enchufarlo, en la electricidad". "Pero si aquí no tenemos luz eléctrica, hijo". "Ah caray. Pues ni modo viejecita, así, como metate. Usalo así. Qué remedio. ¡A ver, traigo filo! ¿Dónde andan las tortillas?" Por nada se cambia la comidita mexicana, *pero el año entrante, otra vez, a jalarle p'al Norte, donde está el dinero, y el trabajo a la mano, y los five and ten, y la luz eléctrica.*

Voy...En el cabaré ese en donde estuve de mozo, pos sí, muy suave. Pero luego les ves los hocicos a los mozos viejos, mano, y sientes rete gacho. Ya no dan una, ya nunca hicieron lana, y como que se les salió todo de adentro. Están pendejos. Y los cabrones lambiscones metidos allí todas las noches, buscando trancazos. No, mano...¿Pero qué te queda entonces? Te vas de paletero y es la misma cosa. No, mano...Vamos al carajo, a buscar chamba al Norte. Ahi te dan dólares, te regresas a gastarlos en tu cantón y ni quien te esté jodiendo. ¿Que te tratan como mierda los gringos? Pos ni modo, para eso te pagan tu buena lana.

—¡Godán sonobich!

—¡Hijos de puta! Caray, Beto, a l'hora que te echan ese argüende para matar pulgas encima y te encueran y a veces hasta te rapan, te entran ganas de...

—De agarrar un chicote y...

—Un montón de pelados metidos en un cuarto para reses, Beto, todos encuerados y oliendo a la chingadera esa...

—Di Di Ti.

—Esa mera. Y un gringote de dos metros gritándote gríser y esculcándote todito. Pero ¡qué caray! A ése no lo vuelves a ver, ni a los otros. Luego, cuando sales del trabajo, pues duermes en un catre a gusto y tienes lana para ir a coger o a tomar. Se acaba la cosecha y te despachan volando. Y cuando cruzas la frontera, mano, pos hasta recuerdas bonito aquellas tierras.

WHERE THE AIR IS CLEAR

carlos fuentes

The stink of vomit, sleep, heavy breathed air lifted the second the bus braked. "*May*-ee-co!" the driver roared. Bird cages were taken down from the windows, passengers stirred awake, chickens moved in their crates, cheap valises and secondhand shoes shuffled. Gabriel tried to clean the window to see to comb his hair; he cocked his baseball cap and took down his leather jacket. Mexico City! Now to run, spend a few pesos for a taxi, and get home quick. With his hand pressed against his wallet, Gabriel pushed to the exit. A group of whores were crossing Netzahualcóyotl Plaza with their knees wrapped and their heels muddy.

"Now, Mac, or don't bother to see me again!"

"With me you'll stop suffering, daddy."

"You name it, I'm for it."

"I'll pay with dollars!"

"Sure, sure, what you'll pay with is the big joke."

Gabriel set off, walking along the street, smelling the pungent odors of brown bodies, looking at his new reflection, crew-cut, prosperous, in the show windows of shoe stores. The city towered over him, crowded down on him as if there were no sky. He'd go back again, every year, from California's open fields to breathe tomato skins. "Taxi!" Straight streets, cluttered with trash, and now low peeling houses. He amused himself reading the signs over bar doors, over the doors of funeral parlors clustered along Tránsito, white store fronts, and outside, on display, always a white-enameled child's coffin. He could smell the dead stiff blood of a child behind every door; in his own home four had died, too young, before they had done anything, neither work nor fuck, nor anything important in life.

Gabriel snapped his fingers with impatience. A wad of dollars in his pocket, shining presents, so they could all live better. It was his first year, and he would go back again every year, legally or not, risking bullets when he crossed the Río. Well, it was that or push an ice-cream cart along the streets of Mexico City. And he had said so to Tuno, when they were together at harvest time in Texas, "So what if they don't let you in their crappy restaurants? You able to get in the Ambassador in Mexico City? Besides, the only thing here is to get money." Gabriel rapped the wooden door of 28-B. "Hey, I'm back!"

His yellow-toothed mother, his father's always drowsy face, his big sister who was beginning to be good-looking, the two little boys in overalls and holey shirts: "Gabriel, Gabriel, you're bigger, you're grown up!"

"This has got everything for all of you, so let's go, open it!" The room lit by candles, prints of virgins and saints over the iron cot. "For you, Pepa, because you're getting fat, this is what the gringo girls use to squeeze themselves in. Very fine."

"Ah, Gabriel, how strange," his mother repeated over and over. "And a baseball cap just like mine for you, old man. The Cleveland Indians, that's where Beto Avila socks his home runs. And old woman, just look. So you won't have to work so hard."

"And what kind of damn thing is this, my son?"

"I'll show you. Where's Fidelio?"

"He's working, Gabriel, in a house in the Lomas. But explain this machine to me."

"Look, you put the glass vase on top of the white machine and you fill it with beans or fruit or whatever you want to grind up, and it grinds it up for you."

"Let's see it. Go ahead."

"No, Mamá, you got to plug it into the lights first."

"But we don't have electricity, child."

"God damn. That's right. Well, just use it as a vase, that's all you can do. Hey, I'm starving! Where're my tortillas?" He would not change Mexican cooking for anything, but next year once again he would take off northward, to the land where there was work and money, and electricity.

You know, I had it made waiting tables in that cabaret. But after a while the old waiters began to snap at me and I felt like shit. They didn't make nothing. I was stealing their bread. They're just goddamn bums. And those slick-talking bastards who come there night after night, looking for a fight. No, *mano,* not this boy. But what the hell is there left? You push an ice-cream cart, it's the same fucking thing. No, *mano.* All day at work you get screwed, and, come evening, you take off and go looking for a screwing. You head for the States. They give you dollars, you come back to live it up at home. To hell with them. So what if the damn gringos treat you like shit? That's why they pay you."

"God damn son of a bitch!"

"Son of a bitch! And jeez, the way they make you strip and they look for your lice, you feel like—"

"Like grabbing something. . ."

"Cut hair laying around the cow-stall to your ankles, everybody naked and stinking like whores with that fucking—"

"D.D.T."

"Shit, yes. And a six-foot-tall gringo hollering 'greaser' at you and snooping through everything you got. But what the hell! you'll never see the bastard again, nor any of the rest of them. And when you finish a day's work, you can sleep in your cot as long as you want to and you got dough for a drunk or a lay. And then the harvest is in and they kick you out on your ass. And when you come back across the border, *mano,* you remember those rich fields. Here there ain't anything but desert and dirty Indians. Nothing grows but the kids, and they don't grow much. But on the other side—"

"Fifo tells me that when they get the dam, there's going to be good land in Sonora, Gabriel."

"We'll see, Christ, what wouldn't you give to be able to work and make a living here in Mexico City?"

"Yeah."

(trans. by Sam Hileman)

Before, during, and after the Bracero Program, a parallel migration of single Mexican men occurred. The Mexican novel, *Murieron a mitad del río,* (1959) by Luis Spota, relates in first person the experience, the hopes, the fears and aspirations of men who crossed the border without papers. Called mojados, wetbacks or alambristas, these men have been preyed upon by unscrupulous growers or middle men for agribusiness who hide them from the immigration authorities during peak harvest time—and frequently report them to "la migra" right before payday.

This novel offers realistic treatment of the conflicts that arise between Mexican nationals and Chicanos as they are pitted against each other for jobs. It also presents a Mexican's view of the Mexican American.

MURIERON A MITAD DEL RÍO

luis spota

¡Perros texanos!

Desde la orilla frontera los reflectores venían peinando el agua del río. Paván calculó que no andaban muy lejos.

—Es la patrulla —reconoció brevemente, y las ingles se le estremecieron con su miedo amargo.

Ni Lupe ni Luis hablaron. Los blancos ojos redondos seguían tercos y oblicuos, con doble luz, cayendo en la corriente, cada vez más cerca; arrinconándolos sobre sí mismos, barriendo la basura de la sombra que los ocultaba, que los protegía. El agua les colgaba del pecho, y no tenían dónde esconderse en aquella soledad ligeramente fría.

—¡Perros! —repitió.

En ese momento no quería pensar en *Cocula,* ni en que volviera a gritar como diez segundos antes. "Que no lo haga ahora el cochino joto..." deseó con toda su alma. No los perdía de vista, y pudo contarlos bien cuando los tuvo más cerca, a un centenar de metros: eran ya cuatro los reflectores, y los chorros de su luz se clavaban en el río o abrían boquetes azulados en la negrura de la orilla mexicana. Se movieron un poco, bruscamente, enfocando hacia la parte en que ellos temían.

—¡Túmbense! —alcanzó a decir Paván, antes de que la sierra luminosa rebanara la noche en dos mitades, sobre sus cabezas.

"Hijos de gringo..." gruñó al hundir la cara, de sopetón, hasta las orejas, en el agua. Sobre las tres bolas peludas y medio sumergidas pasó lentamente el aspa cuadruplicada. Hasta entonces no advirtió que sentía frío, colándosele por su ropa empapada. Hacia la izquierda, al ras, seguía corriendo la barredora de luz.

Ahora los hombres que rastreaban el río estaban casi enfrente, en la ribera. Paván volvió a sumergirse, quedamente. En eso, en la otra orilla a su espalda, escuchó de nuevo el grito: "¡El muy c....!" Los buscadores se detuvieron, anclados, alertas en su brillo de ángulos sobre el agua.

—¡Ese *Cocula*....! —identificó, hablando sobre el hombro.

—¡Idiota! —dijo la otra voz, silbada entre los dientes, con un poco de furia y un poco de temor.

—Seguirá gritando...

—¡Déjalo por maricón!

No podían moverse, porque los brazos de luz se habían puesto a indagar, precisamente, aquella parte del río. Escucharon voces en inglés: voces amortiguadas, ocultas tras el brillo que los encandilaba inmovilizándolos. Volvió a saltar el grito sobre el agua, y Pav_n deseó, con la furia arrugándole los labios, que el carajo cargara con *Cocula*. Sonaba estruendosamente en el reprentino silencio y desde el lejano resplandor amarillento de Matamoros. "¿Estará ciego para no ver la luz que nos anda buscando?"

—¡Espérenme! ¡Espérenme, Pavén!

"Ahora no se largarán por nada del mundo", se dijo furioso. Al oír su nombre, bajo la planta helada se le metió el fondo escurridizo del lecho del río. Los fanales pasaban y repasaban, buscando al que había gritado. Prefirieron no moverse. "No se irán hasta que nos pesquen". La corriente oculta era fuerte, violenta, muy distinta a la apacible superficie. Se pegaba a sus piernas y hacía esfuerzos por arquearlas, como si fueran de chicle.

Sufría deseando que los reflectores se fueran, o que dejaran de alumbrar aquel sitio. "¿Y el bajo?" No podía alzar la cara y buscarlo. Su única defensa, de la que bien podría depender la salvación de todos, era continuar quietos, sin moverse. Maldijo a Pancho Orozco por asegurarles que podían pasar sin cuidados. "Deben traer carabinas", se previno, pensando en los hombres de la patrulla. "Deben traerlas; nunca las dejan, y en el río se puede cazar".

Recordó vagamente que el bajo arenoso estaba un poco a la derecha. Resolvió arriesgarse y caminó hacia allí, con lentos pasos cautelosos. Luchaba contra la fuerza del agua y contra la fuerza de su pavor. Se detuvo a escuchar si los otros le seguían.

—Por acá está el bajo —orientó Pavén, apuntando el ruido ensordinado de su voz hacia donde venía el rumor líquido de sus compañeros.

Por un lado, las cuatro barras de luz tendían un puente sobre el río. Un gran trecho de México se iluminaba, desierto. El bajo era un cocodrilo de arena, con el lomo fuera del agua. De no más de veinte metros, espejeante cuando lo soslayaban los reflectores. Se hicieron garabato, al socaire. Con la pala desesperada de sus uñas, Pavén comenzó a cavar, para formar un agujero y esconderse. "Como los cangrejos", resopló. "O como un muerto que prepara su propio hoyo". Luis y Lupe hacían lo mismo. De pronto, les cayó encima un chaparrón blanco, delator. Se tiraron panza abajo. Deseaban los tres hacerse pequeños, invisibles, transparentes a la terca luz que pasaba, en andanada, sobre sus cabezas; esa terca luz, ahora absorta e inmóvil, precisamente, en el bajo. "¿Cuándo diablos se irán?", pensaban sin decirlo, mirando los reflectores.

De entre los dos pares de luces, del punto mismo donde debía estar el ceño de los ojos mecánicos, salió un flamazo fugazmente anaranjado, y luego el ruido largo y crujiente de la detonación.

—¡Están tirando...!

No pudo reprimir el miedo, arrugado muy al fondo de su piel; pero estaba seguro de que no era contra ellos. No sabía por qué, pero estaba seguro.

Tronó otro disparo y su estrépito tardó mucho en extinguirse. En ese momento, al escuchar en el silencio subsecuente el rumor extranjero de las voces, quiso alcanzar a entender lo que decían, sin conseguirlo. Pasó la eternidad de un minuto. "¿Y *Cocula?*" Con el retumbo del último tiro se había apagado también su voz.

Los reflectores comenzaron a distanciarse.

No dejaron su tumba de arena hasta que la luz fué alejándose; hasta que el peine tenaz comenzó a hundirse en la distancia, navegando lo superficie. El agua, al sacar ellos sus cuerpos, llenó en un triple remolino lodoso los agujeros. Pero, casi al instante, tuvieron que tenderse de nuevo, asustados por uno de esos ecos inexplicables de todos los ríos.

Supo Paván que estaban a mitad del río. Lo supo porque recordó que el bajo de arena marcaba la frontera—la mitad final de México y la mitad inicial de Estados Unidos. Lo había visto durante horas, hasta que oscureció por completo, la tarde anterior. Ya sus pies, ahora, no se apoyaban en su país. Ya aquella no era el agua de su río. Eran barro y agua, y también peligro, extranjeros, diferentes. Porque ya no estaba en éste sino del otro lado, experimentó un gran pellizco de miedo; supo del riesgo de ser un *mojado,* un inmigrante ilegal. Un hombre fuera de la ley americana, pero dentro de la muerte de las pistolas americanas —o de los rifles. Fué por ello que comenzó a sufrir, realmente, con los miedos del otro que habían desencadenado los disparos cuando mediaba esa minúscula raya geográfica, enorme de momento en sus ciento cincuenta metros de corriente.

No hablaron más. Cada uno sabía que los otros dos estaban temerosos de que *Cocula* siguiera gritando, si en el viento le llegaban sus cuchicheos. Volvieron a lanzar sus pies entumidos hacia la tierra de Brownsville, glugluteando a cada paso.

—¡Estamos llegando! —anunció Paván.

—¡Del otro lado! —completaba Lupe, con un eco de satisfacción.

v

Cuando salía el sol, continuaron la búsqueda. Luis por un lado; Paván por el opuesto.

—Paván, Paván...¡Corre!

Fué corriendo. Luis estaba hincado junto a algo, que apenas sobresalía del agua, en el borde mismo del río.

Cuando alzó la cara, se le soltaron las lágrimas:

—Aquí está —y comenzó a sacudir el llanto.

Paván lo tomó de un hombro:...

—¡Lo mataron hijos de su poca madre...!

Abiertos, en blanco, los ojos de Lupe eran pura esclerótica. Su ropa había desaparecido. Tenía un balazo expansivo a media cabeza.

Sin decirse nada, sin mirarse siquiera, permanecieron allí mucho tiempo, hasta que Paván dijo:

—Vamos a sacarlo.

Lo apartaron del agua y, a cuestas, pudieron llevarlo al matorral. Después arreglaron un lecho de pasto triturado.

—¿Y ahora?

—Ya ni que le reces es bueno; ni eso puede servirle para un carajo. ¡Vámonos!

Luis quiso argüir algo. Paván recalcó:

—¡Vámonos!

Regresaron a la orilla, en un retorno inútil. Tranquila y amarillenta corría el agua del Bravo. Nadie en su horizonte.

Paván vació las aspirinas en su bolsa y llenó con tierra el frasco. Con tierra en que desangrara la herida de Lupe, ya muerto.

—¿Qué haces?

—Nada. Es para que siga con nosotros...

El Río Grande, whose murky waters and banks have been an integral part of Chicano history, is poetized by Abelardo. The poet predicts a symbolic end to the river which has historically been synonymous with suffering.

EL RÍO GRANDE

abelardo

jorobado, arrugado, seco, como viejo mal cuidado
va mi río grande, ya menos apurado
con el soquete del tiempo manchado,
por dos países maltratado y decorado.

si en vez de crugir tus aguas platicaran,
qué de hazañas no nos contaran
y si tus granos de arena miraran

cuanta mentira con su mirar nos desataran.
has visto sufrir al mejicano,
cambiar su sudor por tus aguas mano a mano,
tú le has dado a la lechuga el chile como hermano,
y al tomate le cambiaste en halgo humano.

en ancas de una mula cuando niño te cruce,
miras tú el contrabando que el de la aduana no ve,
sirves de espejo a la esperanza que se fue
y vives esperando la lluvia que una nube negra dé.

río grande, polvo de tejas, ramas, de nuevo méjico las ramas,
duermes bajo la luz de luciérnagas y la música de ranas,
para los enamorados tus orillas son mil camas
y de un amarillento carrizo son tus canas.

tu fama nacional es como una noche oscura
y tus aguas tiñen de una sangre insegura,
eres tú la puerta más cruel y la más dura.
separas al hombre y haces de su ambición basura.

leí que se ahogó un mejicano que te quiso cruzar,
venía a los estados unidos y su muerte fue a encontrar,
un día tus fuerzas, como las fronteras, se van a acabar...
háblame pronto, río grande, que el tiempo te va a matar.

Children have a unique way of perceiving their world—what is important, what makes them cry, what makes them glad. Migrant life has created a special set of associations for children of people, places, and things. The following pieces, written by Chicano students, present retrospective views of their childhood experiences in the migrant stream. These texts are from the state of Washington, but the essence of the experience is shared by many migrant children everywhere.

CHILDHOOD IMAGES

and anonymous students

The cabins were simple. Each one had a wood stove, a couple of cots, a table and two benches. The place looked pretty bad when I first saw it, but as soon as my mother took over, and cleaned it up, it took on a different look. One thing about my mother—she can make any place "feel" like home...

There were about fifteen families in that camp—the one we returned to for seven years. There were a lot of single men too. The families were all from the same area in Texas and in most cases were related. The men would get up before sun-up to hitch the asparagus wagons. There was one wagon and one horse for every family and everyone always used the same horse and the same wagon. Those were the days I remember, because everything had a name. The horses had such names as "el macho", "chata"; the asparagus fields, "el veinte", "el triángulo", "el espinaso del diablo". The first because it was twenty acres, the second because it was shaped like a triangle, and the last because it was like a steep hill—hard and difficult to cut. Even some of the single men had names, "el grande", "Don Víctor", "el borrego", and others. . .

Life at a camp is miserable, but Chicanos always found something in which to find joy. Joy is a word that can define many different things in the life of a Chicano child. It could be a new pair of shoes, a new dress, a trip to a movie theatre, but most often it was a needed rest at the end of a hard day's work. For the young men, there were girls, brown girls that toiled alongside the long summer days. Girls whose make-up was the dirt from the fields, but they were beautiful. . .

At the end of the season people would separate and go on their way. Everyone would be glad to leave the camp—always expecting that the next one would be better. . .

In this essay Enriqueta Vásquez presents the view, shared by many Chicanos, of the land as the source of spiritual and material nourishment. In addition, she stresses respect for the knowledge of los ancianos and criticizes Anglo materialism.

The question of land, its ownership and its use contains profound implications for workers who are part of the rapidly drying migrant stream. Many families now engaged in agricultural work and facing displacement by machinery, must soon choose between life in an urban or life in a rural environment. Chicanos in other parts of the country, evaluating their own situations, may have different interpretations of the importance of land.

LA SANTA TIERRA

enriqueta vásquez

Time passes: Thanksgiving, Christmas, New Year's; it could be the cold that is in the air, the season, the coming of winter, the passing of fall. Perhaps it is the drawing to the end of the year and the birth of the new year that tends to remind us of the passage of time. It is healthful, necessary and beneficial for us to sit and meditate about ourselves, our families, our people; La Raza. We must give ourselves time to think, to stop and think of the passing of time; the making of history. Our history is important, for it shows us the present as the product of the past and the key to the future.

We can all remember some of the things that our viejitos and viejitas taught us, the things they showed us. I remember well the things that my father taught in regard to the earth, land and people. Many would say that it was the teaching of daydreams but you know, I now realize it was the teaching of humanity, the teaching of life. For in the wisdom of our viejitos we learned about human beings and the universe; we learned about the earth, the land, and we called it: la madre tierra; la santa tierra; la tierra sagrada. Our viejitos taught us about nature and the creatures of the earth. We would sit for hours and study the sky, its vastness and the cloud formations that travelled and played games as they went by. We would study the birds and we learned the flow of the air currents, how the birds would ride the currents for miles and miles.

DAYDREAMS? No, mi Raza; let us never for an instant dismiss this beauty as only daydreams. We must learn to realize that these things are an important part of reality; of what life is made of. For it is in this knowledge of the earth that we have a good balance of nature and the function of human beings. It is in this that we find a place for ourselves; it is in this that we know what we are.

I recall how I learned about mother earth. I would ask why it was called a mother and I was told that a female is productive of life and the male is not, therefore because the earth gives life to all living things, it is the female. We learned that the earth gives life and feeds us. Thus, we learned to respect the food on our table and we learned to respect and love the laborer and the campesino. These are a special people, special, for they work close to the earth, to nature. And special for they harvest the products that go on our tables and into our bodies to be processed and return to the earth.

These teachings which have been handed down to us are very important for it is here that we see the failings of the Gringo society and his education system. It fails because in all of its technology it does not make a place for HUMANS in relation to NATURE. This is what we mean when we speak of the dangers of the Mechanized Man and of technology in the method the Gringo teaches. You see, we as people, with all of our beautiful daydreams, (philosophies) know that it is through them that we respect and live in harmony with nature. And this is absolutely necessary for us to know if people are to exist at all because we are at the mercy of nature. We should live within the balance of nature.

We don't say that there is anything wrong with machines and technology. On the contrary, we need technicians in all fields. However, realizing that 80% of the Gringo society is reported to be neurotic and 50% of the people are hypochondriacs, we can realize that in the teachings of our viejitos we have the cultural beliefs necessary for the survival of people. We seek to apply and conserve our knowledge, in our own way. This is why Chicanos are making a stand for cultural survival.

These are the things that we must recall, respect and learn to apply. For this knowledge I have a special place in my heart for the viejitos de nuestra raza, I have a very special place for our elders as I recall going to school to get schooling. We must learn, we must study, but to memorize facts and not be able to apply them; to learn and not be able to relate to the realities of life, is criminal. It's like being castrated. Our real education, our realities and philosophies, come from our viejitos. We learn from them, we learn to apply our schooling. Our viejitos are our knowledge and we bury it every time we bury one of our people.

We can well understand why to a people who are capable of living in harmony with nature, it is very difficult to understand the concept of ownership and possession of land. We can understand what stirs in us when we talk of the land in New Mexico. And even further we can understand why there would be conflict over the control of land. We know why the controlling Gringo is playing with fire when he maneuvers politically with lands in the southwest, The indigenous concepts of Aztlán still live here. The concepts of humanity and nature are very much part of every day living here. If there is a whole truth, if there is an answer to the problems of the Gringos and their sick society, it must come from the people who have been able to endure for thousands of years.

This portion of a taped interview with José Angel Gutiérrez, one of the founders of La Raza Unida Party in Texas, discusses the various types of units that operate within Chicano society. The interview focused on an examination of the elements that had unified a town of almost 10,000 Chicanos, most of whom are migrants, into a powerful political body. The investment of people's lives in a particular area, the commonality of experience, language, and culture; parentelas and other relationships are the solidifying ingredients containing the potential for tremendous social change.

CHICANO NETWORK

josé ángel gutiérrez

...take care of your brother, and the way to really tie this up with the network we spoke of, was to tie it with the family. Take care of your real nuclear brother, your blood brother and then your cousin and then you know, start pushing it—your brother-in-law; then you completely change over to another family, and then your compadre, then you've changed to another family, you see—because there's three kinds of units employed in this network. There's three kinds of units you have to look to for value, that's (1) the nuclear family, (2) the extended family and then, (3) the relationship that comes out of geographic areas such as (it's tied to the land) where you were born, where you die, where you were married, these are very significant things in the experience of Chicanos that merit tremendous social worth. And that's the third kind of unit, because people identify donde nacieron, onde se murieron, onde enterraron a güelito, de donde vinieron de México. You know, onde trabajaron en las piscas. All of those things—en cuál iglesia se bautisaron, see that's got nothing to do with family, but that's got something to do with physical stuff that you can touch, you can go look at...

Stereotypes and the American Dream explode as a young poet questions the nature of a society in which being Mexican has been synonymous with "not good enough." He conveys the sense of a spiritual migration—a journey across time in hostile territory. The focus of the poet's anger and pain is turned away from himself as he affirms his Mexicanidad and confronts the society of cokes, hamburgers and Rainbo Bread with its responsibility.

22 MILES ...

josé ángel gutiérrez

From 22 I see my first 8 weren't.
   Around the 9th, I was called "meskin".
   By the 10th, I knew and believed I was.
      I found out what it meant to know, to believe. . before my 13th.

Through brown eyes, seeing only brown colors and feeling only brown feelings. . . I saw. . . I felt. . . I hated. . . I cried. . . I tried. . . I didn't understand during these 4.
      I rested by just giving up.

While, on the side. . . I realized I BELIEVED in
  white as pretty,
    my being governor,
      blond blue eyed baby Jesus,
        cokes and hamburgers,
          equality for all regardless of race, creed, or color,
           Mr. Williams, our banker.
      I had to!
    That was all I had.
    Beans and Communism were bad.
        Past the weeds, atop the hill, I looked back.

Pretty people, combed and squeaky clean, on arrowlike roads.
Pregnant girls, ragged brats, swarthy machos, rosary beads,
and friends waddle clumsily over and across hills, each other,
mud, cold, and woods on caliche ruts.
At the 19th mile, I fought blindly at everything and anything.
  Not knowing, Not caring about WHY, WHEN, or FOR WHAT.
    I fought. And fought.
      By the 21st, I was tired and tried.

          But now. . . . .
I've been told that I am dangerous.
That is because I am good at not being a Mexican.
That is because I know now that I have been cheated.
That is because I hate circumstances and love choices.

You know...chorizo tacos y tortillas ARE good, even at school.
  Speaking Spanish is a talent.
Being Mexican IS as good as Rainbo bread.
And without looking back, I know that there are still too many...
  brown babies,
    pregnant girls,
      old 25 year-old women,
        drunks,
          who should have lived but didn't,
            on those caliche ruts.

            It is tragic that my problems during these past 21 miles
            were/are/might be...
                looking into blue eyes,
              wanting to touch a gringita,
              ashamed of being Mexican,
            believing I could not make it at college,
          pretending that I liked my side of town,
        remembering the Alamo,
      speaking Spanish in school bathrooms only,
and knowing that Mexico's prostitutes like Americans better.
At 22, my problems are still the same but now I know I am your problem.
That farm boys, Mexicans and Negro boys are in Vietnam is but one thing
I think about:

        Crystal City, Texas 78839
        The migrant worker;
        The good gringo:

Staying Mexican enough;
Helping;
Looking at the world from the back of a truck.

The stoop labor with high school rings on their fingers;
The Anglo cemetery,
Joe the different Mexican,
                Damn.
                Damn.
                Damn.

A call to action by and for migrant workers, "El Plan de Delano," is a statement of farm worker determinátion to struggle for economic and social justice.

Incorporating the Mexican tradition of revolutionary commitment, and calling on the Church to respond with genuine Christian compassion, it constitutes a continuation of the prolonged series of earlier labor struggles by Chicanos. The words dignity, justice, liberation, and revolution are not used rhetorically—they reflect the basic beliefs and irreversible direction of migratory farmworkers. Delano and the events since the writing of this historic document are dramatic evidence that the campesinos, who have been the most victimized segment of the Chicano population, are demonstrating their determination to affect their destiny—to act upon history.

PLAN DE DELANO

united farm workers

tema: *peregrinación, penitencia, revolución*

1. Plan para la liberación de los obreros campesinos asociados a la Huelga de la Uva en Delano, en el Estado de California, pidiendo justicia social para el obrero del campo, por medio de aquellas reformas que juzgamos necesarias para nuestro bienestar, como obreros en los Estados Unidos.

2. Este es el comienzo de un movimiento social de hechos, no de meras palabras. Luchamos por nuestros fundamentales derechos, que Dios mismo nos ha concedido, como seres humanos que somos. Porque hemos sufrido para sobrevivir, y porque no nos asusta el sufrimiento, estamos dispuestos a darlo todo, incluso nuestras vidas, en la lucha por la justicia social. Lo vamos a hacer sin violencia, porque ése es nuestro destino. A los rancheros y a cuántos se oponen a nuestra *Causa* les repetimos las palabras de Benito Juárez: "El respeto al derecho ajeno es la paz".

3. El obrero del campo ha sido abandonado a su suerte —sin representación y sin poder— sujeto a la merced y al capricho del ranchero. Estamos cansados de palabras, de traiciones, de indiferencia. A los políticos les decimos que ya pasaron aquellos años cuando el obrero campesino no decía nada, ni hacía nada por su *Causa*. De este movimiento brotarán los líderes que nos comprendan, que nos guíen, que nos sean fieles; los que nosotros eligiremos para que nos representen. ¡Nos escucharán!

4. Todos los hombres somos hermanos, hijos del mismo Dios; por eso nos dirigimos a todos los hombres de buena voluntad con las palabras del Papa León XIII: "El primer deber de todos es el de protejer a los obreros de las avaricias de los especuladores, quienes usan a los seres

humanos como simples instrumentos para hacer dinero. No es ni justo ni humano oprimir a los hombres con trabajo excesivo a tal grado que sus mentes se embrutezcan y sus cuerpos se gasten".

5. Sufriremos ahora con objeto de acabar con la pobreza, la miseria, y la injusticia; con la esperanza de que nuestros hijos no sean explotados como nosotros lo hemos sido. Nos han impuesto el hambre, pero ahora tenemos hambre de justicia. Sacamos fuerzas de la misma desesperación en que se nos ha forzado a vivir. ¡Resistiremos!

6. Iremos a la huelga. Llevaremos a cabo la revolución que nos hemos propuesto hacer. Somos hijos de la Revolución Mexicana, una revolución del pobre que pedía pan y justicia. Nuestra revolución no será armada; pero sí pedimos que desaparezca el presente orden social. Queremos un nuevo orden social. Somos pobres, somos humildes. Nuestro único recurso es ir a la huelga en aquellos ranchos donde no se nos trata con el respeto que merecemos como hombres trabajadores, donde no son reconocidos nuestros derechos como hombres libres y soberanos.

7. No queremos el paternalismo del ranchero; no queremos contratistas; no queremos caridad al precio de nuestra dignidad. Queremos igualdad con los patrones y con todos los trabajadores de la nación; queremos salarios justos, mejores condiciones de trabajo y un porvenir decente para nuestros hijos. A los que se nos oponen, sean ellos rancheros, policías, políticos, o especuladores, les decimos que continuaremos luchando hasta morir o hasta vencer. ¡Triunfaremos!

8. Por todo el Valle de San Joaquín, por toda California, por todo el suroeste de los Estados Unidos; allí donde hay gente mexicana, allí donde hay obreros del campo, nuestro movimiento se extiende ya como voraz fuego en reseca llanura. Nuestra peregrinación es la mecha que encenderá nuestra *Causa*. Así verán todos los obreros del campo lo que aquí está pasando, y se decidirán a hacer lo que nosotros hemos hecho. ¡Ha llegado la hora de la liberación del pobre obrero del campo! Así lo dispone la historia.

    ¡Que siga la huelga! ¡Viva la huelga!
    ¡Viva la causa! ¡Viva César Chávez!
    ¡Viva la Virgen de Guadalupe!

THE DELANO MANIFESTO

united farmworkers

theme: *pilgrimage, penitence, revolution*

1. Plan for the liberation of the Farm Workers associated with the Delano Grape Strike in the State of California, seeking social justice in farm labor with those reforms that they believe necessary for their well-being as workers in these United States.

2. This is the beginning of a social movement in fact and not in pronouncements. We seek our basic God-given rights as human beings. Because we have suffered—and are not afraid to suffer—in order to survive, we are ready to give up everything, even our lives, in our fight for social justice. We shall do it without violence because that is our destiny. To the ranchers and to all those who oppose us we say, in the words of Benito Juárez, "Respect for another's rights is the meaning of Peace."

3. The farm worker has been abandoned to his own fate—without representation, without power—subject to the mercy and caprice of the rancher. But we are tired of words, of betrayals, of indifference. To the politicians we say that the years are gone when the farm worker said nothing and did nothing to help himself. From this movement shall spring leaders who shall understand us, lead us, be faithful to us, and we shall elect them to represent us.

4. All men are brothers, sons of the same God; that is why we say to all men of good will, in the words of Pope Leo XIII, "Everyone's first duty is to protect the workers from the greed of speculators who use human beings as instruments to provide themselves with money. It is neither just nor human to oppress men with excessive work to the point where their minds become enfeebled and their bodies worn out."

5. Now we will suffer for the purpose of ending the poverty, the misery, and the injustice, with the hope that our children will not be exploited as we have been. They have imposed hungers on us, and now we hunger for justice. We draw our strength from the very despair in which we have been forced to live. *We shall endure!*

6. We shall strike. We shall pursue the Revolution we have proposed. We are sons of the Mexican Revolution, a revolution of the poor seeking bread and justice. Our revolution will not be armed, but we want the existing social order to dissolve; we want a new social order. We are poor, we are humble, and our only choice is to strike in those ranches where we are not treated with the respect we deserve as working men, where our rights as free and sovereign men are not recognized.

7. We do not want the paternalism of the ranchers; we do not want the contractor; we do not want charity at the price of our dignity. We want to be equal with all the working men in the nation; we want a just wage, better working conditions, a decent future for our children. To those who oppose us, be they ranchers, police, politicians, or speculators, we say that we are going to continue fighting until we die, or we win. We shall overcome!

8. Across the San Joaquin Valley, across California, across the entire Southwest of the United States, wherever there are Mexican people, wherever there are farm workers, our movement is spreading like flames across a dry plain. Our pilgrimage is the march that will light our cause for all farm workers to see what is happening here, so that they may do as we have done. The time has come for the liberation of the poor farm worker. History is on our side.

> May the srike go on!
> Viva la causa!
> Viva César Chávez!
> Viva la Virgen de Guadalupe!

Literatura de La Raza:
The Context of Chicano Literature

Lo Mexicano
Lo Puertorriqueño
Lo Hispanoamericano

LITERATURA DE LA RAZA— THE CONTEXT OF CHICANO LITERATURE

This unit presents literary examples from beyond the borders of Aztlán. The writers share with Chicanos the same language and cultural origins, tracing back not only to Spain, but also, in the countries of Central America and the Andean highlands, to the pre-Hispanic Indian civilizations. We believe that demonstrating this Latin American context will serve to broaden the horizons of Chicano literature.

We are aware that this is not the only context—that Chicano writers from the nineteenth century on, and increasingly in modern times, have received the influences of the mainstream society of the United States, and of its literature. But this Anglo-American setting is available in most other works which present Chicano writing, and indeed is what underlies many classes in English departments throughout the country which deal with Chicano literary expression.

What interests us here is to show varied points of contact, whether in tone, mood, or theme. To cite a few specific examples, the Argentine poem, "El gaucho Martín Fierro" evokes the tone of the corrido, and brings to mind the experience of the vaquero in Texas. The poetry of the Quechua-speaking Indians of Peru is similar to that of the Aztecs in its use of imagery from nature, but different in its tone of personal mourning. And Piri Thomas's fiction treating ghetto life in Puerto Rican Harlem adds perspective to our understanding of barrio values in urban Chicano communities.

For obvious reasons, the literature of Mexico has prime importance in showing this context. A second area which we felt should receive attention is Puerto Rico, since Puerto Ricans in the United States—the second largest Spanish-speaking minority—have undergone many of the same pressures experienced by the Chicano. This explains the structure of the present unit. It begins with a section presenting some of the major figures in Mexican literature, from Nezahualcóyotl to Carlos Fuentes. A Puerto Rican section follows, with examples both from the island and within the United States. And finally the third section covers all Spanish-speaking America, highlighting important literary figures such as José

Martí and Pablo Neruda. We have attempted also to include important literary currents, such as poesía gauchesca, and significant tendencies, ranging from the poetry of the Indians of Peru to the ideas of the modern writers García Márquez (Colombia) and Vargas Llosa (Peru) on the responsibility of the writer.

We have made an effort to single out how Latin Americans interpret Mexico and the Chicano. The third section includes a cuento by Fernando Alegría of Chile, which is set in East Los Angeles. It also has selections which relate directly or indirectly to Mexico, written by Gabriela Mistral of Chile, Augusto Monterroso of Guatemala, and Alberto Ordóñez Argüello of Nicaragua.

We have constructed this unit with two purposes in mind. The first, mentioned above, is to extend the setting in which the reader perceives Chicano literature. The second, equally important, is to show how other Latin American writers used forms similar to those chosen by Chicano writers, and frequently elaborated themes and ideas which, if not completely similar, strike echoes. Seeing similarities and contrasts, we feel, will serve to illuminate further the Chicano texts presented in other units.

I

lo mexicano

Many Mexican materials have already been presented as integral parts of the preceding units. In addition, we believe that a volume on Chicano literature should include, as background, outstanding literary figures such as Nezahualcóyotl, José Vasconcelos, Octavio Paz, and Carlos Fuentes. Further, important Mexican themes merit attention, such as contemporary views of the Indian, attitudes toward the United States and Latin America, and the question of "mexicanidad."

This Aztec poet, who lived in the fifteenth century, was one of the great figures in Aztec and Mexican history. Nezahualcóyotl was not only a poet but a head of state. For more than forty years, until his death in 1472, he was lord and ruler of Texcoco, one of the key city-states in the Aztec empire. His rule is noted as a period of cultural and material flowering, for he was arquitect of public buildings, botanical gardens, temples and roads, and encouraged the development of legal systems and the arts, especially music and poetry.

In the selection below we see the poet's appreciation of the lyrical quality of nature, his stress on the poetic symbols of "flor y canto," and his enjoyment of the happy moments offered by life, one of which is symbolized by the season of color and sound—the season of spring.

We have presented the original text in *nahuatl* in order to give a feeling for its sounds. By comparing the texts, the interested student can identify a number of words, such as flores (xochitl) and canto (cuicatl).

XOPAN CUICATL

nezahualcóyotl

Amoxcalco
pehua cuica.
yeyecohua.
quimoyahua xochitl,
on ahuia cuicatl.

Icahuaca cuicatl.
oyohualli ehuatihuitz,
zan quinanquiliya
toxochayacach.
Quimoyahua xochitl,
on ahuia cuicatl.

Xochiticpac cuica
in yectli cocoxqui,
ye con ya totoma
aitec.
Zan ye connanquilia
in nepapan quechol,
in yectli quechol,
in huel ya cuica.

Amoxtlacuilol in moyollo,
tocuicaticaco,
in tictzotzona in mohuehueuh,
in ticuicanitl.
Xopan cala itec,
in tonteyahuiltiya.

Zan tic moyahua
in puyuma xochitli,
in cacahua xochitli.

In ticuicanitl.
Xopan cala itec,
in tonteyahuiltiya.

CANTO DE PRIMAVERA

nezahualcóyotl

En la casa de las pinturas
comienza a cantar,
ensaya el canto,
derrama flores,
alegra el canto.

Resuena el canto,
los cascabeles se hacen oír,
a ellos responden
nuestras sonajas floridas.
Derrama flores,
alegra el canto.

Sobre las flores canta
el hermoso faisán,
su canto despliega
en el interior de las aguas.
A él responden
varios pájaros rojos,
el hermoso pájaro rojo
bellamente canta.

Libro de pinturas es tu corazón,
has venido a cantar,
haces resonar tus tambores,
tú eres el cantor.
En el interior de la casa de la primavera,
alegras a las gentes.

Tú sólo repartes
flores que embriagan,
flores preciosas.

Tú eres el cantor.
En el interior de la casa de la primavera,
alegras a las gentes.

SONG OF SPRING

nezahualcóyotl

In the house of paintings
he begins to sing,
he tries out his song,
pouring forth flowers,
the song rejoices.

The singing resounds,
the rattles are heard,
and in turn the response
of our flowery bells,
pouring forth flowers,
the song rejoices.

Over the flowers the song
of the beautiful pheasant
unfolds its melody
in the interior of the waters.
Responding to it,
many red birds,
the beautiful red bird
melodically sings.

A book of paintings is your heart,
you have come to sing,
you sound your drums,
you are the singer.
Inside the house of spring
you bring joy to the people.

You alone give away
flowers that intoxicate,
precious flowers.

You are the singer
inside the house of spring,
you bring joy to the people.

José Vasconcelos was one of the most colorful and controversial intellectuals in Mexico in the half century from the Revolution of 1910 until his death in 1959. He was rector of the National University, Secretary of Education (1921–1924), and unsuccessful candidate for President of the Republic in 1929.

In the late years of his life, Vasconcelos moved toward conservatism, mystical thought, and religious belief. However, as Secretary of Education he made a significant contribution in promoting popular education, in developing libraries and publishing large editions of basic books at low prices, in encouraging poets and artists, and in promoting awareness of Latin American heritage.

This last-mentioned interest is evident in the following selected passages from *La raza cósmica*, written in 1925. Among his major themes are: 1) The need for unity of the Spanish-speaking nations in the face of United States power; 2) the need to validate the strength of the Iberian heritage, as against Anglo-Saxon traditions; 3) the importance of ideals such as liberty by comparison with material aims such as commerce; 4) the racial homogeneity of the United States as a weakness which ultimately will yield leadership to the new strength and new ideology of the great ethnic fusion of Latin America—la raza cósmica.

LA RAZA CÓSMICA

josé vasconcelos

Nadie hubiera imaginado que los humildes colonos del Hudson y el Delaware, pacíficos y hacendosos, se irían apoderando paso a paso de las mejores y mayores extensiones de la tierra, hasta formar la República que hoy constituye uno de los mayores imperios de la Historia.

Pugna de latinidad contra sajonismo ha llegado a ser, sigue siendo nuestra época; pugna de instituciones, de propósitos y de ideales. Crisis de una lucha secular que se inicia con el desastre de la Armada Invencible y se agrava con la derrota de Trafalgar. Sólo que desde entonces el sitio del conflicto comienza a desplazarse y se traslada al continente nuevo, donde tuvo todavía episodios fatales. Las derrotas de Santiago de Cuba y de Cavite y Manila son ecos distantes pero lógicos de las catástrofes de la Invencible y de Trafalgar. Y el conflicto está ahora planteado totalmente en el Nuevo Mundo. En la Historia, los siglos suelen ser como días; nada tiene de extraño que no acabemos todavía de salir de la impresión de la derrota. Atravesamos épocas de desaliento, seguimos perdiendo, no sólo en soberanía geográfica, sino también en poderío moral. Lejos de sentirnos unidos frente al desastre, la voluntad se nos dispersa en pequeños y vanos fines. La derrota nos ha traído la confusión de los valores y los conceptos; la diplomacia de los vencedores nos engaña después de vencernos; el

comercio nos conquista con sus pequeñas ventajas. Despojados de la antigua
grandeza, nos ufanamos de un patriotismo exclusivamente nacional, y ni
siquiera advertimos los peligros que amenazan a nuestra raza en conjunto.
Nos negamos los unos a los otros. La derrota nos ha envilecido a tal punto
que, sin darnos cuenta, servimos los fines de la política enemiga, de batirnos
en detalle, de ofrecer ventajas particulares a cada uno de nuestros hermanos,
mientras al otro se le sacrifica en intereses vitales. No sólo nos derrotaron en
el combate, ideológicamente también, nos siguen venciendo. Se perdió la
mayor de las batallas el día en que cada una de las repúblicas ibéricas se
lanzó a hacer vida propia, vida desligada de sus hermanos, concertando
tratados y recibiendo beneficios falsos, sin atender a los intereses comunes de
la raza. Los creadores de nuestro nacionalismo fueron, sin saberlo, los
mejores aliados del sajón, nuestro rival en la posesión del continente. El des-
pliegue de nuestras veinte banderas en la Unión Panamericana de Wáshing-
ton deberíamos verlo como una burla de enemigos hábiles. Sin embargo,
nos ufanamos cada uno de nuestro humilde trapo, que dice ilusión vana,
y ni siquiera nos ruboriza el hecho de nuestra discordia, delante de la fuerte
unión norteamericana. No advertimos el contraste de la unidad sajona frente
a la anarquía y soledad de los escudos iberoamericanos. Nos mantenemos
celosamente independientes respecto de nosotros mismos; pero de una o de
otra manera nos sometemos o nos aliamos con la Unión Sajona. Una
carencia de pensamiento creador y un exceso de afán crítico que por cierto
tomamos, prestado de otras culturas, nos lleva a discusiones estériles, pero
no advertimos que a la hora de obrar, y pese a todas las dudas de los
sabios ingleses, el inglés busca la alianza de sus hermanos de América y de
Australia, y entonces el yanqui se siente tan inglés como el inglés de In-
glaterra. Nosotros no seremos grandes mientras el español de la América no
se sienta tan español como los hijos de España. Lo cual no impide que
seamos distintos cada vez que sea necesario, pero sin apartarnos de la más
alta misión común. Así es menester que procedamos, si hemos de lograr
que la cultura ibérica acabe de dar todos sus frutos, si hemos de impedir que
en la América triunfe sin oposición la cultura sajona. Inútil es imaginar
otras soluciones. La civilización no se improvisa ni se trunca, ni puede
hacerse partir del papel de una constitución política; se deriva siempre de
una larga, de una secular preparación y depuración de elementos que se
transmiten y se combinan desde los comienzos de la Historia. Por eso resulta
tan torpe hacer comenzar nuestro patriotismo con el grito de independencia
del Padre Hidalgo, o con la conspiración de Quito; o con las hazañas de
Bolívar, pues si no lo arraigamos en Cuauhtémoc y en Atahualpa no tendrá
sostén, y al mismo tiempo es necesario remontarlo a su fuente hispánica y
educarlo en las enseñanzas que deberíamos derivar de las derrotas, que son
también nuestras, de las derrotas de la Invencible y de Trafalgar. Si nuestro
patriotismo no se identifica con las diversas etapas del viejo conflicto de

latinos y sajones, jamás lograremos que sobrepase los caracteres de un regionalismo sin aliento universal y lo veremos fatalmente degenerar en estrechez y miopía de campanario y en inercia impotente de molusco que se apega a su roca.

En los Estados Unidos rechazan a los asiáticos, por el mismo temor del desbordamiento físico propio de las especies superiores; pero también lo hacen porque no les simpatiza el asiático, porque lo desdeñan y serían incapaces de cruzarse con él. Las señoritas de San Francisco se han negado a bailar con oficiales de la marina japonesa, que son hombres tan aseados, inteligentes y, a su manera, tan bellos, como los de cualquiera otra marina del mundo. Sin embargo, ellas jamás comprenderán que un japonés pueda ser bello. Tampoco es fácil convencer al sajón de que si el amarillo y el negro tienen su tufo, también el blanco lo tiene para el extraño, aunque nosotros no nos demos cuenta de ello. En la América Latina existe, pero infinitamente más atenuada, la repulsión de una sangre que se encuentra con otra sangre extraña. Allí hay mil puentes para la fusión sincera y cordial de todas las razas. El amurallamiento étnico de los del Norte frente a la simpatía mucho más fácil de los del Sur, tal es el dato más importante y a la vez el más favorable para nosotros, si se reflexiona, aunque sea superficialmente, en el porvenir. Pues se verá en seguida que somos nosotros de mañana, en tanto que ellos van siendo de ayer. Acabarán de formar los yanquis el último gran imperio de una sola raza: el imperio final del poderío blanco. Entre tanto, nosotros seguiremos padeciendo en el vasto caos de una estirpe en formación, contagiados de la levadura de todos los tipos, pero seguros del avatar de una estirpe mejor. En la América española ya no repetirá la Naturaleza uno de sus ensayos parciales, ya no será la raza de un solo color, de rasgos particulares, la que en esta vez salga de la olvidada Atlántida; no será la futura ni una quinta ni una sexta raza, destinada a prevalecer sobre sus antecesoras; lo que de allí va a salir es la raza definitiva, la raza síntesis o raza integral, hecha con el genio y con la sangre de todos los pueblos y, por lo mismo, más capaz de verdadera fraternidad y de visión realmente universal.

Cada raza que se levanta necesita constituir su propia filosofía, el *deus ex machina* de su éxito. Nosotros nos hemos educado bajo la influencia humillante de una filosofía ideada por nuestros enemigos, si se quiere de una manera sincera, pero con el propósito de exaltar sus propios fines y anular los nuestros. De esta suerte nosotros mismos hemos llegado a creer en la inferioridad del mestizo, en la irredención del indio, en la condenación del negro, en la decadencia irreparable del oriental. La rebelión de las armas no fué seguida de la rebelión de las conciencias. Nos rebelamos contra el poder político de España, y no advertimos que, junto con España, caímos en la dominación económica y moral de la raza que ha sido señora del mundo, desde que terminó la grandeza de España. Sacudimos un yugo para caer bajo otro nuevo. El movimiento de desplazamiento de que fuimos víctimas no se hubiese podido evitar aunque lo hubiésemos comprendido a tiempo. Hay cierta fatalidad en el destino de los pueblos lo mismo que en el destino de los individuos; pero ahora que se inicia una nueva fase de la Historia, se hace necesario reconstituir nuestra ideología y organizar conforme a una nueva doctrina étnica toda nuestra vida continental. Comencemos entonces haciendo vida propia y ciencia propia. Si no se liberta primero el espíritu, jamás lograremos redimir la materia.

Para expresar todas estas ideas que hoy procuro exponer en rápida síntesis, hace algunos años, cuando todavia no se hallaban bien definidas, procuré darles signos en el nuevo Palacio de la Educación Pública de México. Sin elementos bastantes para hacer exactamente lo que deseaba, tuve que conformarme con una construcción renacentista española, de dos patios, con arquerías y pasarelas, que tienen algo de la impresión de un ala. En los tableros de los cuatro ángulos del patio anterior hice labrar alegorías de España, de México, Grecia y la India, las cuatro civilizaciones particulares que más tienen que contribuir a la formación de la América Latina. En seguida, debajo de estas cuatro alegorías, debieron levantarse cuatro grandes estatuas de piedra de las cuatro grandes razas contemporáneas: la Blanca, la Roja, la Negra y la Amarilla, para indicar que la América es hogar de todas, y de todas necesita. Finalmente, en el centro debía erigirse un monumento que en alguna forma simbolizara la ley de los tres estados: el material, el intelectual y el estético. Todo para indicar que, mediante el ejercicio de la triple ley, llegaremos en América, antes que en parte alguna del globo, a la creación de una raza hecha con el tesoro de todas las anteriores, la raza final, la raza cósmica.

THE COSMIC RACE

josé vasconcelos

No one would have imagined that the humble settlers of the Hudson and the Delaware, peaceful and industrious, would seize possession bit by bit of the largest and the best expanses of land, until they had formed the Republic that today stands as one of the greatest empires in history.

Our time in history has come to be a struggle between Latin and Saxon traditions. And it continues: a conflict of institutions, purposes, and ideals. It is the crisis of a secular battle which begins with the disaster of the Invincible Armada, and is sharpened with the defeat at Trafalgar. However, the scene of the conflict then begins to shift, moving to the new continent for further fatal episodes. The defeats at Santiago de Cuba and Cavite and Manila are distant but logical echoes of the disasters of the

Armada and of Trafalgar. And there is now total conflict in the New World. In history, centuries are usually like days; it is hardly strange that we still retain the impression of defeat. We go through periods of discouragement, we continue to lose, not only in geographical control, but also in moral power. Rather than feel united in facing disaster, our collective will is fragmented into small and futile aims. Defeat has brought us confusion of values and concepts; the diplomacy of the winners deceives us after conquering us. Business subdues us with its petty advantages.

Stripped of our ancient grandeur, we boast of a patriotism which is exclusively national in scope, and we hardly notice the dangers which threaten our entire race. We deny each other. Defeat has degraded us to the point that, without knowing it, we serve the purpose of the enemy's policies: to have us struggle with details, to offer advantages to some of our brothers while sacrificing the vital interests of others. Not only did they defeat us in combat, they continue to defeat us ideologically. The greatest battle was lost the day each of the Iberian republics set out to make its own life, separated from brother nations, signing treaties and receiving false benefits, losing sight of common interests of la raza.

The creators of our nationalism, without knowing it, were the best allies of the Saxons, our rivals for control of the continent. The display of our twenty flags at the Pan American Union should be understood by us as a trick by clever enemies. Nevertheless, each of us takes pride in our humble rag, sign of vain illusions, and the fact of our disunity in facing the strong United States does not even embarrass us. We don't even notice the contrast between Saxon unity and the anarchy and loneliness of our national emblems. We jealously guard our independence from each other; but one way or another, we either give in or we align ourselves with the Saxon Union.

A lack of creative thinking and an overly critical attitude, which, to be sure, we borrow from other cultures, carries us into sterile discussions. But we don't notice that, when it is time to act, despite all the doubts of British scholars, the Englishman makes alliances with his brothers in America and Australia, and then the Yankee feels as English as the Englishman from England. We will not be great until the Spanish-speaker of America feels as Spanish as the sons of Spain. This does not prevent us from being distinct when necessary, but without losing sight of our higher common mission. This is the way we must go if we are to see to it that Iberian culture gives all its fruits, if we are to prevent Saxon culture from triumphing unchallenged. There are no other solutions. Civilizations are not created by a whim nor can they be shut off. Nor do they spring from the paper of a political constitution. They always emerge from a long, secular process of preparation and purification of elements that are combined and passed on from the beginnings of history. That is why it is stupid to date our patriotism from *El grito* of Father Hidalgo, or the Quito conspiracy, or the victories of Bolívar; for if we do not root it in Cuauhtémoc and Atahualpa, it will have no real basis; at the same time we must trace it to its Spanish sources, and in the lessons to be learned from the defeats, which are our defeats too, of the Invincible Armada and of Trafalgar. If our patriotism is not identified with the different stages of the old conflict of Latins and Saxons, we will never see it go beyond the limits of a regionalism lacking in universal spirit; and we will see it degenerate inevitably into narrowness and short-sightedness and in the impotent inertia of a mollusk that clings to its rock.

In the United States, they reject Asians, out of the same fear of physical overflow which is found in superior races; but they also do it because they do not like the Asian, they scorn him and would be incapable of mixing with him. Young ladies of San Francisco have refused to dance with officers of the Japanese Navy, who are just as groomed, as intelligent, and, in their way, as handsome, as officers in any other navy in the world. Nonetheless these girls will never understand that a Japanese can be hand-some. Nor is it easy to convince the Saxon that if the yellow and the black man have an odor, so does the white man have one for the other man, though we may not realize it. In Latin America, there does exist, but on a much smaller scale, hostility between different blood lines. There are, though, a thousand bridges for cordial and sincere fusion of all the races. Those in the North have raised ethnic walls; those in the South show a more open sympathy. This is the most important fact and the most favorable one for us, if we think about the future. For we see immediately that we are the people of tomorrow, while they are becoming of yesterday. The Yan-kees will end up being the last great empire based on one race; the final empire of white power. Meanwhile we will keep on suffering in the chaos that is part of the process of forming a lineage; we will be fascinated by the yeast of all ethnic types, but sure of the prediction of a better lineage. In Spanish America, Nature will not repeat one of her partial efforts—it will no longer be the race of one color only, or of particular physical fea-tures, that will arise this time from forgotten Atlantis. The future race will be neither a fifth or a sixth race, destined to win out over its ancestors; what will be coming out is the definitive race, the race of synthesis, that is integral—made of the spirit and the blood of all peoples, and, for that reason, more capable of true fraternity and a really universal vision.

Each race that rises up must build its own philosophy, a higher representation to explain its success. We have been educated under the humiliating influence of a philosophy created by our enemies, certainly in a sincere manner, but designed to praise their aims and to nullify ours. In this way we ourselves have come to believe in the inferiority of the mestizo, in the unredeemable state of the Indian, in the curse of the Negro, and in the permanent decadence of the Oriental. Our military rebellion did not lead to a revolution of our consciences. We rebelled against the political power of

Spain, and we failed to see that, along with Spain, we were falling under the economic and moral control of the race that has been mistress of the world since the decline of Spanish glory. We threw off one yoke only to fall under another. Even if we had understood in time, this process of substitution could not have been avoided. There is a certain fatalism in the destiny of peoples, just as in the destiny of individuals; but now that a new phase of History is beginning, it becomes urgent that we reconstruct our ideology and organize our entire continental life according to a new ethnic doctrine. Let us begin to make our own life and our own knowledge. If first we do not liberate our spirit, we will never redeem our material life.

In order to express all these ideas which today I present in a quick synthesis, some years ago when they were not yet well defined, I tried to design symbols for them at the new national Palace of Public Education. Without enough flexibility to do exactly what I wanted, I had to be satisfied with a structure that was in Spanish Renaissance style, with two patios, with archways and passageways that gave the impression of a wing. On the face boards of the four angles of the first patio, I had them carve allegories of Spain, of Mexico, of Greece and India, the four particular civilizations that have most to contribute to the formation of Latin America. Then, under these four allegories, there were to be placed four large stone statues of the four great races of our time: White, Red, Black, and Yellow, in order to show that America is the home of all, and has need of all. Finally, in the center a monument was to be erected which in some way would symbolize the three states of being: the material, the intellectual, and the esthetic. All this to demonstrate that, by means of this triple law we will arrive, in America sooner than elsewhere on earth, at the creation of a race made out of the treasure of all the earlier ones, the final race, the cosmic race.

Rosario Castellanos (born 1925) is probably Mexico's most distinguished woman writer and intellectual. She is known not only for poetry, but for her cuentos, her novels, and her literary criticism. She has been social worker, journalist, and professor, and at present is Mexican ambassador to Israel.

The poem below deals on one level with the problem of knowing the past in order to understand identity. On another level, it is concerned with the limitations of language and the mystery of poetic creation. These themes of identity, ancestral heritage, language, and the creative process, are familiar to Chicano writers too.

SILENCIO ACERCA DE UNA PIEDRA ANTIGUA

rosario castellanos

Estoy aquí, sentada, con todas mis palabras
como una cesta de fruta verde, intactas.
Los fragmentos
de mil dioses antiguos derribados
se buscan por mi sangre, se aproximan, queriendo
recomponer su estatua.
De las bocas destruidas
quiere subir hasta mi boca un canto,
un olor de resinas quemadas, algún gesto
de misteriosa roca trabajada.
Pero soy el olvido, la traición,
el caracol que no guardó del mar
ni el eco de la más pequeña ola.
Y no miro los templos sumergidos,
sólo miro los árboles que encima de las ruinas
mueven su vasta sombra, muerden con dientes ácidos
el viento cuando pasa.
Y los signos se cierran bajo mis ojos como
la flor bajo los dedos torpísimos de un ciego.
Pero yo sé: detrás
de mi cuerpo otro cuerpo se agazapa,
y alrededor de mí muchas respiraciones
cruzan furtivamente
como los animales nocturnos en la selva.
Yo sé, en algún lugar,
lo mismo
que en el desierto el cacto,
un constelado corazón de espinas

está aguardando un nombre como el cacto la lluvia.
    Pero yo no conozco más que ciertas palabras
en el idioma lápida
bajo el que sepultaron vivo a mi antepasado.

SILENCE CONCERNING AN ANCIENT STONE

rosario castellanos

Here I am, seated, with all my words,
like a basket of green fruit, intact.
The fragments
of a thousand destroyed ancient gods
seek and draw near each other in my blood. They long
to rebuild their statue.
From their shattered mouths
a song strives to rise to my mouth,
a scent of burned resins, some gesture
of mysterious wrought stone.
But I am oblivion, treason,
the shell that did not keep from the sea
even the echo of the smallest wave.
I look not at the submerged temples,
but only at the trees that above the ruins
move their vast shadow, with acid teeth bite
the wind as it passes.
And the seals close under my eyes like
the flower under the searching fingers of a blind man.
But I know: behind
my body another body crouches,
and round about me many breaths
furtively cross
like nocturnal beasts in the jungle.
I know: somewhere,
like the cactus in the desert,
a constellated heart of spines,
it is waiting for a name, as the cactus the rain.

But I know only a few words
in the lapidary language
under which they buried my ancestor alive.

                    (trans. by George Schade)

Leopoldo Zea (born 1912) is one of Mexico's most respected intellectuals. A professor at the National University, he has written numerous books on philosophy and the history of ideas in Mexico. The selection below, from 1952, deals not only with how Mexico sees its past, but also with the philosophy of race. Clearly, Mexican attitudes toward Indian heritage contrast with those of the United States. Although Zea exaggerates when speaking of an absence of prejudice, past and present, against the Indian in Mexico, he does represent the ideals of the Mexican Revolution. These ideas coincide, in attitudes toward race, with Chicano thought today.

EL INDIO

leopoldo zea

... "México debe ser un pueblo de indios". "¿Cómo ha resuelto México el problema indígena?", o más brutalmente, "¿cómo pueden ustedes convivir con los indios?"; tales son las interrogaciones con las cuales se puede tropezar el mexicano en su visita a Iberoamérica. La forma como México haya podido resolver, o trate de resolver, lo que llaman el problema indígena, llama poderosamente la atención a países como la Argentina que lo resolvieron con la casi completa exterminación del indio. O en países como Bolivia, donde ciertas clases privilegiadas de raza criolla, o que cuando menos presumen de ella, consideraron una bendición la guerra del Chaco porque en ella murieron muchos indios. O en el Perú y el Ecuador, donde igualmente ciertos grupos de los llamados blancos o criollos desprecian a la gran masa indígena que forma su principal población, y en donde la palabra "cholo", mestizo de indio y blanco, puede ser un insulto. En fin, en todos aquellos países donde existen grupos sociales que no ven en el indio otra cosa que un instrumento de explotación o el símbolo de la *barbarie*.

Llama mucho la atención la forma como México se siente ligado a su pasado indígena, a diferencia de otros pueblos, inclusive el Perú, que posee un pasado tan valioso como el nuestro. La relación con este pasado se deja ver en los monumentos históricos que hacen referencia a la Conquista. En el Perú podemos encontrar un gran monumento a Pizarro, pero difícilmente uno al último emperador inca. Igualmente en otros países encontramos monumentos a sus conquistadores; en cambio casi se les hace imposible creer que Cortés no tenga un monumento en México y sí lo tenga el "indio" Cuauhtémoc. Otra manera distinta de ver nuestras relaciones con el pasado indígena se hace patente en la forma como el mexicano, común y corriente, se puede referir a episodios de la Conquista y la forma como otros pueblos lo hacen. Nosotros solemos decir con orgullo: "En la noche triste derrotamos a los españoles", o con tristeza, "Después de terrible asedio los mexicanos tuvimos que rendirnos". En cambio aún podemos escuchar en otros países frases como ésta: "Aquí hicimos correr a los indios", "Esta fortaleza que defendían los indios nos costó muchos hombres tomarla".

El orgullo que sentimos por nuestro pasado indígena toma también su expresión en Iberoamérica, que se da cuenta de él. Se expresa en la palabra "azteca", nombre que muchas veces se da al mexicano como su sinónimo. Se oye hablar de "la gran capital azteca", del "pensamiento azteca"; en varias ocasiones se me presentó como "El profesor azteca". En Cuba pude ver en un periódico a grandes titulares: "El próximo domingo celebran comicios los aztecas". En lo azteca se pone énfasis, porque para estos pueblos expresa una tradición autóctona, propia de América, la cual ven continuada en nosotros. Llamar a un mexicano "azteca" es una forma de admiración y respeto por lo que consideran es la fuente de ese nacionalismo cuyas raíces están en la propia tierra, y parece caracterizarnos. Lo "azteca" es también expresión de una resistencia heroica. Expresión de esa resistencia que cada iberoamericano alberga en el fondo de su corazón, situado en un mundo en el que se siente impotente, simple satélite, colonial. Una vez más México vuelve a ser objeto de utopía, sublimando así impotencias de las cuales también participamos los mexicanos.

La mejor explicación racional de esa nuestra capacidad de resistencia, la encuentran nuestros admiradores en ese apoyarnos en la tradición, en la misma tierra americana. Lo que aparecía como milagroso ante los ojos ingenuos del pueblo aparece ya racionalizado. "Ustedes tienen hueso, son vertebrados—me decía la ya citada intelectual argentina—, a diferencia de nosotros que hemos carecido de esa tradición". "Todo lo que ustedes hacen y admiramos, todo aquello de que son ustedes capaces, se ha de deber a esas raíces tan hondas que tienen con la tierra —me decía un joven pensador uruguayo—. Nosotros carecemos de ellas, nuestros antepasados sólo encontraron pueblos nómadas, a los cuales fue menester rechazar para poder vivir". "Nuestros antepasados indígenas lo fueron los belicosos guaraníes, siempre en lucha con sus vecinos e incapaces de realizar una alta cultura, de aquí que siempre, al igual que la Argentina, tengamos que buscar nuestra tradición en Europa". "Todos los actos de ustedes los mexicanos muestran sus ligas con la tierra americana; por esto están llamados a realizar una auténtica cultura americana".

La crisis sufrida por la cultura occidental, y de la cual somos ahora testigos, ha hecho más patente que nunca a Iberoamérica, la necesidad de buscar dentro de sí misma los valores que la han de salvar. Así nos encontramos ahora a ésta con los ojos vueltos sobre sí misma, buscando o fabricando tradiciones. La misma Argentina ha ido, con Ricardo Rojas, hacia el Alto Perú en busca de la tradición indígena de que carece. En el Perú, su gran pasado indígena empieza a dejar de ser simple curiosidad arqueológica para convertirse en política, arte y cultura. El indígena preocupa ya al estadista. Se habla de su asimilación, de la justicia a que tiene derecho.

Argentina celebra "El día del indio"; se realizan o preparan congresos indígenas. El Aprismo reclama para nuestra América el nombre de Indoamérica. Se hace con el indio política sincera o demagógica, pero lo importante es que ahora ya se le toma en cuenta.

Ahora bien, en muchos de estos casos el modelo para este tipo de política lo ha sido México. Unos lo han reconocido abiertamente; otros indirectamente, al apresurarse a negar tal influencia. Y aquí surge nuevamente la experiencia de México por comparación. La política indigenista que se empieza a realizar en los países de que se habla se diferencia de la nuestra en el hecho de que la primera es una política dirigida, hecha desde arriba, mientras que la nuestra viene de abajo, nuestras circunstancias la han impuesto. El indio ha estado siempre latente en nuestra historia; siempre se ha contado con él en forma positiva. Lo encontramos en todas nuestras luchas libertarias, no sólo como masa, sino también como caudillo. El más alto símbolo de esta realidad de que hablo lo reconoce Iberoamérica en la figura de nuestro gran patricio Benito Juárez. En México el tener sangre india no ha sido nunca motivo de afrenta. El ser mestizo, el llevar la sangre india junto con la española, nunca ha sido degradante ni menos un insulto. Justo Sierra ha hecho la apología del mestizo considerándolo como el elemento dinámico de nuestra historia, a diferencia del criollo, que se presentaba siempre como un elemento negativo, raíz y fuente de todo conservadurismo. Nuestra revolución, lo comprenden bien en Iberoamérica, no es sino expresión de la más pura realidad mexicana en marcha, reclamando siempre sus derechos. No hay en esta realidad nuestra, filosofías o políticas dirigidas. Esta política se ha impuesto porque representa la más real de nuestras realidades. Nuestra revolución ha encontrado su mayor apoyo en el campo, es decir, en las masas indígenas. De aquí la razón por la cual nuestra política indigenista no sea una política que venga de arriba hacia abajo, sino de abajo hacia arriba. Se trata de una política impuesta por la propia realidad mexicana.

Leopoldo Zea
(1912–   )

THE INDIAN

leopoldo zea

"Mexico must be a country of Indians." "How has Mexico solved its Indian problem?" or more brutally, "How can you people live together with Indians?"; these are the questions a Mexican encounters on a visit to Latin America. The manner in which Mexico has solved, or tries to solve, what they call the Indian problem, arouses deep interest in countries like Argentina, whose solution was the almost complete extermination of the Indian. Or in Bolivia, where certain privileged classes of criollo origin, or who at least claim this origin, considered the Chaco war a blessing because it involved many Indian deaths. Or in Peru and Ecuador, where certain groups of so-called "whites" or criollos look down on the great Indian mass which is the bulk of the population, and where the word "cholo," a mixture of Indian and white, can be an insult. In short, in all those countries with social groupings who see in the Indian only an instrument for exploitation or a symbol of barbarism.

They take notice of how Mexico feels linked with its indigenous past, unlike other nations, including Peru which has a heritage just as valuable as ours. Our relation to this past is evident in the historical monuments which refer to the Conquest. In Peru we can find a great monument to Pizarro, but hardly any recognition of the last Inca emperor. Similarly, in other countries we find statues of their conquistadores; on the other hand, they find it hard to believe that Cortés has no statue in Mexico, while the "Indian" Cuauhtémoc does. Another view of our relation to the Indian past is evident in the way the average Mexican refers to episodes from the Conquest, and the way in which other peoples do this. We are used to saying with pride, "On the Night of Sorrows we defeated the Spaniards," or with sadness, "After the terrible siege, we Mexicans had to surrender." By contrast, in other countries, one still hears expressions like this: "Here's where we drove off the Indians," "This fort was defended by the Indians and it cost us many men to take it."

The pride that we feel in our Indian past is seen in Latin America, where people realize it. It is expressed in the word "Aztec," a word used often as synonymous with Mexican. One sees reference to "The great Aztec capital" or "Aztec intellectual thought." Several times I was introduced as "The Aztec professor." In Cuba I saw newspaper headlines, "Next Sunday the Aztecs vote in elections." They stress the Aztec concept, because in these countries it expresses a native tradition, peculiar to America, which they see as maintained in us. To call a Mexican "Aztec" is to show admiration and respect, since it signifies the source of a nationalism rooted in the earth, and seems to characterize us. "Aztec" also implies heroic resistance— that quality of resistance that every Latin American nourishes deep in his heart, finding himself as he does in a world where he feels impotent, dependent, colonized. Again Mexico comes to be an image of Utopia, by which feelings of impotence, which we Mexicans ourselves share, are sublimated.

The best rational explanation of our capacity for resistance is found, by our admirers, in our ability to draw strength from tradition, from our very soil. "You people have bones, your structures are all defined," said that Argentine woman intellectual, "unlike we Argentines who have always lacked that tradition." A young Uruguayan intellectual said, "Everything you people do, which we admire, all your capabilities, they must stem from those roots that you people have so deep in the earth. We miss that; our ancestors found only nomad peoples here, and had to reject them in order to survive." "Our Indian ancestors were the warlike Guaranís, always fighting their neighbors and unable to develop a high culture, so that we, like the Argentines, have always had to look for our traditions in Europe." "You Mexicans in all your actions show your bonds with America; for that reason it's you who will attain a genuine American culture."

The crisis of Western culture which we are witnessing now has made clearer than ever to Latin America the need to search within itself for the values which will save it. Thus we see the continent with eyes turned inward upon itself, seeking or formulating a sense of tradition. Argentina itself, with Ricardo Rojas, has moved toward the Peruvian highlands in search of the Indian tradition that it lacks. In Peru, the great indigenous past is losing its role as a mere archeological curiosity and becoming converted into politics, art, and culture. The statesmen are now concerned about the Indian—they talk of acculturation, of the Indian right to justice. Argentina celebrates "the Day of the Indian." Congresses are held and planned on Indian matters. The APRA movement claims for our America the name, Indoamerica. They may be making sincere or demagogic politics with the Indian, but the important thing is that now they take him into account.

Now, in many of these cases the model for this type of policy has been Mexico. Some recognize it openly; others do so indirectly by their haste in denying this influence. And here again the Mexican experience lends itself to comparison. The Indian policy that some countries are beginning to put in effect differs from ours in that it is a directed policy, handed down from above, while ours comes from below; our circumstances have imposed it. The Indian has always been on the scene in our history; he has always been involved in an affirmative way. We find him in all our struggles for liberty, not only among the masses, but also as leader. The highest symbol of this reality is recognized by Latin America in the figure of our great countryman, Benito Juárez.

In Mexico to have Indian blood has never been the reason for insult. To be mestizo, bearing Indian blood together with Spanish, has never been degrading. Justo Sierra has spoken on behalf of the mestizo, judging him as the dynamic element in our history, as compared with the criollo, who always played a negative role, origin and source of all conservatism. Our revolution, they understand well in Latin America, is merely an expression of the most essential Mexican reality on the move, in quest of its rights. In this reality of ours, there are no directed philosophies or policies. This policy has been adopted because it represents the most actual reality for us. Our revolution has found its greatest support in the countryside, that is from the Indian peoples. For this reason our Indian policy is not a policy coming from above to below, but rather the reverse. We are dealing with a policy imposed by our own Mexican reality.

Octavio Paz, born in 1914, is Mexico's most renowned poet of modern times. His work is known the world over, having been translated into many languages. Paz has also published essays on philosophy, art, and literary criticism.

Widely traveled, Paz was with the Spanish Republicans during the Civil War in Spain, and later lived as a diplomat in Paris and Bombay until he lost his appointment for having criticised (in a poem) the government's suppression of the university students' strike in 1968.

His most widely read essay and his most ambitious poem are available in English: *El laberinto de la soledad* (*The Labyrinth of Solitude*), and *Piedra de sol* (*Sun Stone*).

The poem below is representative of Paz in its use of elements of the natural world as the measures by which man comes to understand his limitations and his capacities. Man is a voyager on a permanent journey toward knowledge of the past, of time—a journey which leads him to find, through his encounter with the colors, the sounds, the objects of nature, that the more he learns of time, the more he is its victim. In his turning to nature, as he asks basic questions about life, about time, about history, Paz has much to say to Chicano readers.

EL REGRESO

octavio paz

A mitad del camino
me detuve. Le di la espalda al tiempo
y en vez de caminar lo venidero
"nadie me espera allá",
volví a caminar lo caminado.

Abandoné la fila en donde todos,
desde el principio del principio, aguardan
un billete, una llave, una sentencia,
mientras desengañada la esperanza espera
que se abra la puerta de los siglos
y alguien diga: no hay puertas ya, ni siglos...

Crucé calles y plazas,
estatuas grises en el alba fría
y solo el viento vivo entre los muertos.

Tras la ciudad el campo y tras el campo
la noche en el desierto:
mi corazón fue noche y fue desierto.

Después fui piedra al sol, piedra y espejo.
Y luego del desierto y de las ruinas,
el mar y sobre el mar el cielo negro,
inmensa piedra de gastadas letras:
nada me revelaron las estrellas.

Llegué al cabo. Las puertas derribadas
y el angel sin espada, dormitando.
Dentro, el jardín: hojas entrelazadas,
respiración de piedras casi vivas,
sopor de las magnolias y, desnuda,
la luz entre los troncos tatuados.

El agua en cuatro brazos abrazada
al prado verde y rojo.
Y en medio, el árbol y la niña,
cabellera de pájaros de fuego.

La desnudez no me pesaba:
ya era como el agua y como el aire.

Bajo la verde luz del árbol,
dormida entre la yerba,
era una larga pluma
abandonada por el viento, blanca.

Quise besarla, mas el son del agua
tentó mi sed y allí su transparencia
me invitó a contemplarme.
Vi temblar una imagen en su fondo:
una sed encorvada y una boca deshecha,
¡oh viejo codicioso, sarmiento, fuego fatuo!
Cubrí mi desnudez. Salí despacio.

El ángel sonreía. Sopló el viento
y me cegó la arena de aquel viento.

Viento y arena fueron mis palabras:
no vivimos, el tiempo es quien nos vive.

THE RETURN

octavio paz

In the middle of the road I
stopped. I turned my back on time
and rather than continuing into the future
—where no one was waiting for me—
I turned back, traveling the traveled road.

I left that line where everyone
since the beginning of beginning waits
some ticket, some key, some verdict,
while hope hopes hopelessly
for the door of the centuries to open,
for someone to say: now there are no doors, nor centuries...

I crossed streets and squares,
grey statues in the chilly dawn
and only the wind lived among the dead things.
Beyond the city the country and beyond the country
the night in the desert:
my heart was night, was desert.
Then I was a stone in the sun, a stone and a mirror.
And then the sea out of the desert and the ruins
and over the sea the black sky,
huge stone of spent letters:
nothing showed me the stars.

I came to the end. The doors torn down
and the angel, weaponless and sleeping.
Inside, the garden: intertwined leaves,
a breathing of stones almost alive,
drowse of magnolias and naked
light between tattooed trunks.

The water embraced the red
and green meadow with four arms.
And at the center the woman, the tree,
hair of fiery birds.

My nakedness seemed natural:
I was like water, like air.
Under the tree's green light,
sleeping in the grass,
was a long feather
abandoned by the wind, white.

I wanted to kiss it, but the water-sound
touched my thirst and the transparence there
invited me to contemplate myself.
I saw an image trembling in the depths:
a curved thirst, a destroyed mouth,
oh old miser, creeper, fatuous fire,
cover my nakedness. I went, slowly.
The angel smiled. The wind woke
and the sand of that wind blinded me.

My words were wind, were sand:
it is not we who live, it is time lives us.

(trans. by Tim Reynolds)

One of the fruits of the Revolution has been the ongoing process begun in the 1930s of defining "mexicanidad." What is the real Mexican heritage, what are the lessons of Mexican history, what does it mean to say that Mexico is a mestizo nation, in what ways is the Mexican unique, in what ways like other Latin Americans, like all men? These are some of the questions underlying the writing of Samuel Ramos, Leopoldo Zea, and Octavio Paz over the past three decades.

Carlos Fuentes (born 1928), Mexico's most important novelist today, has been much influenced by this process of definition, and has incorporated his own contribution in novels such as *La muerte de Artemio Cruz* (*The Death of Artemio Cruz*, 1962). The selection below is from a play he wrote in 1970, *Todos los gatos son pardos* (*All Cats are Gray*). It contains the seeds of an interpretation of "mexicanidad" which is provocative not only for Mexicans, but for Chicanos as well.

The anguished and angry lament of La Malinche as she is about to give birth to the son of Cortés, a son who will be the first Mexican mestizo, is heavy with militant and vengeful prophesy. Fuentes implies that the Conquest, out of which Mexico was born, has signified a double legacy: firstly a sense of betrayal and violation, and secondly a drive to undo in vengeance this inherited curse, which is almost like original sin. It is as though Mexico, conceived in violence, must continue to exist in violence.

Many Mexicans have criticised this line of thought, which they also find in the recent essay by Octavio Paz, *Posdata*. They see a new version of fatalism embedded in this notion that the past determines the present, that hovering over the Mexican is the consciousness of origins in a betraying mother and a plundering father. They agree that Mexican history has been a sequence of violent struggles, but they find the causes to be more concrete than the need to undo the myth of original betrayal. In their view Mexico's struggles—those of the Revolution, or those of the students at Tlatelolco in 1968—are rooted in the fight for self-determination, in the need to better the lot of the dispossessed classes, in the desire for authentic national ideals, and in the will to resist outside (United States) domination.

As the Chicano process of definition continues, building on the base established by intellectuals such as George I. Sánchez, Ernesto Galarza, and Octavio I. Romano–V., many more Chicanos will propose answers to questions similar to those formulated by the Mexicans. Who is the Chicano, how does he evaluate his past, what is the real meaning of his complex heritage, is his sense of identity a product primarily of cultural factors, or is it due more to socio-economic factors, or perhaps to *both* culture and class considerations. Ramos, Zea, Paz, and Fuentes—the lessons of Mexico—may be useful in this Chicano process. But the differences must also be defined and understood, and this must be done in the first place by Chicano writers and thinkers.

LA HERENCIA DE LA MALINCHE

carlos fuentes

Marina

Oh, sal ya, hijo mío, sal, sal entre mis piernas...Sal, hijo de la traición...sal, hijo de puta...sal, hijo de la chingada...adorado hijo mío, sal ya...cae sobre la tierra que ya no es mía ni de tu padre, sino tuya... sal, hijo de las dos sangres enemigas...sal, mi hijo, a recobrar tu tierra maldita, fundada sobre el crimen permanente y los sueños fugitivos...ve si puedes recuperar tu tierra y tus sueños, hijo mío, blanco y moreno, ve si puedes lavar toda la sangre de las pirámides y de las espadas y de las cruces manchadas que son como los terribles y ávidos dedos de tu tierra...sal a tu tierra, hijo de la madrugada, sal lleno de rencor y miedo, sal lleno de burla y engaño y falsa sumisión...sal, mi hijo, sal a odiar a tu padre y a insultar a tu madre...habla quedo, hijo mío, como conviene a un esclavo; inclínate, sirve, padece y ármate de un secreto odio para el día de tu venganza; entonces, sal de la entraña de la miserable y opulenta tierra que heredaste, como ahora sales de mi vientre, y habla fuerte, pisa fuerte el suelo de plata y polvo, canta, cabalga, hijo mío, en los corceles de tu padre; quema las casas de tu padre como él quemó las de tus abuelos, clava a tu padre contra los muros de México como él clavó a su dios contra la cruz, mata a tu padre con sus propias armas; mata, mata, mata, hijo de puta, para que no te vuelvan a matar a ti; hay demasiados hombres blancos en el mundo, y todos quieren lo mismo: la sangre, el trabajo y el culo de los hombres oscurecidos por el sol; vendrá oleada tras oleada de hombres blancos a adueñarse de nuestra tierra; contra todos deberás luchar y tu lucha será triste porque pelearás contra una parte de tu propia sangre. Tu padre nunca te reconocerá, hijito prieto; nunca verá en ti a su vástago, sino a su esclavo; tú tendrás que hacerte reconocer en la orfandad, sin más apoyo que las manos de espina de tu chingada madre. Emborráchate, hijo de la tristeza, fornica, canta, baila, vístete con los colores de la tierra, huerfanito hijo de la tierra, para que la tierra resucite en el barro de tu cuerpo hambriento: haz de nuestra tierra una gran fiesta secreta, subterránea, invisible...una fiesta: no tendrás otra comunión en tu soledad, ni otra riqueza en tu miseria, ni otra voz en tu silencio, que las de las grandes fiestas de la muerte y el sueño, de la insurrección y del amor; sueño, amor, insurrección y muerte serán todo lo mismo para ti: la fiesta delirante en la que te rebelarás para amar y amarás para soñar y soñarás para morir; embárrate bien de tierra el cuerpo, hijo mío, hasta que la tierra sea tu máscara y los señores no puedan distinguir, detrás de ella, ni tus sueños, ni tu amor, ni tu rebelión, ni tu

From *Todos los gatos son pardos.*

muerte; cúbrete de polvo, mi hijo, para que aun muerto parezca que sigues vivo y te teman, pícaro, ratero, borracho, estuprador, rebelde armado de cohetes y navajas y aullidos y colores, amenazante hasta en tu sometimiento terco y mudo: sabrás esperar, esperar, esperar como nuestros ancestros esperaron la llegada del dios Quetzalcóatl, el dios que huyó espantado de su propio rostro para que tu propio rostro espantable, hijo mío, apareciese con los rasgos de la niebla y el jade, con la máscara del polvo y del llanto; algún día, hijo mío, tu espera será recompensada y el dios del bien y la felicidad reaparecerá detrás de una iglesia o de una pirámide en el espejismo de la vasta meseta mexicana; pero sólo reaparecerá si desde ahora te preparas para reencarnarlo tú, tú mismo, mi hijito de la chingada; tú deberás ser la serpiente emplumada, la tierra con alas, el ave de barro, el cabrón y encabronado hijo de México y España: tú eres mi única herencia, la herencia de Malintzin, la diosa, de Marina, la puta, de Malinche, la madre...

THE LEGACY OF LA MALINCHE

carlos fuentes

Marina

Oh, come out, son of mine, come out, come out between my legs... Come, son of betrayal...come, son of a whore...come out, hijo de la chingada...my beloved son, come out onto the land that no longer is mine or your father's, but yours...Come out, son of two warring bloods...come, son, to recover your accursed land, founded on permanent crime and fugitive dreams...see if you can regain your land and your dreams, son of mine, white and brown, see if you can wash all the blood from the pyramids and the swords and the stained crosses which seem like terrible, greedy fingers of the earth. Come out upon your land, son of dawn, come out full of anger and fear, full of mockery and deceit and false submissiveness...come out, my son, to hate your father and insult your mother...speak softly, as befits a slave; bend down, serve your master, suffer, and arm yourself with a secret hate for the day of your vengeance; then, emerge from the womb of the miserable and abundant land you inherited, as now you emerge from my womb; and speak strongly, stride strongly on the earth of silver and dust, sing, gallop on your father's chargers, son of mine; burn your father's houses as he burned those of your grandfathers, nail your father to the walls of Mexico as he nailed his god to the cross, kill your father with his own weapons; kill, kill, son of a whore, so that they may not kill you; there are too many white men in the world, and they all want the same thing: the blood, the labor, and the bodies of the people who have been darkened by the sun; wave after wave of white men will come to take over our land;

you must fight them all, and your struggle will be a sad one, for you will be fighting against a part of your own blood. Your father will never recognize you, my dark-skinned son; he will never see you as an heir, but rather as a slave; you will have to make your way as an orphan, with the help only of the thorny fingers of your outcast mother. Get drunk, son of sadness, fornicate, sing, dance, dress in all the colors of the earth, my orphan son of the earth, so that the earth may be reborn in the clay of your hungry body; turn our land into a great secret celebration, underground and invisible...a fiesta; you shall have no other communion in your loneliness; no other riches in your poverty; no other voice in your silence, except those of the great fiestas of death, dreaming, rebellion, and love; dreaming, loving, rebelling and dying will all be the same for you—the delirious fiesta in which you rebel in order to love, and you love in order to dream and you will dream in order to die; cover your body well with earth, son of mine, until the earth becomes your mask, and the masters are unable to recognize, behind it, your dreams, your love, your revolt or your death. Cover yourself with dust, my son, so that even when you are dead, you will seem alive and they will fear you, pícaro, thief, drunk, rapist, rebel armed with firecrackers and razors and shrill shrieks, threatening even in your stubborn, silent submission. You will know how to wait and wait, as our ancestors awaited the arrival of the god Quetzalcóatl, the god who fled in fright from his own face, so that your own face, easily frightened, my son, would have the features of mist and jade, with a mask of dust and weeping. Someday, my son, your wait will be rewarded, and the god of good and happiness will reappear behind a church or a pyramid on the mirage of the vast Mexican plateau; but he will only appear to you if from now on you prepare to reencarnate him, you yourself, my little hijito de la chingada; you must be the feathered serpent, the winged earth, the clay bird, the screwed and doubly screwed son of Mexico and Spain: you are my only legacy, the legacy of Malintzin, the goddess; Marina, the whore; of Malinche, the mother.

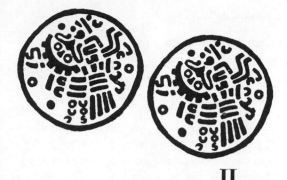

II

lo puertorriqueño

Except for certain cities in the Midwest, such as Chicago, there are few places where Chicanos and Puertorriqueños have ongoing communication. The gap was bridged at the historic Chicano Youth Conferences at Denver in 1968 and 1969, when Puerto Rican groups attended and participated. The purpose of highlighting Puerto Rican selections in this book on Chicano literature is to create the mutual appreciation needed to strengthen that bridge.

The fact is that Puerto Ricans and Chicanos, the major Spanish-speaking minorities in the United States, have many experiences in common. Both groups have encountered similar brands of racism, based on skin color, language, or culture. Both groups know the meaning, in human terms, of economic repression. And both have confronted the pressures to acculturate by forfeiting language and cultural loyalty.

Puerto Rican Studies programs are now being developed at numerous campuses in the East. They emphasize study of the history and culture of the Puerto Rican, both on the island and in the United States. One important component is literary expression, which has a long and rich tradition. It begins in Puerto Rico under Spanish colonial rule, and continues in modern times in all the urban barrios of the East where Puerto Rican emigrants have settled, and where new generations have been born.

We have chosen selections written in both Puerto Rico and the United States. Our aim has been to show both parallels with Chicano expression (Piri Thomas, José Luis González), and contrasts stemming from the uniqueness of the Puerto Rican experience (Julia de Burgos, Luis Palés Matos.)

Everywhere in the Spanish-speaking world, folk poetry is created from the people's blending of language and music to express emotions and reflect experience.

The anonymous poem below seems to begin with a note of humor, but by the final stanza it takes on a note of bitterness as it stresses the inevitable doom of the illusion of love. But it also includes a note of protest, in the second stanza, against foreign control of the Puerto Rican economy.

We have left the spelling intact in order to convey the feeling of Puerto Rican Spanish. The final -s in *sembrarlos* disappears in pronunciation. *Hacer* in popular speech is closer to *jasel*. *Extrangís*, we think, is another form for *extranjeros*.

POEMA POPULAR

Si quieres estar contento,
manda comprar, buen amigo,
un quintal de indiferencia
y tres arrobas de olvido.

El café y la caña tienen
la culpa de tanto amor
de extrangís a Puerto Rico.
¡No sembrarlo es lo mejor!

Quítate de esa ventana,
no te baya a jasel daño,
como a flor de la ilusión
el viento del desengaño.

FOLK POEM

If you want to be happy,
have someone buy you, my friend
a sackful of indifference
and three large loads of forgetfulness.

Coffee and sugar cane should get
the blame for all that love
those foreigners have for Puerto Rico.
Don't plant them, is our best bet!

Come away from that window
so you won't do yourself any harm,
as is done to the flower of illusion
by that old wind of disenchantment.

José de Diego, patriot, civil leader, and advocate of Puerto Rican independence, wrote this poem in the early twentieth century. He was a contemporary of Santiago de la Hoz, the Chicano poet of Laredo (see unit I, subunit 1) and the high-sounding tone of his sonnet reminds us of the "Sinfonía de combate." Both writers conceive of poetry as a call to arms.

EN LA BRECHA

josé de diego

Oh desgraciado, si el dolor te abate,
si el cansancio tus miembros entumece;
haz como el árbol seco: Reverdece;
y como el germen enterrado: Late.

Resurge, alienta, grita, anda, combate,
vibra, ondula, retruena, resplandece...
Haz como el río con la lluvia: ¡Crece!
y como el mar contra la roca: ¡Bate!

De la tormenta al iracundo empuje,
no has de balar, como el cordero triste,
sino rugir, como la fiera ruge.

¡Levántate! ¡Revuélvete! ¡Resiste!
Haz como el toro acorralado: ¡Muge!
O como el toro que no muge: ¡¡Embiste!!

Unlike what they did in Mexico, the Spaniards in Puerto Rico in the sixteenth century completely eliminated the native Indian population. African slaves were imported to the island for three centuries, to replace Indian labor. As a result, Puerto Ricans have incorporated African influences in their language, their religion, and many other aspects of their culture.

In the 1920s and 1930s Luis Palés Matos was Puerto Rico's outstanding contributor to a movement that became known in the Caribbean as "Poesía negra." Poets in Cuba and Puerto Rico affirmed pride in the African heritage of the islands, and tried to reflect it in their poetry. The poem below integrates African symbols, sounds, words, geographical references, and especially rhythms.

DANZA NEGRA

luis palés matos

Calabó y bambú.
Bambú y calabó.
El Gran Cocoroco dice: tu-cu-tú.
La Gran Cocoroca dice: to-co-tó.
Es el sol de hierro que arde en Tombuctú.
Es la danza negra de Fernando Póo.
El cerdo en el fango gruñe: pru-pru-prú
El sapo en la charca sueña: cro-cro-cró.
Calabó y bambú
Bambú y calabó.

Rompen los junjunes en furiosa ú.
Los gongos trepidan con profunda ó.
Es la raza negra que ondulando va

en el ritmo gordo del mariyandá.
Llegan los botucos a la fiesta ya.
Danza que te danza la negra se da.

   Calabó y bambú.
Bambú y calabó.
El Gran Cocoroco dice: tu-cu-tú.
La Gran Cocoroca dice: to-co-tó.

   Pasan tierras rojas, islas de betún:
Haití, Martinica, Congo, Camerún;
las papiamentosas antillas del ron
y las patualesas islas del volcán,
que en el grave son
del canto se dan.

   Calabó y bambú.
Bambú y calabó.
Es el sol de hierro que arde en Tombuctú
Es la danza negra de Fernando Póo.
El alma africana que vibrando está.
en el ritmo gordo del mariyandá.

   Calabó y bambú.
Bambú y Calabó.
El Gran Cocoroco dice: tu-cu-tú.
La Gran Cocoroca dice: to-co-tó.

Julia de Burgos, who died in New York in 1953, spent much of her unhappy life away from Puerto Rico—a fact which made her appreciate it all the more. In her love for the natural landscape she knew as a child, Julia de Burgos shares the emotions of many Chicanos in the Southwest who have been uprooted. What is different here is the specific importance which the ocean, in all its colors and moods, has for Puerto Rican consciousness.

LETANÍA DEL MAR

julia de burgos

> Mar mío,
> mar profundo que comienzas en mí,
> mar subterráneo y solo
> de mi suelo de espadas apretadas.
>
> Mar mío,
> mar sin nombre,
> desfiladero turbio de mi canción despedazada,
> roto y desconcertado silencio transmarino,
> azul desesperado,
> mar lecho,
> mar sepulcro...
>
> Azul,
> lívido azul,
> para mis capullos ensangrentados,
> para la ausencia de mi risa,
> para la voz que oculta mi muerte con poemas...
>
> Mar mío,
> mar lecho,
> mar sin nombre,
> mar a deshoras,
> mar en la espuma del sueño,
> mar en la soledad desposando crepúsculos,
> mar viento descalzando mis últimos revuelos,
> mar tú,
> mar universo...

Luis Rafael Sánchez, a young writer (born 1936), teaches literature at the University of Puerto Rico. In this story he tries to communicate the notion that humanity and decency belong as much—or more—to the social outcast as to those who live hypocritically by social convention. The story is ironic because it contrasts the internal decency of Gurdelia with the external respectability of her neighbors.

The meaning of the prostitute who, as a woman, rises above the degradation of prostitution, and the boy who is on the borderline between innocence and the most negative variety of machismo, should be of interest both to Chicano and Chicana readers.

TIENE LA NOCHE UNA RAÍZ

luis rafael sánchez

A las siete el dindón. Las tres beatísimas con unos cuantos pecados a cuestas marcharon a la iglesia a rezongar el ave nocturnal. Iban de prisita, todavía el séptimo dindón agobiando, con la sana esperanza de acabar de prisita el rosario para regresar al beatario y echar, ¡ya libres de pecados!, el ojo por las rendijas y saber quién alquilaba esa noche el colchón de la Gurdelia. ¡La Gurdelia Grifitos nombrada! ¡La vergüenza de los vergonzosos, el pecado del pueblo todo!

Gurdelia Grifitos, el escote y el ombligo de manos, al oír el séptimo dindón se paró detrás del antepecho con su lindo abanico de nácar, tris-tras-tris-tras, y empezó a anunciar la mercancía. En el pueblo el negocio era breve. Uno que otro majadero cosechando los treinta, algún viejo verdérrimo o un tipitejo quinceañero debutante. Total, ocho o diez pesos por semana que sacando los tres del cuarto, los dos de la fiambrera y los dos para polvos, meivelines y lipstis, se venían a quedar en la dichosa porquería que sepultaba en una alcancía hambrienta.

Gurdelia no era hermosa. Una murallita de dientes le combinaba con los ojos saltones y asustados que tenía, ¡menos mal!, en el sitio en que todos tenemos los ojos. Su nariguda nariz era suma de muchas narices que podían ser suyas o prestadas. Pero lo que redondeaba su encanto de negrita bullanguera era el buen par de metáforas —princesas cautivas de un sostén cuarenticinco— que encaramaba en el antepecho y que le hacían un suculento antecedente. Por eso, a las siete, las mujeres decentes, y cotidianas, oscurecían sus balcones, y sólo quedaba como anuncio luminoso el foco de la Gurdelia.

Gurdelia se rescotaba del antepecho y esperaba. No era a las siete ni a las ocho que venían sino más tarde. Por eso aquel toc único en su persiana la asombró. El gato de la vecina, pensó. El gato maullero encargado de asustarla. Desde su llegada había empezado la cuestión. Mariposas negras prendidas con un alfiler, cruces de fósforos sobre el antepecho, el miau en stacatto, hechizos, maldiciones y fufús desde la noche de tormenta en que llegó al pueblo. Pero ella era valiente. Ni la asustaba eso, ni las sartas de insultos en la madrugada, ni las piedras en el techo. Así que cuando el toc se hizo de nuevo agarró la escoba, se echó un coño en la boca y abrió la puerta de sopetón. Y al abrir:

—Soy yo doñita, soy yo que vengo a entrar. Míreme la mano apretá. Es un medio peso afisiao. Míreme el puño doñita. Le pago éste ahora y después cada sábado le lavo el atrio al cura y medio y medio y medio hasta pagar los dos que dicen que vale.

La jerigonza terminó en la sala ante el asombro de la Grifitos, que no veía con buenos ojos el que un muchachito se le metiera en la casa. No por ella, que no comía niños, sino por los vecinos. Un muchachito allí afilaba las piedras y alimentaba las lenguas. Luego, un muchachito bien chito, ni siquiera tirando a mocetón, un muchachito con gorra azul llamado...

—¿Cómo te llamas?

—Cuco.

Un muchachito llamado Cuco, que se quitó la gorra azul y se dejó al aire el cholo pelón.

—¿Qué hace aquí?

—Vine con este medio peso doñita.

—Yo no vendo dulce.

—Yo no quiero dulce doñita.

—Pues yo no tengo ná.

—Ay sí doñita. Dicen lo que han venío que...Cosa que yo no voy a decir pero dicen cosa tan devina que yo he mancao este medio peso porque tengo gana del amor que dicen que usté vende.

—¿Quién dice?

Gurdelia puso cara de vecina y se llevó las manos a la cintura como cualquier señora honrada que pregunta lo que se le venga en ganas.

—Yo oí que mi pai se lo decía a un compai, doñita. Que era devino. Que él venía de cuando en ve porque era devino, bien devino, tan devino que él pensaba golver.

—¿Y qué era lo devino?

—Yo no sé pero devino, doñita.

Gurdelia Grifitos, lengüetera, bembetera, solariega, güíchara registrada, lavá y tendía en tó el pueblo, bocona y puntillosa, como que no encontraba por dónde agarrar el muerto. Abría los ojos, los cerraba, se daba tris-tras en las metáforas pero sólo lograba decir "ay virgen, ay virgen". Gurdelia Grifitos, loba vieja en los menesteres de vender amor, como que no encontraba por dónde desenredar el enredo, porque era la primera vez en su perra vida que se veía requerida por un...por un...¡Dios Santo! Era desenvuelta, cosa que en su caso venía como anillo, argumentosa, pico de oro, en fin, ¡águila! Pero ahora de pronto el muchachito Cuco la había callado. Precisamente por ser el muchachito Cuco. ¡Precisamente por ser el muchachito! En todos sus afanados años se había enredado con viejos solteros, viejos casados, viejos viudos, solteros sin obligación o maridos cornudos o maridos corneando. Pero un mocosillo, ¡Santa Cachucha!, que olía a trompo y chiringa. Un mocosillo que podía ser, claro que sí, su hijo. Esto último la mareó un poco. El vientre le dió un sacudón y las palabras le salieron.

—Usté e un niño. Eso son mala costumbre.

—Aquí viene to el mundo. Mi pai dijo...

Ahora no le quedaban razones. Los dientes, a Gurdelia, se le salían en fila, luego en un desplazamiento de retaguardia volvían a acomodarse, tal la rabia que tenía.

Usté e un niño.

—Yo soy un hombre.

—¿Cuánto año tiene?

—Dié pa once.

—Mire nenine. Voy a llamar a su pai.

Pero Cuco puso la boca apucherada, como para llorar hasta mañana y entre puchero y gemido decía —que soy un hombre, que soy un hombre. Gurdelia, el tris-tras por las metáforas, harta ya de la histeria y la historia le dijo que estaba bien, que le daría del amor. Bien por dentro empezó a dibujar una idea.

—Venga acá...a mi falda.

Cuco estrenó una sonrisa de demonio junior.

—Cierre lo ojito.

—Pai decía que en la cama doñita.

—La cama viene despué.

Cuco, tembloroso, fue a acurrucarse por la falda de la Gurdelia. Esta se estaba quieta pero el vientre volvió a darle otro salto magnífico. Cuando Gurdelia sintió la canción reventándole por la garganta Cuco dijo —oiga, oiga. Pero el sillón que se mecía y la luz que era mediana y el vaivén del que no tiene vaca no bebe leche empezaron a remolcarlo hasta la zona rotunda del sueño. Gurdelia lo cambió a la cama y allí lo dejó un buen rato. Al despertar, como sin creerlo, como si se hubiese vuelto loco, Cuco preguntó bajito

—¿Ya doñita?

Ella, como sin creerlo, como si se hubiese vuelto loca, le contestó más bajo aún

—Ya Cuco.

Cuco salió corriendo diciendo devino, devino. Gurdelia al verlo ir sintió el vaivén del que no tiene vaca no bebe leche levantándole una parcela de la barriga. Esa noche apagó temprano. Y un viejo borracho se cansó de tocar.

This story by Jesús Colón, written in the 1950s, focuses on the conflict faced by Puerto Ricans in New York, in their daily encounters with race prejudice. Only a few changes, for example, in locale (New York to, say, Los Angeles), and skin color (black to brown) would be needed to convert the story from a Puerto Rican to a Chicano experience.

LITTLE THINGS ARE BIG

jesús colón

It was very late at night on the eve of Memorial Day. She came into the subway at the 34th Street Pennsylvania Station. I am still trying to remember how she managed to push herself in with a baby on her right arm, a valise in her left hand and two children, a boy and girl about three and five years old, trailing after her. She was a nice looking white lady in her early twenties.

At Nevins Street, Brooklyn, we saw her preparing to get off at the next station—Atlantic Avenue—which happened to be the place where I too had to get off. Just as it was a problem for her to get on, it was going to be a problem for her to get off the subway with two small children to be taken care of, a baby on her right arm and a medium sized valise in her left hand.

And there I was, also preparing to get off at Atlantic Avenue, with no bundles to take care of—not even the customary book under my arm without which I feel that I am not completely dressed.

As the train was entering the Atlantic Avenue station, some white man stood up from his seat and hleped her out, placing the children on the long, deserted platform. There were only two adult persons on the long platform some time after midnight on the eve of last Memorial Day.

I could perceive the steep, long concrete stairs going down to the Long Island Railroad or into the street. Should I offer my help as the American white man did at the subway door placing the two children outside the subway car? Should I take care of the girl and the boy, take them by their hands until they reached the end of the steep long concrete stairs of the Atlantic Avenue station?

Courtesy is a characteristic of the Puerto Rican. And here I was—a Puerto Rican—hours past midnight, a valise, two white children and a white lady with a baby on her arm palpably needing somebody to help her at least until she descended the long concrete stairs.

But how could I, a Negro and a Puerto Rican approach this white lady who very likely might have preconceived prejudices against Negroes and everybody with foreign accents, in a deserted subway station very late at night?

What would she say? What would be the first reaction of this white

American woman, perhaps coming from a small town, with a valise, two children and a baby on her right arm? Would she say: Yes, of course, you may help me. Or would she think that I was just trying to get too familiar? Or would she think worse than that perhaps? What would I do if she let out a scream as I went toward her to offer my help?

Was I misjudging her? So many slanders are written every day in the daily press against the Negroes and Puerto Ricans. I hesitated for a long, long minute. The ancestral manners that the most illiterate Puerto Rican passes on from father to son were struggling inside me. Here was I, way past midnight, face to face with a situation that could very well explode into an outburst of prejudices and chauvinistic conditioning of the "divide and rule" policy of present day society.

It was a long minute. I passed on by her as if I saw nothing. As if I was insensitive to her need. Like a rude animal walking on two legs, I just moved on half running by the long subway platform leaving the children and the valise and her with the baby on her arm. I took the steps of the long concrete stairs in twos until I reached the street above and the cold air slapped my warm face.

This is what racism and prejudice and chauvinism and official artificial divisions can do to people and to a nation!

Perhaps the lady was not prejudiced after all. Or not prejudiced enough to scream at the coming of a Negro toward her in a solitary subway station a few hours past midnight.

If you were not that prejudiced, I failed you, dear lady. I know that there is a chance in a million that you will read these lines. I am willing to take that millionth chance. If you were not that prejudiced, I failed you, lady, I failed you, children. I failed myself to myself.

I buried my courtesy early on Memorial Day morning. But here is a promise that I make to myself here and now; if I am ever faced with an occasion like that again, I am going to offer my help regardless of how the offer is going to be received.

Then I will have my courtesy with me again.

Pedro Juan Soto is a contemporary cuentista and novelista. This story is from a volume entitled *Spiks*, published in 1956. Soto condenses in the dialogue the sense of frustration that results when the institutions of a society—personified in the policeman with his book of citations and his attitude of suspicion—close the doors of language, employment, and cultural acceptance.

BAYAMINIÑA

pedro juan soto

De lejos, si uno se dejaba llevar por los colores de su fachada, era un carrito pizpireto estacionado en una esquina de la Calle 116. Tenía franjas azules, rojas y amarillas, y la caja en el tope —llena de fritas de bacalao, morcilla y alcapurrias— tenía cristal por los cuatro costados. De cerca, sin embargo, se notaba que su pizpiretería no era más que un frente: con ella disimulaba un desgaste y una pudrición que le consumían desde las ruedas hasta la barra de empuje. En un pedazo de hojalata claveteado al frente, se leía en letras rojas y deformes: BAYAMINIÑA.

Pero nadie hacía caso del carro. El gentío estaba atento a la discusión del vendedor con el policía. Las negras que desfilaban rumbo a la Avenida Lennox detenían su rápido culipandeo para ver en qué paraba aquello. Los parroquianos del bar próximo descuidaban las bebidas y el televisor para seguir el altercado a través de la vidriera. Y la curiosidad también hacía volver los rostros en los automóviles y autobuses que iban de paso.

—I no pay more —decía, tenso, el vendedor—. I pay las' year other fine...

Y el policía sólo sacudía la cabeza a medida que terminaba de garrapatear en su libreta.

—This has nothing to do with last year, buddy.

—I got no money. I no pay more.

—And the fine you'll have to pay next year will be a bigger one, if you don't get rid of that *thing* there.

—You're killing me —dijo el vendedor—. Why you do this?

—The Department of Health...

—Okay, you gimme a job an' I...

—...is after all you guys.

—I have to eat —dijo el vendedor—. Don't gimme no fine, gimme a job.

—I have nothing to do with that —dijo el policía. Le metió la papeleta en un bolsillo de la camisa y añadió—: You keep that...And remember to go to court.

El vendedor sacó la papeleta, enfurecido, e intentó leerla. Pero no acertó a entender más que los números.

—All right, break it up —díjole el policía al gentío. Y al vendedor—: And you get going before I lose my patience.

El vendedor se dio vuelta hacia los escolares que tenían su misma delgadez y su mismo acanelamiento en el cutis.

—Ehtos abusadores —masculló—. ¡Sia la madre d'ehtos policías!

—C'mon —dijo el policía—. Get the hell out of here.

De súbito, el vendedor se inclinó, recogió la piedra que servía de freno al carrito y volvió a alzarse con ella en el puño. Ya el rostro se le descomponía con el presagio del llanto.

—Gimme a job, saramambich!

—You'd better get your ass out of this neighborhood before I throw you in jail!—dijo el policía sin levantar la vista del puño amenazante, alzando la mano hacia la vaqueta.

El vendedor vaciló, hizo una mueca airada, y se dio vuelta para abalanzarse sobre el carro. ¡Kirilín! los cristales y ¡pon! ¡pon! la madera. Y él chillaba:

—Gimme a job, saramambich, gimme a job!

Y la hojalata —¡clan! ¡clan!—, donde mismo se leía BAYAMINIÑA, ya se ensuciaba de sangre, ya se salpicaba de lágrimas, y ya se libraba de clavos para recobrar su antigua forma de cacharro.

In Puerto Rico, as in the Southwestern United States, many rural families face economic hardships because the small farmer or the tenant farmer is at a disadvantage in competing with large-scale mechanized agriculture. For this reason many young men migrate to the cities in hopes of finding better jobs in factories.

This story written by José Luis González in 1948, conveys the personal suffering that is part of this migratory process. Its impact is heightened by the boy's sense of dignity and his obvious love of family, as well as by the fact that he has had only a minimal exposure to education.

José Luis González has lived in Mexico for many years, teaching at the National University and translating into Spanish important works in history and philosophy.

LA CARTA

josé luis gonzález

San Juan, Puerto Rico
8 de marso de 1947

Querida bieja:
Como yo le desia antes de venirme, aqui las cosas me van vién. Desde que llegé enseguida incontré trabajo. Me pagan 8 pesos la semana y con eso vivo igual que don Pepe el alministradol de la central allá.

La ropa aquella que quedé de mandale, no la he podido compral pues quiero buscarla en una de las tiendas mejores. Digale a Petra que cuando valla por casa le boy a llevar un regalito al nene de ella.

Voy a ver si me saco un retrato un día de estos para mandálselo a uste.

El otro día vi a Felo el hijo de la comai María. El esta trabajando pero gana menos que yo.

Bueno recueldese de escrivilme y contarme todo lo que pasa por allá.
Su ijo que la quiere y le pide la bendision.

Juan.

Después de firmar, dobló cuidadosamente el papel ajado y lleno de borrones y se lo guardó en el bolsillo de atrás del pantalón. Caminó hasta la estación de correos más cercana, y al llegar se echó la gorra raída sobre la frente y se acuclilló en el umbral de una de las puertas. Dobló la mano izquierda, como la tienen los mancos, y extendió la derecha abierta.

Cuando reunió los cuatro centavos necesarios, compró el sobre y el sello y despachó la carta.

THE LETTER

josé luis gonzález

San Juan, Puerto Rico
March 8, 1947

Dear Ma,

Like I was telling you before I came, things go good for me here. Right away when I got here I found work. They pay me 8 dollers a week, and I can live on that as good as Don Pepe the boss of the sugar mill back home.

Those clothes I said I was gonna send you, I haven't got them yet cause I want to bye them in one of the best stores. Tell Petra that when I come home I'm gonna bring a present for her baby.

I'm gonna try one of these days to have my picture taken and send it to you.

The other day I ran into Felo, the son of auntie María. He's working but he don't make as much as me.

Well don't forget to wright and tell me bout what's happening there. Your son who loves you and asks your blessing.

Juan.

After signing his name, he carefully folded the wrinkled paper, with its smudges, and tucked it in his rear pants pocket. He walked to the nearest post office. On arrival, he pulled his ragged cap over his forehead and squatted in one of the doorways. He bent his left hand over, like amputees hold them, and stretched out his right hand, holding it open.

When he finally collected the four cents, he bought the envelope and stamp, and mailed his letter.

The selections below are from *Down These Mean Streets* (1968), by Piri
Thomas, an ex-convict with great literary talent. The first chapter highlights
the contrast, through the eyes of they boy, between the harsh reality of their
life in Puerto Rican Harlem, and the sweet illusions of his mother's memories
of life back in Puerto Rico. The second chapter focuses on the "initiation"
process in the barrio, and on what Chicano readers will recognize is a code of
behavior involving manliness, bravery, and loyalty.

PUERTO RICAN PARADISE

piri thomas

Poppa didn't talk to me the next day. Soon he didn't talk much to
anyone. He lost his night job—I forget why, and probably it was worth forgetting—and went back on home relief. It was 1941, and the Great Hunger
called Depression was still down on Harlem.

But there was still the good old WPA. If a man was poor enough, he
could dig a ditch for the government. Now Poppa was poor enough again.

The weather turned cold one more time, and so did our apartment.
In the summer the cooped-up apartments in Harlem seem to catch all the
heat and improve on it. It's the same in the winter. The cold, plastered walls
embrace that cold from outside and make it a part of the apartment, till
you don't know whether it's better to freeze out in the snow or by the stove,
where four jets, wide open, spout futile, blue-yellow flames. It's hard on
the rats, too.

Snow was falling. "My *Cristo*," Momma said, "*qué frío*. Doesn't that
landlord have any *corazón*? Why don't he give more heat?" I wondered
how Pops was making out working a pick and shovel in that falling snow.

Momma picked up a hammer and began to beat the beat-up radiator
that's copped a plea from so many beatings. Poor steam radiator, how could
it give out heat when it was freezing itself? The hollow sounds Momma
beat out of it brought echoes from other freezing people in the building.
Everybody picked up the beat and it seemed a crazy, good idea. If everybody took turns beating on the radiators, everybody could keep warm from
the exercise.

We drank hot cocoa and talked about summertime. Momma talked
about Puerto Rico and how great it was, and how she'd like to go back
one day, and how it was warm all the time there and no matter how poor
you were over there, you could always live on green bananas, *bacalao,* and
rice and beans. "*Dios mío*," she said, "I don't think I'll ever see my island
again."

"Sure you will, Mommie," said Miriam, my kid sister. She was eleven.
"Tell us, tell us all about Porto Rico."

"It's not Porto Rico, it's Puerto Rico," said Momma.

"Tell us, Moms," said nine-year-old James, "about Puerto Rico."

"Yeah, Mommie," said six-year-old José.

Even the baby, Paulie, smiled.

Moms copped that wet-eyed look and began to dream-talk about her *isla verde,* Moses' land of milk and honey.

"When I was a little girl," she said, "I remember the getting up in the morning and getting the water from the river and getting the wood for the fire and the quiet of the greenlands and the golden color of the morning sky, the grass wet from the *lluvia...Ai, Dios,* the *coquís* and the *pajaritos* making all the *música...*"

"Mommie, were you poor?" asked Miriam.

"*Sí, muy pobre,* but very happy. I remember the hard work and the very little bit we had, but it was a good little bit. It counted very much. Sometimes when you have too much, the good gets lost within and you have to look very hard. But when you have a little, then the good does not have to be looked for so hard."

"Moms," I asked, "did everybody love each other—I mean, like if everybody was worth something, not like if some weren't important because they were poor—you know what I mean?"

"*Bueno hijo,* you have people everywhere who, because they have more, don't remember those who have very little. But in Puerto Rico those around you share *la pobreza* with you and they love you, because only poor people can understand poor people. I like *los Estados Unidos,* but it's sometimes a cold place to live—not because of the winter and the landlord not giving heat but because of the snow in the hearts of the people."

"Moms, didn't our people have any money or land?" I leaned forward, hoping to hear that my ancestors were noble princes born in Spain.

"Your grandmother and grandfather had a lot of land, but they lost that."

"How come, Moms?"

"Well, in those days there was nothing of what you call *contratos,* and when you bought or sold something, it was on your word and a handshake, and that's the way your *abuelos* bought their land and then lost it."

"Is that why we ain't got nuttin' now?" James asked pointedly.

"Oh, it—"

The door opened and put an end to the kitchen yak. It was Poppa coming home from work. He came into the kitchen and brought all the cold with him. Poor Poppa, he looked so lost in the clothes he had on. A jacket and coat, sweaters on top of sweaters, two pairs of long johns, two pairs of pants, two pairs of socks and a woolen cap. And under all that he was cold. His eyes were cold; his ears were red with pain. He took off his gloves and his fingers were stiff with cold.

"*Cómo está?*" said Momma. "I will make you coffee."

Poppa said nothing. His eyes were running hot frozen tears. He worked his fingers and rubbed his ears, and the pain made him make faces. "Get me some snow, Piri," he said finally.

I ran to the window, opened it, and scraped all the snow on the sill into one big snowball and brought it to him. We all watched in frozen wonder as Poppa took that snow and rubbed it on his ears and hands.

"Gee, Pops, don't it hurt?" I asked.

"*Sí*, but it's good for it. It hurts a little first, but it's good for the frozen parts."

I wondered why.

"How was it today?" Momma asked.

"Cold. My God, ice cold."

Gee, I thought, *I'm sorry for you, Pops. You gotta suffer like this.*

"It was not always like this," my father said to the cold walls. "It's all the fault of the damn depression."

"Don't say 'damn,' " Momma said.

"Lola, I say 'damn' because that's what it is—*damn.*"

And Momma kept quiet. She knew it was "damn."

My father kept talking to the walls. Some of the words came out loud, others stayed inside. I caught the inside ones—the damn WPA, the damn depression, the damn home relief, the damn poorness, the damn cold, the damn crummy apartments, the damn look on his damn kids, living so damn damned and his not being able to do a damn thing about it.

And Momma looked at Poppa and at us and thought about her Puerto Rico and maybe being there where you didn't have to wear a lot of extra clothes and feel so full of damns, and how when she was a little girl all the green was wet from the *lluvias.*

And Poppa looking at Momma and us, thinking how did he get trapped and why did he love us so much that he dug in damn snow to give us a piece of chance? And why couldn't he make it from home, maybe, and keep running?

And Miriam, James, José, Paulie, and me just looking and thinking about snowballs and Puerto Rico and summertime in the street and whether we were gonna live like this forever and not know enough to be sorry for ourselves.

IF YOU AIN'T GOT HEART,
YOU AIN'T GOT NADA

piri thomas

We were moving—our new pad was back in Spanish Harlem—to 104th Street between Lex and Park Avenue.

Moving into a new block is a big jump for a Harlem kid. You're torn up from your hard-won turf and brought into an "I don't know you" block where every kid is some kind of enemy. Even when the block belongs to your own people, you are still an outsider who has to prove himself a down stud with heart.

As the moving van rolled to a stop in front of our new building, number 109, we were all standing there, waiting for it—Momma, Poppa, Sis, Paulie, James, José, and myself. I made out like I didn't notice the cats looking us over, especially me—I was gang age. I read their faces and found no trust, plenty of suspicion, and a glint of rising hate. I said to myself, *These cats don't mean nothin'. They're just nosy.* But I remembered what had happened to me in my old block, and that it had ended with me in the hospital.

This was a tough-looking block. That was good, that was cool; but my old turf had been tough, too. *I'm tough enough.* A voice within said. *I hope I'm tough enough. I am tough enough. I've got* mucho corazón, *I'm king wherever I go. I'm a killer to my heart. I not only* can *live, I* will *live, no punk out, no die out, walk bad; be down, cool breeze, smooth.* My mind raced, and thoughts crashed against each other, trying to reassemble themselves into a pattern of rep. I turned slowly and with eyelids half-closed I looked at the rulers of this new world and with a cool shrug of my shoulders I followed the movers into the hallway of number 109 and dismissed the coming war from my mind.

The next morning I went to my new school, called Patrick Henry, and strange, mean eyes followed me.

"Say, pops," said a voice belonging to a guy I later came to know as Waneko, "where's your territory?"

In the same tone of voice Waneko had used, I answered, "I'm on it, dad, what's shaking?"

"Bad, huh?" He half-smiled.

"No, not all the way. Good when I'm cool breeze and bad when I'm down."

"What's your name, kid?"

"That depends. 'Piri' when I'm smooth and 'Johnny Gringo' when stomping time's around."

"What's your name now?" he pushed.

"You name me, man," I answered, playing my role like a champ.

He looked around, and with no kind of words, his boys cruised in. Guys I would come to know, to fight, to hate, to love, to take care of. Little Red, Waneko, Little Louie, Indio, Carlito, Alfredo, Crip, and plenty more. I stiffened and said to myself, *Stomping time, Piri boy, go with heart.*

I fingered the garbage-can handle in my pocket—my homemade brass knuckles. They were great for breaking down large odds into small, chopped-up ones.

Waneko, secure in his grandstand, said, "We'll name you later, *panín.*"

I didn't answer. Scared, yeah, but wooden-faced to the end, I thought, *Chévere, panín.*

It wasn't long in coming. Three days later, at about 6 p.m., Waneko and his boys were sitting around the stoop at number 115. I was cut off from my number 109. For an instant I thought, *Make a break for it down the basement steps and through the back yards—get away in one piece!* Then I thought, *Caramba! Live punk, dead hero. I'm no punk kid. I'm not copping any pleas.* I kept walking, hell's a-burning, hell's a-churning, rolling with cheer. *Walk on, baby man, roll on without fear. What's he going to call?*

"Whatta ya say, Mr. Johnny Gringo?" drawler Waneko.

Think, man, I told myself, *think your way out of a stomping. Make it good.* "I hear you 104th Street coolies are supposed to have heart," I said. "I don't know this for sure. You know there's a lot of streets where a whole 'click' is made out of punks who can't fight one guy unless they all jump him for the stomp." I hoped this would push Waneko into giving me a fair one. His expression didn't change.

"Maybe we don't look at it that way."

Crazy, man. I cheer inwardly, the cabrón *is falling into my setup. We'll see who gets messed up first, baby!* "I wasn't talking to you," I said. "Where I come from, the pres is president 'cause he got heart when it comes to dealing."

Waneko was starting to look uneasy. He had bit on my worm and felt like a sucker fish. His boys were now light on me. They were no longer so much interested in stomping me as in seeing the outcome between Waneko and me. "Yeah," was his reply.

I smiled at him. "You trying to dig where I'm at and now you got me interested in you. I'd like to see where you're at."

Waneko hesitated a tiny little second before replying, "Yeah."

I knew I'd won. Sure, I'd have to fight; but one guy, not ten or fifteen. If I lost I might still get stomped, and if I won I might get stomped.

I took care of this with my next sentence. "I don't know you or your boys," I said, "but they look cool to me. They don't feature as punks."

I had left him out purposely when I said "they." Now his boys were in a separate class. I had cut him off. He would have to fight me on his own, to prove his heart to himself, to his boys, and most important, to his turf. He got away from the stoop and asked, "Fair one, Gringo?"

"Uh-uh," I said, "roll all the way—anything goes." I thought, *I've got to beat him bad and yet not bad enough to take his prestige all away.* He had *corazón.* He came on me. *Let him draw first blood,* I thought, *it's his block.* Smish, my nose began to bleed. His boys cheered, his heart cheered, his turf cheered. "Waste this chump," somebody shouted.

Okay, baby, now it's my turn. He swung. I grabbed innocently, and my forehead smashed into his nose. His eyes crossed. His fingernails went for my eye and landed in my mouth—crunch, I bit hard. I punched him in the mouth as he pulled away from me, and he slammed his foot into my chest.

We broke, my nose running red, my chest throbbing, his finger—well, that was his worry. I tied up with body punching and slugging. We rolled onto the street. I wrestled for acceptance, he for rejection or, worse yet, acceptance on his terms. It was time to start peace talks. I smiled at him. "You got heart, baby," I said.

He answered with a punch to my head. I grunted and hit back, harder now. I had to back up my overtures of peace with strength. I hit him in the ribs, I rubbed my knuckles in his ear as we clinched. I tried again. "You deal good," I said.

"You too," he muttered, pressuring out. And just like that, the fight was over. No more words. We just separated, hands half up, half down. My heart pumped out, *You've established your rep. Move over, 104th Street. Lift your wings, I'm one of your baby chicks now.*

Five seconds later my spurs were given to me in the form of introductions to streetdom's elite. There were no looks of blankness now; I was accepted by heart.

"What's your other name, Johnny Gringo?"

"Piri."

"Okay, Pete, you wanna join my fellows?"

"Sure, why not?"

III

lo hispanoamericano

The following selections provide the basis for the title phrase, "literatura de la raza" which applies to the present unit. The term, "raza," as used today, is flexible in its range of coverage. When a Chicano lettuce-striker in the Salinas Valley of California shouts "¡Viva la raza!", he likely is referring to Chicano unity. But in another, noncontradictory sense, the term "raza" may also refer to the Spanish speaking peoples of North and South America, for there are bonds—linguistic, cultural, and historic—which link these peoples to Aztlán.

In this sense Chicano literature has connections with the literatures of Argentina, Cuba, Peru, and the other Hispanic nations of this hemisphere. Not only is there a shared language, but also a shared Hispano-Indian cultural heritage, and a shared history which includes the oppressive experience of colonization, in its Spanish and North American variations.

We have selected, to serve as a context of Chicano literature, a small number of samples from the tremendous range of possible material. The selections are by famous and less famous authors, from the large and the small nations, dating from both past and present. Each piece, we feel, has some special relevance in its own way to the student of Chicano literature. This relevance was our prime basis of choice.

ARGENTINA

The long epic poem of Martín Fierro, written in the 1870s, is a classic in Argentina. It tells of the gaucho, his struggle for freedom against the forces of society and of nature, and of his system of values, stressing independence, self-reliance, closeness to nature, love of music and popular verse, the capacity to find strength in suffering.

The poem, so deeply Argentine, still reminds us in many ways of Mexican and Chicano expression. The opening verse, like the corrido, carries the self-introduction of the poet. The form is that of the décima, with the first four lines omitted. And the figure of the gaucho in his life style, his personal pride and dignity, his feeling of being a social outcast, is comparable to the vaquero of the Southwest. We have selected the stanzas below as typical of the language, the tone and the themes of the gaucho, Martín Fierro.

EL GAUCHO MARTÍN FIERRO

josé hernández

Aquí me pongo a cantar
al compás de la vigüela,
que el hombre que lo desvela
una pena estrordinaria,
como la ave solitaria
con el cantar se consuela.

Cantando me he de morir,
cantando me han de enterrar,
y cantando he de llegar
al pie del Eterno Padre;
dende el vientre de mi madre
vine a este mundo a cantar.

Que no se trabe mi lengua
ni me falte la palabra;
el cantar mi gloria labra
y, poniéndomé a cantar,
cantando me han de encontrar
aunque la tierra se abra.

Yo no soy cantor letrao,
mas si me pongo a cantar
no tengo cuándo acabar
y me envejezco cantando:

THE GAUCHO MARTÍN FIERRO

josé hernández

Here I come to sing
to the beat of my guitar;
because a man who is kept
   from sleep
by an uncommon sorrow
comforts himself with singing
like a solitary bird.

Singing I'll die,
singing they'll bury me,
and singing I'll arrive
at the Eternal Father's feet—
out of my mother's womb I came
into this world to sing.

Let me not be tongue-tied
nor words fail me:
singing carves my fame,
and once I set myself to sing
they'll find me singing even though
the earth should open up.

I'm no educated singer,
but if I start to sing
there's nothing to make me stop
and I grow old singing—

las coplas me van brotando
como agua de manantial.

Yo soy toro en mi rodeo
y torazo en rodeo ajeno;
siempre me tuve por güeno
y si me quieren probar
salgan otros a cantar
y veremos quién es menos.

Soy gaucho, y entiéndanló
como mi lengua lo esplica:
para mí la tierra es chica
y pudiera ser mayor;
ni la víbora me pica
ni quema mi frente el sol.

Mi gloria es vivir tan libre
como el pájaro del cielo;
no hago nido en este suelo
ande hay tanto que sufrir,
y naides me ha de seguir
cuando yo remuento el vuelo.

Y sepan cuantos escuchan
de mis penas el relato
que nunca peleo ni mato
sino por necesidá
y que a tanta alversidá
sólo me arrojó el mal trato.

Y atiendan la relación
que hace un gaucho perseguido,
que padre y marido ha sido
empeñoso y diligente,
y sin embargo la gente
lo tiene por un bandido.

Junta esperencia en la vida
hasta pa dar y prestar
quien la tiene que pasar
entre sufrimiento y llanto;
porque nada enseña tanto
como el sufrir y el llorar.

the verses go spouting from me
like water from a spring.

I'm the bull in my own herd
and a braver bull in the next one;
I always thought I was pretty good
and if anyone else wants to try me
let them come out and sing
and we'll see who comes off worst.

I am a gaucho, and take this from me
as my tongue explains to you:
for me the earth is a small place
and it could well be bigger—
the snake does not bite me
nor the sun burn my brow.

It is my glory to live as free
as a bird in the sky:
I make no nest on this ground
where there's so much to be suffered,
and no one will follow me
when I take to flight again.

Let whoever may be listening
to the tale of my sorrows—
know that I never fight nor kill
except when it has to be done,
and that only injustice threw me
into so much adversity.

And listen to the story told
by a gaucho who's hunted
    by the law;
who's been a father and husband
hard-working and willing—
and in spite of that, people take him
to be a criminal.

You gather experience in life,
enough to lend and give away,
if you have to go through it
between tears and suffering—
because nothing teaches you
    so much
as to suffer and cry.

(trans. by C.E. Ward)

CUBA

José Martí (1853–1895) lived and died for the cause of freedom. His death in 1895 came on the battlefield in the struggle for Cuban independence from Spain.

His inspirational role as leader of the forces of national liberation did not conflict with his literary activities. On the contrary, for Martí literature was a means of communicating both the enjoyment of beauty and the enrichment of ethical concepts.

Martí was a prolific writer. His *Obras completas,* in twenty-six volumes, include poetry, novel, children's stories, and essays on themes of history, politics, and literature. His ideas on literature were in sharp contrast with those of the artepuristas. For them poetry and art, written for aesthetic reasons only, were the property of the upper strata of society. In Martí's view poetry was a spiritual necessity for the people.

The verses below, selected fragments from *Versos sencillos* (1891), show Martí using the popular eight syllable form, usually with a simple rhyme scheme, in treating themes which for him were important: the beauty of nature, the struggle for freedom, the need for simplicity and basic morality, his loyalty to "los pobres de la tierra." The final lines provide an accurate poetic forecast of his death, which came four years later.

VALOR DE LA POESÍA

josé martí

¿Quién es el ignorante que sostiene que la poesía no es necesaria a los pueblos? Hay gente de tan corta vista mental que creen que toda la fruta se acaba en la cáscara.

La poesía que congrega o disgrega, que fortifica o angustia, que apuntala o derriba las almas, que da o quita a los hombres la fe y el aliento, es más necesaria a los pueblos que la industria misma, pues ésta les proporciona el modo de subsistir mientras que aquélla las da el deseo y la fuerza de la vida.

Pero la poesía es a la vez obra del bardo y del pueblo que la inspira.

La poesía es durable cuando es obra de todos. Tan autores son de ella los que la comprenden como los que la hacen. Para sacudir todos los corazones con las vibraciones del propio corazón, es preciso tener los gérmenes e inspiración de la humanidad. Para andar entre las multitudes, de cuyos sufrimientos y alegrías quiere hacerse intérprete, el poeta ha de oír todos los suspiros, presenciar todas las agonías, sentir todos los goces, e inspirarse en las pasiones comunes a todos. Principalmente es preciso vivir entre los que sufren.

THE VALUE OF POETRY

josé martí

Who is the fool that maintains that the people do not need poetry? There are those with such short sight that they think that the peel is all there is to the fruit.

Poetry, that brings together or breaks apart, that strengthens or saddens, that shores up or bowls over our very souls, that can give faith and spirit to men or take them away, is more necessary to people than work itself; for work gives them the means to survive while poetry gives them the desire and the force of life.

But poetry is both the work of the poet and of the people who inspire it.

Poetry is durable when it is the work of all. Those who understand it are as much its authors as those who compose it. To thrill all hearts by the vibrations of one's own, one must have the germs and the inspiration of humanity. To walk among the multitudes whose sufferings and joys he wants to interpret, the poet must hear all the sighs, witness all the agonies, feel all the happy moments, and be inspired by the passions common to all. Above all, he must live among those who suffer.

VERSOS SENCILLOS

josé martí

Yo soy un hombre sincero
De donde crece la palma,
Y antes de morirme quiero
Echar mis versos del alma.

Yo sé bien que cuando el mundo
Cede, lívido, al descanso,
Sobre el silencio profundo
Murmura el arroyo manso.

Oculto en mi pecho bravo
La pena que me lo hiere:
El hijo de un pueblo esclavo
Vive por él, calla y muere.

Todo es hermoso y constante,
Todo es música y razón,
Y todo, como el diamante,
Antes que luz es carbón.

Yo sé que el necio se entierra
Con gran lujo y con gran llanto,—
Y que no hay fruta en la tierra
Como la del camposanto.

Con los pobres de la tierra
Quiero yo mi suerte echar:
El arroyo de la sierra
Me complace más que el mar.

Denle al vano el oro tierno
Que arde y brilla en el crisol:
A mí denme el bosque eterno
Cuando rompe en él el Sol.

Yo he visto el oro hecho tierra
Barbullendo en la redoma:
Prefiero estar en la sierra
Cuando vuela una paloma.

Si ves un monte de espumas,
Es mi verso lo que ves:
Mi verso es un monte, y es
Un abanico de plumas.

Mi verso es como un puñal
Que por el puño echa flor:
Mi verso es un surtidor
Que da un agua de coral.

Mi verso es de un verde claro
Y de un carmín encendido:
Mi verso es de un ciervo herido
Que busca en el monte amparo.

Mi verso al valiente agrada:
Mi verso, breve y sincero,
Es del vigor del acero
Con que se funde la espada.

Yo quiero salir del mundo
Por la puerta natural:
En un carro de hojas verdes
A morir me han de llevar.

No me pongan en lo oscuro
A morir como un traidor:
Yo soy bueno, y como bueno
Moriré de cara al Sol!

Born in 1902, Nicolás Guillén has been a major poet in Cuba for more than forty years. He is known especially for his Afro-Cuban poetry which used the sounds, symbols, images and rhythms of Africa which in Cuba have blended with Hispanic elements to forge a new mixed culture.

The poem below is one of his more complex compositions, searching back in history for the roots of the poet's (and Cuba's) identity. Like many Chicanos, Guillén identifies his personal destiny with that of his people.

BALADA DE LOS DOS ABUELOS

nicolás guillén

Sombras que sólo yo veo,
me escoltan mis dos abuelos.

Lanza con punta de hueso,
tambor de cuero y madera:
mi abuelo negro.

Gorguera en el cuello ancho,
gris armadura guerrera:
mi abuelo blanco.

Africa de selvas húmedas
y de gordos gongos sordos...
—¡Me muero!
(Dice mi abuelo negro).
Aguaprieta de caimanes,
verdes mañanas de cocos...
—¡Me canso!
(Dice mi abuelo blanco).
Oh velas de amargo viento,
galeón ardiendo en oro...
—¡Me muero!
(Dice mi abuelo negro).
¡Oh costas de cuello virgen
engañadas de abalorios...!
—¡Me canso!
(Dice mi abuelo blanco).
¡Oh puro sol repujado,
preso en el aro del trópico;
oh luna redonda y limpia
sobre el sueño de los monos!

BALLAD OF THE TWO GRANDFATHERS

nicolás guillén

Shadows that I alone can see
shadow two grandfathers
following me.

A lance with a point of bone,
drum of skin and a hollow log,
my black grandfather.

White ruff on strong neck,
grey warrior's armor,
my white grandfather.

Africa of the humid forests
and the great songless drums.
I'm dying!
says my black grandfather.
Muddy water of alligators,
green mornings of palm trees.
I'm tired!
says my white grandfather.
Oh, sails in the bitter wind,
galleons of burning gold.
I'm dying!
says my black grandfather:
Oh, virgin shores undefiled,
deceived by beads of glass.
I'm tired!
says my white grandfather.
Oh, solid sun of beaten brass,
prisoner in the ring of the tropics!
Oh, round clean moon
above the monkeys' dream.

¡Qué de barcos, qué de barcos!
¡Qué de negros, qué de negros!
¡Qué largo fulgor de cañas!
¡Qué látigo el del negrero!
Piedra de llanto y de sangre,
venas y ojos entreabiertos,
y madrugadas vacías,
y atardeceres de ingenio,
y una gran voz, fuerte voz,
despedazando el silencio.
¡Qué de barcos, qué de barcos,
qué de negros!

Sombras que sólo yo veo,
me escoltan mis dos abuelos.

Don Federico me grita
y Taita Facundo calla;
los dos en la noche sueñan
y andan, andan.
Yo los junto.

    —¡Federico!
¡Facundo! Los dos se abrazan.
Los dos suspiran. Los dos
las fuertes cabezas alzan;
los dos del mismo tamaño,
bajo las estrellas altas;
los dos del mismo tamaño,
ansia negra y ansia blanca,
los dos del mismo tamaño,
gritan, sueñan, lloran, cantan.
Sueñan, lloran, cantan.
Lloran, cantan.
¡Cantan!

So many ships, so many ships!
So many Negroes, so many Negroes!
What a vast glow of canefields!
What a whip has the slave trader.
Blood? Blood...Tears? Tears.
Half-opened veins and
 half-opened eyes
and empty mornings
and sunsets at the sugarmill
and a great voice, a strong voice,
bursting the silence.
So many ships, so many ships!
So many Negroes!

Shadows I alone can see
Shadow two grandfathers
 following me.

Don Federico shouts at me,
but Taita Facundo says nothing.
At night they both walk
dreaming, dreaming.
In me they meet.

Federico!...Facundo!
They embrace. Both sigh.
Both throw back their strong heads.
Both the same size,
beneath the distant stars.
Both the same size
black longing and white longing,
both the same size,
they shout, they dream,
they cry, they sing.
They dream, they cry, they sing.
They cry, they sing.
They sing!

      (trans. by Langston Hughes
      and Ben F. Carruthers)

NICARAGUA

Rubén Darío (1867–1916) was one of the great poets in the Spanish language, and one of the leaders of "modernismo," a movement which brought originality and innovation to the poetry of Hispanoamérica. "Lo fatal" (1905), the poem we have selected, stresses the poet's anguish in his efforts to understand the nature of life, in which the only certainty is death.

Darío in this poem is really asking the same question as Jesús Maldonado, the Chicano poet, in "Under a Never Changing Sun" (see unit I, subunit 1). However, Darío's terms are more individualistic and less socially developed, and his poem reflects more stress on traditional form in the external sense of rhyme and meter.

LO FATAL

rubén darío

Dichoso el árbol que es apenas sensitivo,
y más la piedra dura, porque ésta ya no siente,

pues no hay dolor más grande que el dolor de ser vivo,
ni mayor pesadumbre que la vida consciente.

Ser, y no saber nada, y ser sin rumbo cierto,
y el temor de haber sido y un futuro terror...
Y el espanto seguro de estar mañana muerto,
y sufrir por la vida y por la sombra y por

lo que no conocemos y apenas sospechamos,
y la carne que tienta con sus frescos racimos
y la tumba que aguarda con sus fúnebres ramos,
¡y no saber adónde vamos,
ni de dónde venimos...!

FATALITY

rubén darío

The tree is happy because it is scarcely sentient;
the hard rock is happier still, it feels nothing:
there is no pain as great as being alive,
no burden heavier than that of conscious life.

To be, and to know nothing, and to lack a way,
and the dread of having been, and future terrors...
And the sure terror of being dead tomorrow,
and to suffer all through life and through the darkness,

and through what we do not know and hardly suspect...
And the flesh that tempts us with bunches of cool grapes,
and the tomb that awaits us with its funeral sprays,
and not to know where we go,
nor whence we came!...

(trans. by Lysander Kemp)

Born in 1914 in the town of Rivas, on the shores of Lake Nicaragua, this writer has published one volume of poetry, a play, and a novel. Here he has taken his theme from an ancient Mayan poem—in the italicized stanzas—and has embroidered his own pattern upon it. The volcano of Izalco, referred to in the poem, has been active since 1777; its glow can be seen from the Pacific Ocean.

CANCIÓN DE NEZAHUALCÓYOTL

alberto ordóñez argüello

i

Madre mía, cuando muera
sepúltame en el hogar
y al hacer el pan, espera
y por mí ponte a llorar.

Siguapil de luz primera,
la mañana ha de aromar
entre la tierra y el mar,
madre mía, cuando muera.

No sobre tierra cualquiera,
sí donde habrá de cantar
la tórtola en Primavera,
¡allí quiero descansar!
Madre mía, cuando muera,
sepúltame en el hogar.

Un abril de llama entera
vendrá el maizal a dorar;
madre mía, cuando muera
enciende el fuego del lar
y al hacer el pan, espera.

Sobre su verde bandera
levantará el platanar
la roja flor que yo era.
Habrás la flor de cortar
madre mía, cuando muera
y por mí ponte a llorar.

ii

Y si uno en saber se empeña
la causa de tu penar,
dile que verde es la leña
y que el humo hace llorar.

Y si uno en saber se empeña
por qué la espuma del mar
deja su amargo en la peña.

Y si uno en saber se empeña
bajo la noche mareña
la causa de tu penar,
dile, madre, al suspirar:
"a quien ya mi sueño sueña,
nunca más ha de soñar."

Y si uno en saber se empeña
—cuando en la piedra y la breña
el río rompe a cantar—
la causa de tu penar,
di que una dicha pequeña
dejó en tu pecho por seña
la herida del balsamar.

Y si uno en saber se empeña
por qué tu cara trigueña
mira las nubes pasar,
di que la nube te enseña
—madre mía, dulce dueña—,
la causa de tu penar.

Y si uno en saber se empeña
si es la luna volcaneña
la causa de tu penar,
brisa de huerta izalqueña
mi amor te hará recordar;
y ante la lumbre hogareña,
dile que verde es la leña
y que el humo hace llorar.

SONG OF NEZAHUALCÓYOTL

alberto ordóñez argüello

i

Mother of mine, when I die
bury me 'neath the hearth
and when you make the bread, pause
and weep a little for me.

Maiden of early dawn,
morning will spread its fragrance
between the earth and the sea,
mother of mine, when I die.

Not upon any earth,
but only where rises the song
of the turtle dove in spring,
there I wish to rest!
Mother of mine, when I die,
bury me 'neath the hearth.

An April completely aflame
will come to gild the cornfield;
mother of mine, when I die
light the fire in the hearth
and when you make the bread, pause.

Above its green pennant
the banana tree will raise
the red blossom which was I.
You must pluck that blossom,
mother of mine, when I die
and weep a little for me.

ii

And if someone seeks to know
the reason for your sorrow,
tell him the wood is green
and the smoke makes you cry.

And if someone seeks to know
why the salt spray of the sea
leaves its bitterness on the rock.

And if someone seeks to know
under the wave-wasted night
the reason for your sorrow,
tell him, mother, as you sigh:
"The one my dreams now dream of
never, nevermore will dream."

And if someone seeks to know
—when among the rocks and the tangle
the river breaks into song—
the reason for your sorrow,
say an infinitesimal happiness
left in your breast as remembrance
the wound of the balsam tree.

And if someone seeks to know
why your golden-hued face
watches the passing clouds,
say that the cloud has taught you
—mother of mine, gentle mistress—
the reason for your sorrow.

And if someone seeks to know
whether the volcano moon
is the reason for your sorrow,
a breeze from the groves of Izalco
shall remind you of my love;
and as you sit before the hearth
tell him the wood is green
and the smoke makes you cry.

COLOMBIA

Gabriel García Márquez, born in 1928, is one of Latin America's outstanding novelists. His recent work, *Cien años de soledad* (*One Hundred Years of Solitude*) is a remarkable blend of history, myth, fantasy, satire, protest, and pessimism.

We chose to present the author's statement rejecting diplomatic honors. Its satirical impact, its fierce independence, its protest against dehumanization—these are qualities which Chicanos and Latin Americans alike see as basic to survival.

EL ESCRITOR Y EL SISTEMA

gabriel garcía márquez

He dicho varias veces y se ha publicado que no acepto puestos públicos ni subvenciones de ninguna clase, que nunca he recibido un centavo que no me haya ganado trabajando con la máquina de escribir, que cualquier auxilio extraño al oficio compromete la independencia del escritor, y que ésta es para él, según mi modo de pensar, algo tan esencial como saber escribir. Más aún: si no he asistido a la entrega de los premios que se me han otorgado en distintos países, ni participo nunca en ninguna clase de promociones públicas, no es solamente por pudor sino porque creo que en el fondo son actos de publicidad para que los libros se vendan más. Y yo pienso que lo único decente que puede hacer un escritor para que sus libros se vendan es escribirlos bien.

Así pensaba cuando era un escritor tan poco conocido que nadie me ofrecía un consulado, y ahora que vivo del favor de mis lectores, tengo menos motivos y ningún derecho para cambiar de opinión. Sin embargo, aunque no estuvieran de por medio estos inconvenientes éticos, hubiera declinado de todos modos el ofrecimiento del consulado en Barcelona. Esta es la esquina adonde quería llegar, y explico los motivos con tanta solemnidad como sólo somos capaces de hacerlo los colombianos: no puedo ponerme al servicio del gobierno de mi país, y no por su soberbia dogmática, ni por el machismo vengativo con que quiere tener manos arriba a los estudiantes, ni por sus explosiones de rabia que retumban en el exterior con un estruendo mayor que el de sus buenas obras, sino porque estoy en desacuerdo con el sistema entero a todo lo ancho y a todo lo profundo de su estructura anacrónica.

THE WRITER AND THE SYSTEM

gabriel garcía márquez

I have said many times and in print that I accept no public positions or grants of any kind, that I have never received a penny that has not been earned with my typewriter, that any assistance which comes from outside his profession limits the independence of the writer, and that independence is for him, as I see it, something as basic as knowing how to write. I'll go further: if I have failed to attend the awarding of prizes that have been given me in different countries, if I never participate in any kind of public promotions, it is not only due to bashfulness but because I believe that these really are publicity scenes designed to sell more books. And I think that the only decent thing a writer can do so that his books will sell is write them well.

That is how I felt when I was a writer so unknown that no one offered me a consul's job; and now that I can live from the generosity of my readers I have less motives and no right to change my views. Anyhow even if all these bothersome moral questions were not in the way, I would have refused anyway the offer to be consul in Barcelona. This is the spot I wanted to reach, and I'll explain my motives, taking myself seriously like only we Colombians know how to do. I can't place myself at the service of my government, and it's not because of their dogmatic arrogance, or because of the vengeful brutality with which they keep the students up against the wall, or because of their angry rhetoric that resounds abroad with a noise much larger than anything caused by their positive deeds, but because I am in disagreement with the entire system in all the length and the breadth of its obsolete structure.

PERU

Chicanos and Latin Americans alike are familiar with stereotyped labels such as "fatalist," "passive," and "resigned." César Vallejo, Peru's outstanding poet of this century, gives the lie to these labels in the poem below, as he did in his life of political commitment (1892–1938).

This poem dates from his visit to Spain in 1937, to support the Loyalist forces fighting against General Franco. Its central theme is the triumph of human solidarity over death.

MASA

césar vallejo

Al fin de la batalla,
y muerto el combatiente, vino hacia él un hombre
y le dijo: "¡No mueras; te amo tanto!"
Pero el cadáver ¡ay!, siguió muriendo.

Se le acercaron dos y repitiéronle:
"¡No nos dejes! ¡Valor! ¡Vuelve a la vida!"
Pero el cadáver ¡ay!, siguió muriendo.

Acudieron a él veinte, cien, mil, quinientos mil,
clamando: "¡Tanto amor, y no poder nada contra la muerte!"
Pero el cadáver ¡ay!, siguió muriendo.

Le rodearon millones de individuos,
con un ruego común "¡Quédate hermano!"
Pero el cadáver ¡ay!, siguió muriendo.

Entonces, todos los hombres de la tierra
le rodearon; les vió el cadáver triste, emocionado;
incorporóse lentamente,
abrazó al primer hombre; echóse a andar...

España, aparta de mí este cáliz

MASSES

césar vallejo

At the end of the battle,
When the fighter was dead, a man came toward him
And said to him "Do not die, I love you so!"
But the corpse, alas, went on dying!

Then two approached him and repeated it,
"Do not leave us! Courage! Come back to life!"
But the corpse, alas, went on dying.

Then twenty came, a hundred, a thousand, five hundred thousand,
Clamoring, "So much love and nothing can be done about death!"
But the corpse, alas, went on dying.

Millions of individuals surrounded him,
With a common entreaty, "Stay with us, brother!"
But the corpse, alas, went on dying.

Then all the men of the earth
Surrounded him; the corpse looked at them sadly, full of emotion;
Sat up slowly,
Embraced the first man; and began to walk...

(trans. by H.R. Hays)

JOSÉ MARÍA ARGUEDAS
Y LA POESÍA INDÍGENA DEL PERÚ

The translations and the introduction below are by José María Arguedas, one of Peru's leading *indigenista* novelists, who died in 1969. Arguedas was a bilingual writer who until twelve years of age lived in an Indian community and spoke only Quechua. His novels and stories use Quechua expressions and language patterns. Bilingualism (Indian languages and Spanish) is common in Peru, as it is in Mexico.

Arguedas' concern here, as in his works of fiction, is to show the uniqueness and the sensitivity of the world view of the Quechua-speaking Indians, descendants of the Incas, who inhabit the Andean highlands.

The poems illustrate the Indian consciousness of himself as a fragile being in a harsh universe; his constant use of imagery based on his knowledge of nature; and his faith in natural forces as the basis of human conduct and human decision.

Tengo la esperanza de que este libro cumplirá su objetivo: demostrar la capacidad de creación artística del pueblo indio y mestizo, haciendo conocer uno de los aspectos de la belleza que hay en el arte popular indígena y mestizo; y cómo este arte popular podrá ser el fermento, la raíz primaria de una gran producción nacional en todos los aspectos del arte.

I hope that this book will fulfill its objective—to demonstrate that capacity for artistic creativity in the Indian and mestizo people; to help make known one of the aspects of beauty to be found in their popular art; and to show how this popular art can be the ferment, the primary source of a great national outpouring in all art forms.

MANA PIYNILLAYOK'

> Sapay rikukuni
> mana piynillayok'
> puna wayta jina
> llaki llantullayok'.
>
> Tek'o pinkulluypas
> chakañas rikukun
> nunaypa kirinta
> k' apark' achask' ampi.
>
> Imatak' kausayniy
> maytatak' ripusak'
> maytak' tayta mamay
> ¡lliusi tukukapun!

SIN NADIE, SIN NADIE...

> Qué solo me veo,
> sin nadie sin nadie.
> Como flor de la puna,
> mi sombra nomás tengo,
> como flor de la puna.
>
> Mi pinkullo también está ronco,
> con nervios de toro estaba apretado
> ¡pero tanto ha llorado
> el dolor de mi alma!
> Ahora está ronco.
>
> ¡Qué es, pues, esta vida!
> Sin padre, sin madre,
> sin pueblo donde ir.
> ¡Todo se ha acabado!
> Como un ojo ciego
> ya no sirvo.
> Por gusto sigo en el mundo
> como un ojo ciego.

WITH NO ONE, WITH NO ONE

How lonely I feel,
with no one, with no one.
Like a flower on the open plain,
all I have is my own shadow
Like a flower on the open plain.

My flute too is hoarse,
It had been tight as the nerves of a bull
but so much has it wept
at the pain in my soul!
Now it sings hoarsely.

What, then, is this life!
No father, no mother,
no village to go to.
Everything has ended!
Like a blinded eye,
I've lost my use.
For selfish joy I keep going in this world
like a blinded eye.

KAY TUTAYAYPI

Intillay, killallay,
maychallantam llok' simunki,
chaychallantam ripukusak'
maychallantam kutipusak'.

Intillay, killallay,
maypi kanaykikamatak'
kay tutapi wak' achkani,
kay tutayaypi suyachkaiki.

Intillay killallay,
maychallantam llok' simunki,
chaychallantam ripukusak'
maychallantam chinkaykusak'.

EN ESTE OSCURECER ...

¡Oh mi Sol, mi Luna!
por donde sales
por donde alumbras, amaneciendo,
por esa abra me iré.

¡Oh mi Sol, mi Luna!
hasta que estés dónde,
yo lloro en este oscurecer
esperando en tanta noche.

¡Oh, mi Sol, mi Luna!
por donde alumbras, amaneciendo,
por esa abra, por ese filo del cielo
me he de volver, me he de volver.

IN THIS DARKNESS

Oh my Sun, my Moon!
wherever you come out
wherever you light up, dawning,
that is the path I will take.

Oh my Sun, my Moon!
until you come forth,
I weep in this darkness
waiting in all this night.

Oh my Sun, my Moon!
Wherever you light up, dawning,
by that path, by that sliver of sky
I will come back, I will come back.

Mario Vargas Llosa, author of *La ciudad y los perros* (*The Time of the Hero*) and other novels, is Peru's most widely known writer today (born 1936). Below are excerpts from his courageous and thoughtful acceptance speech, in Caracas, 1969, of El Premio Rómulo Gallegos, the most important literary award in Latin America. This speech, with its image of literature as symbolic "fuego" and its view of the writer in his dissenting relation to society, has had a deep impact throughout Latin America.

While Vargas Llosa refers to the literature of the middle class, popular literature also fits into his definition. We feel that his concepts in most respects are applicable to the Chicano literature we have presented.

LA LITERATURA ES FUEGO

mario vargas llosa

Lentamente se insinúa en nuestros países un clima más hospitalario para la literatura. Los círculos de lectores comienzan a crecer, las burguesías descubren que los libros importan, que los escritores son algo más que locos benignos, que ellos tienen una función que cumplir entre los hombres. Pero entonces, a medida que comience a hacerse justicia al escritor latinoamericano, o más bien, a medida que comience a rectificarse la injusticia que ha pesado sobre él, una amenaza puede surgir, un peligro endiabladamente sutil. Las mismas sociedades que exilaron y rechazaron al escritor, pueden pensar ahora que conviene asimilarlo, integrarlo, conferirle una especie de estatuto oficial. Es preciso, por eso, recordar a nuestras sociedades lo que les espera. Advertirles que la literatura es fuego, que ella significa inconformismo y rebelión, que la razón de ser del escritor es la protesta, la contradicción y la crítica. Explicarles que no hay término medio: que la sociedad suprime para siempre esa facultad humana que es la creación artística y elimina de una vez por todas a ese perturbador social que es el escritor, o admite la literatura en su seno y en ese caso no tiene más remedio que aceptar un perpetuo torrente de agresiones, de ironías, de sátiras, que irán de lo adjetivo a lo esencial, de lo pasajero a lo permanente, del vértice a la base de la pirámide social. Las cosas son así y no hay escapatoria: el escritor ha sido, es y seguirá siendo un descontento. Nadie que esté satisfecho es capaz de escribir, nadie que esté de acuerdo, reconciliado con la realidad, cometería el ambicioso desatino de inventar realidades verbales. La vocación literaria nace del desacuerdo de un hombre con el mundo, de la intuición de deficiencias, vacíos y escorias a su alrededor. La literatura es una forma de insurrección permanente y ella no admite las camisas de fuerza. Todas las tentativas destinadas a doblegar su naturaleza airada, díscola, fracasarán. La literatura puede morir pero no será nunca conformista.

Sólo si cumple esta condición es útil la literatura a la sociedad. Ella contribuye al perfeccionamiento humano impidiendo el marasmo espiritual, la autosatisfacción, el inmovilismo, la parálisis humana, el reblandecimiento intelectual o moral. Su misión es agitar, inquietar, alarmar, mantener a los hombres en una constante insatisfacción de sí mismos: su función es estimular sin tregua la voluntad de cambio y de mejora, aun cuando para ello deba emplear las armas más hirientes y nocivas. Es preciso que todos lo comprendan de una vez: mientras más duros y terribles sean los escritos de un autor contra su país, más intensa será la pasión que lo una a él. Porque en el dominio de la literatura la violencia es una prueba de amor.

La realidad americana, claro está, ofrece al escritor un verdadero festín de razones para ser un insumiso y vivir descontento. Sociedades donde la injusticia es ley, paraísos de ignorancia, de explotación, de desigualdades cegadoras, de miseria, de alienación económica, cultural y moral, nuestras tierras tumultuosas nos suministran materiales suntuosos, ejemplares, para mostrar en ficciones, de manera directa o indirecta, a través de hechos, sueños, testimonios, alegorías, pesadillas o visiones, que la realidad está mal hecha, que la vida debe cambiar. Pero dentro de diez, veinte o cincuenta años habrá llegado, a todos nuestros países como ahora a Cuba, la hora de la justicia social y América Latina entera se habrá emancipado del imperio que la saquea, de las castas que la explotan, de las fuerzas que hoy la ofenden y reprimen. Yo quiero que esa hora llegue cuanto antes y que América Latina ingrese de una vez por todas en la dignidad y en la vida moderna, que el socialismo nos libere de nuestro anacronismo y nuestro horror. Pero cuando las injusticias sociales desaparezcan, de ningún modo habrá llegado para el escritor la hora del consentimiento, la subordinación o la complicidad oficial. Su misión seguirá, deberá seguir siendo la misma; cualquier transigencia en este dominio constituye, de parte del escritor, una traición.

Nuestra vocación ha hecho de nosotros, los escritores, los profesionales del descontento, los perturbadores consciente o inconscientes de la sociedad, los rebeldes con causa, los insurrectos irredentos del mundo, los insoportables abogados del diablo. No sé si está bien o si está mal, sólo sé que es así. Esta es la condición del escritor y debemos reivindicarla tal como es. En estos años en que comienza a descubrir, aceptar y auspiciar la literatura, América Latina debe saber, también, la amenaza que se cierne sobre ella, el duro precio que tendrá que pagar por la cultura. Nuestras sociedades deben estar alertadas: rechazado o aceptado, perseguido o premiado, el escritor que merezca este nombre seguirá arrojándoles a los hombres el espectáculo no siempre grato de sus miserias y tormentas.

LITERATURE IS FIRE

mario vargas llosa

Little by little a climate more hospitable to literature can be felt in our countries. The circles of readers are beginning to grow, the bourgeoisie is discovering that books matter, that writers are more than gentle fools, that they have a role to play. But then, as justice begins to appear for the Latin American writer, or rather, as former injustices are corrected, a new threat can be felt, a diabolically subtle danger. The same societies that rejected and exiled the writer, now are likely to see the convenience of assimilating him, integrating him, awarding a sort of official status to him. That is why it is necessary to remind our societies what awaits them. To warn them that literature is fire, signifying nonconformism and rebellion, that the writer's very way of being is protest, contradiction, and criticism. To explain to them that there is no middle way—that society can suppress forever that human faculty for artistic creativity, eliminating once and for all that disturbing social element, the writer; or it can admit literature into its heart, in which case it will be accepting an endless outpouring of aggression, irony, satire that range from the secondary to the essential, from the temporary to the permanent, from the top to the bottom of the social pyramid. Things are that way, and there is no escaping: The writer has been, is, and will continue to be a malcontent. No one who is satisfied is capable of writing; no one who is in harmony and accepts his reality would commit the ambitious foolishness of inventing new realities. A literary vocation arises from a man's disagreement with the world, from his intuition of deficiencies, emptiness and waste in the world around him. Literature is a form of permanent rebellion, and it cannot tolerate straitjackets. All efforts to subdue its angry, aggravated nature, will fail. It may die, but it will never be conformist.

Only if it meets this condition can literature be useful to society. It contributes to human perfection by preventing spiritual starvation, self-satisfaction, human paralysis, intellectual or moral softening. Its mission is to agitate, disturb, alarm, to keep men constantly dissatisfied with themselves; its function is to stimulate increasingly the will to change and betterment, even when to do this it has to use the most damaging, harmful weapons. Everyone should understand this from the beginning: The more harsh and terrible an author's writings against his country, the more intense the passion he feels for it. For in the world of literature, violence is proof of love.

Latin American reality, of course, offers the writer a wealth of reasons to be rebellious and malcontent. Societies where injustice is the rule, paradises of ignorance, of exploitation, of blinding inequalities and misery, of economic, cultural and moral alienation, our tumultuous lands offer us beautiful models to demonstrate in fiction, directly or indirectly, through facts, dreams, memories, allegories, nightmares or visions, that reality is badly constructed, that life must change. But within ten, twenty or fifty years the hour of social justice will have arrived in our countries, as it has in Cuba, and all Latin America will have emancipated itself from the empire that now is sacking it, from the castes that exploit it, from the forces that insult and repress it. I want this hour to arrive as soon as possible, so that Latin America may finally know dignity and begin a modern existence, liberated by socialism from our obsolete, horrible state. But when social injustices disappear, the hour of consent, submission or official collaboration will in no way have arrived for the writer. His mission must keep on being the same—any compromise in this area would mean, for the writer, betrayal.

Our vocation as writers has made us the professionals of discontent, the conscious or unconscious disturbers of society, the agitators with a cause, the hopeless rebels of the world, the intolerable devil's advocates. I don't know if this is good or bad—I only know it is. Such is the writer's condition, and so must we see him. In this period, when it is beginning to discover, accept, and sponsor literature, Latin America must also know the threat that hangs over it, the high price it will have to pay for culture. We must alert our societies: rejected or accepted, persecuted or prized, the writer who deserves that title will continue to throw in men's faces the hardly pleasing spectacle of their misery and their anguish.

GUATEMALA

Beneath the surface of this simple cuento, with its objective, emotionless style, is a satirical treatment of the attitude of superiority with which the Spaniards viewed Indian cultural and scientific achievements. The reference to Carlos Quinto situates the story in the first half of the sixteenth century.

Augusto Monterroso has lived more or less in political exile in Mexico since the right-wing military group seized power in Guatemala in 1954 (aided by the U.S. government).

EL ECLIPSE

augusto monterroso

Cuando fray Bartolomé Arrazola se sintió perdido aceptó que ya nada podría salvarlo. La selva poderosa de Guatemala lo había apresado, implacable y definitiva. Ante su ignorancia topográfica se sentó con tranquilidad a esperar la muerte. Quiso morir allí, sin ninguna esperanza, aislado, con el pensamiento fijo en la España distante, particularmente en el convento de Los Abrojos, donde Carlos Quinto condescendiera una vez a bajar de su eminencia para decirle que confiaba en el celo religioso de su labor redentora.

Al despertar se encontró rodeado por un grupo de indígenas de rostro impasible que se disponían a sacrificarlo ante un altar, un altar que a Bartolomé le pareció como el lecho en que descansaría, al fin, de sus temores, de su destino, de sí mismo.

Tres años en el país le habían conferido un mediano dominio de las lenguas nativas. Intentó algo. Dijo algunas palabras que fueron comprendidas.

Entonces floreció en él una idea que tuvo por digna de su talento y de su cultura universal y de su arduo conocimiento de Aristóteles. Recordó que para ese día se esperaba un eclipse total de sol. Y dispuso, en lo más íntimo, valerse de aquel conocimiento para engañar a sus opresores y salvar la vida.

—Si me matáis —les dijo— puedo hacer que el sol se oscurezca en su altura.

Los indígenas lo miraron fijamente y Bartolomé sorprendió la incredulidad en sus ojos. Vio que se produjo un pequeño consejo, y esperó confiado, no sin cierto desdén.

Dos horas después el corazón de fray Bartolomé Arrazola chorreaba su sangre vehemente sobre la piedra de los sacrificios (brillante bajo la opaca luz de un sol eclipsado), mientras uno de los indígenas recitaba sin ninguna inflexión de voz, sin prisa, una por una, las infinitas fechas en que se producirían eclipses solares y lunares, que los astrónomos de la comunidad maya habían previsto y anotado en sus códices sin la valiosa ayuda de Aristóteles.

THE ECLIPSE

augusto monterroso

When Fray Bartolomé Arrazola found himself lost, he accepted the fact that nothing could save him now. The powerful Guatemalan jungle had taken him prisoner, relentlessly and unmistakably. Knowing he was ignorant of the topography, he sat down peacefully to await death. He wanted to die there, with no hope, cut off, with his thoughts fixed on distant Spain, especially the monastery at Los Abrojos, where King Carlos the Fifth had come down one day from his eminent royal posture to voice confidence in the religious spirit of his holy labor.

On awakening he found himself surrounded by a group of natives with emotionless expressions, who were preparing to sacrifice him before an altar—an altar which seemed to Bartolomé like the bed in which he would rest, at last, from his fears, from his destiny, from himself.

Three years in this country had given him a moderate command of the native languages. He tried something. He spoke a few words which were understood.

Then an idea blossomed forth that he felt was worthy of his talent and universal culture, and his hard-earned knowledge of Aristotle. He remembered that on that day a total eclipse of the sun was calculated. And he determined, in his own mind, to make use of that knowledge to fool his captors and save his life.

"If you kill me," he told them, "I can have the sun go dark while still on high."

The natives look at him firmly and Bartolomé spied a look of disbelief in their eyes. He watched as they held a brief council, and he waited, confident, not without a touch of contempt.

Two hours later, Fray Bartolomé's heart poured out its steaming blood on the sacrificial stone (which shone in the dark light of the sun in its eclipse), while one of the Indians recited, in a voice with no inflection, unhurriedly, one by one, the infinite series of dates on which there would be solar eclipses and lunar eclipses, that the astronomers of the Maya community had foretold and noted in their codices without the valued assistance of Aristotle.

CHILE

Gabriela Mistral is one of three Latin Americans to be honored with the Nobel Prize for literature (the others were Miguel Angel Asturias of Guatemala and Pablo Neruda of Chile). She lived through a period of social turmoil and struggle in Latin America (1889–1957) and consistently aligned herself with the cause of the poor and the suffering. She was especially sensitive to the problems of women. The prose selection below, addressed to the women of Mexico, was inspired by her stay in Mexico in 1922, working with José Vasconcelos in the Revolution's program of educational reform. The poem conveys Gabriela's poetic response to loneliness and suffering, as represented in the vast forces of nature and symbolic night. Man's (and woman's) hope is to come together in love, whether of man and woman, or mother and child.

MADRE MEXICANA

gabriela mistral

Madre mexicana: reclama para tu hijo, vigorosamente, lo que la existencia debe a los seres que nacen sin que pidieran nacer. Por él tienes derecho a las grandes solicitaciones. Pide para él la escuela soleada y limpia; pide los alegres parques; pide las fiestas de las imágenes, en el libro y en el cinema educador; exige colaborar en las leyes, pero cuando se trate de las cosas que te manchan o te empequeñecen la vida, puedes pedir leyes que limpien de vergüenza al hijo ilegítimo al que se hace nacer paria y vivir paria en medio de los otros hijos, y leyes que reglamenten vuestro trabajo y el de los niños, que se agotan en la faena brutal de las fábricas.

Para eso podréis ser vehementes sin dejar de ser austeras; vuestra palabra no será grotesca; hasta tendrá santidad.

Te oirán, tarde o temprano, madre mexicana; volverán a ti la mirada los hombres justos, que todavía son muchos porque tu majestad quiebra, vencidas, a todas las demás majestades, y el verso de Walt Whitman se recuerda cuando se te ve cruzar "¡Yo os digo que no hay nada más grande que la madre de los hombres!"

Yo te amo, madre mexicana, hermana de la mía, que bordas exquisitamente y tejes la estera color de miel; que pintas la jícara coloreada y que cruzas el campo vestida de azul, como la mujer de la Biblia, para llevar el sustento del hijo o del esposo que riegan los maizales.

Nuestra raza se probará en tus hijos; en ellos hemos de salvarnos o de perecer. Dios les fijó la dura suerte de que la marejada del Norte rompa sobre su pecho. Por eso, cuando tus hijos luchan o cantan, los rostros del Sur se vuelven hacia acá, llenos de esperanza y de inquietud a la par.

Mujer mexicana: en tus rodillas se mece la raza entera, y no hay destino más grande y más tremendo que el tuyo en esta hora.

MEXICAN MOTHER

gabriela mistral

Mexican mother: claim for your child, with vigor, what life owes to all beings who are born and never asked to be born. For him you have the right to make great demands. Demand a school that is sunny and clean; demand happy parks; demand a fiesta of images, in books and in educational films; insist on helping make the laws, but when they deal with things that dirty you, or make your life petty, you can demand laws that wash away the shame of the illegitimate child, who is made an outcast from birth, and must live an outcast among other children; and demand laws that regulate your labor and the labor of your children, who work to exhaustion in the brutal routine of the factory.

For that cause you can speak loudly and still be austere; your words will not seem peculiar, they will even be saintly.

You will be heard, sooner or later, Mexican mother. The eyes of honest men will turn to you, for there still are many, because your dignity defeats other kinds of pride; and they will remember the poem of Walt Whitman when they see you: "I tell you there is none greater than the mother of men!"

I have love for you, Mexican mother, sister of my mother, as you embroider exquisitely, and you weave honey-colored mats, as you paint a flowered jar, or cross a field dressed in blue like the women of the Bible, carrying food to a son or husband watering the field of corn.

Our raza will be proven in your sons; in them will we be saved or will we perish. God assigned to them the difficult fate of having the tide from the North break against their chests. That is why, when your sons are fighting or singing, other eyes from farther South look toward here, full of hope and worry at the same time.

Mexican mother; on your knees you rock the entire raza; there is no greater destiny than yours in our time.

YO NO TENGO SOLEDAD	I AM NOT LONELY
gabriela mistral	**gabriela mistral**

Es la noche desamparo	The night is left lonely
de las sierras hasta el mar.	from the hills to the sea.
Pero yo, la que te mece,	But I, who cradle you,
¡yo no tengo soledad!	I am not lonely!
Es el cielo desamparo	The sky is left lonely
pues la luna cae al mar.	should the moon fall in the sea.
Pero yo, la que te estrecha,	But I, who cling to you,
¡yo no tengo soledad!	I am not lonely!
Es el mundo desamparo.	The world is left lonely
Toda carne triste va.	and all know misery.
Pero yo, la que to oprime	But I, who hug you close,
¡yo no tengo soledad!	I am not lonely!

(trans. by Langston Hughes)

Fernando Alegría is one of the few Latin American authors who write about the United States from personal experience. Having lived in California as professor of literature many years, he has been aware of the hardships and mistreatment suffered by the thousands of Chileans who in the last century came in search of a better life during the Gold Rush. This concern, as might be expected, motivated his interest in the Chicano. This story, written in 1956, is realistic, almost documentary, and strikes a note of social protest. Published in Mexico, it helped Latin Americans understand the difficult reality of the Pachucos in Los Angeles during World War II.

¿A QUÉ LADO DE LA CORTINA?

fernando alegría

En un teatro a oscuras se puede expresar el amor de muchas maneras. Los pies se hunden en una alfombra espesa cubierta de papeles, pulgas, chicle y maní tostado. Hay un rumor sordo durante la función. Mezcla de murmullos, de pasos, de tímidos avances por encima de las ropas y un ruido más líquido y profundo, difícil de identificar, que es el ruido de la sangre y de la digestión colectiva.

"Se estima que treinta mil jóvenes mexicanos y veinticinco mil negros, más o menos, se visten de pachucos en Los Angeles".

En la película Gary Cooper usa uniforme de marino. Naturalmente, no se va a vestir de pachuco si combate en la guerra. Además es blanco. Si fuera negro o mexicano no sería oficial de marina y Ginger Rogers, que hace de enfermera en la película, no estaría tratando de meterse debajo de las sábanas con él. La escena ocurre en un hospital. Cooper se ve muy pálido a causa de la sangre que ha perdido desde el comienzo de la historia. Ginger frunce los ojos como gallina que va a poner. Por los cristales relumbran los reflectores en busca de los bombarderos enemigos. Una bomba cae cerca del hospital.

Pancho estiró la mano para sacar un puñado de maní y, sin querer, le palpó los muslos a Nancy.

Cooper parece al borde de la muerte, pero así y todo consigue atraer a Ginger hacia su lecho.

¿Quién va a comer maní en tales circunstancias? Pancho se metió entre los brazos de Nancy y empezó a mordisquearle el cuello. Alguien tuvo que acomodarse en la butaca de atrás para seguir mirando por encima de los enamorados. "Honey" le dijo Nancy a Pancho devolviéndole la caricia. En los labios floreció la sal del maní fresco y caliente. A los pocos instantes es un solo beso de cuatro bocas. Un beso de setenta y cinco centavos para Pancho y Nancy. Un beso de cinco mil dólares por segundo —Paramount— para Cooper y Ginger.

"El 90 por ciento de los pachucos trabajan en industrias de guerra y no tienen más de dieciocho años. Los que pasan de esa edad son llamados a servir en el ejército".

Pancho no tiene más que catorce, así es que va al liceo, cuando no va al cine o a los billares. ¡Ah si lo viera Ginger Rogers! Quiero decir si lo viera tal como es. No como una fotografía del *Los Angeles Times* —bandido de pelo negro, de boca torcida, de cicatriz en la mejilla y complejo de inferioridad— sino este Pancho de las tres de la tarde, ni alto ni bajo, delgado pero firme y duro, cabello negro crespo, ojos oscuros y tristes, boca gruesa, chaqueta hasta la rodilla, pantalones negros con listas blancas apretados sobre los calcetines de todos colores. Este Pancho de la calle Broadway que lleva a su novia al cine y tiene un compás de guitarra en cada paso, un chasquido de maracas en cada sonrisa. ¡Si lo viera Ginger como lo ve Nancy! Porque Nancy lo ve moreno y de piel sedosa —y como ella es rubia y tiene los pechos grandes y las piernas duras y blancas, como viste de negro y no usa medias y al sentarse se levanta la falda y muestra los muslos de melocotón, como tiene los ojos azules y desde pequeña jugó con muñecos que vestía de toreros y les pintaba largas pestañas—, por eso Nancy olvidó la Constitución y se prendó de Pancho y, a pesar de vivir en Los Angeles, todavía no llega a ser actriz de cine. ¿Qué influencia va a tener la pobre sobre Ginger Rogers?

Todas las tardes, al regresar del liceo, Pancho pasaba por una tienda de San Gabriel, su barrio. En la vidriera había un maniquí de pelo negro engominado y mejillas de color ladrillo. ¡Quién iba a fijarse en la cara! En cambio, la chaqueta de color crema, de hombros gigantes, de bolsillos plisados, angosta en la cintura, larga, larga, hasta la rodilla, quizás más abajo de la rodilla, y ese clavel de seda roja en la solapa y esa cadena... Se puede ser artillero en un portaaviones o piloto de un cohete, se puede ser comandante galoneado de estrellas y hojas de laurel, se puede ser capitán de un equipo de fútbol, tener a todas las bellezas de Hollywood con hipo de admiración, pero Pancho sólo quería esa chaqueta de pachuco, esa elegancia para llevarse la mirada de Nancy, nada más que la mirada de Nancy en los corredores de la escuela, en el baile del viernes por la noche; esa elegancia de la era atómica. Y por eso se la compró y para no desentonar con su generación se dejó crecer el pelo a la manera de Tarzán con una colilla de pato en la nuca.

Pero resulta que Gary Cooper está casado con Irene Dunne. Pero le vuelve loco Ginger Rogers. Hay el asunto de hijos por medio, el qué dirán de los vecinos de la Paramount, el qué dirán de los cronistas de cine y de la Censura, de manera que, al volver del frente, después de haber derrotado a los japoneses y no obstante su entrañable amor por Ginger Rogers, tiene que someterse a la fuerza del destino, servir en su antiguo empleo, acariciar a los hijos y...¿qué otra cosa va a hacer uno en su caso? ¿de qué le serviría quedarse con la enfermera en Saipán? Aún si no estuviera legalmente casado en los Estados Unidos ¿dónde encontrará consuelo para su corazón democrático en una tierra primitiva, pueblo con disenteria, explotado, elefantiásico y comido por los mosquitos? Además Irene Dunne no es ningún saco de papas.

"Durante dos noches multitudes de marineros y soldados anduvieron de caza por las calles de Los Angeles".

Con Irene Dunne y tres robustos chiquillos, sin contar el nuevo Oldsmobile, la cocina a gas, y los palos de golf, ya se puede pensar en hacer patria. Una patria grande, generosa, que sea como la hermana mayor de las naciones. Una patria cristiana, muy respetuosa de la tradición, sólida para trabajar, serena y tolerante, una patria que le abra los brazos al boxeador italiano tanto como a la cocinera holandesa, al físico austriaco y al cantor tropical.

"En largas caravanas de taxis, jeeps y autos particulares, recorrieron los barrios mexicanos, armados de palos y manoplas".

Gary Cooper ofrece seguridad, es sano, buenmozo, tiene un excelente empleo. Ginger Rogers es sana, hermosa, tiene un excelente empleo. Los niños son sanos, hermosos. Es un encanto ocupar una de esas casitas del suburbio californiano, tibias y cómodas, florecidas y alegres de colores, llegar todas las noches al hogar, recoger el periódico, besar a la esposa y los niños, arrellanarse en el sofá, sacarse los zapatos y leer las aventuras de Tarzán al mismo tiempo que se oyen las noticias mundiales en el radio. Placer auténtico, de significado metafísico, un dominar la naturaleza sin lucha.

Entonces Gary Cooper volvió a la patria, capitán de un buque mercante, herido pero seductor, afirmado en la borda, con una cachimba en los labios. El barco va surgiendo de la niebla. Cooper no sabe que es Ginger Rogers quien lo espera en el muelle, porque Irene Dunne murió durante la guerra y le pidió a Ginger que se casara con Cooper y cuidara de los hijos. Pero Pancho y Nancy sí lo saben. Desde la alfombra pegajosa sube un murmullo de asombro, una ansiedad, un éxtasis que busca la culminación en el beso final. El beso final de la película debe realizarse porque es el acto de procreación del que nace otra película y sin el cual se interrumpe la proyección, se encienden las luces, el cine muere y las gentes enloquecidas, atacan la obra del Señor.

"Le quebraron la mandíbula a un niñito mexicano de doce años".

Hasta el reloj luminoso junto al escenario parece gritar sus segundos.

"Desnudaron a los pachucos, los patearon en el suelo".

Pancho acercó los labios a la oreja de Nancy y en esos momentos un golpe como de cuchillo cortó por el pecho la imagen del héroe en la pantalla. El teatro quedó a oscuras unos instantes. Se oyó el tropel de patas que venía de la calle; gritos, portazos, carcajadas. Una botella se estrelló contra el mosaico del *foyer* y el whiskey buscó los rincones avergonzado de verse expuesto en el suelo bajo tantas luces. Pancho y Nancy se miraron con incredulidad. Era como ver morir a un transeúnte de un ataque al corazón. ¿Pero es que estas máquinas de cine también pueden detenerse? ¿Se puede ver uno de estos cines a plena luz? ¿Después de tantos años de funcionar día y noche? Había algo de monstruoso en la interrupción. Sorprendidos miraron las paredes, el yeso dorado retorciéndose en mil filigranas para imitar una catedral o un catre de bronce o un ídolo azteca. Las lámparas enormes, rosadas, repugnantes como pústulas; las cortinas de pelos de ratón o de araña. Bajo la luz rojiza la muchedumbre se revolvió incómoda. Bajaban la vista, se escarbaban los pantalones y las faldas avergonzados, como si les hubieran cogido *in fraganti* en una aberración.

Pancho se miró en los ojos de Nancy y dicidió que nada había cambiado en el mundo. En la platea se oían gritos, blasfemias y risas sofocadas. El tropel parecía correr ahora por los pasillos. De súbito la escalera del balcón se llenó de gente y unos marineros saltaron por encima de los asientos vacíos en dirección a Pancho. Veinte, treinta, cincuenta individuos, con el pelo engrifado, sucios de tierra y sangre, se le abalanzaron. Pancho vio una frente moreteada con el cabello rojizo pegado de sudor y luego sintió un golpe horrible en las narices. Saltó la sangre manchando la chaqueta crema. Un segundo golpe lo derribó al suelo, alguien le tomó de una pierna y le arrastró hasta el pasillo.

—Con permiso, hijo de...—un marinero le puso de pie y empezó a arreglarle la corbata y a limpiarle las manchas de sangre. Por detrás sintió una patada que le hizo rodar por la escalera. Desde el suelo, con los ojos espantados, mudo en la inconsciencia, Pancho miró a Nancy. Le sacaron a empujones hasta el *foyer*, de ahí, entre filas de gentes enfurecidas que trataban de golpearle, le llevaron hasta la calle. Todo había sucedido en pocos segundos. Afuera, el ambiente era festivo. Pancho veía ahora caras burlonas y trataba de limpiarse la sangre que sentía pesar sobre los ojos. Había espectadores sobre el techo de los automóviles, sobre los tranvías. Como exhalaciones de júbilo salían de en medio de la multitud los relámpagos de los fotógrafos. El mismo pelirrojo que le golpeara la nariz le cogió ahora por detrás y, viéndole inmovilizado, los demás comenzaron a desnudarle. Dos manos fortísimas le rasgaron la chaqueta como si hubiera sido de seda. La muchedumbre dio un aullido de satisfacción. Las viejas se codeaban ahora con los marineros y trataban de ganar la primera fila cuando las prendas íntimas empezaron a caer destrozadas. Pancho creyó oír la voz de Nancy entre el clamor de los marineros y viéndose desnudo quiso correr, pero los brazos le sujetaban firmemente, trató de patear al más cercano y un golpe de manopla le sacudió la cabeza. Babeando sangre se dobló. Una patada le echó de bruces. Los de la primera fila saltaron para no ser salpicados por la sangre.

—*O. K., O. K. break it up...*

Los policías avanzaron resueltamente. Llevaban bombas lacrimógenas en las manos, máscaras contra gases, garrotes y rifles ametralladoras. Avanzaron sin romper la formación. El capitán dirigía la maniobra con un altoparlante desde la capota de un automóvil colorado. Tres *cameramen* le tomaban película y había en su mandíbula inferior la solidez del deber cumplido. La policía dominó el área de peligro en pocos instantes. Con gesto rápido y seguro, sonriente, uno de los policías recogió a Pancho del suelo y lo depositó en el interior de un camión. Hubo aplausos entre la concurrencia.

—¿Qué tal Bill? —alguien reconoció al policía y le saludaba orgullosamente.

El capitán dio la voz de mando y, con el prisionero bien seguro, se replegaron las fuerzas balanceando elegantemente los garrotes ante la mirada satisfecha de la muchedumbre. El camión soltó un bocinazo y se lanzó a toda velocidad por entre los tranvías, taxis y mirones.

En el interior del teatro se apagaron las luces. La banda de marineros y soldados se echó a correr nuevamente olfateando las barriadas mexicanas de Belvedere, Boyle Heights, El Monte y Montebello. El mismo ataque sufrieron otros cines y de la misma manera, suave y silenciosa, volvió a correr la sangre por los proyectores y Gary Cooper pudo, al fin, besar legalmente a Ginger Rogers. Y como el beso es la procreación de otra película, al beso siguió nueva joya de arte: una fábula de Walt Disney. El marinero pelirrojo, aprovechando la entrada gratis, se instaló en el balcón, mientras tanto, para comunicarse con el infinito.

Y los asientos de Pancho y Nancy continuaron tomados del brazo.

Pablo Neruda of Chile is one of the world's great poets in our time. Born in 1904, he has been writing poetry for fifty years now, and has evolved in style, from an early stress on personal themes to a later expansion that not only included love and nature, but social, political, and historical themes. From the time of the Spanish Civil War, when he supported the Republic against General Franco, Neruda has been an active Communist. His career includes residence in prison as well as the Chilean Senate. At present he represents Chile in Paris. Neruda received the Nobel Prize for Literature in 1971.

"Poema 20" ("Tonight I Can Write"), written in 1924, is an early work treating the mixed emotions and sensations—the paradoxes—that come to the surface when we contemplate a lost love. Careful in his rhythm, the poet held to the fourteen-syllable verse, with each line divided in two seven-syllable halves. Other internal rhythms are set up by assonant rhyme (quiso, infinito) and by repetition of the key verse of the first line, which is emphatically reversed at the end.

The "Canción," clearly meant to be sung, with its changing rhymes, is from a play written in 1966, "Fulgor y muerte de Joaquín Murieta." His loose interpretation of history, which casts Murieta (sic) as a Chilean, does not carry over to his poetic sense. "Canción" is a poem carried along by rhythm to express the poet's anger, and his final vigorous affirmation of life over death.

XX
PUEDO ESCRIBIR

pablo neruda

Puedo escribir los versos más tristes esta noche.

Escribir, por ejemplo: 'La noche está estrellada,
y tiritan, azules, los astros, a lo lejos.'

El viento de la noche gira en el cielo y canta.

Puedo escribir los versos más tristes esta noche.
Yo la quise, y a veces ella también me quiso.

En las noches como ésta la tuve entre mis brazos.
La besé tantas veces bajo el cielo infinito.

Ella me quiso, a veces yo también la quería.
Cómo no haber amado sus grandes ojos fijos.

Puedo escribir los versos más tristes esta noche.
Pensar que no la tengo. Sentir que la he perdido.

Oir la noche inmensa, más inmensa sin ella.
Y el verso cae al alma como al pasto el rocío.

Qué importa que mi amor no pudiera guardarla.
La noche está estrellada y ella no está conmigo.

Eso es todo. A lo lejos alguien canta. A lo lejos.
Mi alma no se contenta con haberla perdido.

Como para acercarla mi mirada la busca.
Mi corazón la busca, y ella no está conmigo.

La misma noche que hace blanquear los mismos árboles.
Nosotros, los de entonces, ya no somos los mismos.

Ya no la quiero, es cierto, pero cuánto la quise.
Mi voz buscaba el viento para tocar su oído.

De otro. Será de otro. Como antes de mis besos.
Su voz, su cuerpo claro. Sus ojos infinitos.

Ya no la quiero, es cierto, pero tal vez la quiero.
Es tan corto el amor, y es tan largo el olvido.

Porque en noches como ésta ta tuve entre mis brazos,
mi alma no se contenta con haberla perdido.

Aunque éste sea el último dolor que ella me causa,
y éstos sean los últimos verso que yo le escribo.

XX
TONIGHT I CAN WRITE

pablo neruda

Tonight I can write the saddest lines.

Write, for example, 'The night is shattered
and the blue stars shiver in the distance.'

The night wind revolves in the sky and sings.

Tonight I can write the saddest lines.
I loved her, and sometimes she loved me too.

Through nights like this one I held her in my arms.
I kissed her again and again under the endless sky.

She loved me, sometimes I loved her too.
How could one not have loved her great still eyes.

Tonight I can write the saddest lines.
To think that I do not have her. To feel that I have lost her.

To hear the immense night, still more immense without her.
And the verse falls to the soul like dew to the pasture.

What does it matter that my love could not keep her.
The night is shattered and she is not with me.

This is all. In the distance someone is singing. In the distance.
My soul is not satisfied that it has lost her.

My sight searches for her as though to go to her.
My heart looks for her, and she is not with me.

The same night whitening the same trees.
We, of that time, are no longer the same.

I no longer love her, that's certain, but how I loved her.
My voice tried to find the wind to touch her hearing.

Another's. She will be another's. Like my kisses before.
Her voice, her bright body. Her infinite eyes.

I no longer love her, that's certain, but maybe I love her.
Love is so short, forgetting is so long.

Because through nights like this one I held her in my arms
my soul is not satisfied that it has lost her.

Though this be the last pain that she makes me suffer
and these the last verses that I write for her.

(trans. by W.S. Merwin)

CANCIÓN

pablo neruda

Los ojos que se murieron,
no murieron, los mataron,
los matarán.
Todos los ojos del mundo
morirán,
porque el mundo está muriendo
en Vietnam.

SONG

pablo neruda

Those eyes that died,
they didn't die; they killed them,
they will kill them.
All the eyes of the world
will die,
because the world is dying
in Vietnam.

Porque manejan la historia	Because history is the plaything
los crueles y los ariscos	of the cruel and the crude
y ustedes ven la victoria	and you see the triumph
de la muerte en San Francisco.	of death in San Francisco.
Pregunta el hombre:	The man asks:
Algún día	Some day
terminará la agonía?	will the agony end?
Maldición!	A curse!
Terminará la crueldad	Will cruelty end
y reinará la alegría?	and happiness flower?
Maldición!	A curse!
Los nazis con su guadaña	The Nazis with their swords
cortaron el corazón	pierced the heart
de España!	of Spain!
Maldición!	A curse!
Y ladra el perro a la luna	And the dog barks at the moon
y el niño desde la cuna	and the child from the cradle on
crece sin duda ninguna	grows up, there's no doubt,
en la opresión.	in oppression.
Maldición!	A curse!
Proclamamos la alegría!	We proclaim happiness!
Reclamamos rebeldía!	We demand rebellion!
Bendición!	A blessing!
Para que el hombre algún día	So that man some day
se case con la alegría!	may wed with joy!
Bendición!	A blessing!
Si la vida es buena o mala	Whether life is good or bad
ustedes lo dirán:	you'll be the one to say;
ésta es una suave sala,	this is a lovely room,
pero matan en Vietnam.	but they're killing in Vietnam.
Sigamos viendo esta farsa	Let's go on viewing this comedy
del dolor	of pain
para continuar la vida	so we may continue life
y el amor.	and love.
Porque si muere la muerte	Because if death dies
no la matarán los otros:	it won't be others who kill her;
la lucha la matará	the struggle will kill her
antes	before
de que nos mate a nosotros.	it gets to kill us.

Ecuador, which once formed part of the Inca empire, shares with Peru and Bolivia the consciousness of an ancient heritage. It is this awareness which underlies the poem by Hugo Salazar Tamariz, an important writer in Ecuador today. Like Chicano poets, Salazar Tamariz affirms not only the heritage of the past, but his people's vigor in the present.

LAS RAÍCES

hugo salazar tamariz

Somos un pueblo antiguo,
                viejo como la miel,
como la sombra,
            como las altas hojas,
tan pegado a la áspera corteza que,
                   de lejos
nadie nos diría seres sino topografía.
Zurcidos a la tierra hemos estado siglos azules
y amargos siglos,
               hollando la ya enterrada
edad de la montaña,
               los sucesivos cauces de los ríos
y comiendo del ácimo concepto de los frutos.
De jaguares,
         de sol
            y hachas de piedra,
hemos ido viviendo
            y falleciendo.
Regados entre guerras
            y mujeres adelantamos nuestro rumor
y la intacta sangre que nos golpea entera.
Viejo pueblo no envejecido porque tiene millones de luz
y de hierba,
         creciendo;
            de puertas
              y ventanas
                 abiertas.
Hemos estado viniendo hasta ser tres millones,
una espiga gigante,
            una inmensa mano,
              una red,

un ramal,
           un pueblo entero.
Somos,
       terriblemente,
                   un grito.
Un viejo pueblo definitivamente verde
                           y rumoroso.
Un pueblo con tres millones de ventanas,
en voluntad de abrirse.
Nadie que nos viera,
                 de lejos
                       nos creyera,
sin acaso
       ni ocaso,
                 sino una audaz topografía.

THE ROOTS

hugo salazar tamariz

We are an ancient people,
                       as old as honey,
as shadow,
         as the high leaves,
so united to the rough bark that, from a distance,
no one would call us beings, but rather topography.
Stitched to the earth, we have been blue centuries
and bitter centuries, trampling the already interred
age of the mountain,
                   the successive courses of the rivers
and eating the azymous concept of fruits.
Of jaguars,
         of sun
               and stone hatchets,
we have gone on living
                   and dying.
Strewn between wars
                 and women we advance our murmuring
and the unaltered blood that buffets us.

An old people not grown old, we have a multitude of light
and of grass,
                   growing;
                           of doors
                                   and windows,
                                             opened.
We have been coming until we number three million,
a gigantic wheat stalk,
                       an immense hand,
                                       a net,
a branch,
         an entire people!
We are,
       with a vengeance,
                        a shout.
An old people, definitively green
                               and murmurous.
A people with three million windows
determined to open themselves.
No one seeing us,
                 from a distance,
                                would think us to be,
without chance
              or sunset,
                       but an audacious topography.

                   (trans. by Darwin Flakoll and Claribel Alegría)

MEXICO
(CERRANDO EL CÍRCULO)

By way of closing this unit, it seemed appropriate to choose a song by a Mexican which appeals to the common history of Latin America, to the libertarian traditions of Hidalgo and Bolívar, as it sings of uniting la raza, from North to South, in a struggle for revolutionary change.

DEL BRAVO A LA PATAGONIA

josé de molina

Nacido en Sonora, tierra mexicana,
cantará mi voz latinoamericana,
pues del Río Bravo hasta la Patagonia
nos une la raza, nos une la sangre,
nos une la gloria.

En estos momentos de fieros combates
que han organizado los gringos orates,
yo llamo a las armas para liberarnos,
para sacudirnos de esa plaga inmunda
de yanquis magnates.

Se roban la fruta y nuestro petróleo,
desde un kilo de oro a una simple banana.
Ya nomás nos falta, queridos hermanos,
que nos asesinen, que también nos violen
a nuestras hermanas.

Si Bolívar viera nuestra cobardía
de pesar quizás otra vez moriría.
Si Miguel Hidalgo se resucitara,
de castrados hombres, de viles mujeres
nos acusaría.

Tomemos las armas sin miedo ninguno,
tomemos ejemplo del pueblo cubano,
que más inspirado y con Castro de guía
rompió las cadenas, se llenó de gloria
venciendo al tirano.

Si la sangre corre será necesario
¡adelante siempre, revolucionario!
Que para salvar el honor de los pueblos
no bastan promesas ni los crucifijos,
menos los rosarios.

Obreros, empleados, universitarios,
con los campesinos cantemos victoria,
¡ya se acabarán esas castas sociales
y no habrá frontera desde el Río Bravo
hasta la Patagonia!

VALS DEL AUTOR MEXICANO JOSÉ DE MOLINA. 1965